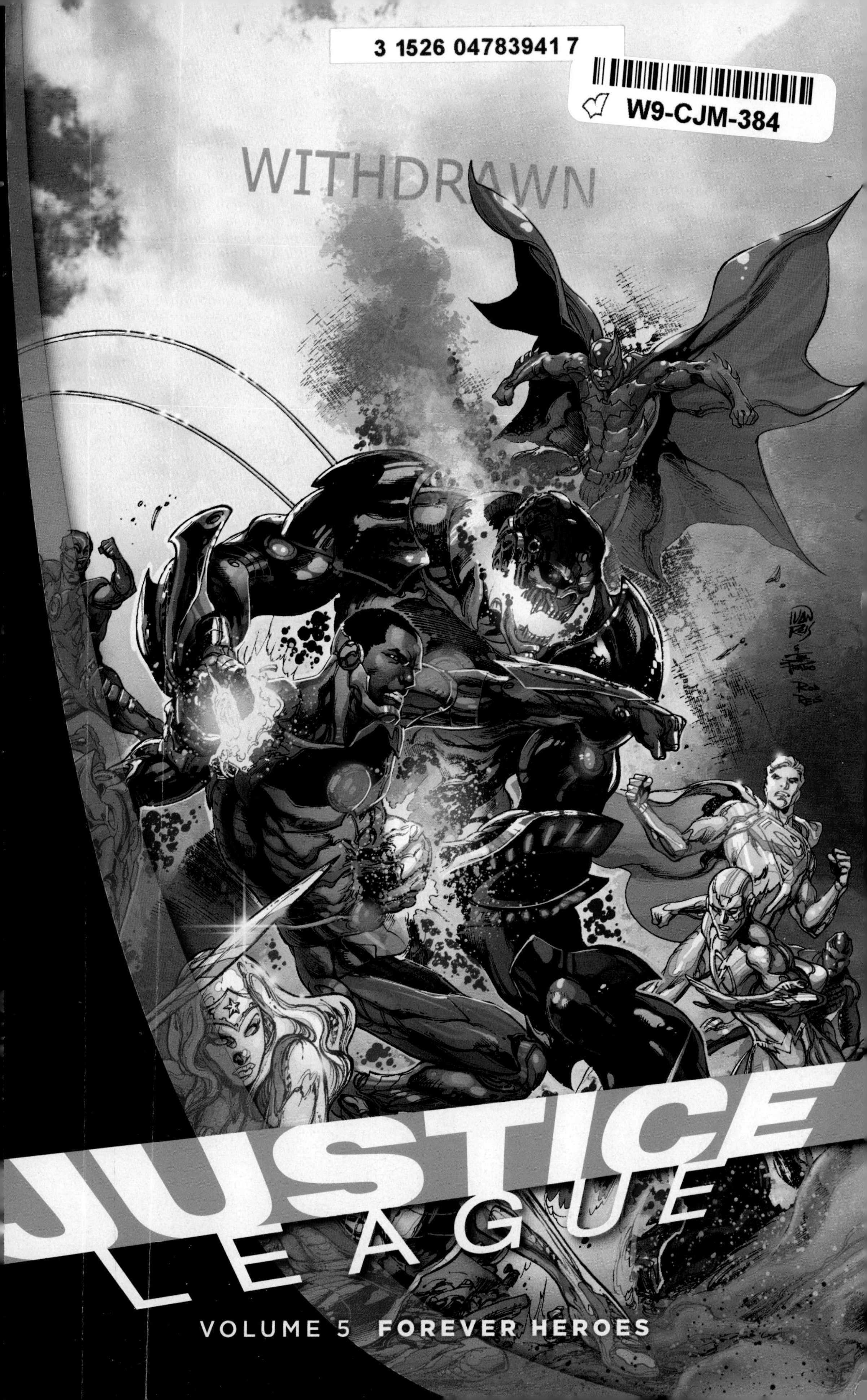
JUSTICE
LEAGUE
VOLUME 5 FOREVER HEROES

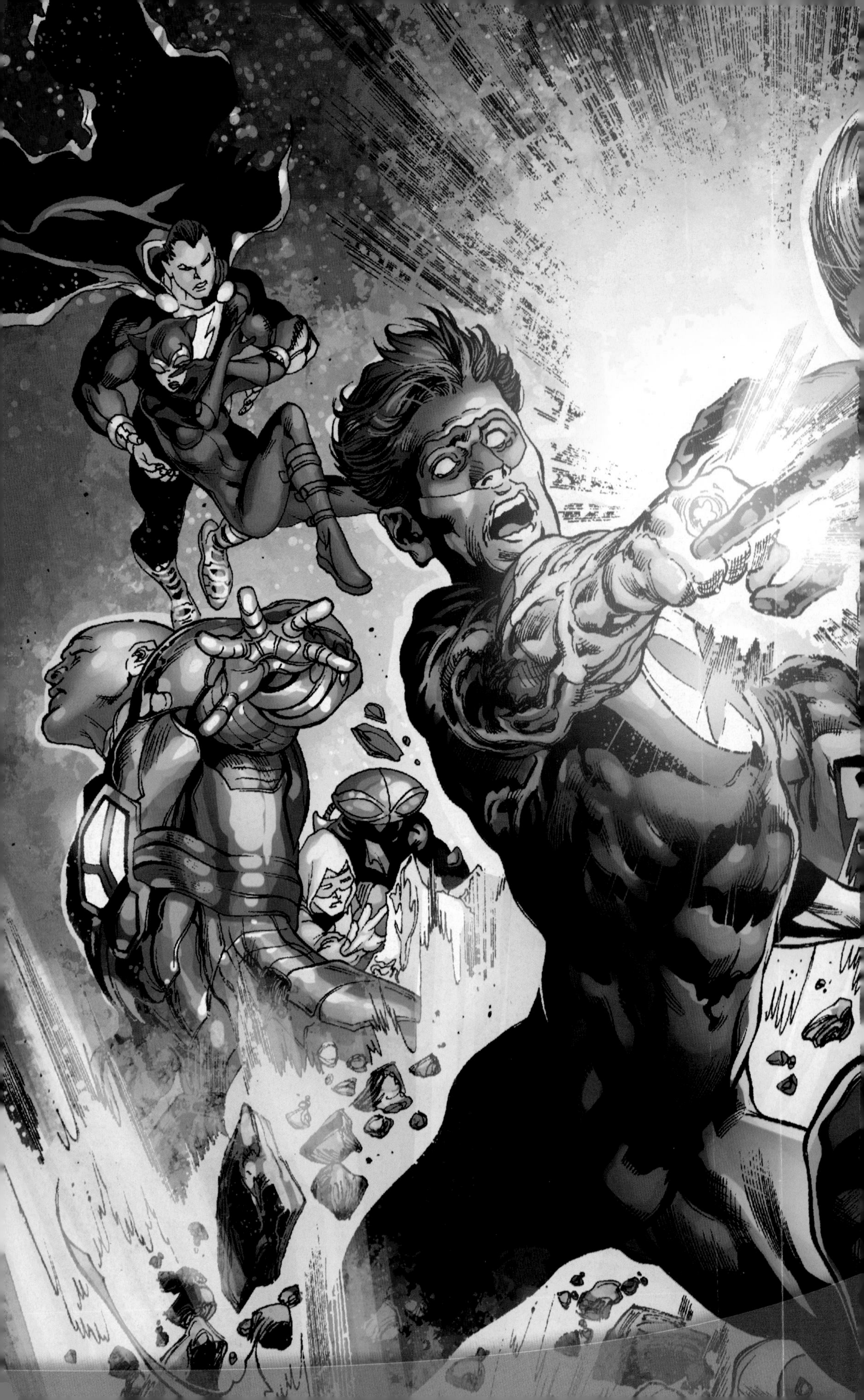

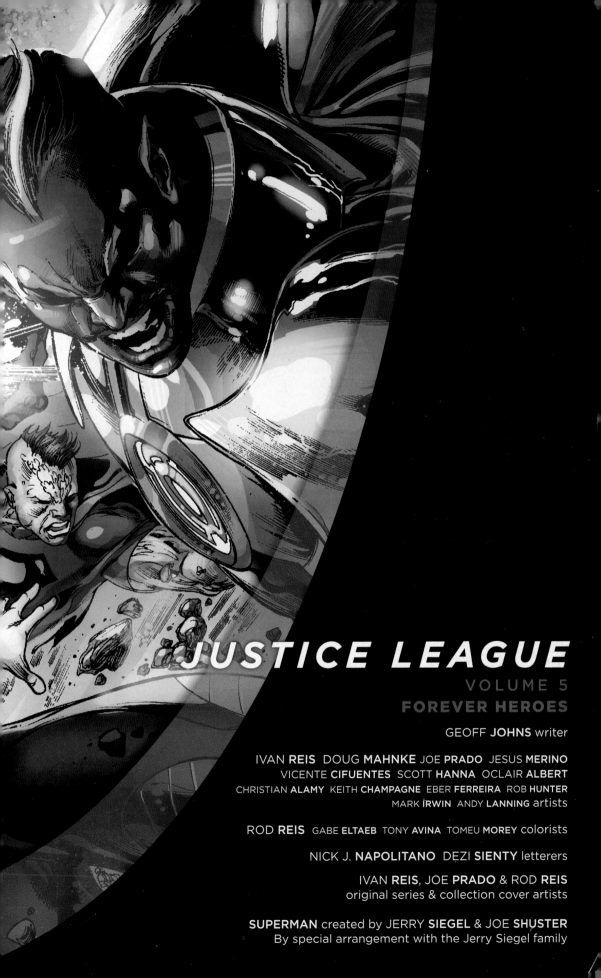

JUSTICE LEAGUE
VOLUME 5
FOREVER HEROES

GEOFF JOHNS writer

IVAN **REIS** DOUG **MAHNKE** JOE **PRADO** JESUS **MERINO**
VICENTE **CIFUENTES** SCOTT **HANNA** OCLAIR **ALBERT**
CHRISTIAN **ALAMY** KEITH **CHAMPAGNE** EBER **FERREIRA** ROB **HUNTER**
MARK **IRWIN** ANDY **LANNING** artists

ROD **REIS** GABE **ELTAEB** TONY **AVINA** TOMEU **MOREY** colorists

NICK J. **NAPOLITANO** DEZI **SIENTY** letterers

IVAN **REIS**, JOE **PRADO** & ROD **REIS**
original series & collection cover artists

SUPERMAN created by JERRY **SIEGEL** & JOE **SHUSTER**
By special arrangement with the Jerry Siegel family

BRIAN CUNNINGHAM Editor – Original Series KATE DURRÉ Assistant Editor – Original Series ROBIN WILDMAN Editor
ROBBIN BROSTERMAN Design Director – Books ROBBIE BIEDERMAN Publication Design

BOB HARRAS Senior VP – Editor-in-Chief, DC Comics

DIANE NELSON President DAN DIDIO and JIM LEE Co-Publishers GEOFF JOHNS Chief Creative Officer
AMIT DESAI Senior VP – Marketing and Franchise Management
AMY GENKINS Senior VP – Business and Legal Affairs NAIRI GARDINER Senior VP – Finance
JEFF BOISON VP – Publishing Planning MARK CHIARELLO VP – Art Direction and Design
JOHN CUNNINGHAM VP – Marketing TERRI CUNNINGHAM VP – Editorial Administration
LARRY GANEM VP – Talent Relations and Services ALISON GILL Senior VP – Manufacturing and Operations
HANK KANALZ Senior VP – Vertigo and Integrated Publishing JAY KOGAN VP – Business and Legal Affairs, Publishing
JACK MAHAN VP – Business Affairs, Talent NICK NAPOLITANO VP – Manufacturing Administration SUE POHJA VP – Book Sales
FRED RUIZ VP – Manufacturing Operations COURTNEY SIMMONS Senior VP – Publicity BOB WAYNE Senior VP – Sales

JUSTICE LEAGUE VOLUME 5: FOREVER HEROES

DC Comics, 1700 Broadway, New York, NY 10019
A Warner Bros. Entertainment Company.
Printed by RR Donnelley, Owensville, MO. USA. 2/6/15. First Printing.

ISBN: 978-1-4012-5419-3

Library of Congress Cataloging-in-Publication Data

Johns, Geoff, 1973- author.
Justice League. Volume 5, Forever Heroes / Geoff Johns, Ivan Reis.
pages cm. — (The New 52!)
ISBN 978-1-4012-5419-3
1. Graphic novels. I. Reis, Ivan, illustrator. II. Title. III. Title: Forever Heroes.
PN6728.J87J6544 2014
741.5'973—dc23
                    2014011708

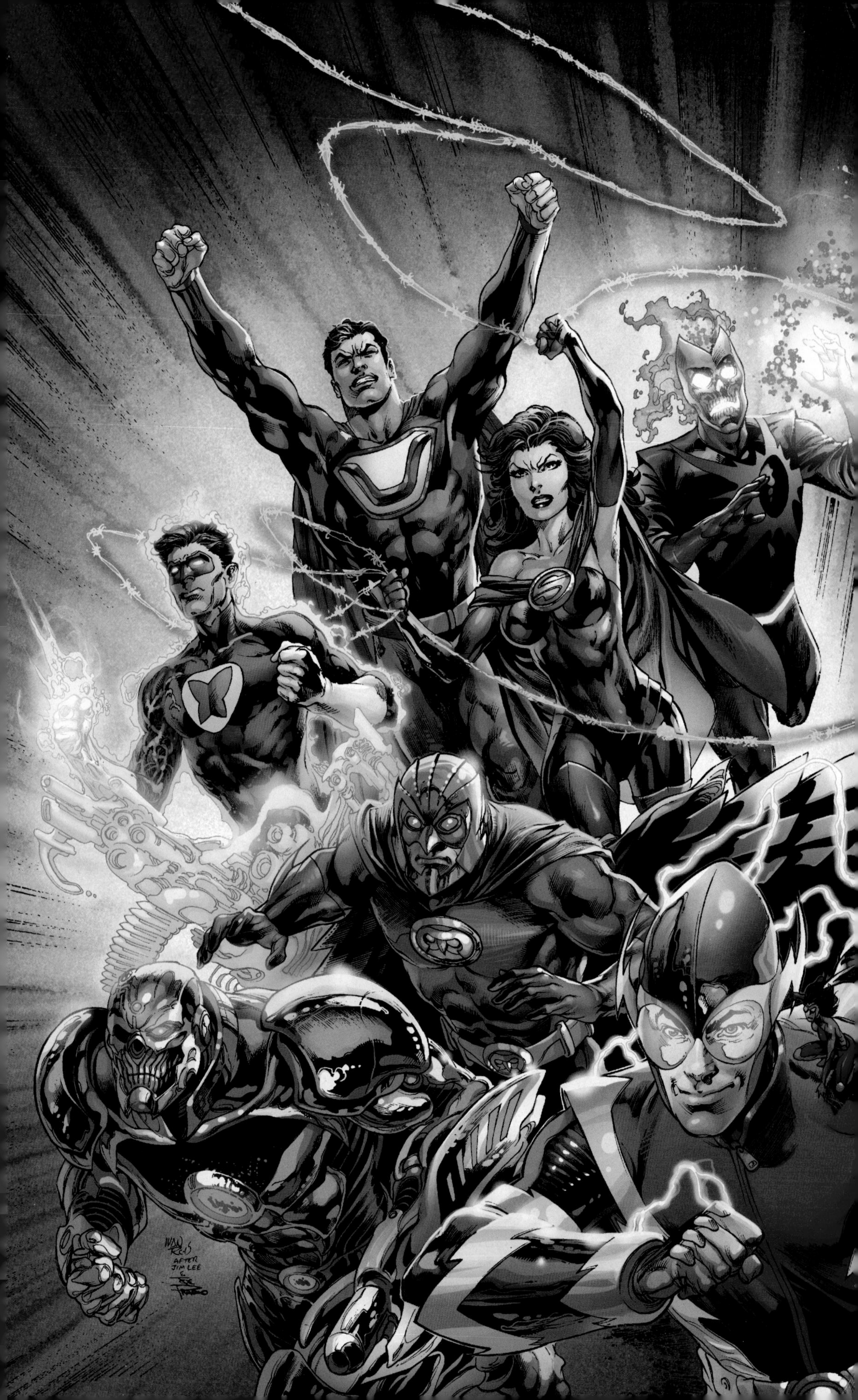
IVAN REIS
AFTER
JIM LEE
&

FOREVER STRONG

GEOFF JOHNS writer **IVAN REIS** penciller **JOE PRADO, OCLAIR ALBERT** and **EBER FERREIRA** inkers

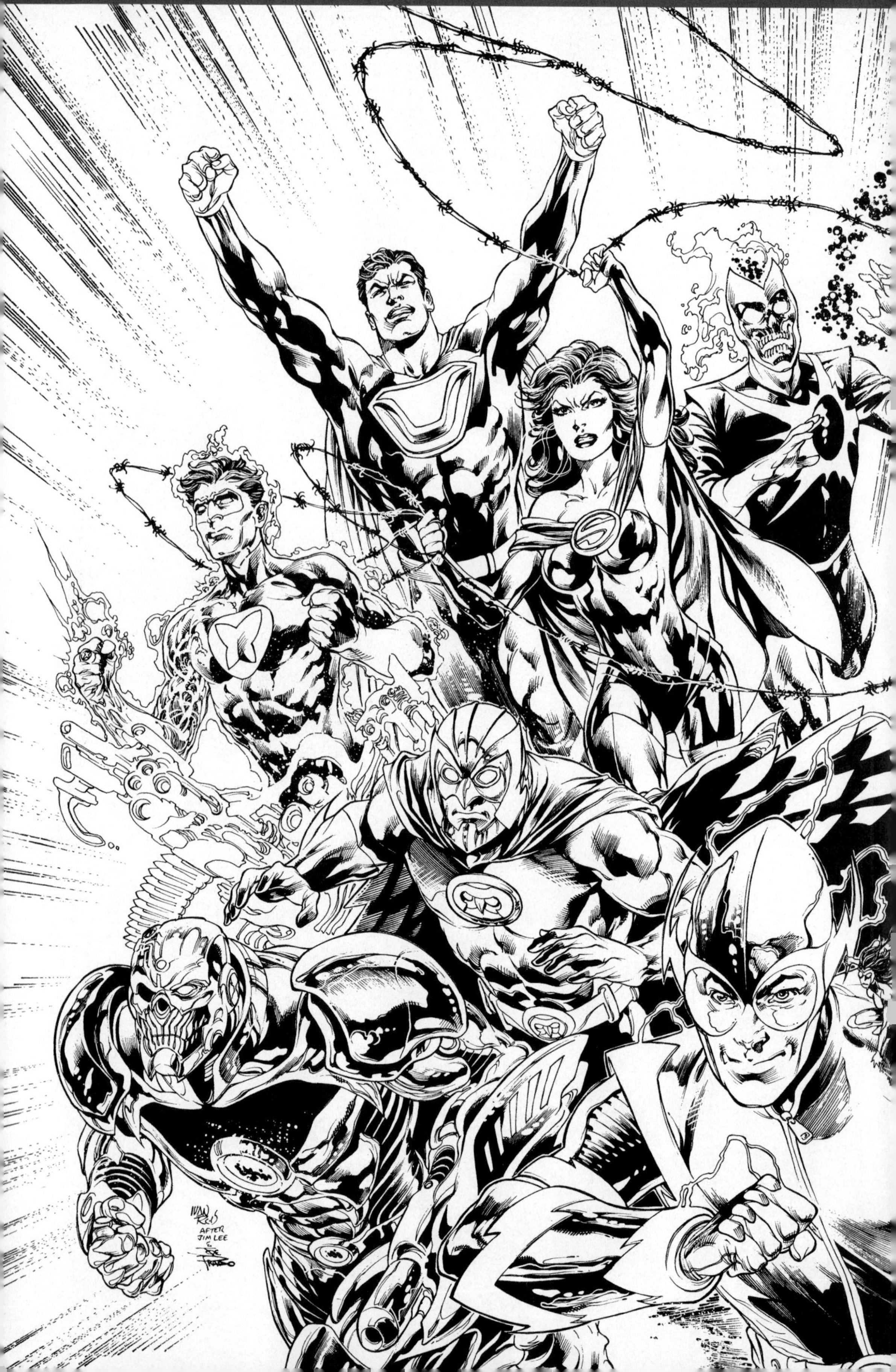

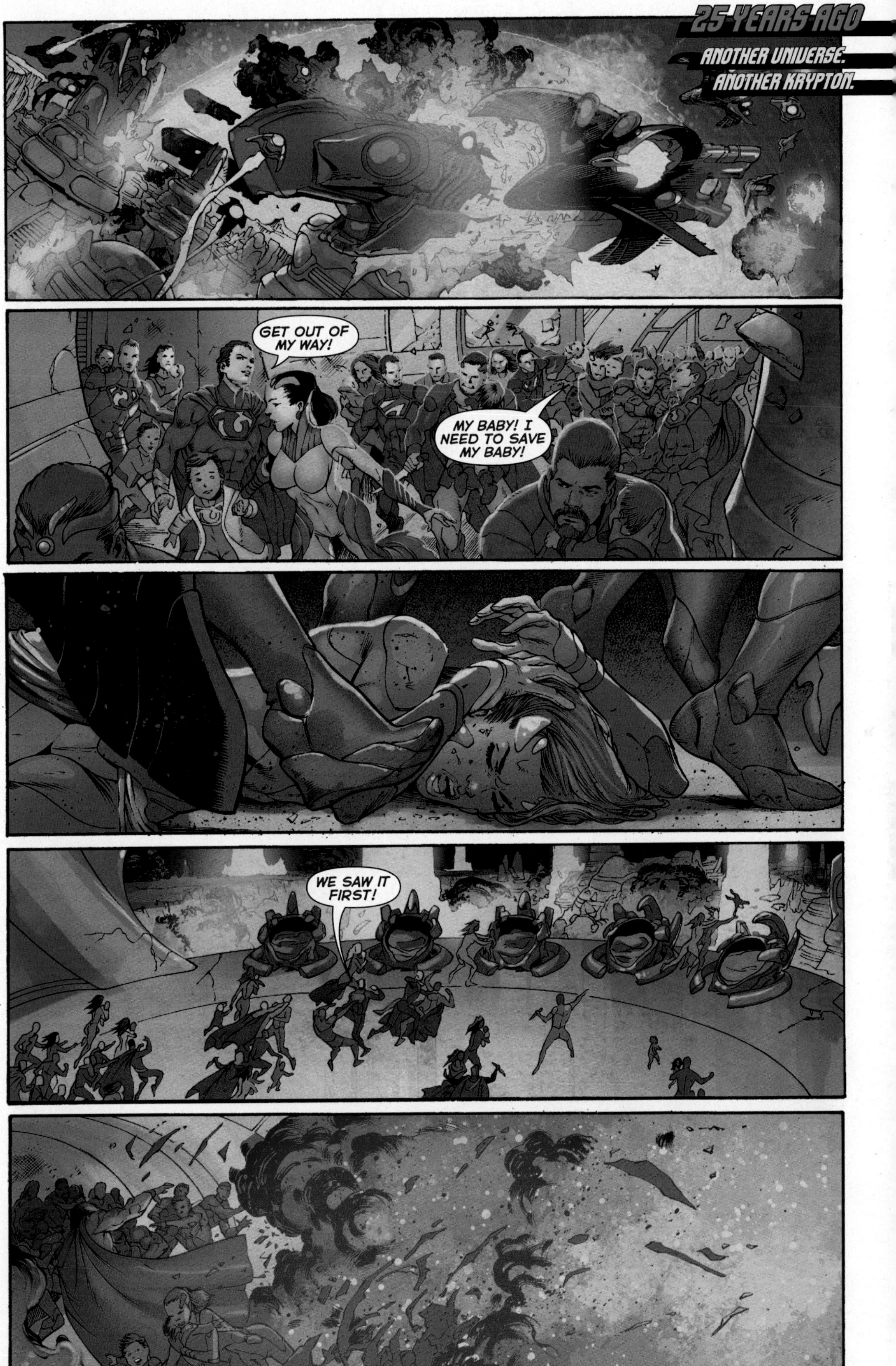
25 YEARS AGO
ANOTHER UNIVERSE. ANOTHER KRYPTON.
GET OUT OF MY WAY!
MY BABY! I NEED TO SAVE MY BABY!
WE SAW IT FIRST!

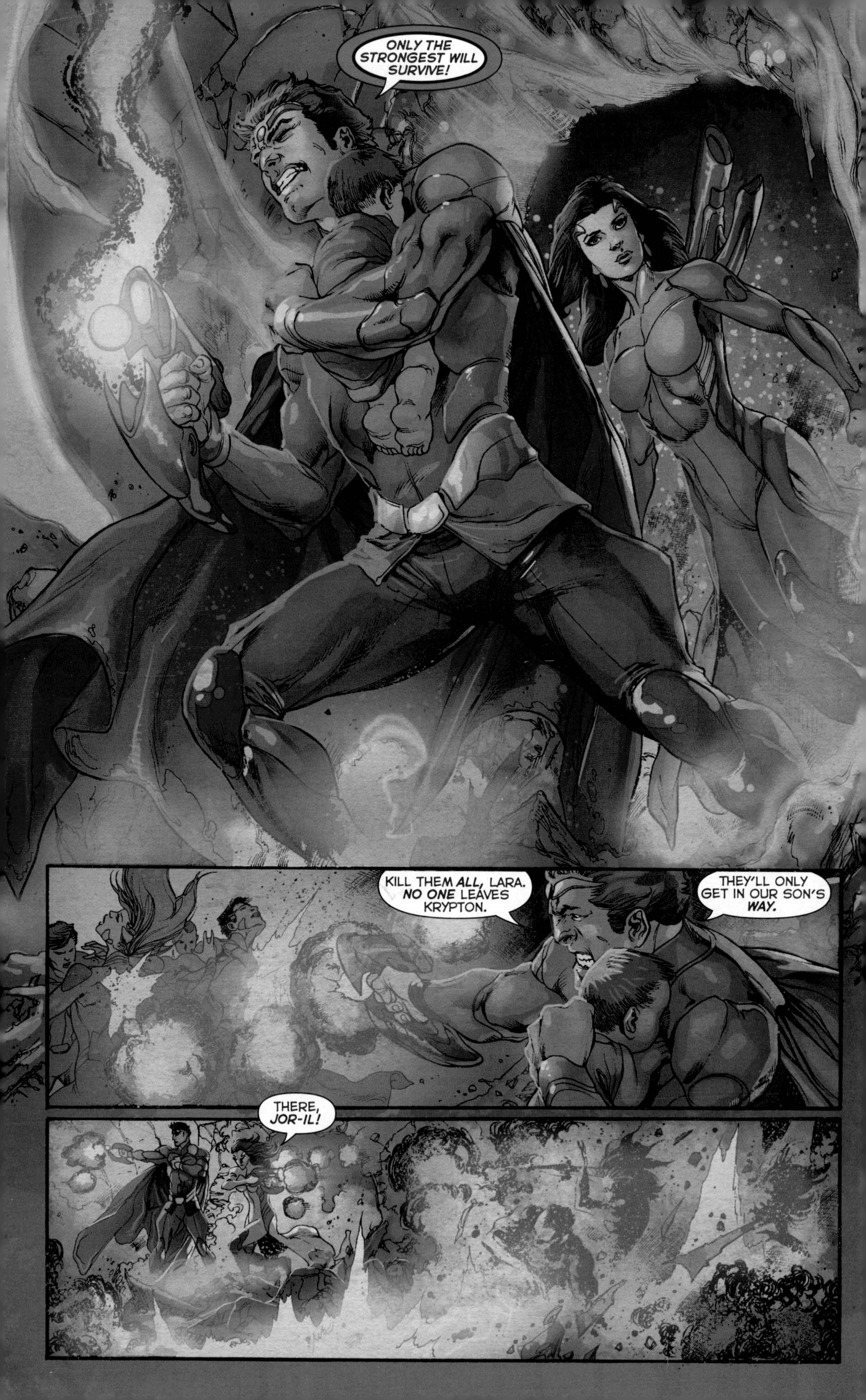
ONLY THE STRONGEST WILL SURVIVE!
KILL THEM ALL, LARA. NO ONE LEAVES KRYPTON.
THEY'LL ONLY GET IN OUR SON'S WAY.
THERE, JOR-IL!

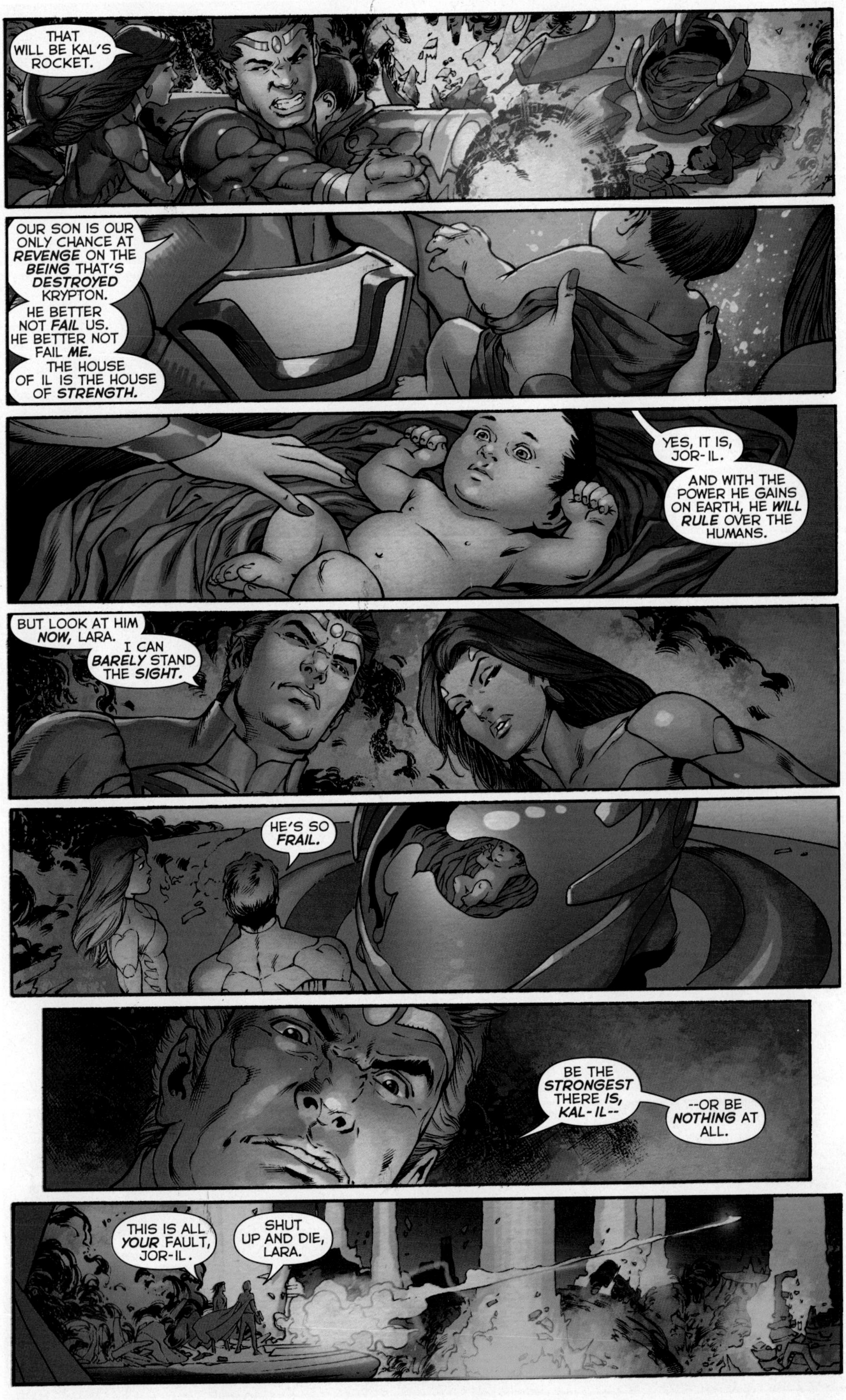
THAT WILL BE KAL'S ROCKET.
OUR SON IS OUR ONLY CHANCE AT *REVENGE* ON THE *BEING* THAT'S *DESTROYED* KRYPTON.
HE BETTER NOT *FAIL* US. HE BETTER NOT FAIL *ME.*
THE HOUSE OF IL IS THE HOUSE OF *STRENGTH.*
YES, IT IS, JOR-IL.
AND WITH THE POWER HE GAINS ON EARTH, HE *WILL RULE* OVER THE HUMANS.
BUT LOOK AT HIM *NOW,* LARA.
I CAN *BARELY* STAND THE *SIGHT.*
HE'S SO *FRAIL.*
BE THE *STRONGEST* THERE *IS, KAL-IL--*
--OR BE *NOTHING* AT ALL.
THIS IS ALL *YOUR* FAULT, JOR-IL.
SHUT UP AND DIE, LARA.

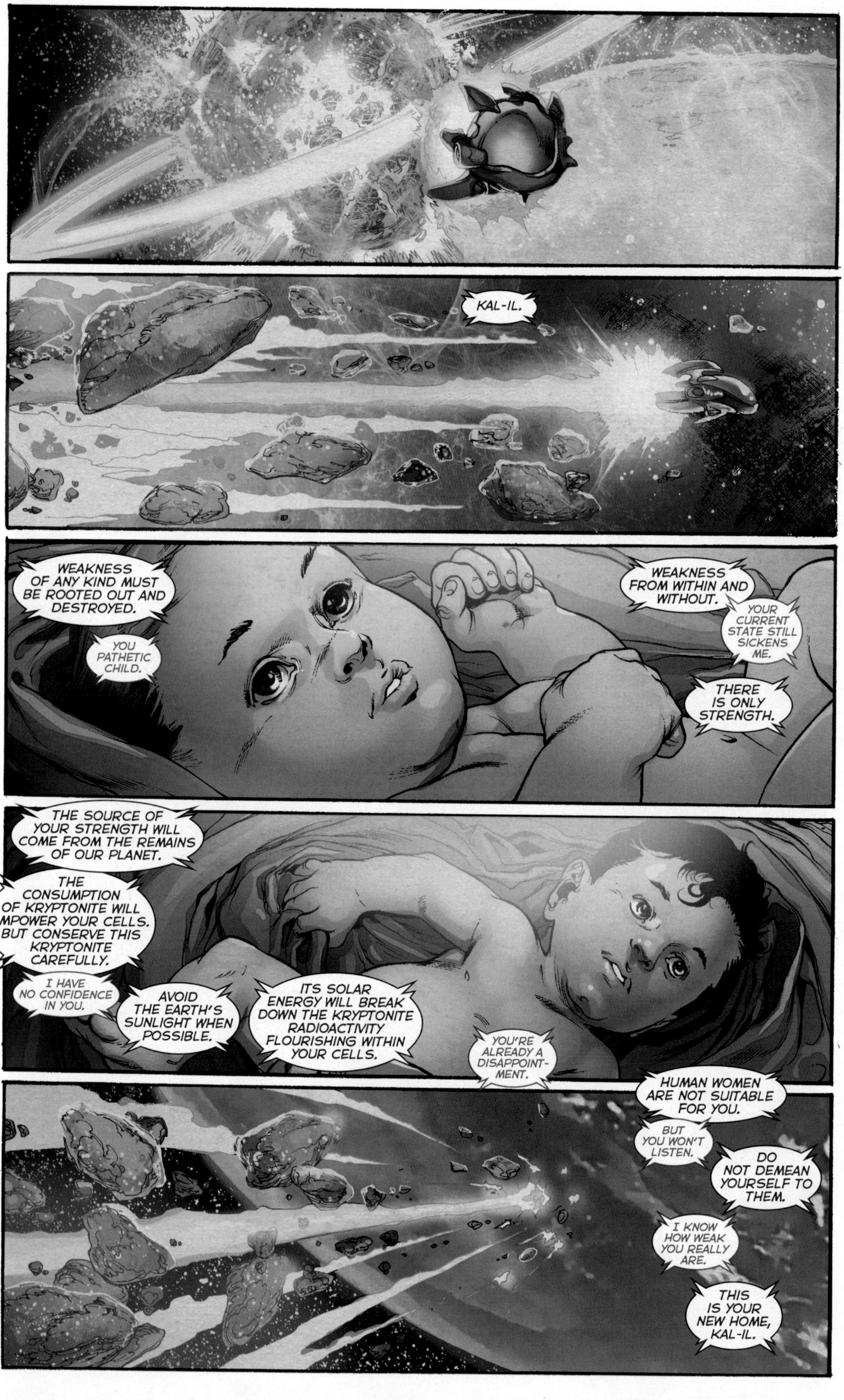
KAL-IL.
WEAKNESS OF ANY KIND MUST BE ROOTED OUT AND DESTROYED.
YOU PATHETIC CHILD.
WEAKNESS FROM WITHIN AND WITHOUT.
YOUR CURRENT STATE STILL SICKENS ME.
THERE IS ONLY STRENGTH.
THE SOURCE OF YOUR STRENGTH WILL COME FROM THE REMAINS OF OUR PLANET.
THE CONSUMPTION OF KRYPTONITE WILL EMPOWER YOUR CELLS. BUT CONSERVE THIS KRYPTONITE CAREFULLY.
I HAVE NO CONFIDENCE IN YOU.
AVOID THE EARTH'S SUNLIGHT WHEN POSSIBLE.
ITS SOLAR ENERGY WILL BREAK DOWN THE KRYPTONITE RADIOACTIVITY FLOURISHING WITHIN YOUR CELLS.
YOU'RE ALREADY A DISAPPOINT-MENT.
HUMAN WOMEN ARE NOT SUITABLE FOR YOU.
BUT YOU WON'T LISTEN.
DO NOT DEMEAN YOURSELF TO THEM.
I KNOW HOW WEAK YOU REALLY ARE.
THIS IS YOUR NEW HOME, KAL-IL.

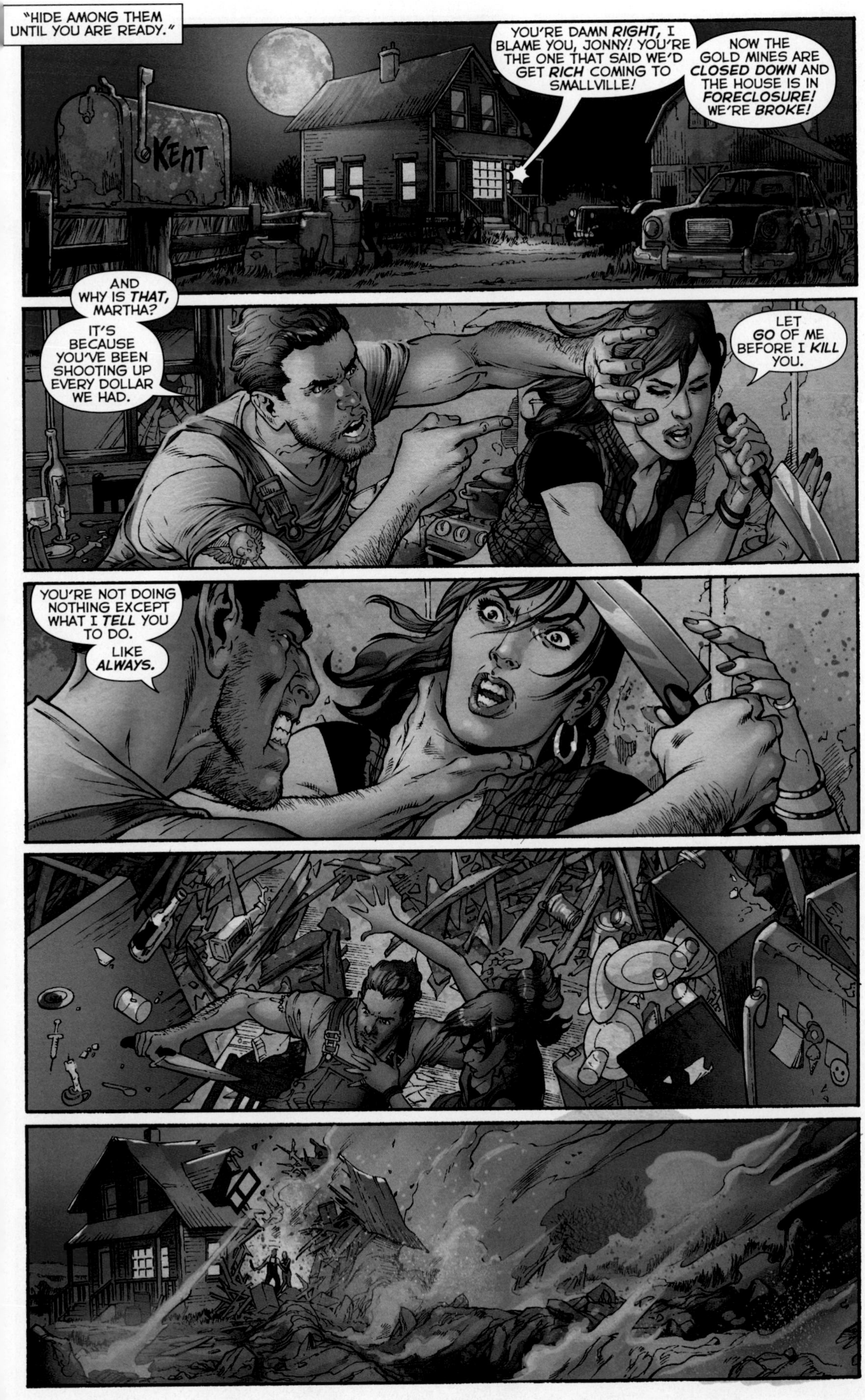
"HIDE AMONG THEM UNTIL YOU ARE READY."
KENT
YOU'RE DAMN RIGHT, I BLAME YOU, JONNY! YOU'RE THE ONE THAT SAID WE'D GET RICH COMING TO SMALLVILLE!
NOW THE GOLD MINES ARE CLOSED DOWN AND THE HOUSE IS IN FORECLOSURE! WE'RE BROKE!
AND WHY IS THAT, MARTHA?
IT'S BECAUSE YOU'VE BEEN SHOOTING UP EVERY DOLLAR WE HAD.
LET GO OF ME BEFORE I KILL YOU.
YOU'RE NOT DOING NOTHING EXCEPT WHAT I TELL YOU TO DO.
LIKE ALWAYS.

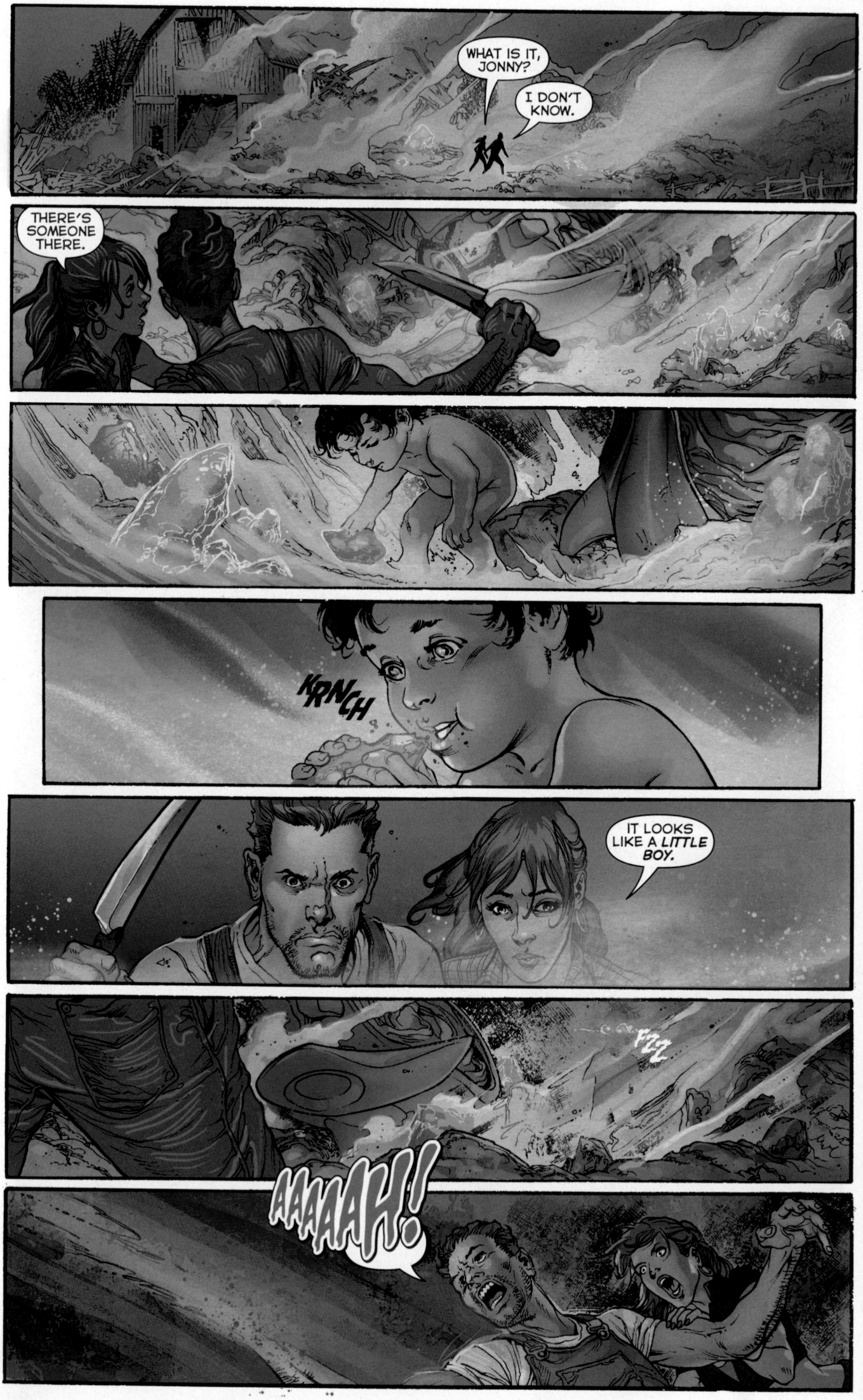
WHAT IS IT, JONNY?
I DON'T KNOW.
THERE'S SOMEONE THERE.
KRNCH
IT LOOKS LIKE A *LITTLE BOY.*
FZZ
AAAAAH!

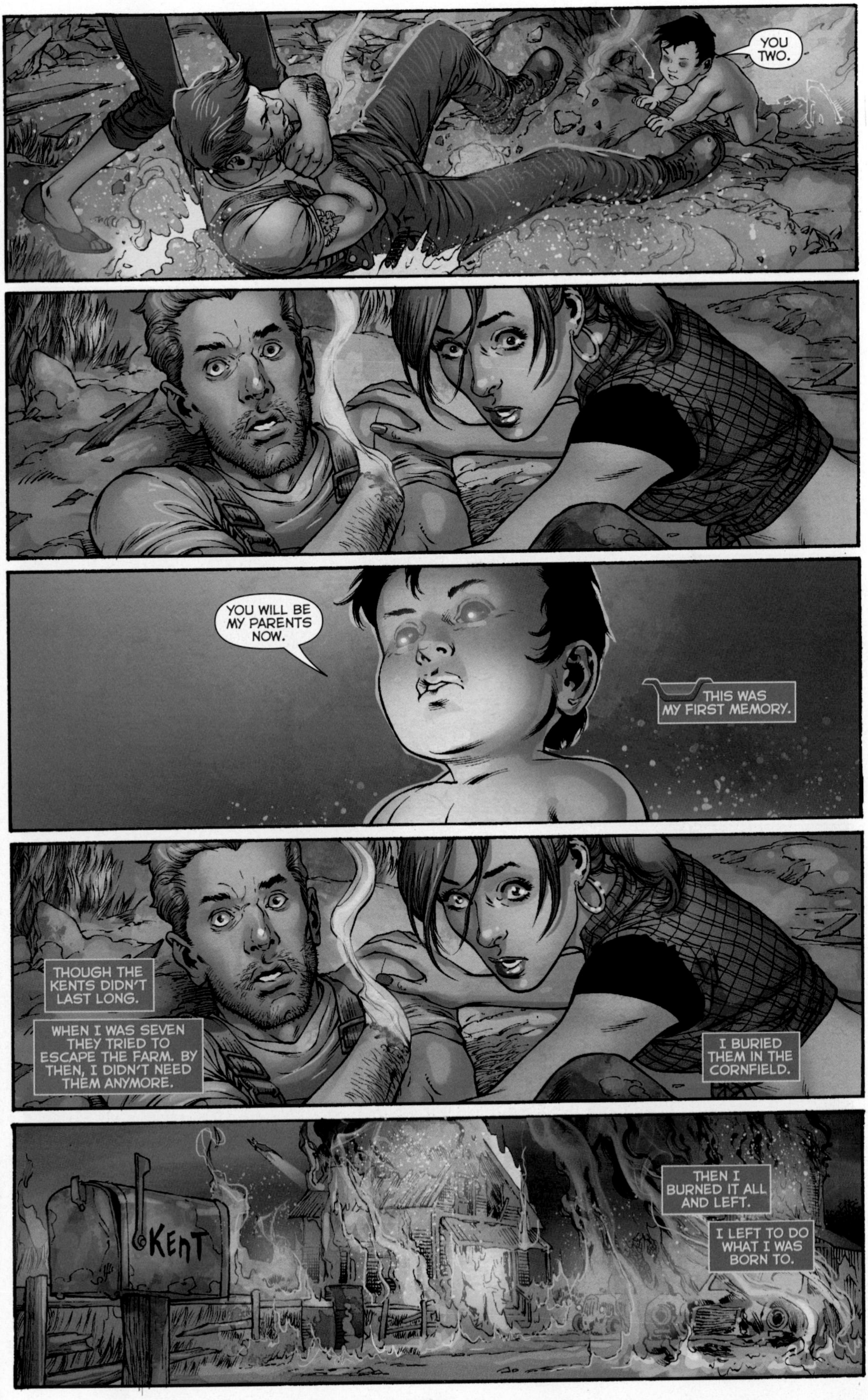
YOU TWO.
YOU WILL BE MY PARENTS NOW.
THIS WAS MY FIRST MEMORY.
THOUGH THE KENTS DIDN'T LAST LONG.
WHEN I WAS SEVEN THEY TRIED TO ESCAPE THE FARM. BY THEN, I DIDN'T NEED THEM ANYMORE.
I BURIED THEM IN THE CORNFIELD.
KENT
THEN I BURNED IT ALL AND LEFT.
I LEFT TO DO WHAT I WAS BORN TO.

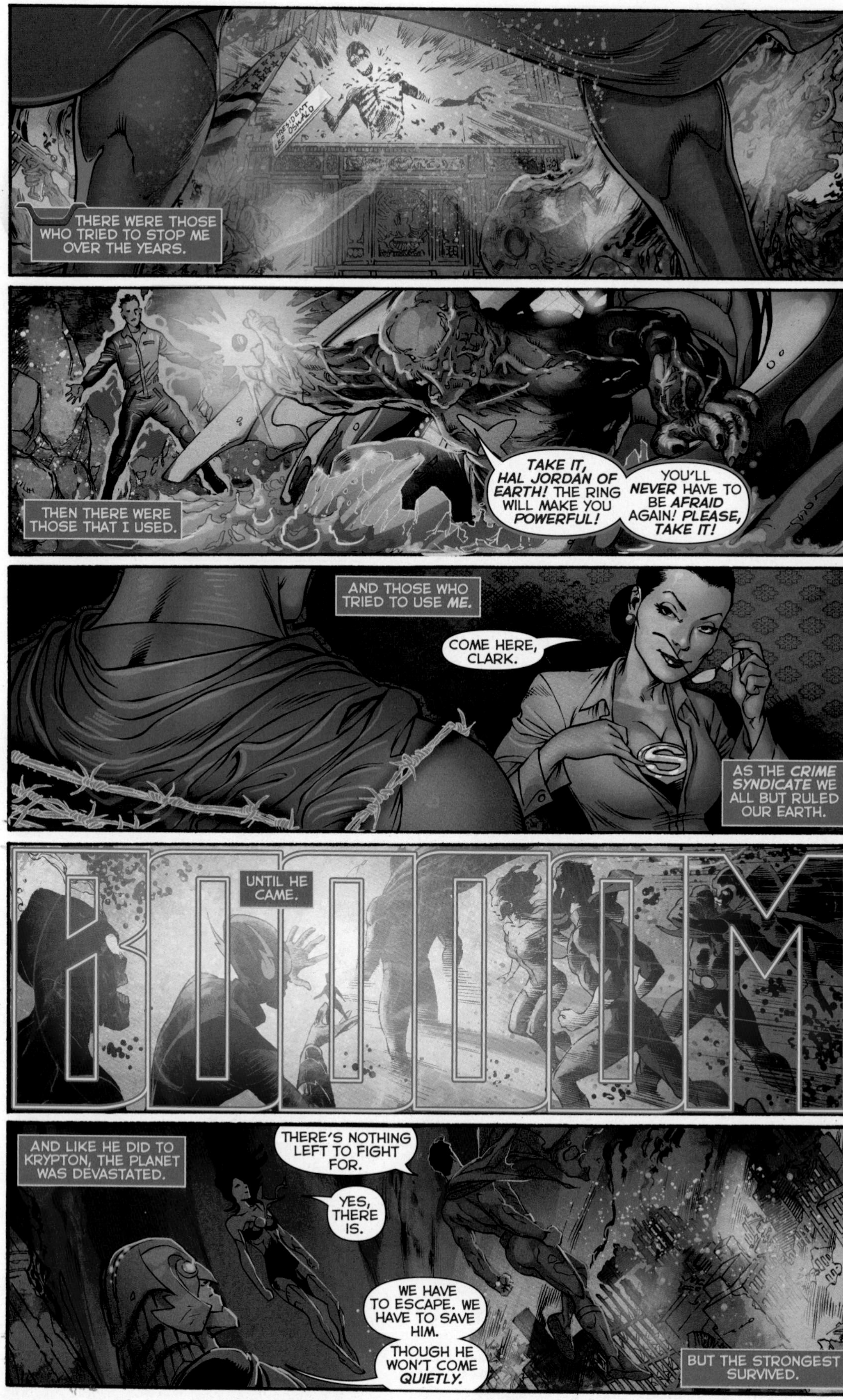
PRESIDENT LEE OSWALD
THERE WERE THOSE WHO TRIED TO STOP ME OVER THE YEARS.
THEN THERE WERE THOSE THAT I USED.
TAKE IT, HAL JORDAN OF EARTH! THE RING WILL MAKE YOU POWERFUL!
YOU'LL NEVER HAVE TO BE AFRAID AGAIN! PLEASE, TAKE IT!
AND THOSE WHO TRIED TO USE ME.
COME HERE, CLARK.
AS THE CRIME SYNDICATE WE ALL BUT RULED OUR EARTH.
UNTIL HE CAME.
AND LIKE HE DID TO KRYPTON, THE PLANET WAS DEVASTATED.
THERE'S NOTHING LEFT TO FIGHT FOR.
YES, THERE IS.
WE HAVE TO ESCAPE. WE HAVE TO SAVE HIM.
THOUGH HE WON'T COME QUIETLY.
BUT THE STRONGEST SURVIVED.

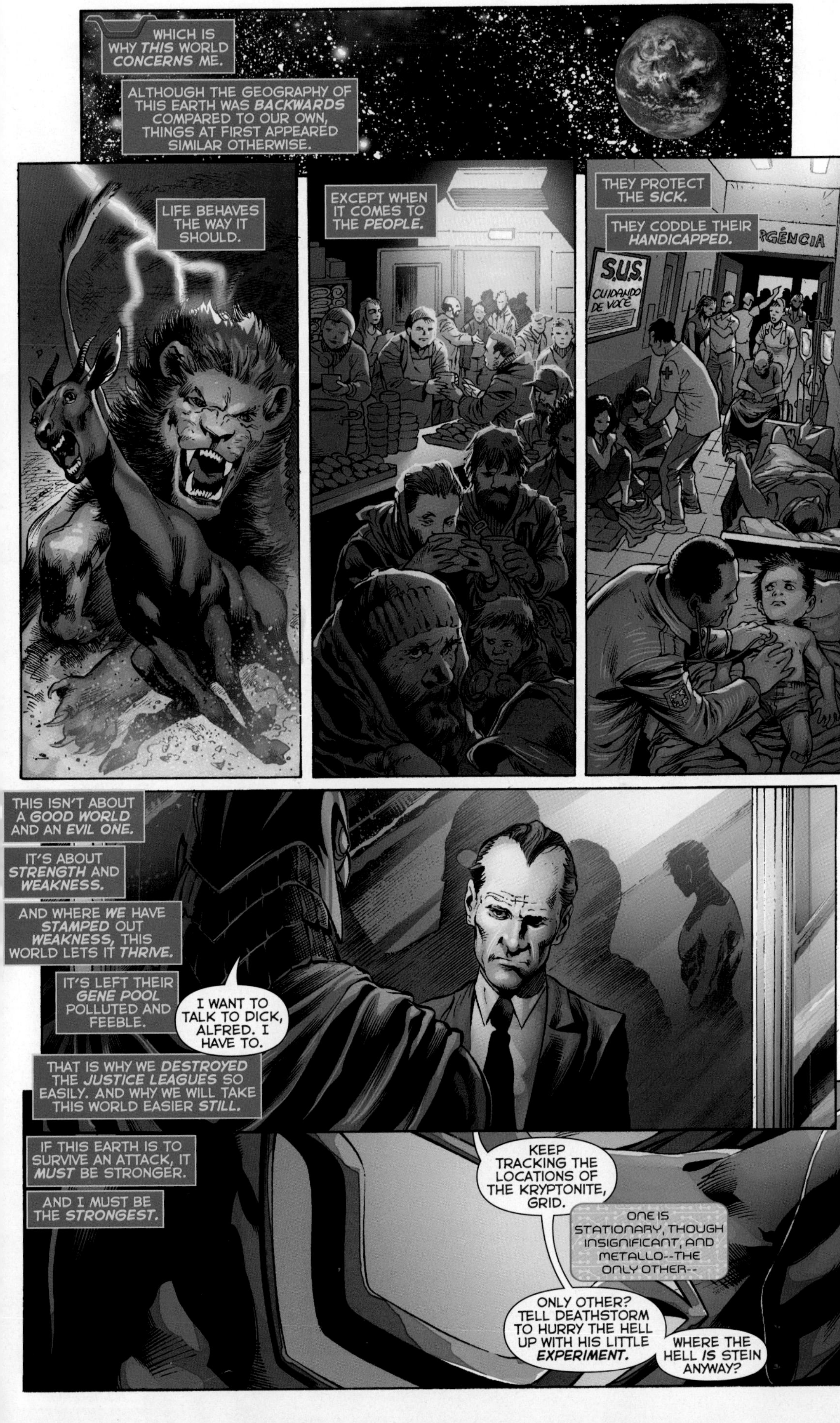

WHICH IS WHY THIS WORLD CONCERNS ME.
ALTHOUGH THE GEOGRAPHY OF THIS EARTH WAS BACKWARDS COMPARED TO OUR OWN, THINGS AT FIRST APPEARED SIMILAR OTHERWISE.
LIFE BEHAVES THE WAY IT SHOULD.
EXCEPT WHEN IT COMES TO THE PEOPLE.
THEY PROTECT THE SICK.
THEY CODDLE THEIR HANDICAPPED.
RGÊNCIA
S.U.S. CUIDANDO DE VOCÊ
THIS ISN'T ABOUT A GOOD WORLD AND AN EVIL ONE.
IT'S ABOUT STRENGTH AND WEAKNESS.
AND WHERE WE HAVE STAMPED OUT WEAKNESS, THIS WORLD LETS IT THRIVE.
IT'S LEFT THEIR GENE POOL POLLUTED AND FEEBLE.
I WANT TO TALK TO DICK, ALFRED. I HAVE TO.
THAT IS WHY WE DESTROYED THE JUSTICE LEAGUES SO EASILY. AND WHY WE WILL TAKE THIS WORLD EASIER STILL.
IF THIS EARTH IS TO SURVIVE AN ATTACK, IT MUST BE STRONGER.
AND I MUST BE THE STRONGEST.
KEEP TRACKING THE LOCATIONS OF THE KRYPTONITE, GRID.
ONE IS STATIONARY, THOUGH INSIGNIFICANT, AND METALLO--THE ONLY OTHER--
ONLY OTHER? TELL DEATHSTORM TO HURRY THE HELL UP WITH HIS LITTLE EXPERIMENT.
WHERE THE HELL IS STEIN ANYWAY?

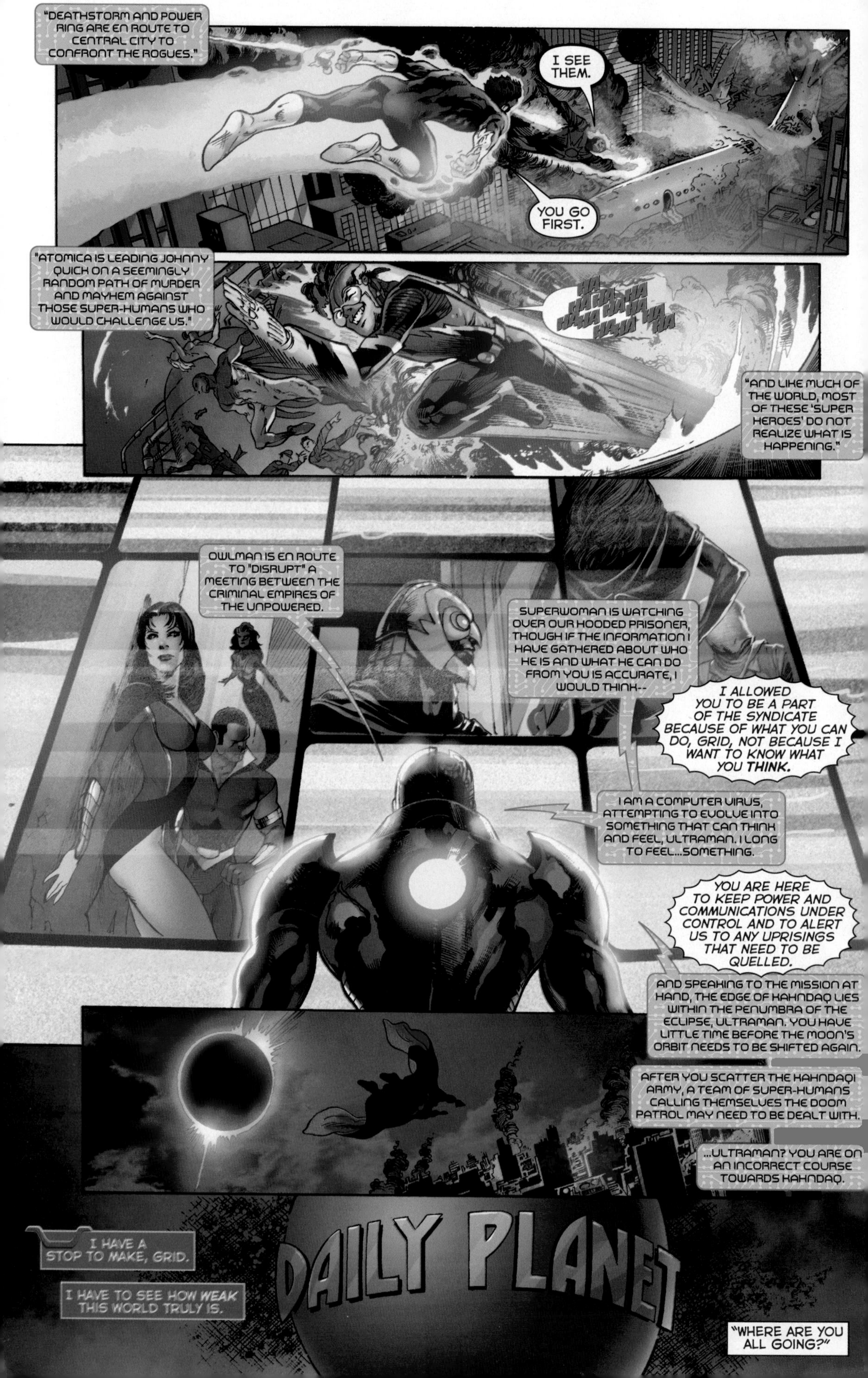
"DEATHSTORM AND POWER RING ARE EN ROUTE TO CENTRAL CITY TO CONFRONT THE ROGUES."
I SEE THEM.
YOU GO FIRST.
"ATOMICA IS LEADING JOHNNY QUICK ON A SEEMINGLY RANDOM PATH OF MURDER AND MAYHEM AGAINST THOSE SUPER-HUMANS WHO WOULD CHALLENGE US."
HA HAHA HAHAHA HAHAHA HA HA
"AND LIKE MUCH OF THE WORLD, MOST OF THESE 'SUPER HEROES' DO NOT REALIZE WHAT IS HAPPENING."
OWLMAN IS EN ROUTE TO "DISRUPT" A MEETING BETWEEN THE CRIMINAL EMPIRES OF THE UNPOWERED.
SUPERWOMAN IS WATCHING OVER OUR HOODED PRISONER, THOUGH IF THE INFORMATION I HAVE GATHERED ABOUT WHO HE IS AND WHAT HE CAN DO FROM YOU IS ACCURATE, I WOULD THINK--
I ALLOWED YOU TO BE A PART OF THE SYNDICATE BECAUSE OF WHAT YOU CAN DO, GRID, NOT BECAUSE I WANT TO KNOW WHAT YOU **THINK.**
I AM A COMPUTER VIRUS, ATTEMPTING TO EVOLVE INTO SOMETHING THAT CAN THINK AND FEEL, ULTRAMAN. I LONG TO FEEL...SOMETHING.
YOU ARE HERE TO KEEP POWER AND COMMUNICATIONS UNDER CONTROL AND TO ALERT US TO ANY UPRISINGS THAT NEED TO BE QUELLED.
AND SPEAKING TO THE MISSION AT HAND, THE EDGE OF KAHNDAQ LIES WITHIN THE PENUMBRA OF THE ECLIPSE, ULTRAMAN. YOU HAVE LITTLE TIME BEFORE THE MOON'S ORBIT NEEDS TO BE SHIFTED AGAIN.
AFTER YOU SCATTER THE KAHNDAQI ARMY, A TEAM OF SUPER-HUMANS CALLING THEMSELVES THE DOOM PATROL MAY NEED TO BE DEALT WITH.
...ULTRAMAN? YOU ARE ON AN INCORRECT COURSE TOWARDS KAHNDAQ.
I HAVE A STOP TO MAKE, GRID.
I HAVE TO SEE HOW *WEAK* THIS WORLD TRULY IS.
DAILY PLANET
"WHERE ARE YOU ALL GOING?"

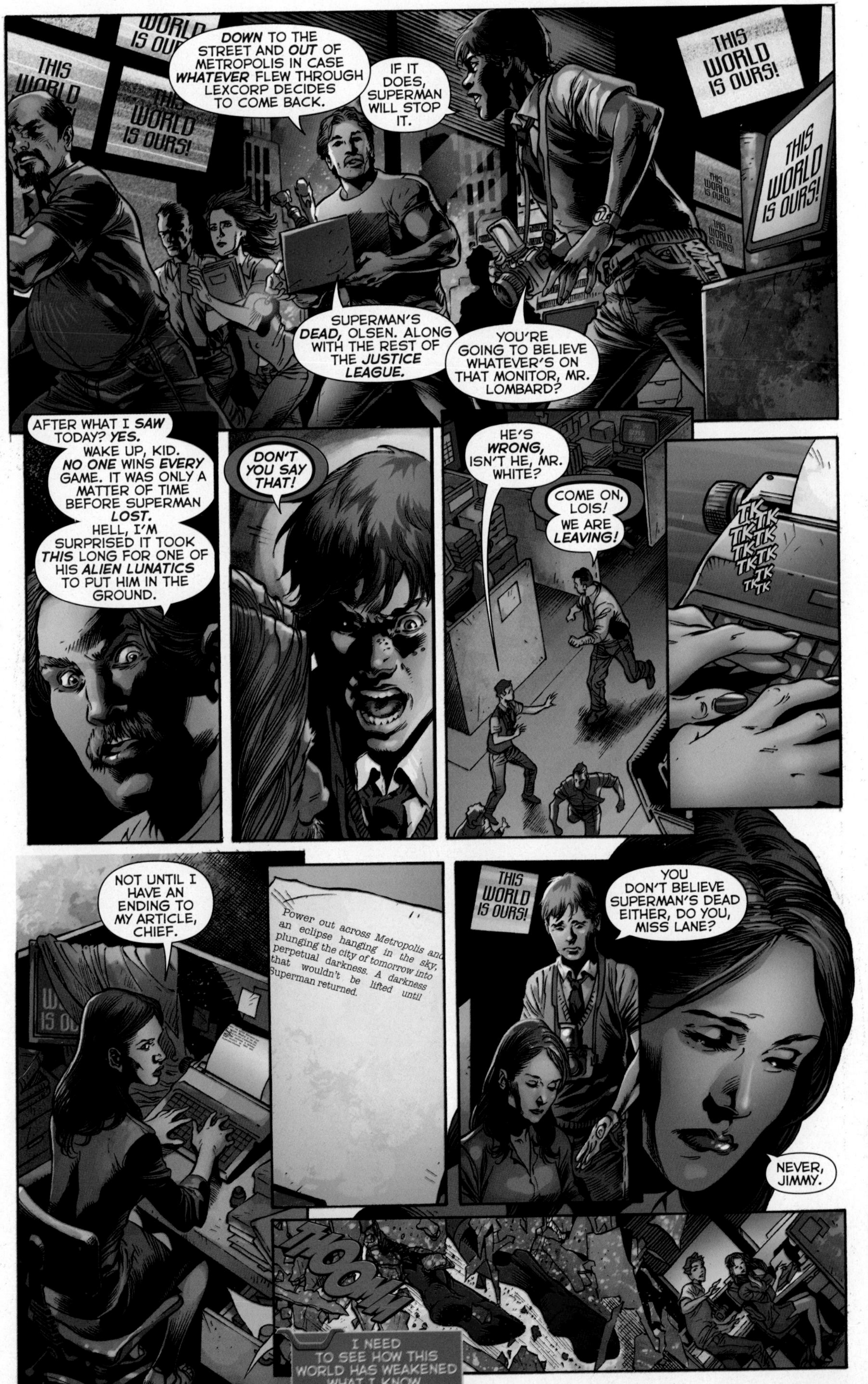

WORLD IS OURS!
THIS WORLD
THIS WORLD IS OURS!
DOWN TO THE STREET AND OUT OF METROPOLIS IN CASE WHATEVER FLEW THROUGH LEXCORP DECIDES TO COME BACK.
IF IT DOES, SUPERMAN WILL STOP IT.
THIS WORLD IS OURS!
THIS WORLD IS OURS!
THIS WORLD IS OURS!
THIS WORLD IS OURS!
SUPERMAN'S DEAD, OLSEN. ALONG WITH THE REST OF THE JUSTICE LEAGUE.
YOU'RE GOING TO BELIEVE WHATEVER'S ON THAT MONITOR, MR. LOMBARD?
AFTER WHAT I SAW TODAY? YES.
WAKE UP, KID. NO ONE WINS EVERY GAME. IT WAS ONLY A MATTER OF TIME BEFORE SUPERMAN LOST.
HELL, I'M SURPRISED IT TOOK THIS LONG FOR ONE OF HIS ALIEN LUNATICS TO PUT HIM IN THE GROUND.
DON'T YOU SAY THAT!
HE'S WRONG, ISN'T HE, MR. WHITE?
COME ON, LOIS! WE ARE LEAVING!
TK TK TK TK TK TK TK TK TK TK TK TK
NOT UNTIL I HAVE AN ENDING TO MY ARTICLE, CHIEF.
Power out across Metropolis and an eclipse hanging in the sky, plunging the city of tomorrow into perpetual darkness. A darkness that wouldn't be lifted until Superman returned.
THIS WORLD IS OURS!
YOU DON'T BELIEVE SUPERMAN'S DEAD EITHER, DO YOU, MISS LANE?
NEVER, JIMMY.
THOOM
I NEED TO SEE HOW THIS WORLD HAS WEAKENED WHAT I KNOW.

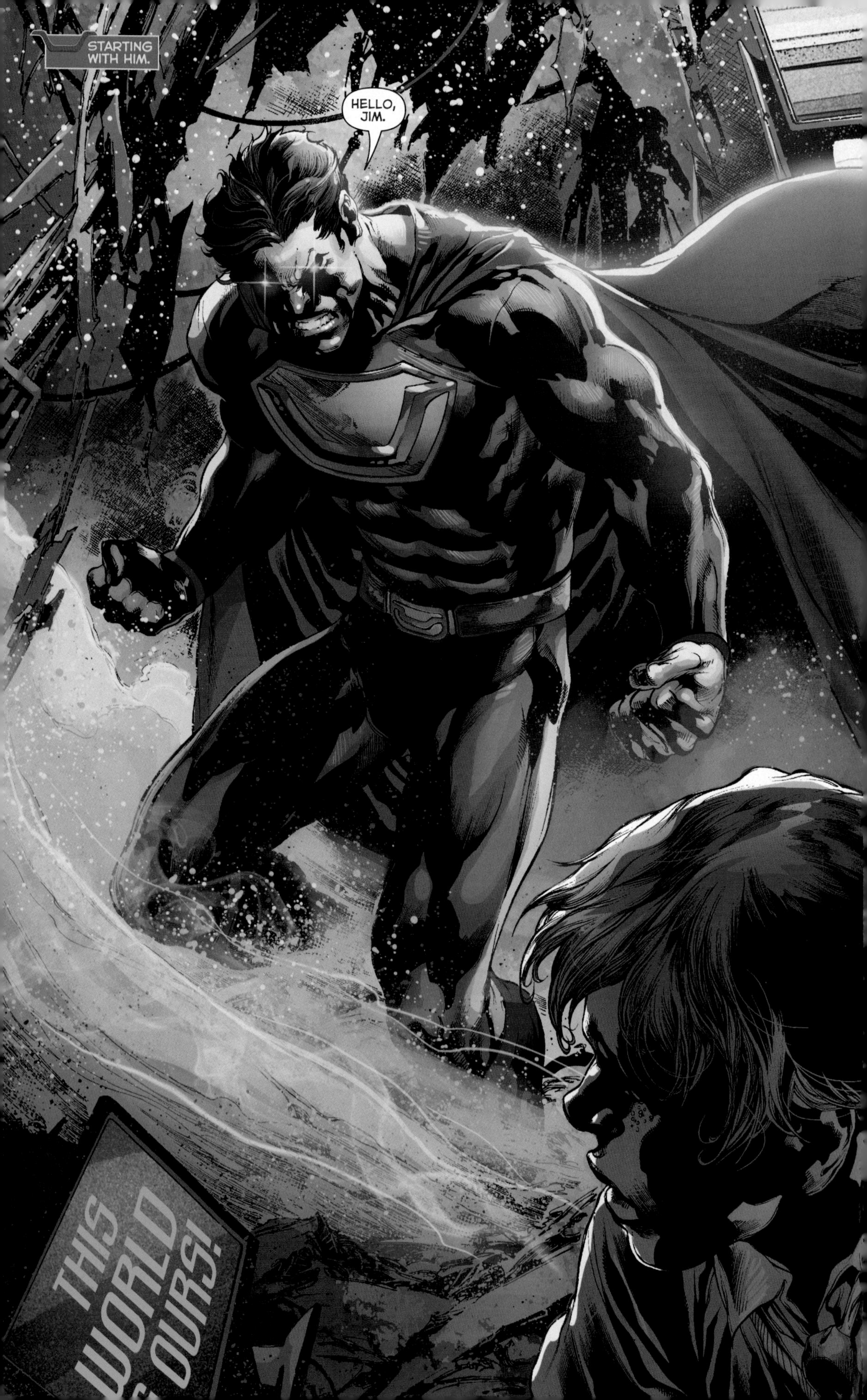
STARTING WITH HIM.
HELLO, JIM.
THIS WORLD IS OURS!

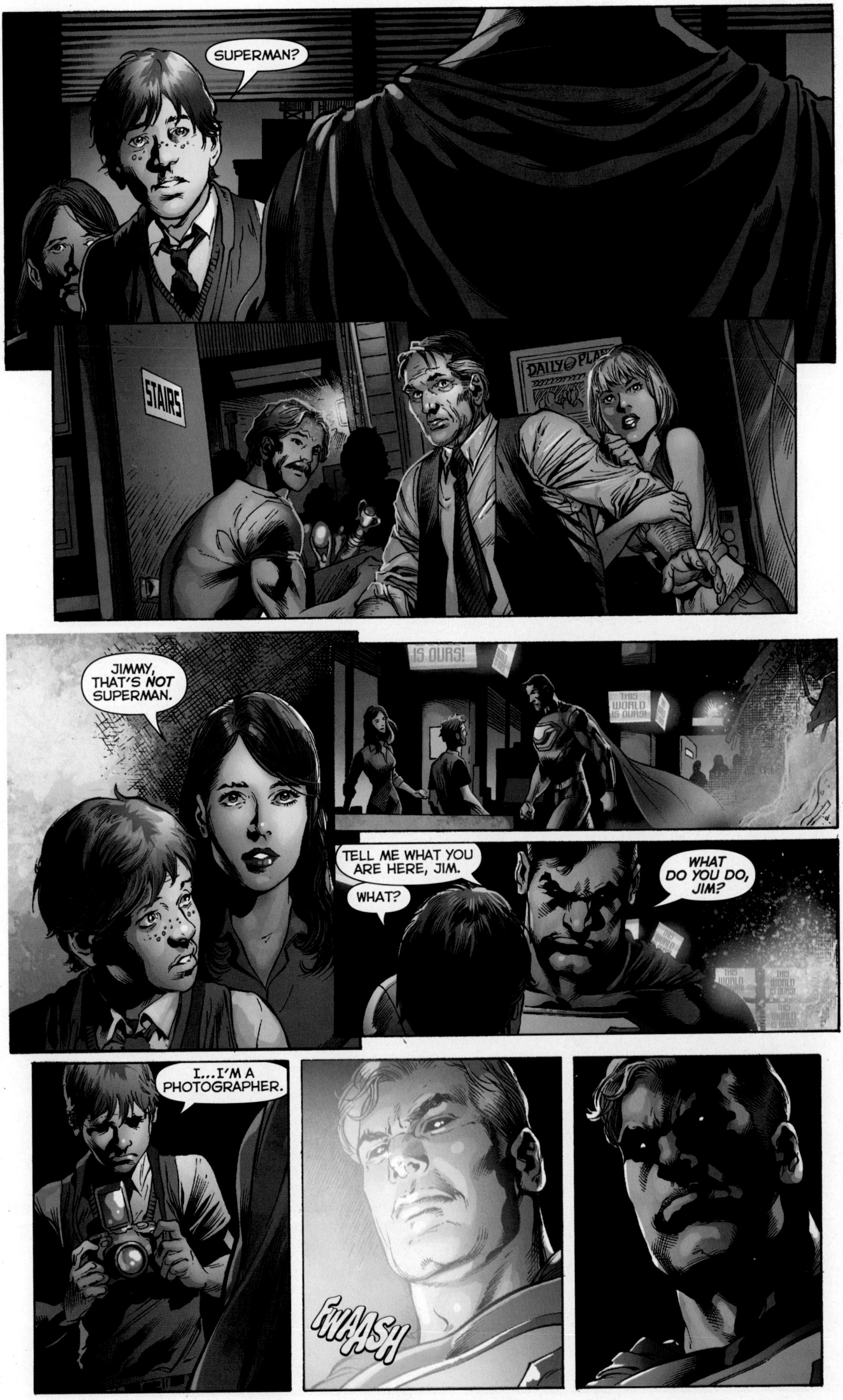
SUPERMAN?
STAIRS
DAILY PLA
JIMMY, THAT'S *NOT* SUPERMAN.
IS OURS!
THIS WORLD IS OURS!
TELL ME WHAT YOU ARE HERE, JIM.
WHAT?
WHAT DO YOU DO, JIM?
I...I'M A PHOTOGRAPHER.
FWAASH

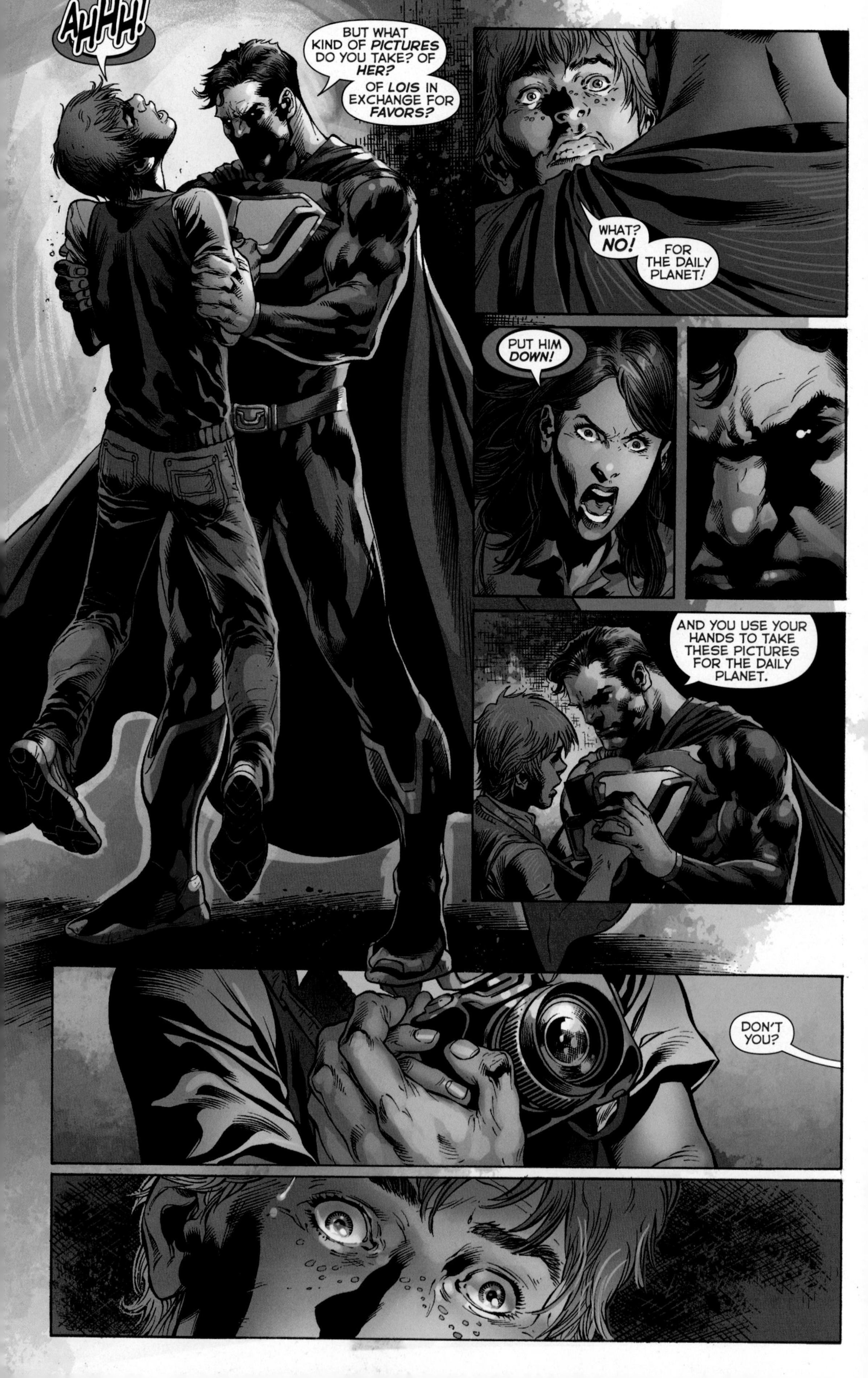
AHHH!
BUT WHAT KIND OF PICTURES DO YOU TAKE? OF HER?
OF LOIS IN EXCHANGE FOR FAVORS?
WHAT? NO!
FOR THE DAILY PLANET!
PUT HIM DOWN!
AND YOU USE YOUR HANDS TO TAKE THESE PICTURES FOR THE DAILY PLANET.
DON'T YOU?

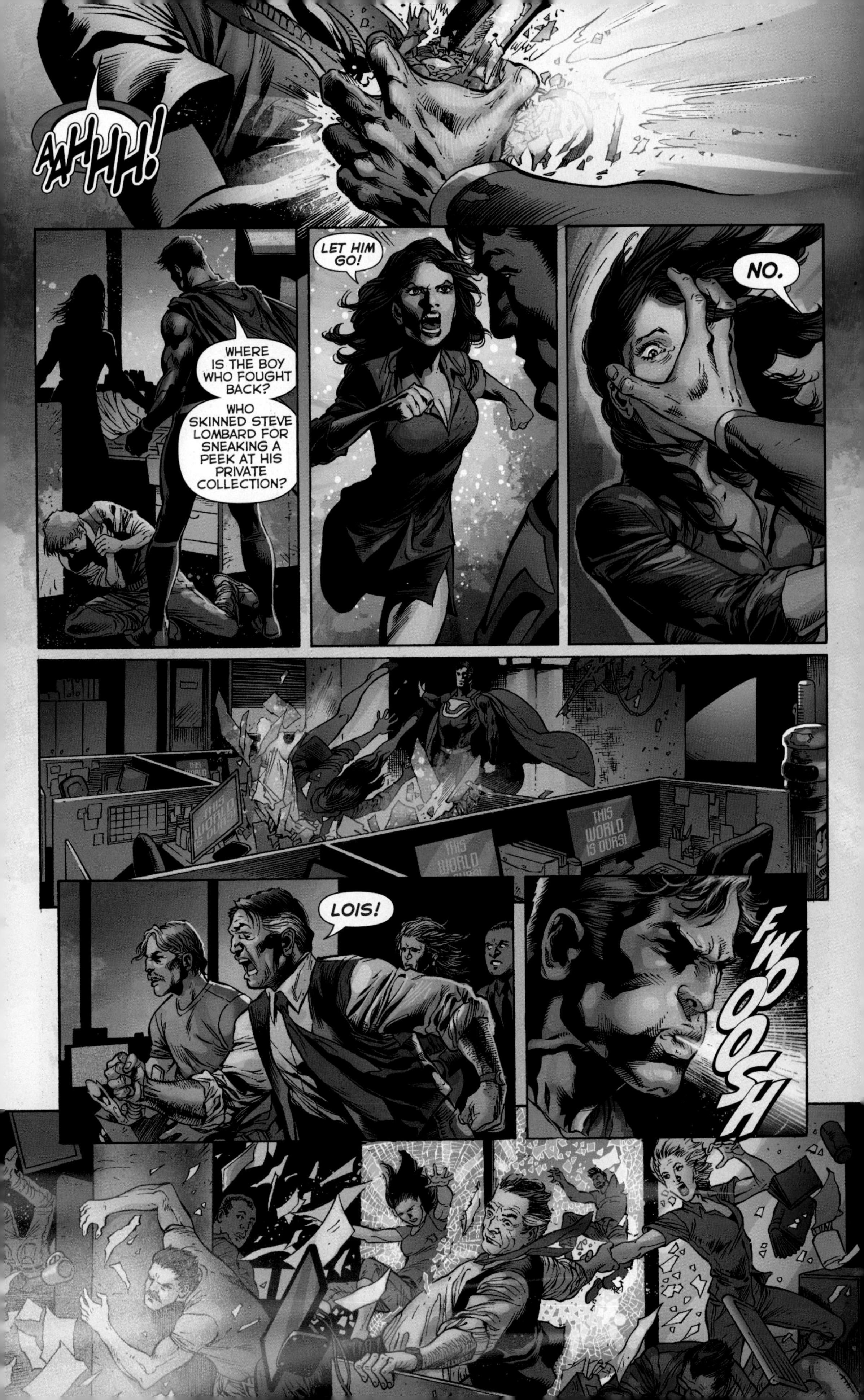
AAHHH!
WHERE IS THE BOY WHO FOUGHT BACK?
WHO SKINNED STEVE LOMBARD FOR SNEAKING A PEEK AT HIS PRIVATE COLLECTION?
LET HIM GO!
NO.
THIS WORLD IS OURS!
THIS WORLD IS OURS!
LOIS!
FWOOOOSH

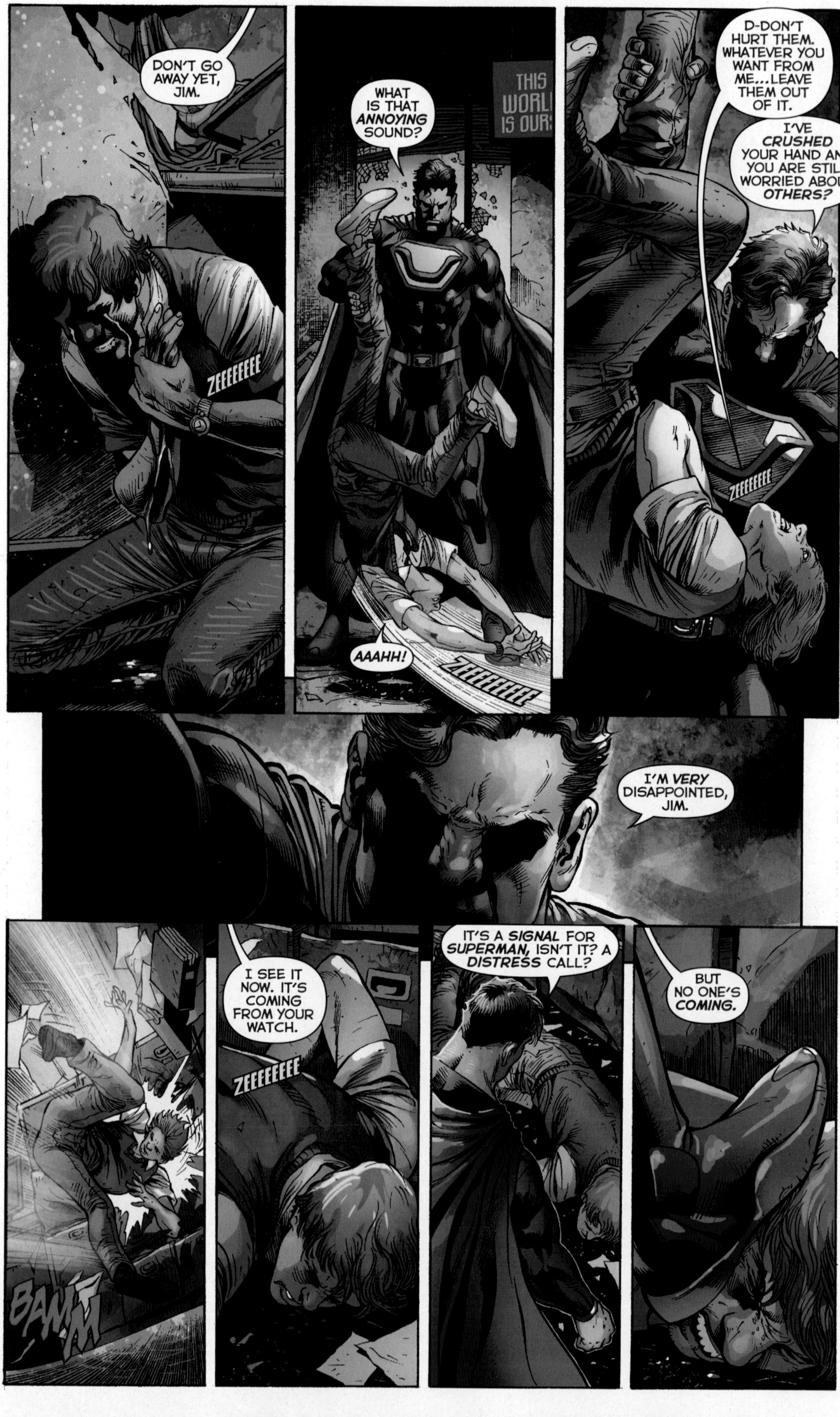
DON'T GO AWAY YET, JIM.
ZEEEEEEE
THIS WORLD IS OURS
WHAT IS THAT ANNOYING SOUND?
AAAHH!
ZEEEEEEEE
D-DON'T HURT THEM. WHATEVER YOU WANT FROM ME...LEAVE THEM OUT OF IT.
I'VE CRUSHED YOUR HAND AND YOU ARE STILL WORRIED ABOUT OTHERS?
ZEEEEEEE
I'M VERY DISAPPOINTED, JIM.
BAMM
I SEE IT NOW. IT'S COMING FROM YOUR WATCH.
ZEEEEEEE
IT'S A SIGNAL FOR SUPERMAN, ISN'T IT? A DISTRESS CALL?
BUT NO ONE'S COMING.

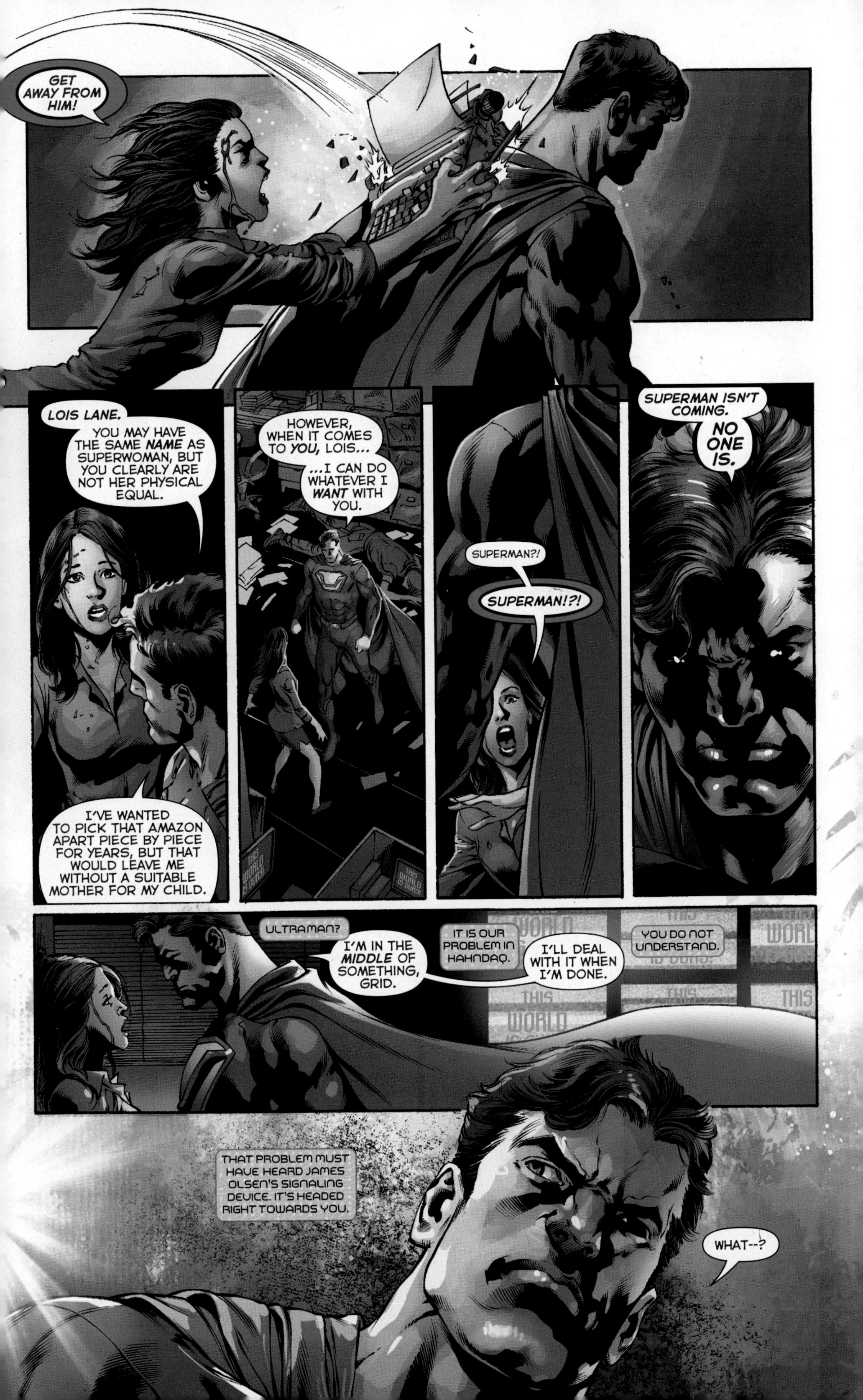
GET AWAY FROM HIM!
LOIS LANE.
YOU MAY HAVE THE SAME NAME AS SUPERWOMAN, BUT YOU CLEARLY ARE NOT HER PHYSICAL EQUAL.
I'VE WANTED TO PICK THAT AMAZON APART PIECE BY PIECE FOR YEARS, BUT THAT WOULD LEAVE ME WITHOUT A SUITABLE MOTHER FOR MY CHILD.
HOWEVER, WHEN IT COMES TO YOU, LOIS...
...I CAN DO WHATEVER I WANT WITH YOU.
SUPERMAN?!
SUPERMAN!?!
SUPERMAN ISN'T COMING.
NO ONE IS.
ULTRAMAN?
I'M IN THE MIDDLE OF SOMETHING, GRID.
IT IS OUR PROBLEM IN KAHNDAQ.
I'LL DEAL WITH IT WHEN I'M DONE.
YOU DO NOT UNDERSTAND.
THAT PROBLEM MUST HAVE HEARD JAMES OLSEN'S SIGNALING DEVICE. IT'S HEADED RIGHT TOWARDS YOU.
WHAT--?

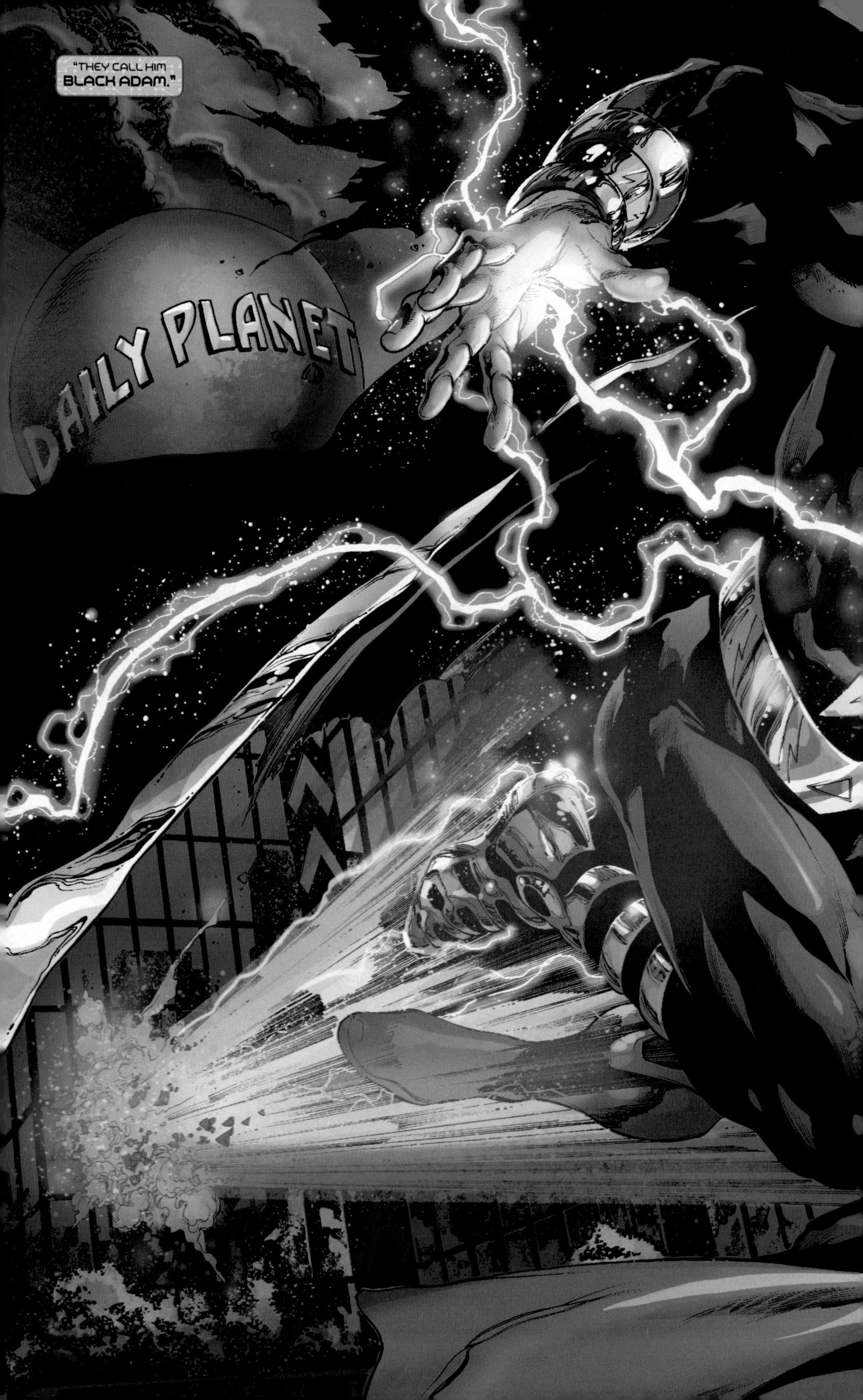
"THEY CALL HIM BLACK ADAM."
DAILY PLANET

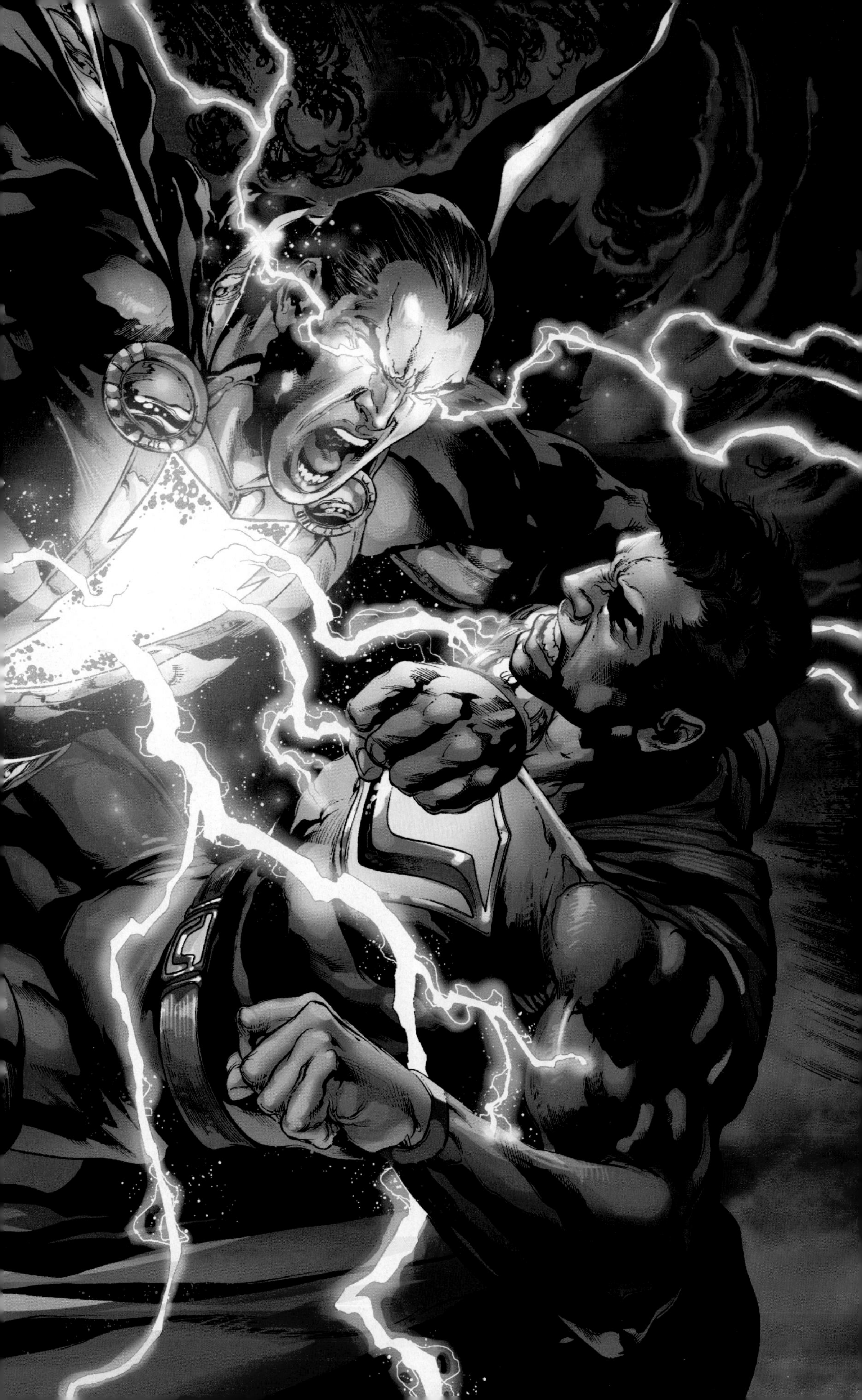

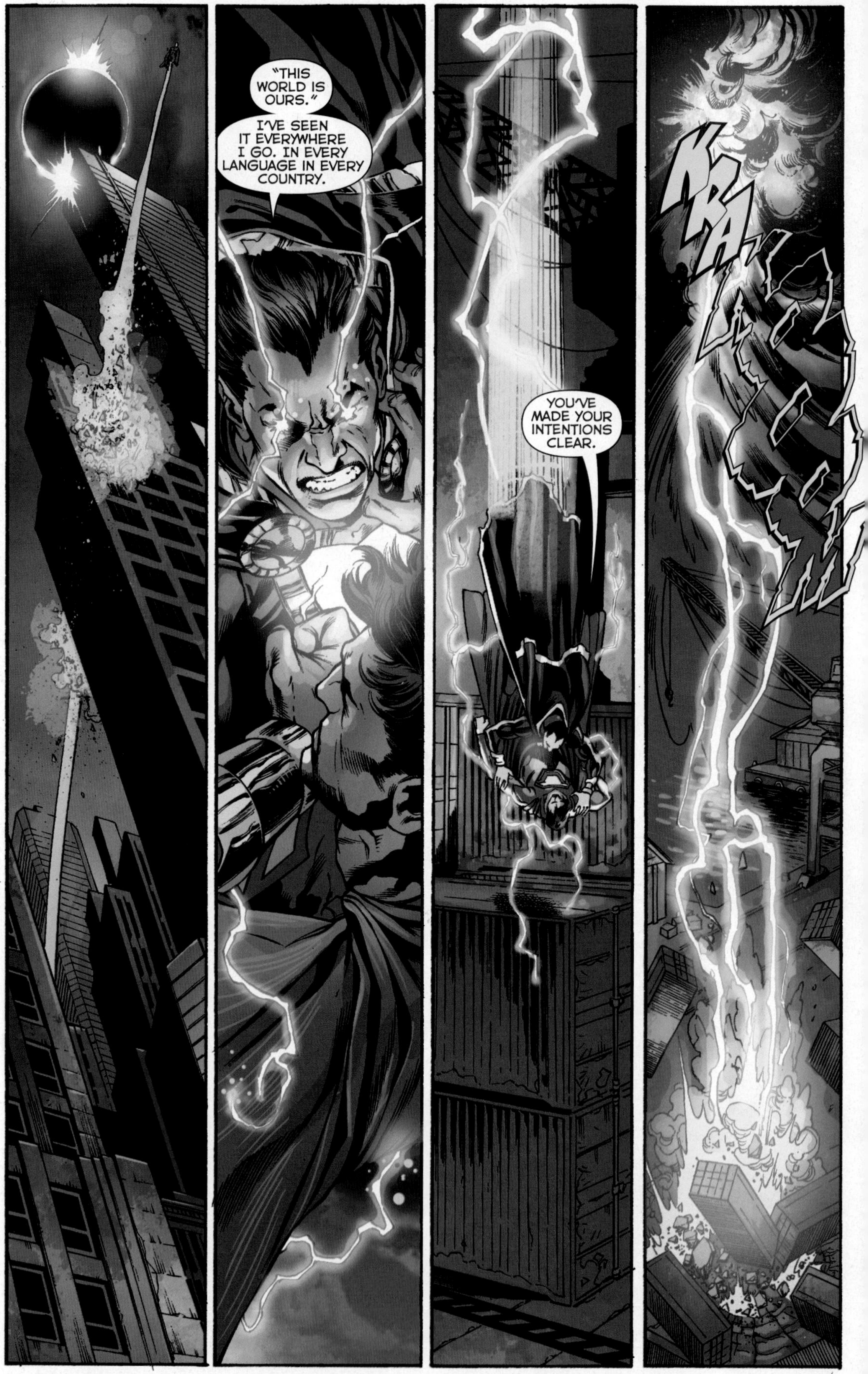
"THIS WORLD IS OURS."
I'VE SEEN IT EVERYWHERE I GO. IN EVERY LANGUAGE IN EVERY COUNTRY.
YOU'VE MADE YOUR INTENTIONS CLEAR.
KRA

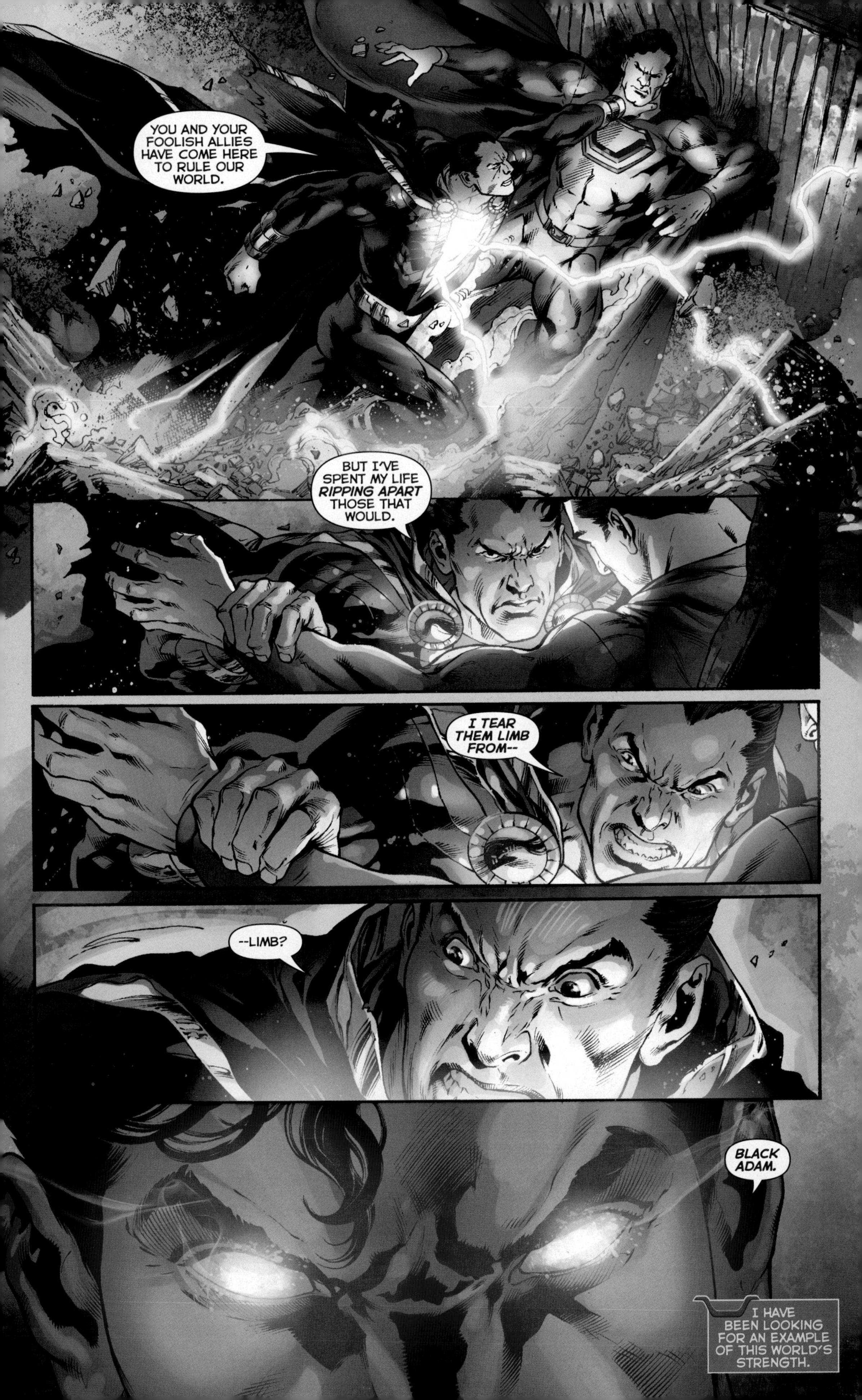
YOU AND YOUR FOOLISH ALLIES HAVE COME HERE TO RULE OUR WORLD.
BUT I'VE SPENT MY LIFE *RIPPING APART* THOSE THAT WOULD.
I TEAR THEM LIMB FROM--
--LIMB?
BLACK ADAM.
I HAVE BEEN LOOKING FOR AN EXAMPLE OF THIS WORLD'S STRENGTH.

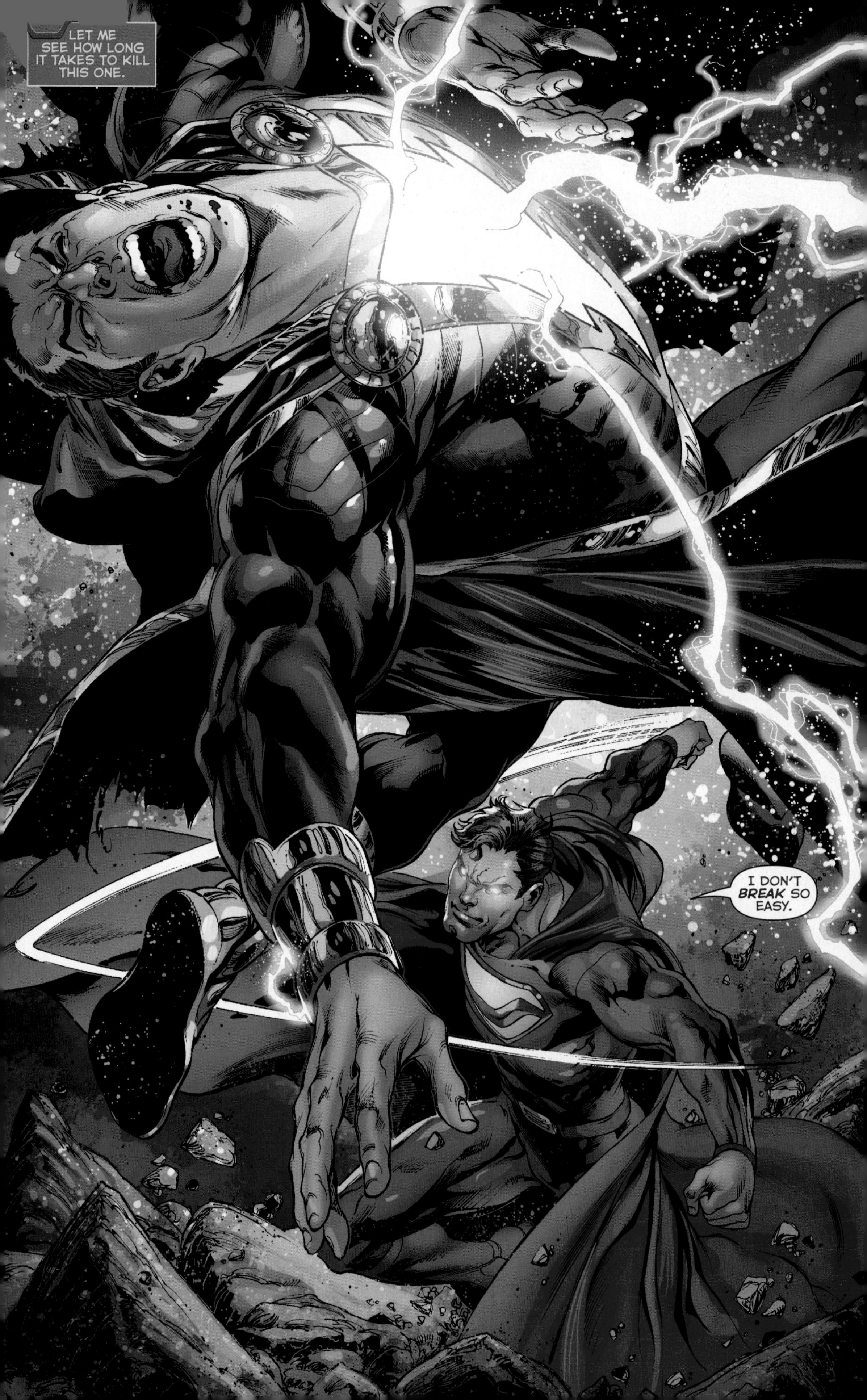
LET ME SEE HOW LONG IT TAKES TO KILL THIS ONE.
I DON'T *BREAK* SO EASY.

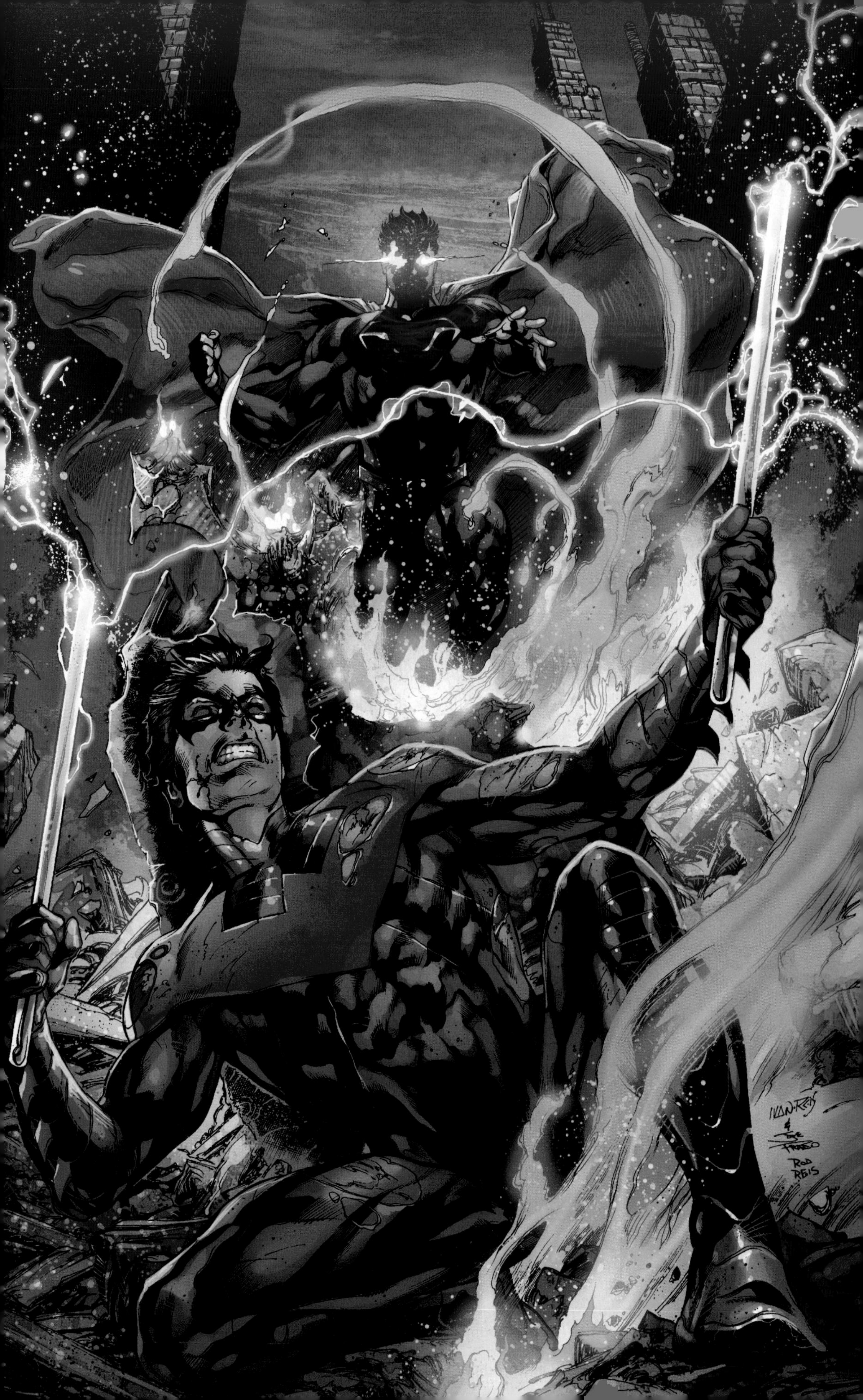
ROD REIS

FOREVER LOST

GEOFF JOHNS writer **DOUG MAHNKE** penciller

CHRISTIAN ALAMY, MARK IRWIN, KEITH CHAMPAGNE and **DOUG MAHNKE** inkers

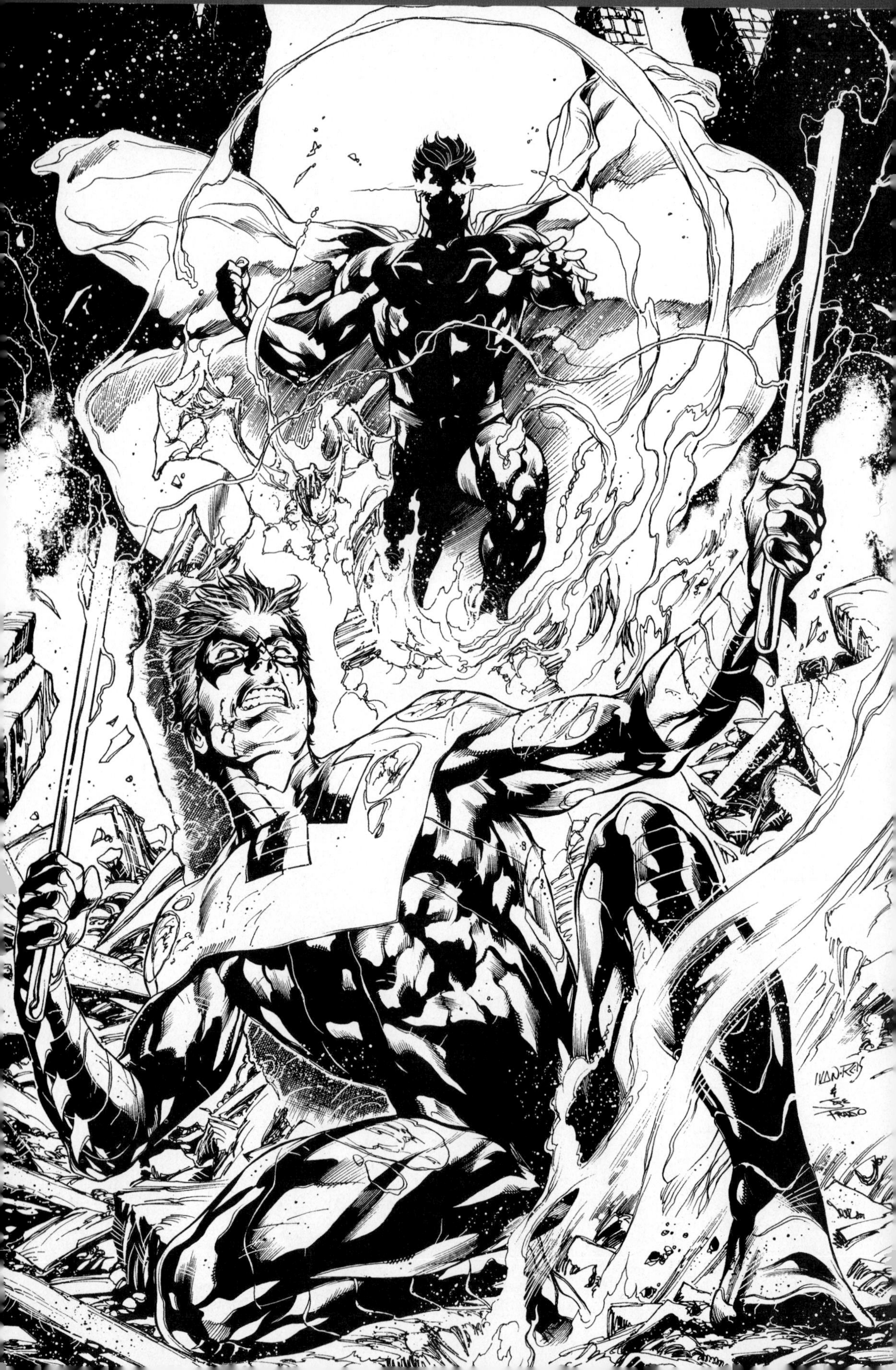

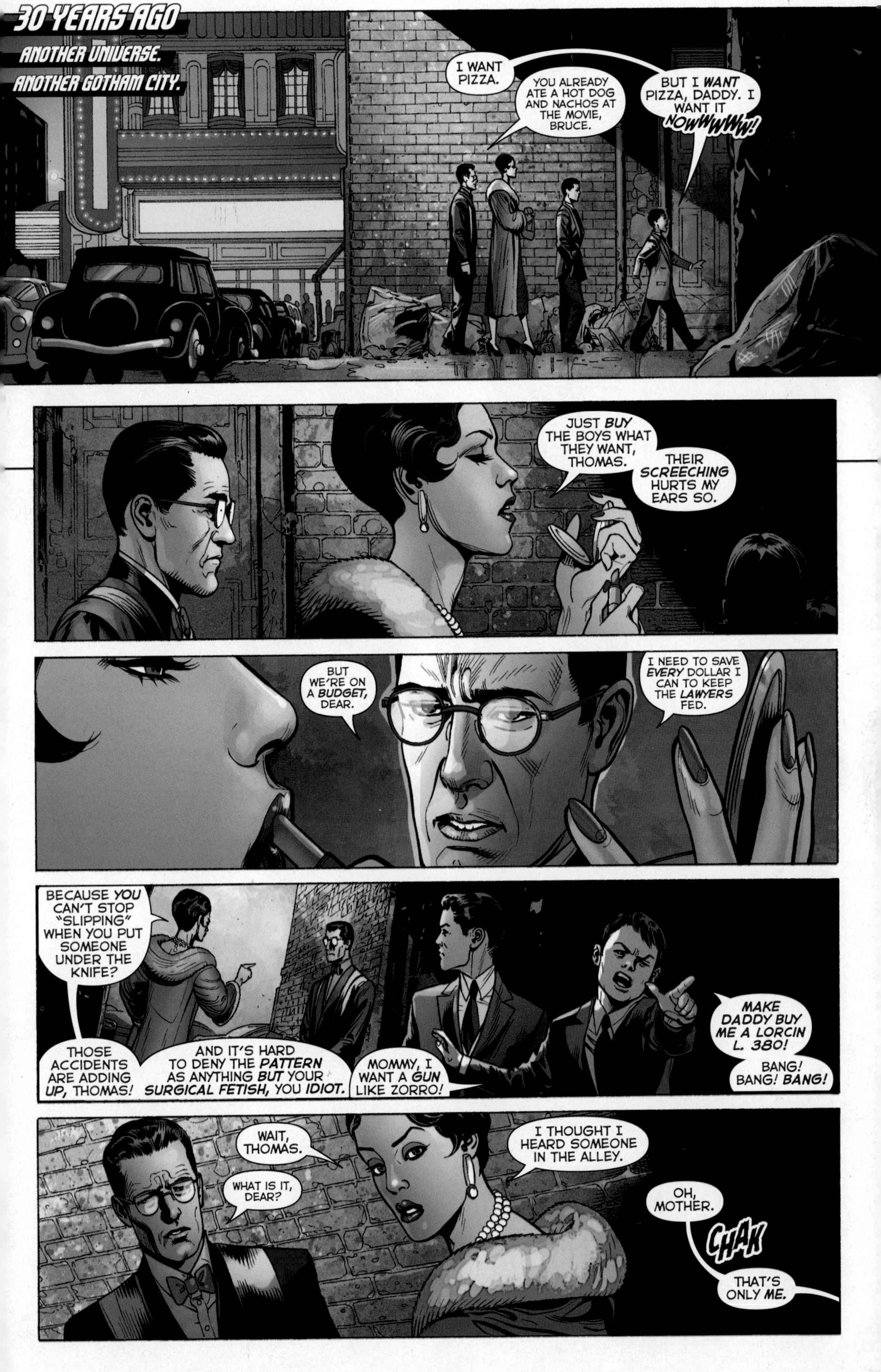
30 YEARS AGO
ANOTHER UNIVERSE.
ANOTHER GOTHAM CITY.
I WANT PIZZA.
YOU ALREADY ATE A HOT DOG AND NACHOS AT THE MOVIE, BRUCE.
BUT I WANT PIZZA, DADDY. I WANT IT NOWWWWW!
JUST BUY THE BOYS WHAT THEY WANT, THOMAS.
THEIR SCREECHING HURTS MY EARS SO.
BUT WE'RE ON A BUDGET, DEAR.
I NEED TO SAVE EVERY DOLLAR I CAN TO KEEP THE LAWYERS FED.
BECAUSE YOU CAN'T STOP "SLIPPING" WHEN YOU PUT SOMEONE UNDER THE KNIFE?
THOSE ACCIDENTS ARE ADDING UP, THOMAS!
AND IT'S HARD TO DENY THE PATTERN AS ANYTHING BUT YOUR SURGICAL FETISH, YOU IDIOT.
MOMMY, I WANT A GUN LIKE ZORRO!
MAKE DADDY BUY ME A LORCIN L. 380!
BANG! BANG! BANG!
WAIT, THOMAS.
WHAT IS IT, DEAR?
I THOUGHT I HEARD SOMEONE IN THE ALLEY.
OH, MOTHER.
CHAK
THAT'S ONLY ME.

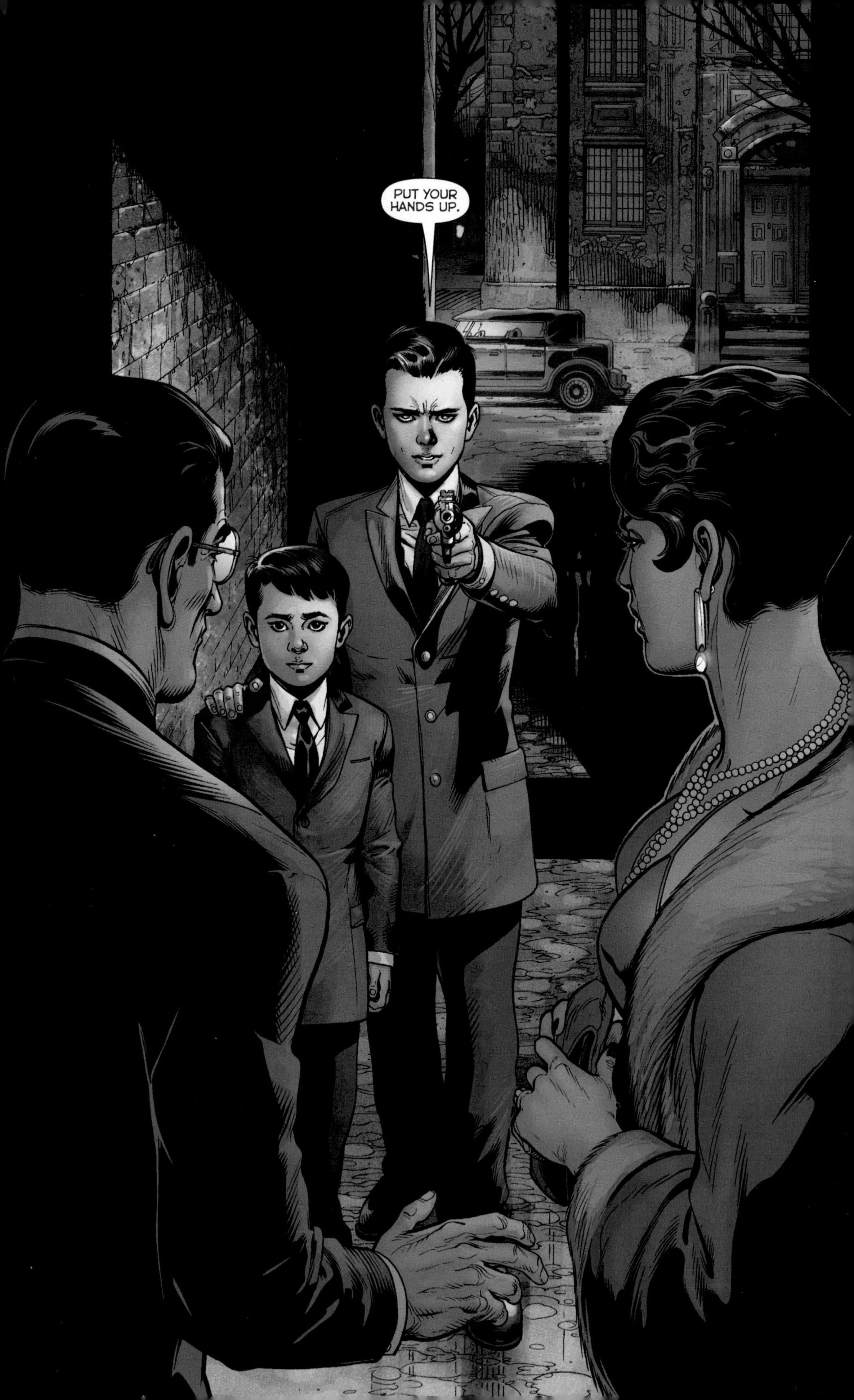
PUT YOUR HANDS UP.

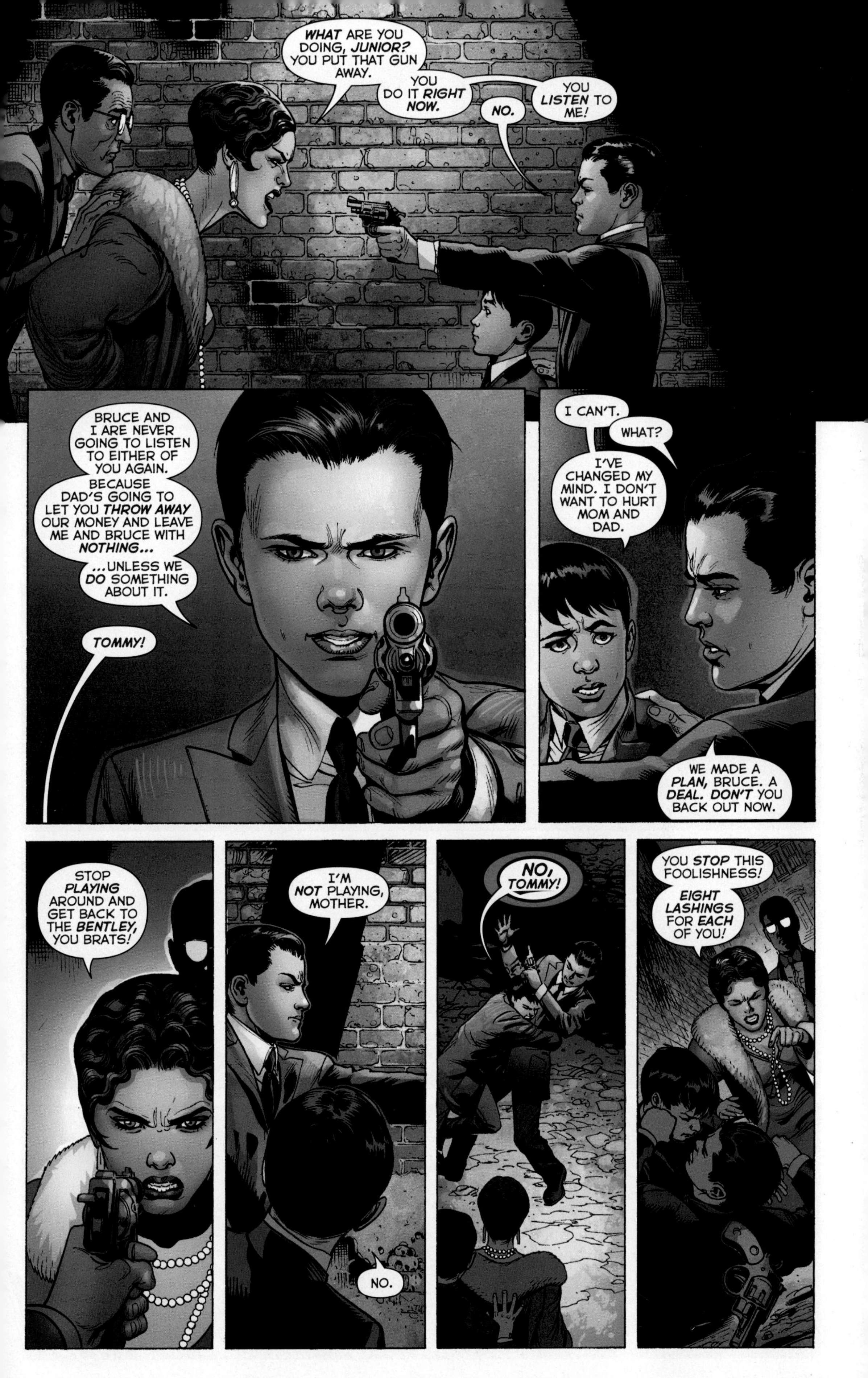
WHAT ARE YOU DOING, JUNIOR? YOU PUT THAT GUN AWAY.
YOU DO IT RIGHT NOW.
NO.
YOU LISTEN TO ME!
BRUCE AND I ARE NEVER GOING TO LISTEN TO EITHER OF YOU AGAIN.
BECAUSE DAD'S GOING TO LET YOU THROW AWAY OUR MONEY AND LEAVE ME AND BRUCE WITH NOTHING...
...UNLESS WE DO SOMETHING ABOUT IT.
TOMMY!
I CAN'T.
WHAT?
I'VE CHANGED MY MIND. I DON'T WANT TO HURT MOM AND DAD.
WE MADE A PLAN, BRUCE. A DEAL. DON'T YOU BACK OUT NOW.
STOP PLAYING AROUND AND GET BACK TO THE BENTLEY, YOU BRATS!
I'M NOT PLAYING, MOTHER.
NO.
NO, TOMMY!
YOU STOP THIS FOOLISHNESS!
EIGHT LASHINGS FOR EACH OF YOU!

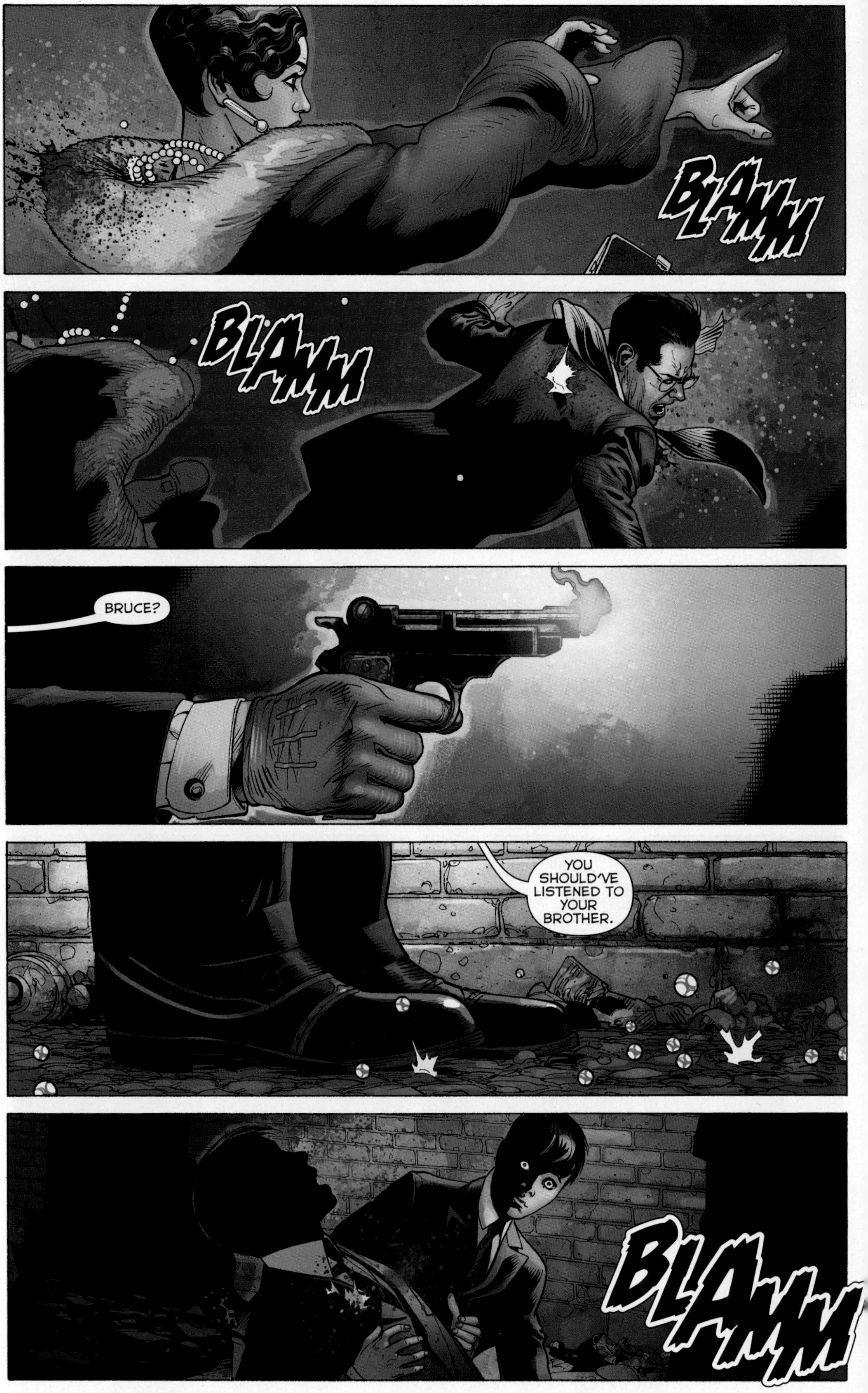
BLAMM
BLAMM
BRUCE?
YOU SHOULD'VE LISTENED TO YOUR BROTHER.
BLAMM

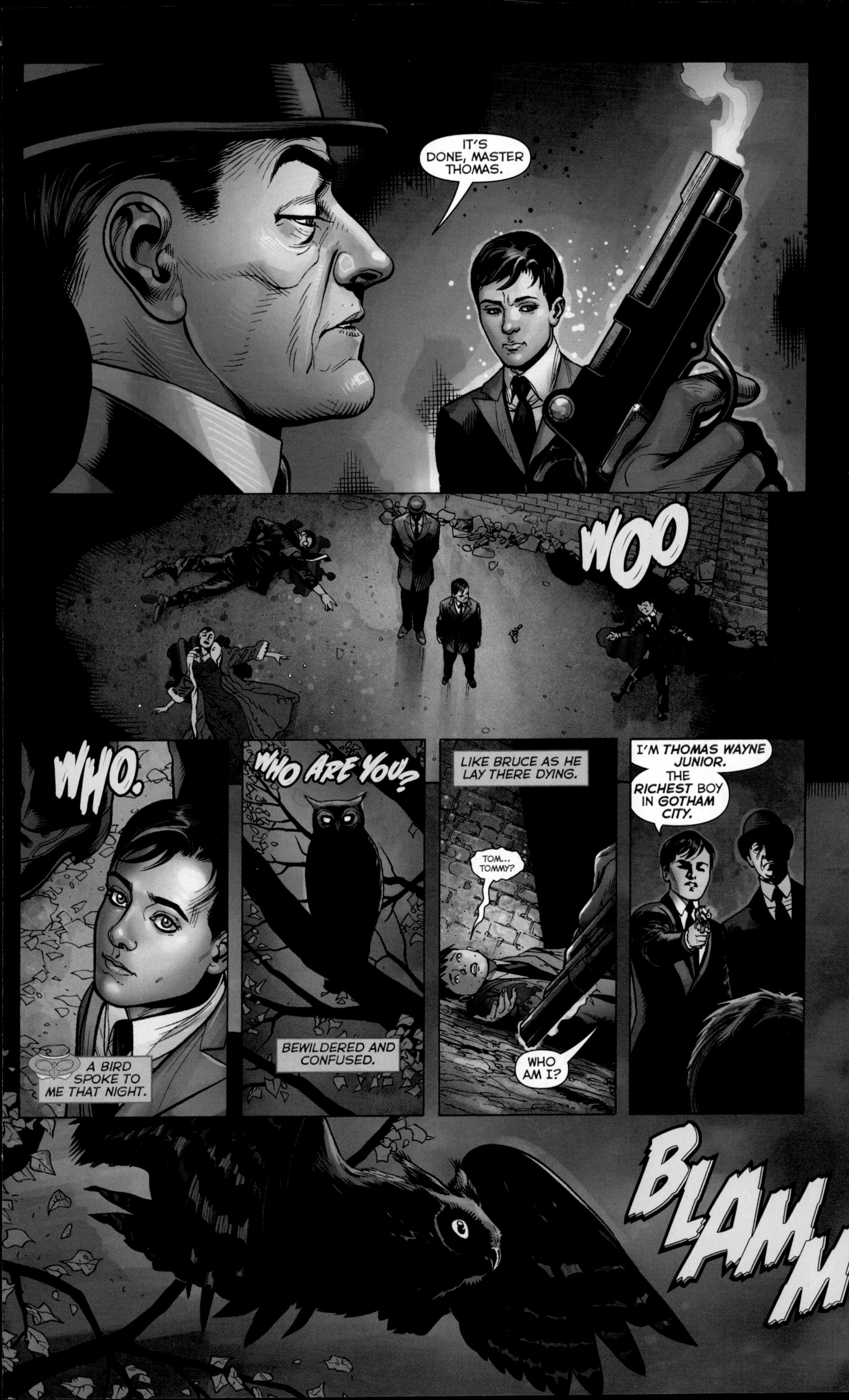

IT'S DONE, MASTER THOMAS.
WOO
WHO.
A BIRD SPOKE TO ME THAT NIGHT.
WHO ARE YOU?
BEWILDERED AND CONFUSED.
LIKE BRUCE AS HE LAY THERE DYING.
TOM... TOMMY?
WHO AM I?
I'M THOMAS WAYNE JUNIOR. THE RICHEST BOY IN GOTHAM CITY.
BLAMM

STRIITCH

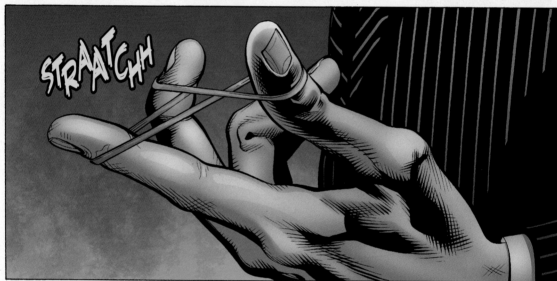

STRAATCHH

SNP

OW!

JEEZUS, EEL, WILL YOU *QUIT* PLAYING WITH THOSE DAMN THINGS?

IT WAS ONLY A MATTER OF TIME BEFORE THEIR WORLD BROKE.

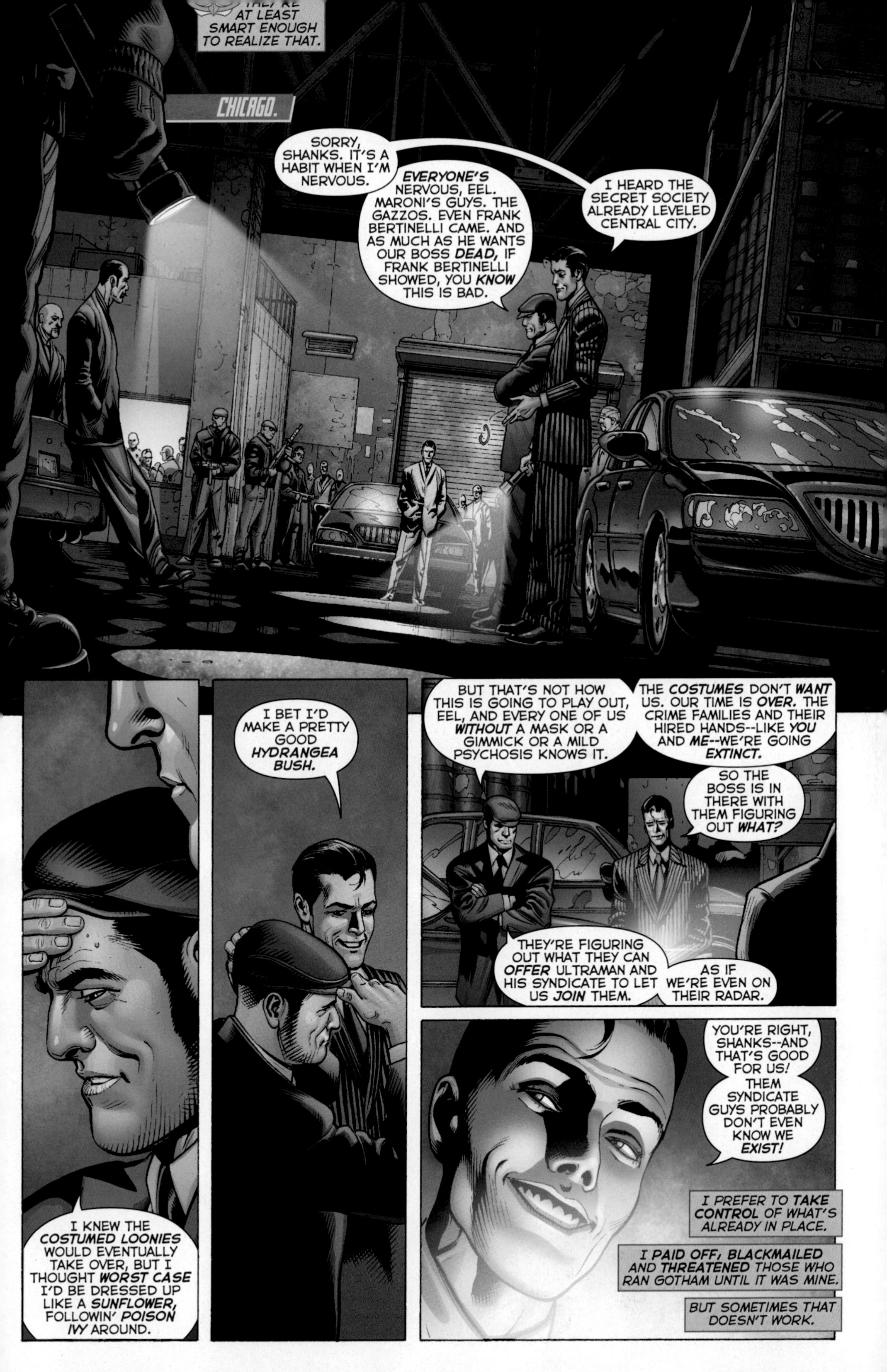

THEY'RE AT LEAST SMART ENOUGH TO REALIZE THAT.
CHICAGO.
SORRY, SHANKS. IT'S A HABIT WHEN I'M NERVOUS.
EVERYONE'S NERVOUS, EEL. MARONI'S GUYS. THE GAZZOS. EVEN FRANK BERTINELLI CAME. AND AS MUCH AS HE WANTS OUR BOSS DEAD, IF FRANK BERTINELLI SHOWED, YOU KNOW THIS IS BAD.
I HEARD THE SECRET SOCIETY ALREADY LEVELED CENTRAL CITY.
I KNEW THE COSTUMED LOONIES WOULD EVENTUALLY TAKE OVER, BUT I THOUGHT WORST CASE I'D BE DRESSED UP LIKE A SUNFLOWER, FOLLOWIN' POISON IVY AROUND.
I BET I'D MAKE A PRETTY GOOD HYDRANGEA BUSH.
BUT THAT'S NOT HOW THIS IS GOING TO PLAY OUT, EEL, AND EVERY ONE OF US WITHOUT A MASK OR A GIMMICK OR A MILD PSYCHOSIS KNOWS IT.
THE COSTUMES DON'T WANT US. OUR TIME IS OVER. THE CRIME FAMILIES AND THEIR HIRED HANDS--LIKE YOU AND ME--WE'RE GOING EXTINCT.
SO THE BOSS IS IN THERE WITH THEM FIGURING OUT WHAT?
THEY'RE FIGURING OUT WHAT THEY CAN OFFER ULTRAMAN AND HIS SYNDICATE TO LET US JOIN THEM.
AS IF WE'RE EVEN ON THEIR RADAR.
YOU'RE RIGHT, SHANKS--AND THAT'S GOOD FOR US!
THEM SYNDICATE GUYS PROBABLY DON'T EVEN KNOW WE EXIST!
I PREFER TO TAKE CONTROL OF WHAT'S ALREADY IN PLACE.
I PAID OFF, BLACKMAILED AND THREATENED THOSE WHO RAN GOTHAM UNTIL IT WAS MINE.
BUT SOMETIMES THAT DOESN'T WORK.

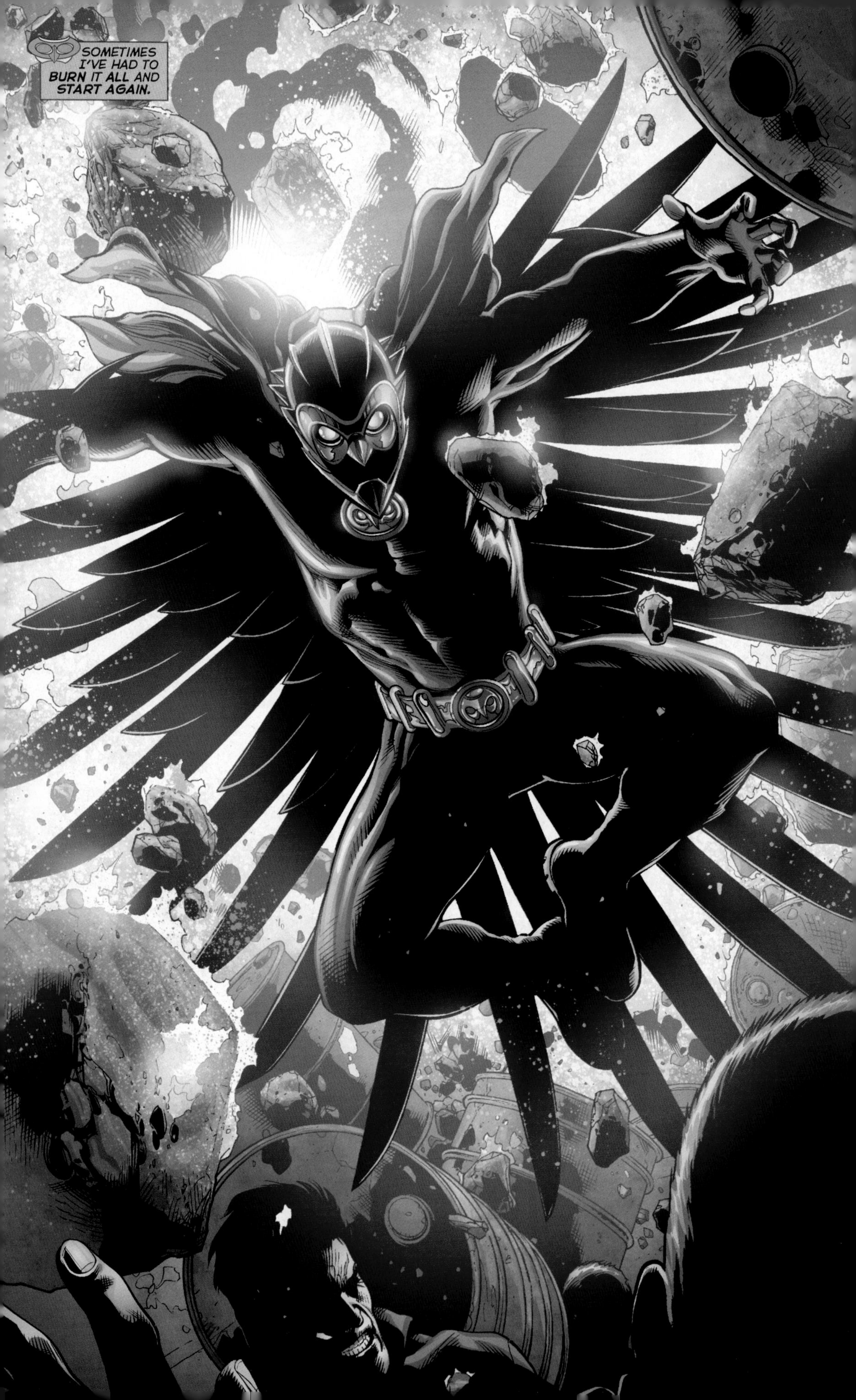
SOMETIMES I'VE HAD TO BURN IT ALL AND START AGAIN.

THAT'S WHAT HAPPENED WITH MY FAMILY.

MY FATHER WAS A WEAK MAN.

MY MOTHER AN OVERBEARING SADIST.

MY BROTHER A RAT.

MY SERVANT, ALFRED, WAS THE ONLY ONE I COULD CONTROL.

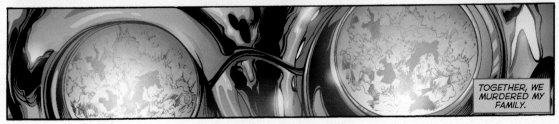

TOGETHER, WE MURDERED MY FAMILY.

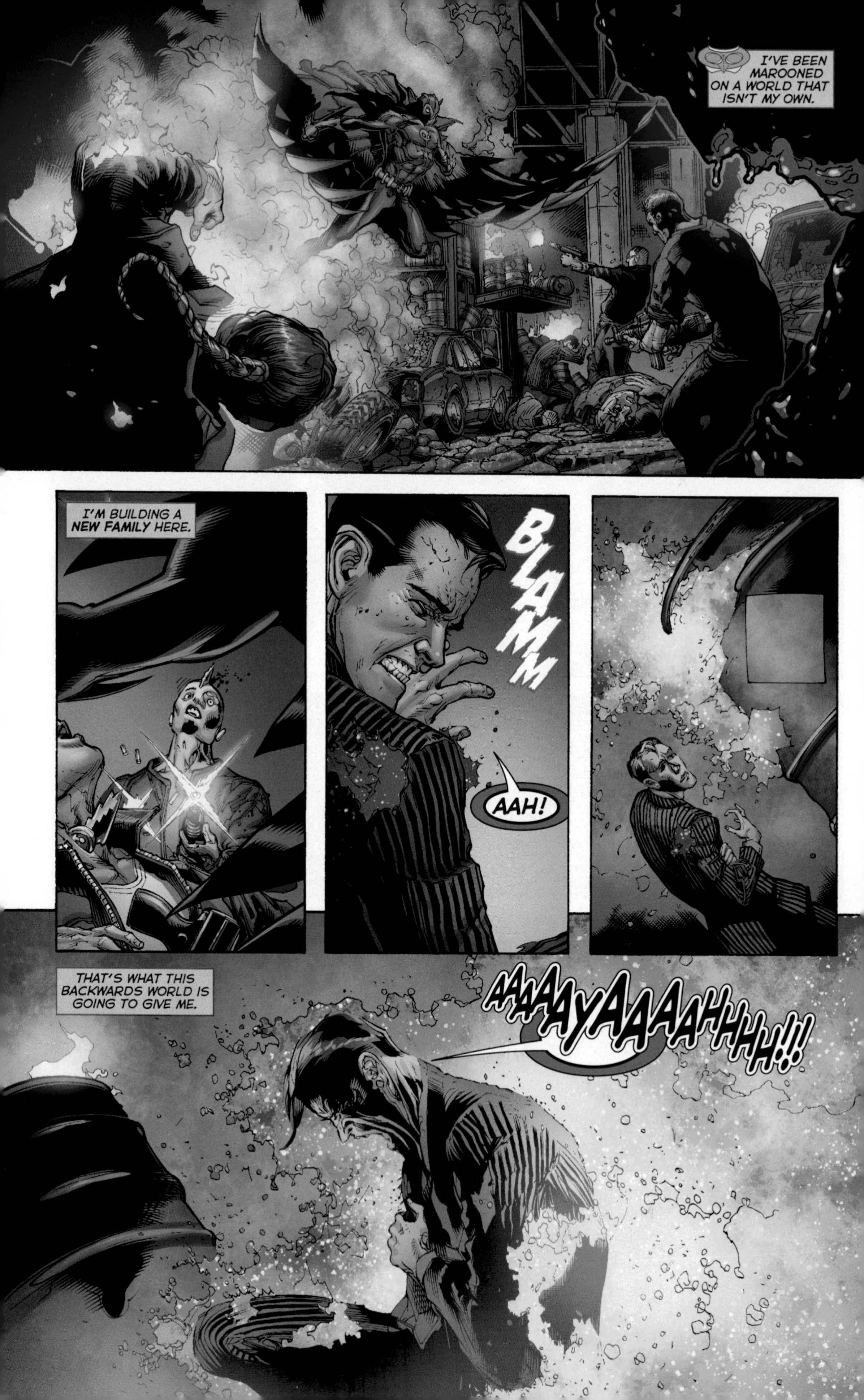

I'VE BEEN MAROONED ON A WORLD THAT ISN'T MY OWN.
I'M BUILDING A NEW FAMILY HERE.
BLAMM
AAH!
THAT'S WHAT THIS BACKWARDS WORLD IS GOING TO GIVE ME.
AAAAAYAAAAHHHH!!!

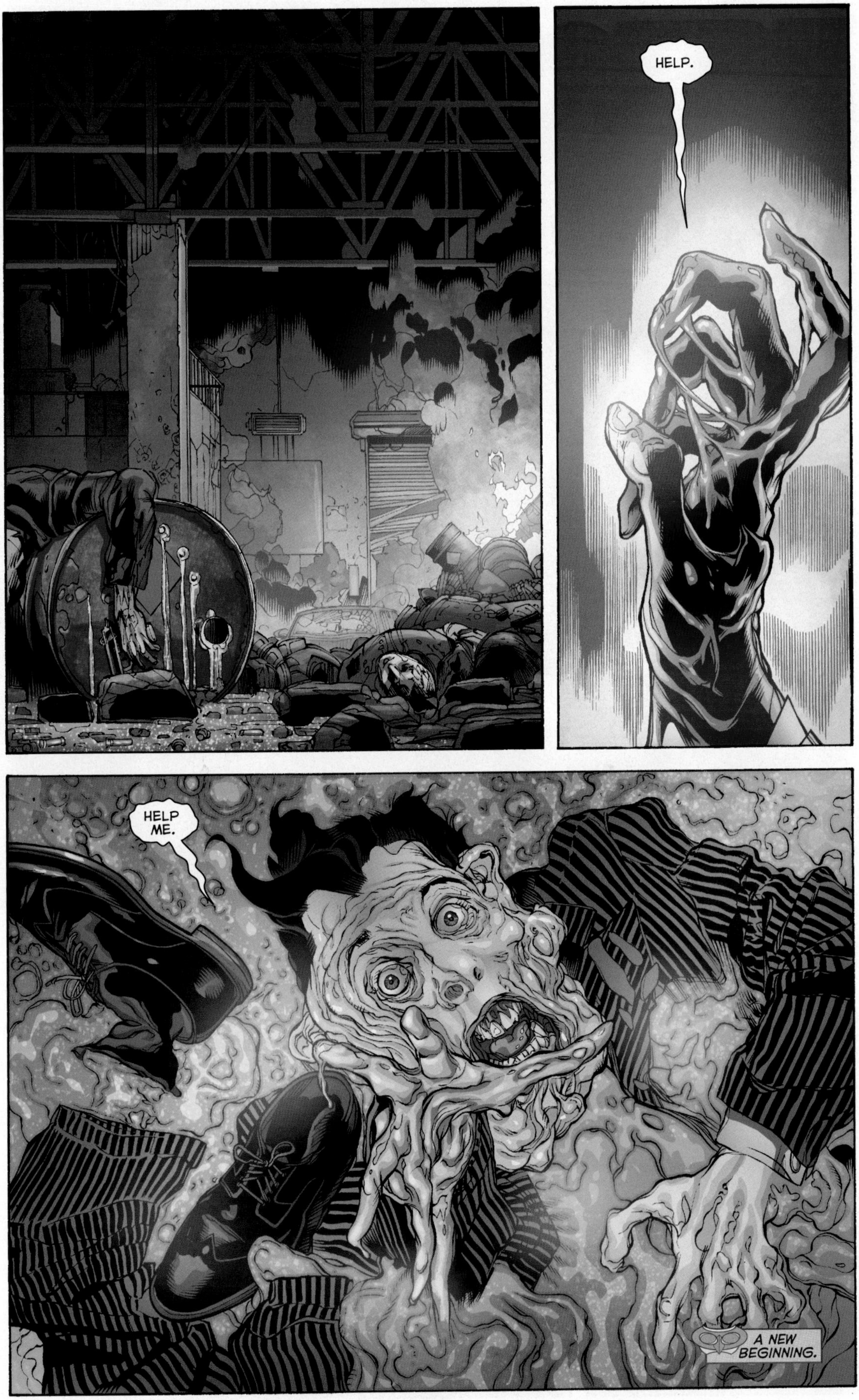
HELP.
HELP ME.
A NEW BEGINNING.

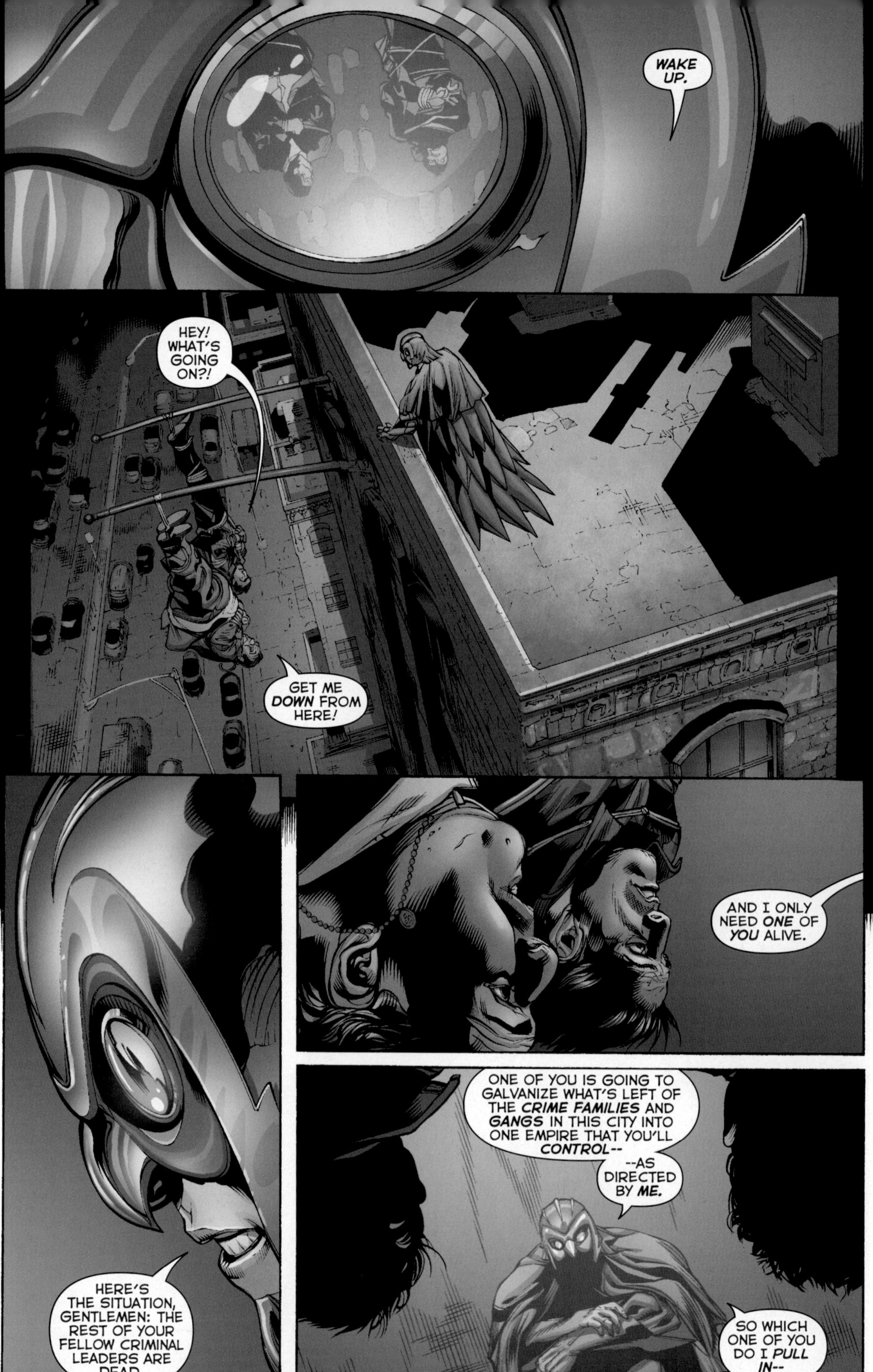
WAKE UP.
HEY! WHAT'S GOING ON?!
GET ME DOWN FROM HERE!
AND I ONLY NEED ONE OF YOU ALIVE.
HERE'S THE SITUATION, GENTLEMEN: THE REST OF YOUR FELLOW CRIMINAL LEADERS ARE DEAD.
ONE OF YOU IS GOING TO GALVANIZE WHAT'S LEFT OF THE CRIME FAMILIES AND GANGS IN THIS CITY INTO ONE EMPIRE THAT YOU'LL CONTROL--
--AS DIRECTED BY ME.
SO WHICH ONE OF YOU DO I PULL IN--
--AND WHICH ONE OF YOU DO I DROP?

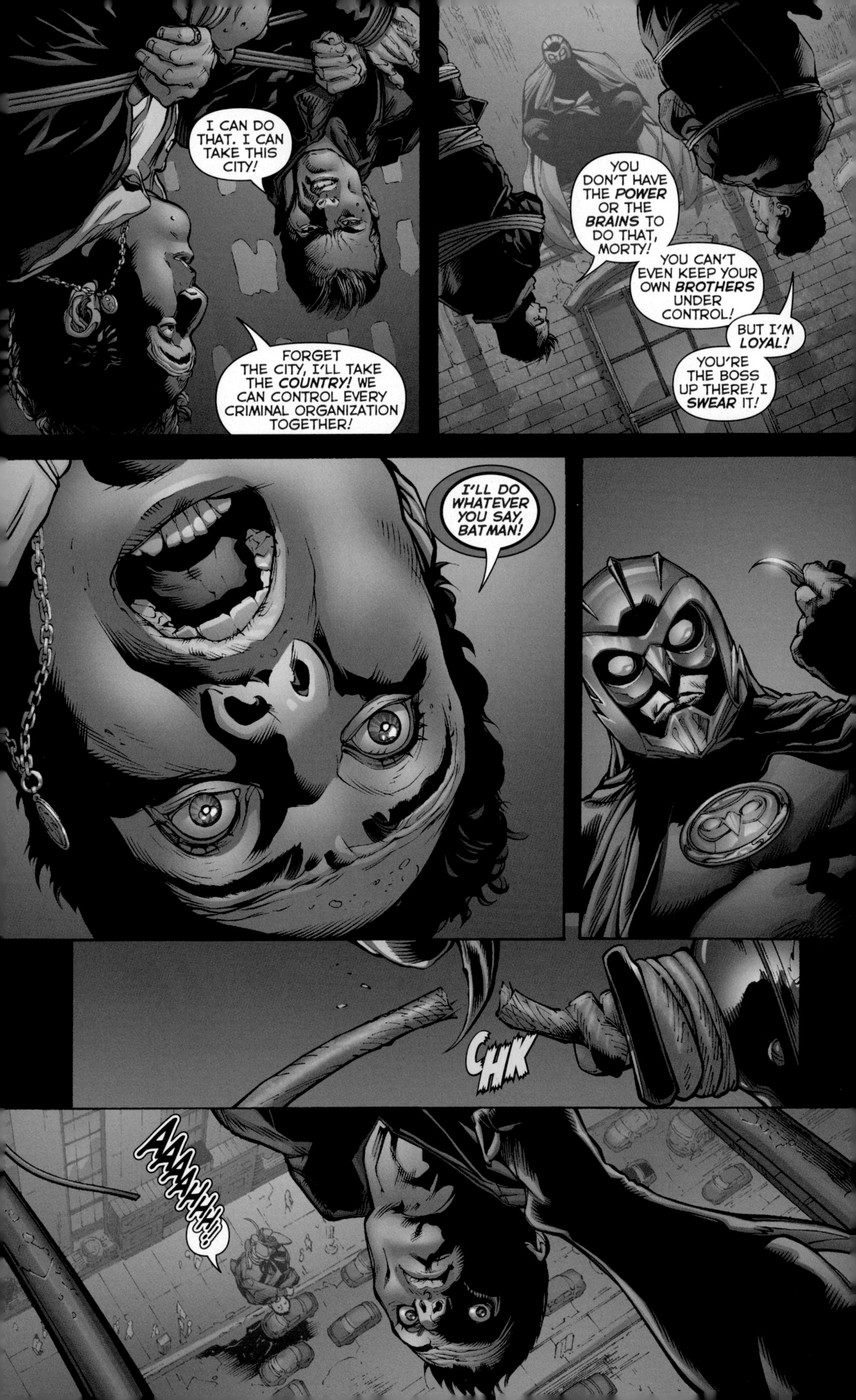
I CAN DO THAT. I CAN TAKE THIS CITY!
FORGET THE CITY, I'LL TAKE THE COUNTRY! WE CAN CONTROL EVERY CRIMINAL ORGANIZATION TOGETHER!
YOU DON'T HAVE THE POWER OR THE BRAINS TO DO THAT, MORTY!
YOU CAN'T EVEN KEEP YOUR OWN BROTHERS UNDER CONTROL!
BUT I'M LOYAL!
YOU'RE THE BOSS UP THERE! I SWEAR IT!
I'LL DO WHATEVER YOU SAY, BATMAN!
CHK
AAAAHHH!!

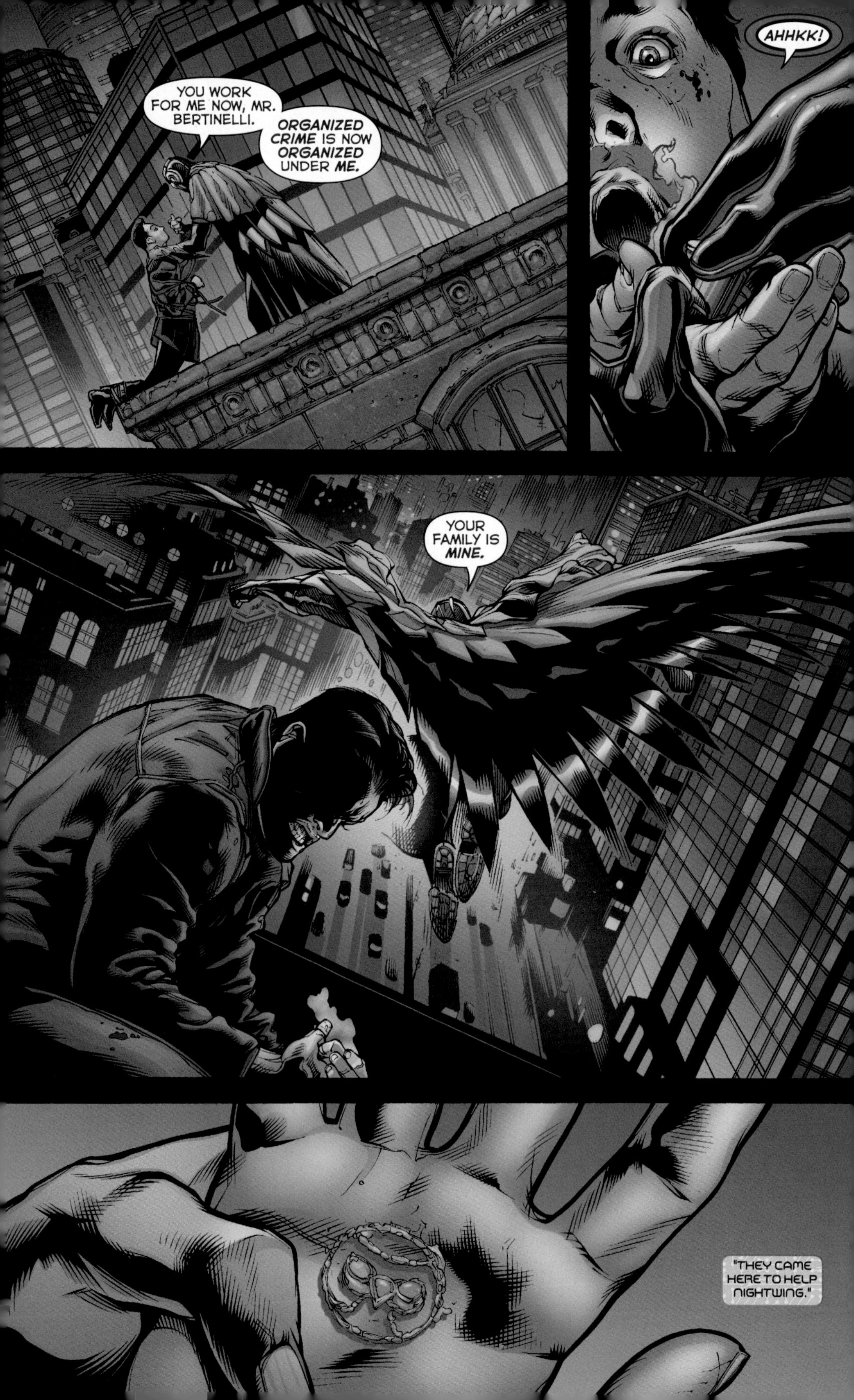
YOU WORK FOR ME NOW, MR. BERTINELLI.
ORGANIZED CRIME IS NOW ORGANIZED UNDER ME.
AHHKK!
YOUR FAMILY IS MINE.
"THEY CAME HERE TO HELP NIGHTWING."

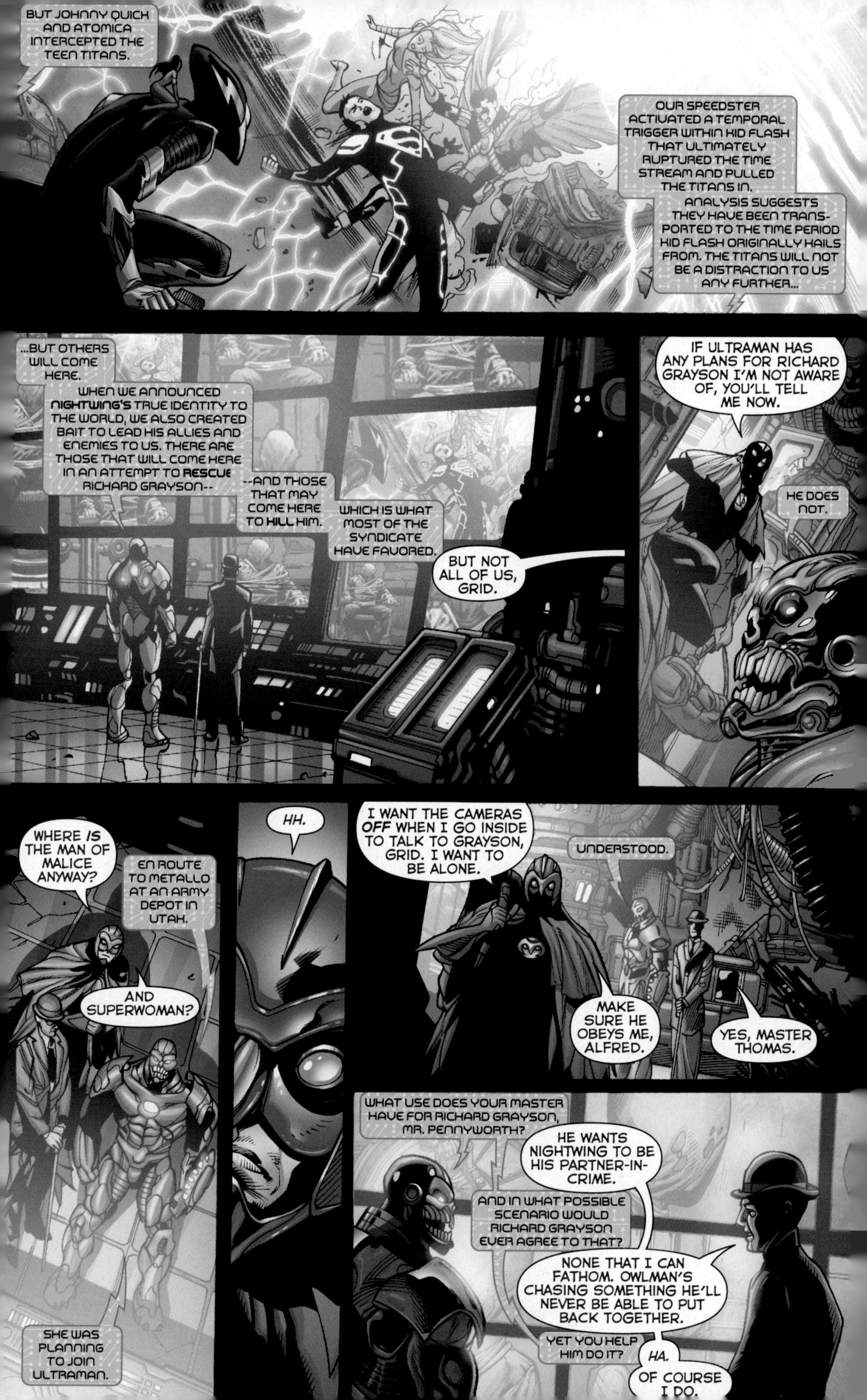

BUT JOHNNY QUICK AND ATOMICA INTERCEPTED THE TEEN TITANS.
OUR SPEEDSTER ACTIVATED A TEMPORAL TRIGGER WITHIN KID FLASH THAT ULTIMATELY RUPTURED THE TIME STREAM AND PULLED THE TITANS IN.
ANALYSIS SUGGESTS THEY HAVE BEEN TRANSPORTED TO THE TIME PERIOD KID FLASH ORIGINALLY HAILS FROM. THE TITANS WILL NOT BE A DISTRACTION TO US ANY FURTHER...
...BUT OTHERS WILL COME HERE.
WHEN WE ANNOUNCED NIGHTWING'S TRUE IDENTITY TO THE WORLD, WE ALSO CREATED BAIT TO LEAD HIS ALLIES AND ENEMIES TO US. THERE ARE THOSE THAT WILL COME HERE IN AN ATTEMPT TO RESCUE RICHARD GRAYSON--
--AND THOSE THAT MAY COME HERE TO KILL HIM.
WHICH IS WHAT MOST OF THE SYNDICATE HAVE FAVORED.
BUT NOT ALL OF US, GRID.
IF ULTRAMAN HAS ANY PLANS FOR RICHARD GRAYSON I'M NOT AWARE OF, YOU'LL TELL ME NOW.
HE DOES NOT.
WHERE IS THE MAN OF MALICE ANYWAY?
EN ROUTE TO METALLO AT AN ARMY DEPOT IN UTAH.
AND SUPERWOMAN?
SHE WAS PLANNING TO JOIN ULTRAMAN.
HH.
I WANT THE CAMERAS OFF WHEN I GO INSIDE TO TALK TO GRAYSON, GRID. I WANT TO BE ALONE.
UNDERSTOOD.
MAKE SURE HE OBEYS ME, ALFRED.
YES, MASTER THOMAS.
WHAT USE DOES YOUR MASTER HAVE FOR RICHARD GRAYSON, MR. PENNYWORTH?
HE WANTS NIGHTWING TO BE HIS PARTNER-IN-CRIME.
AND IN WHAT POSSIBLE SCENARIO WOULD RICHARD GRAYSON EVER AGREE TO THAT?
NONE THAT I CAN FATHOM. OWLMAN'S CHASING SOMETHING HE'LL NEVER BE ABLE TO PUT BACK TOGETHER.
YET YOU HELP HIM DO IT?
HA.
OF COURSE I DO.

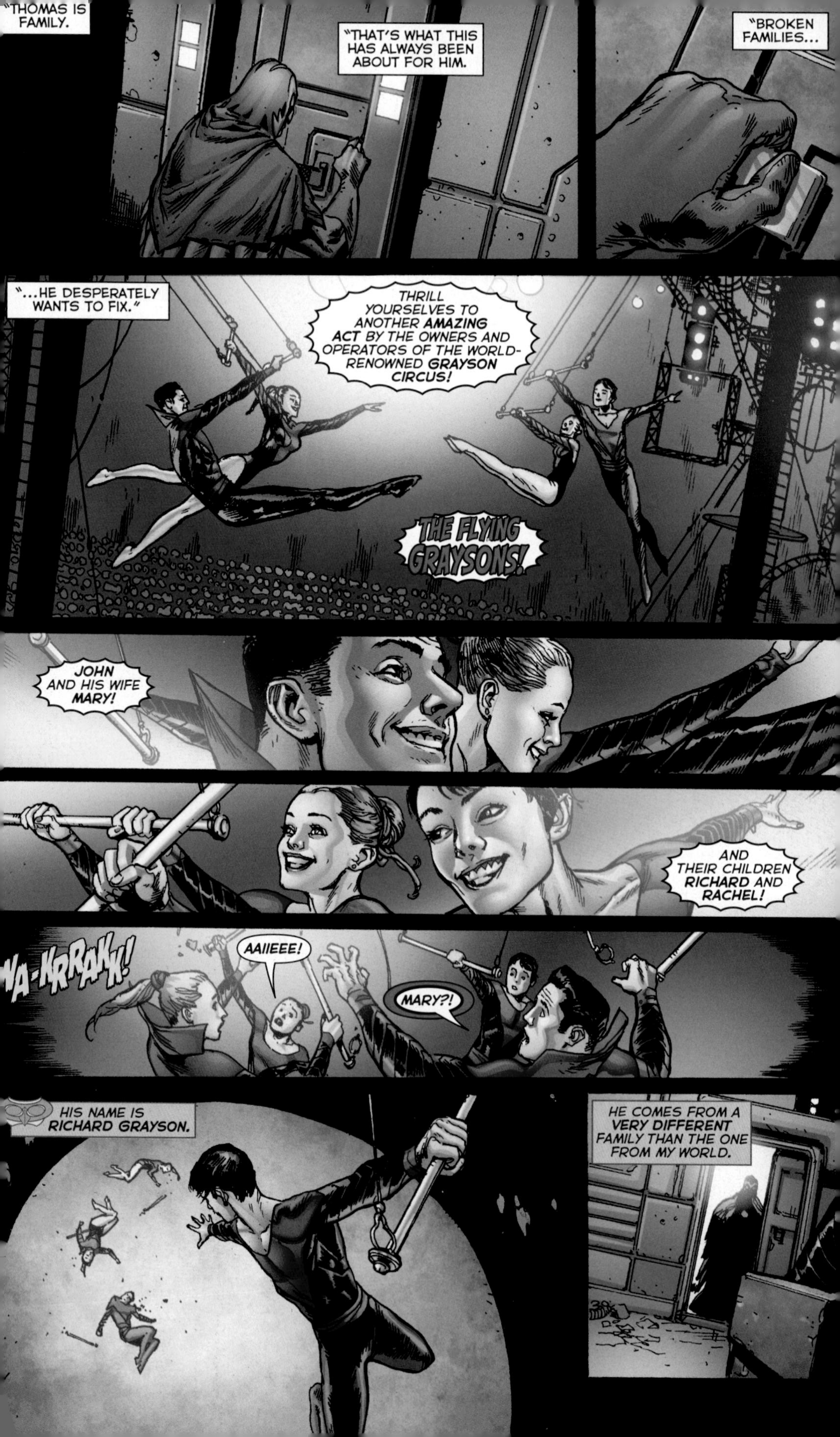
"THOMAS IS FAMILY.
"THAT'S WHAT THIS HAS ALWAYS BEEN ABOUT FOR HIM.
"BROKEN FAMILIES...
"...HE DESPERATELY WANTS TO FIX."
THRILL YOURSELVES TO ANOTHER AMAZING ACT BY THE OWNERS AND OPERATORS OF THE WORLD-RENOWNED GRAYSON CIRCUS!
THE FLYING GRAYSONS!
JOHN AND HIS WIFE MARY!
AND THEIR CHILDREN RICHARD AND RACHEL!
WA-KRRAKK!
AAIIEEE!
MARY?!
HIS NAME IS RICHARD GRAYSON.
HE COMES FROM A VERY DIFFERENT FAMILY THAN THE ONE FROM MY WORLD.

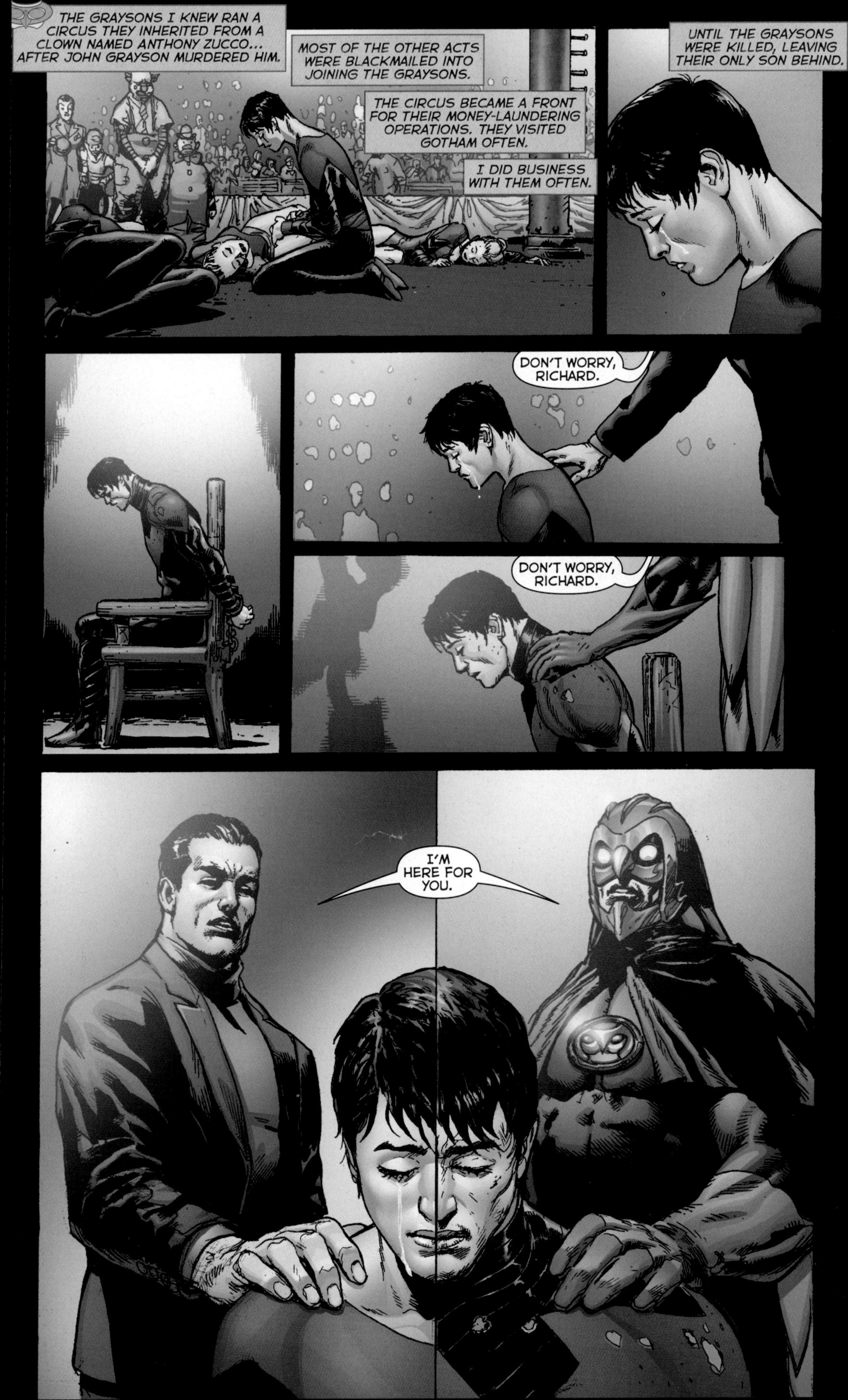
THE GRAYSONS I KNEW RAN A CIRCUS THEY INHERITED FROM A CLOWN NAMED ANTHONY ZUCCO... AFTER JOHN GRAYSON MURDERED HIM.
MOST OF THE OTHER ACTS WERE BLACKMAILED INTO JOINING THE GRAYSONS.
THE CIRCUS BECAME A FRONT FOR THEIR MONEY-LAUNDERING OPERATIONS. THEY VISITED GOTHAM OFTEN.
I DID BUSINESS WITH THEM OFTEN.
UNTIL THE GRAYSONS WERE KILLED, LEAVING THEIR ONLY SON BEHIND.
DON'T WORRY, RICHARD.
DON'T WORRY, RICHARD.
I'M HERE FOR YOU.

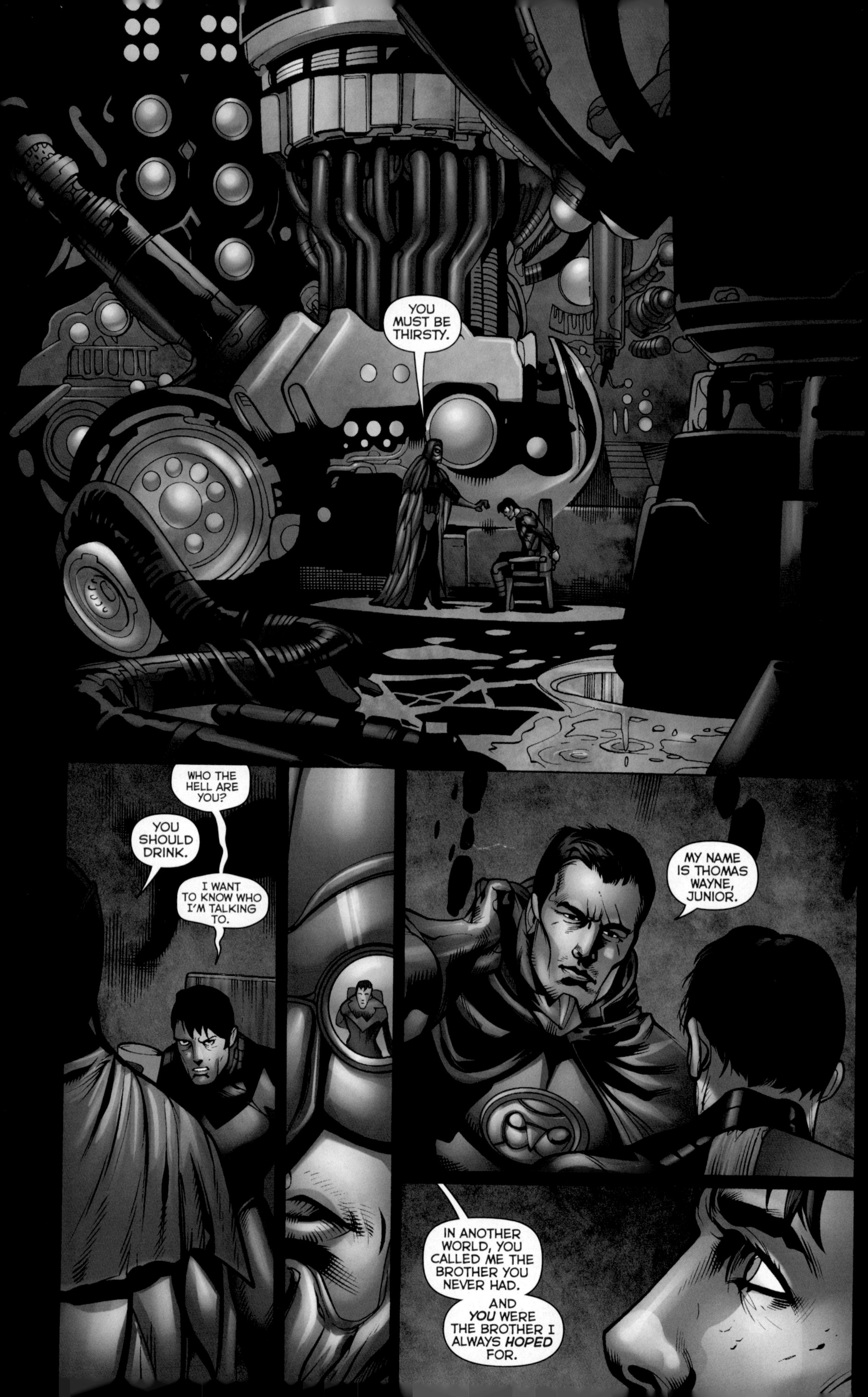
YOU MUST BE THIRSTY.
WHO THE HELL ARE YOU?
YOU SHOULD DRINK.
I WANT TO KNOW WHO I'M TALKING TO.
MY NAME IS THOMAS WAYNE, JUNIOR.
IN ANOTHER WORLD, YOU CALLED ME THE BROTHER YOU NEVER HAD.
AND *YOU* WERE THE BROTHER I ALWAYS *HOPED* FOR.

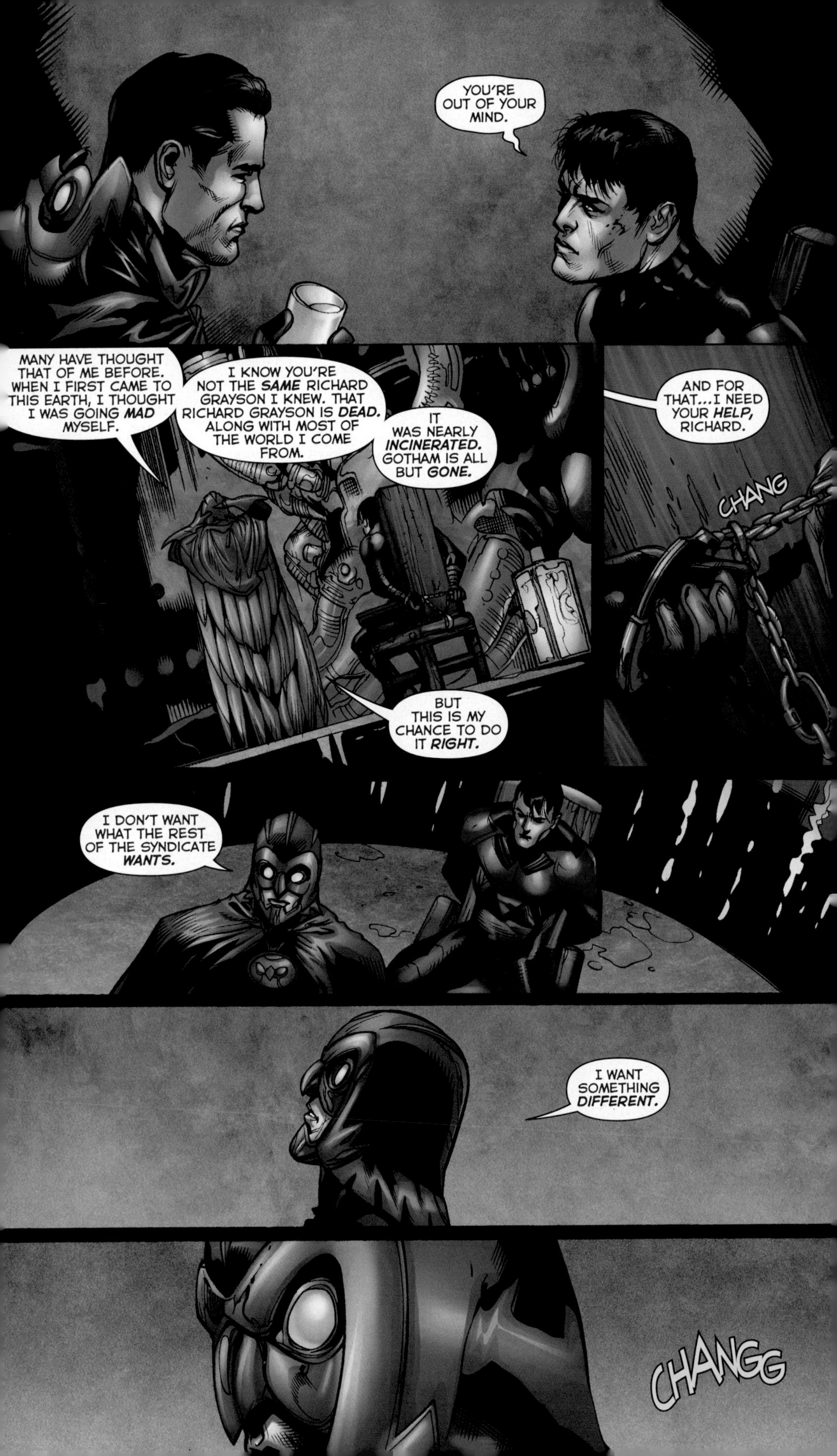
YOU'RE OUT OF YOUR MIND.
MANY HAVE THOUGHT THAT OF ME BEFORE. WHEN I FIRST CAME TO THIS EARTH, I THOUGHT I WAS GOING MAD MYSELF.
I KNOW YOU'RE NOT THE SAME RICHARD GRAYSON I KNEW. THAT RICHARD GRAYSON IS DEAD. ALONG WITH MOST OF THE WORLD I COME FROM.
IT WAS NEARLY INCINERATED. GOTHAM IS ALL BUT GONE.
BUT THIS IS MY CHANCE TO DO IT RIGHT.
AND FOR THAT...I NEED YOUR HELP, RICHARD.
CHANG
I DON'T WANT WHAT THE REST OF THE SYNDICATE WANTS.
I WANT SOMETHING DIFFERENT.
CHANGG

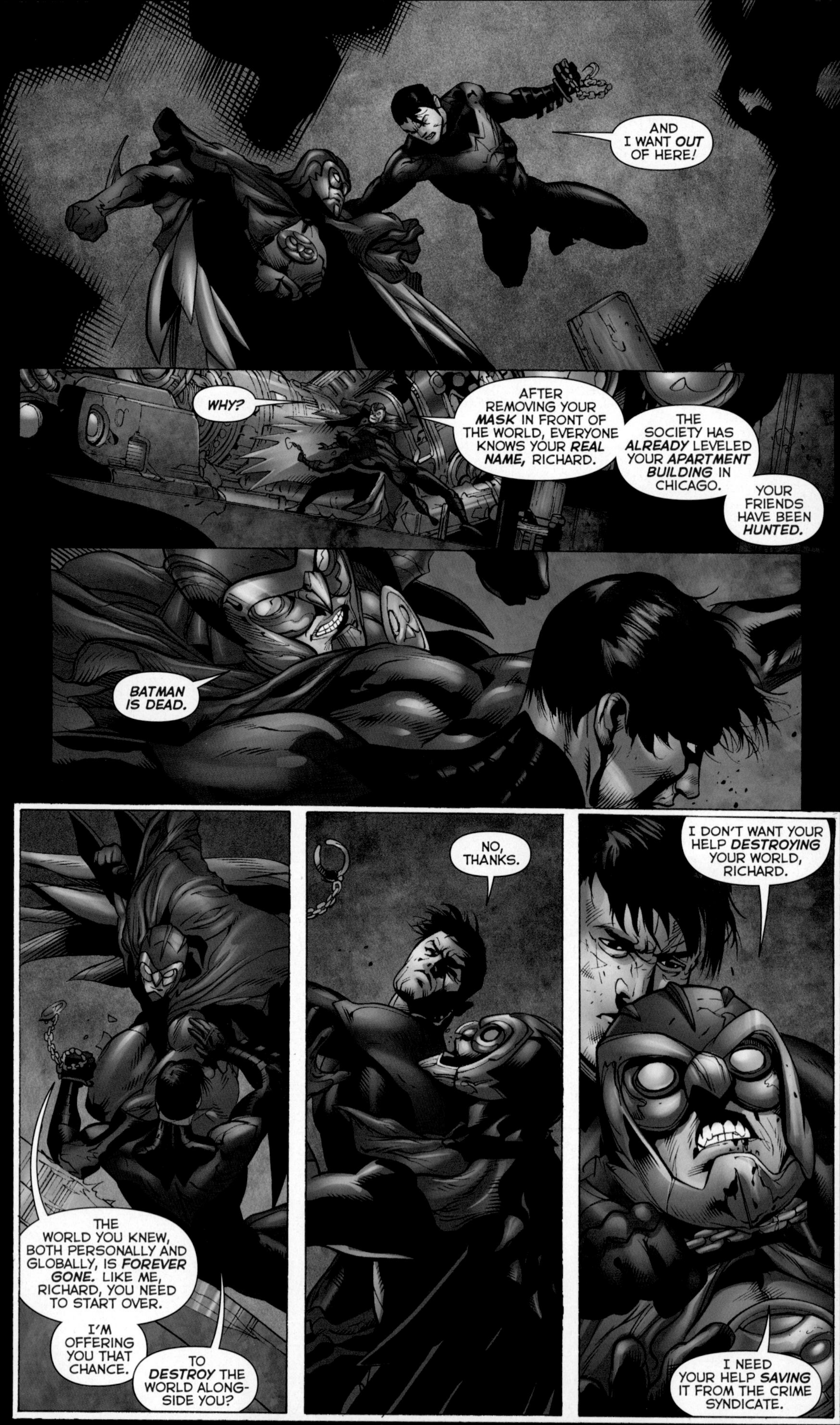
AND I WANT OUT OF HERE!
WHY?
AFTER REMOVING YOUR MASK IN FRONT OF THE WORLD, EVERYONE KNOWS YOUR REAL NAME, RICHARD.
THE SOCIETY HAS ALREADY LEVELED YOUR APARTMENT BUILDING IN CHICAGO.
YOUR FRIENDS HAVE BEEN HUNTED.
BATMAN IS DEAD.
THE WORLD YOU KNEW, BOTH PERSONALLY AND GLOBALLY, IS FOREVER GONE. LIKE ME, RICHARD, YOU NEED TO START OVER.
I'M OFFERING YOU THAT CHANCE.
TO DESTROY THE WORLD ALONGSIDE YOU?
NO, THANKS.
I DON'T WANT YOUR HELP DESTROYING YOUR WORLD, RICHARD.
I NEED YOUR HELP SAVING IT FROM THE CRIME SYNDICATE.

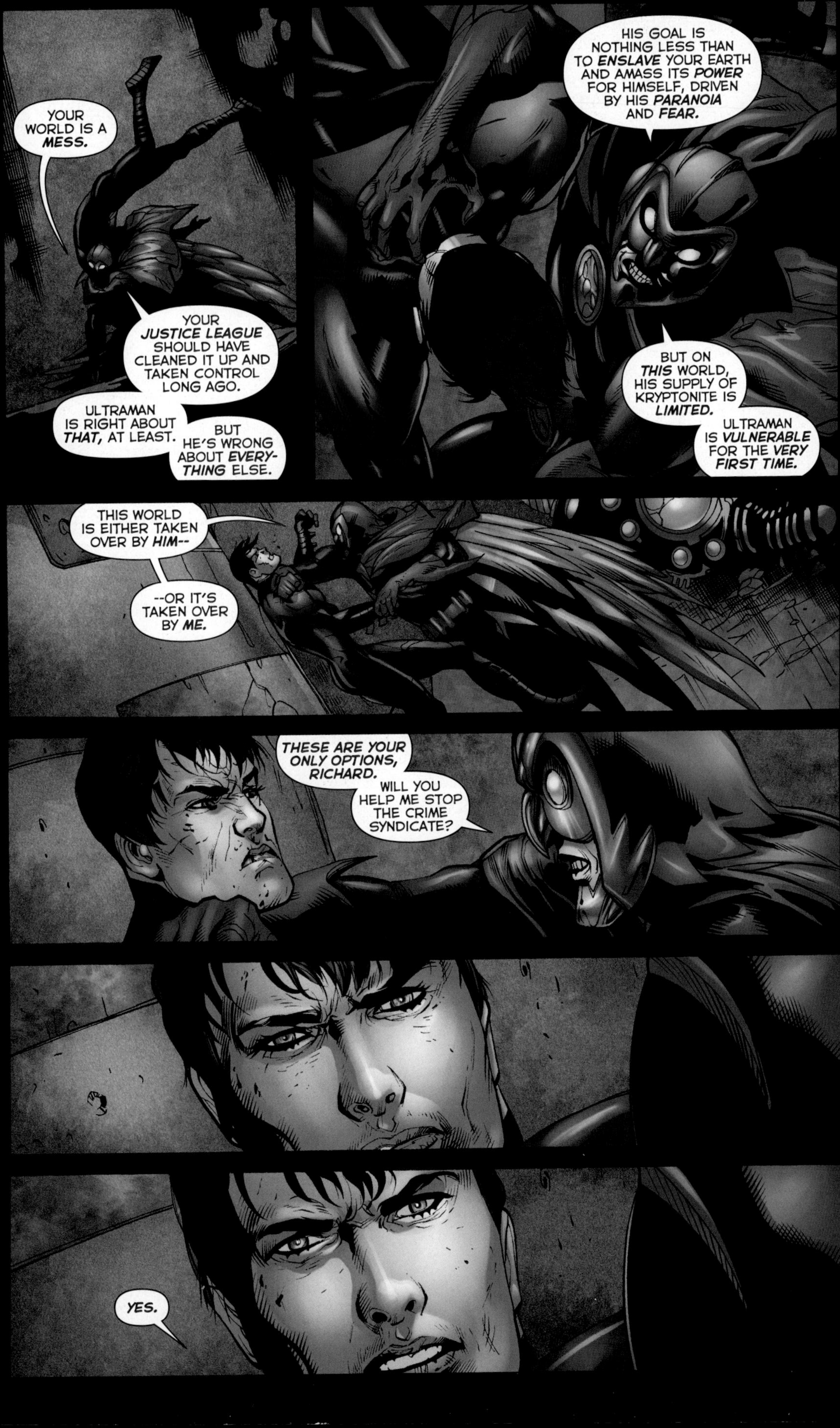

YOUR WORLD IS A MESS.
YOUR JUSTICE LEAGUE SHOULD HAVE CLEANED IT UP AND TAKEN CONTROL LONG AGO.
ULTRAMAN IS RIGHT ABOUT THAT, AT LEAST.
BUT HE'S WRONG ABOUT EVERY-THING ELSE.
HIS GOAL IS NOTHING LESS THAN TO ENSLAVE YOUR EARTH AND AMASS ITS POWER FOR HIMSELF, DRIVEN BY HIS PARANOIA AND FEAR.
BUT ON THIS WORLD, HIS SUPPLY OF KRYPTONITE IS LIMITED.
ULTRAMAN IS VULNERABLE FOR THE VERY FIRST TIME.
THIS WORLD IS EITHER TAKEN OVER BY HIM--
--OR IT'S TAKEN OVER BY ME.
THESE ARE YOUR ONLY OPTIONS, RICHARD.
WILL YOU HELP ME STOP THE CRIME SYNDICATE?
YES.

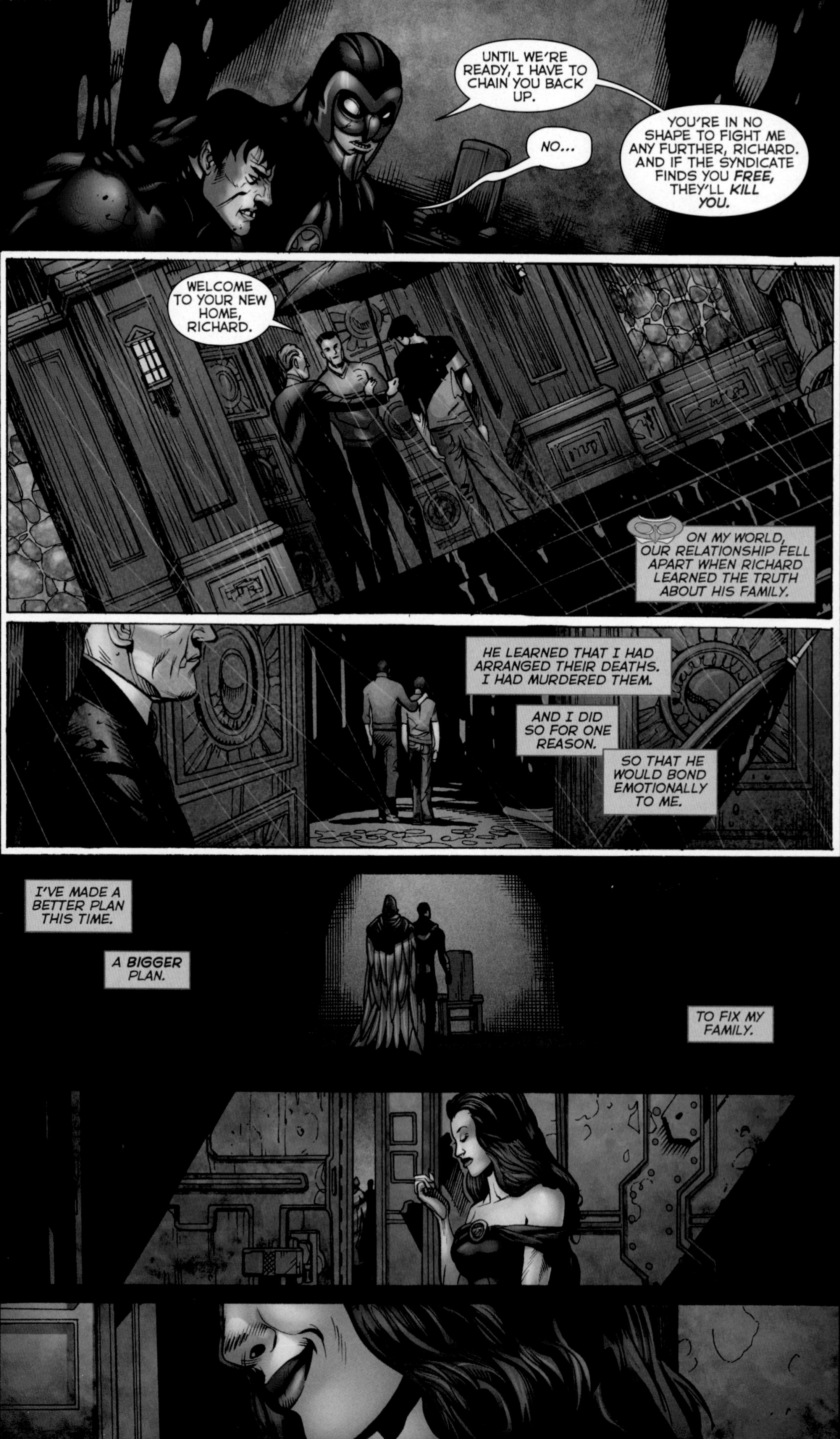
UNTIL WE'RE READY, I HAVE TO CHAIN YOU BACK UP.
NO...
YOU'RE IN NO SHAPE TO FIGHT ME ANY FURTHER, RICHARD. AND IF THE SYNDICATE FINDS YOU FREE, THEY'LL KILL YOU.
WELCOME TO YOUR NEW HOME, RICHARD.
ON MY WORLD, OUR RELATIONSHIP FELL APART WHEN RICHARD LEARNED THE TRUTH ABOUT HIS FAMILY.
HE LEARNED THAT I HAD ARRANGED THEIR DEATHS. I HAD MURDERED THEM.
AND I DID SO FOR ONE REASON.
SO THAT HE WOULD BOND EMOTIONALLY TO ME.
I'VE MADE A BETTER PLAN THIS TIME.
A BIGGER PLAN.
TO FIX MY FAMILY.

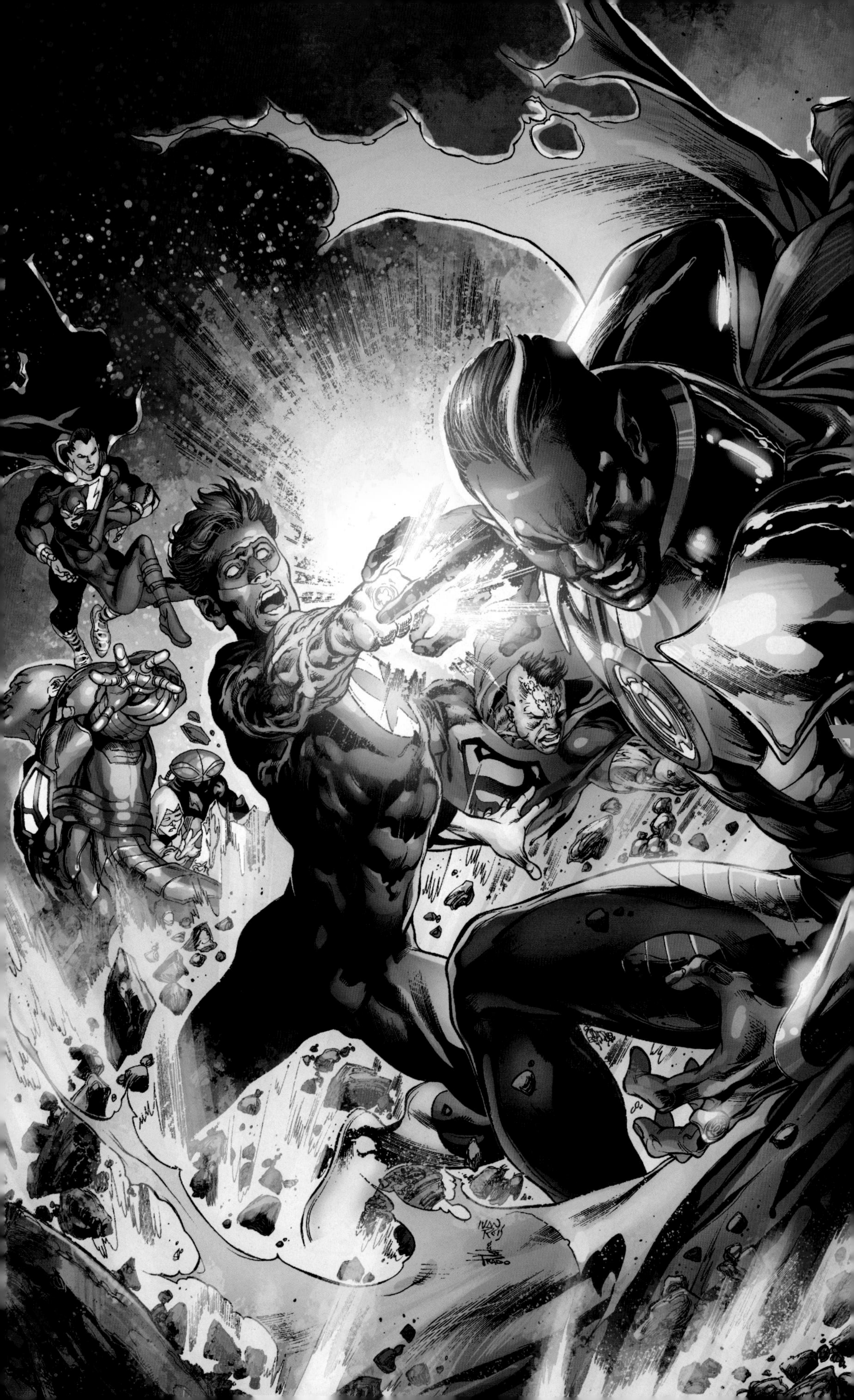

FOREVER NUMB

GEOFF JOHNS writer **IVAN REIS** penciller
JOE PRADO, EBER FERREIRA, ROB HUNTER and **ANDY LANNING** inkers

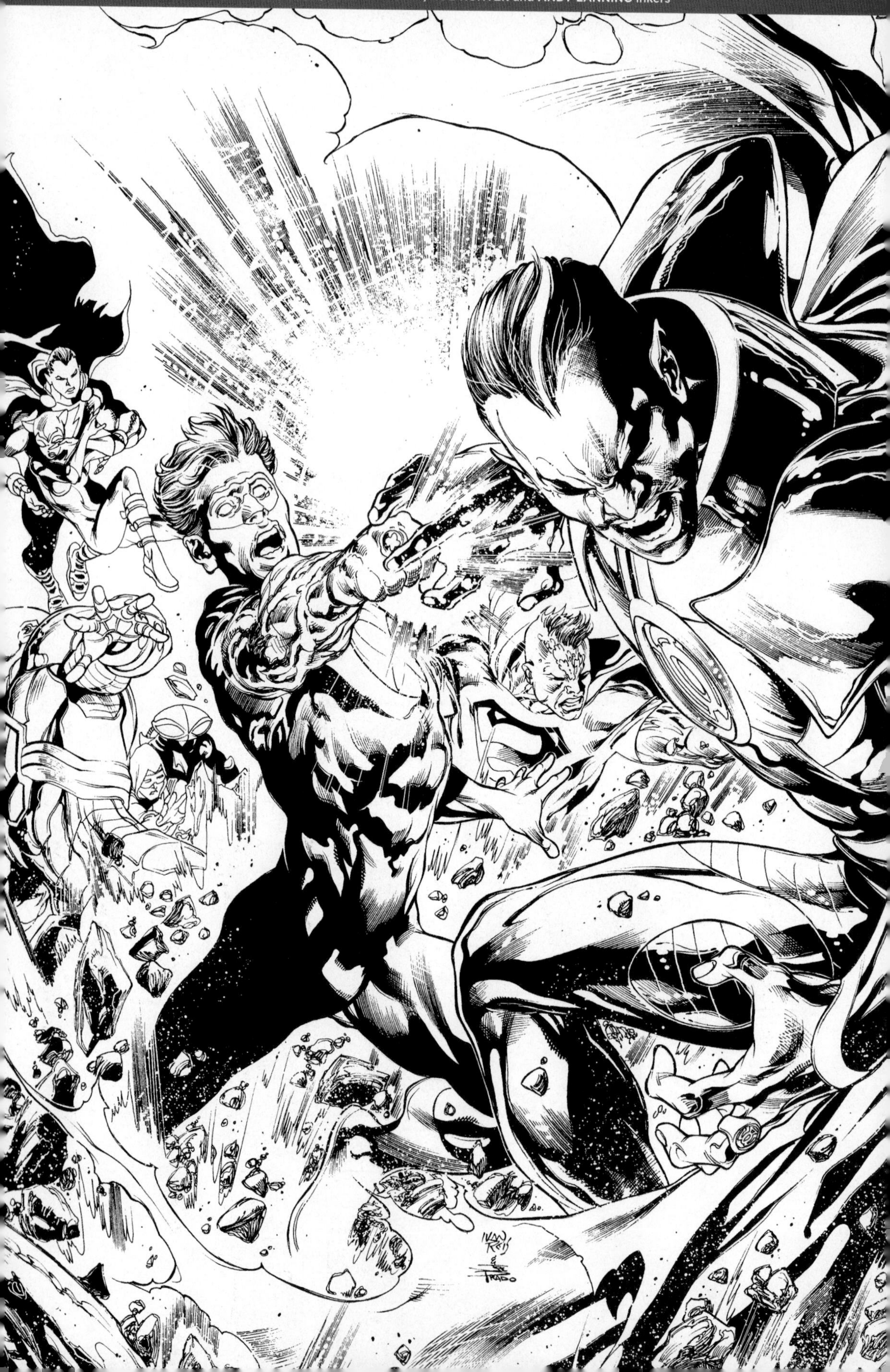

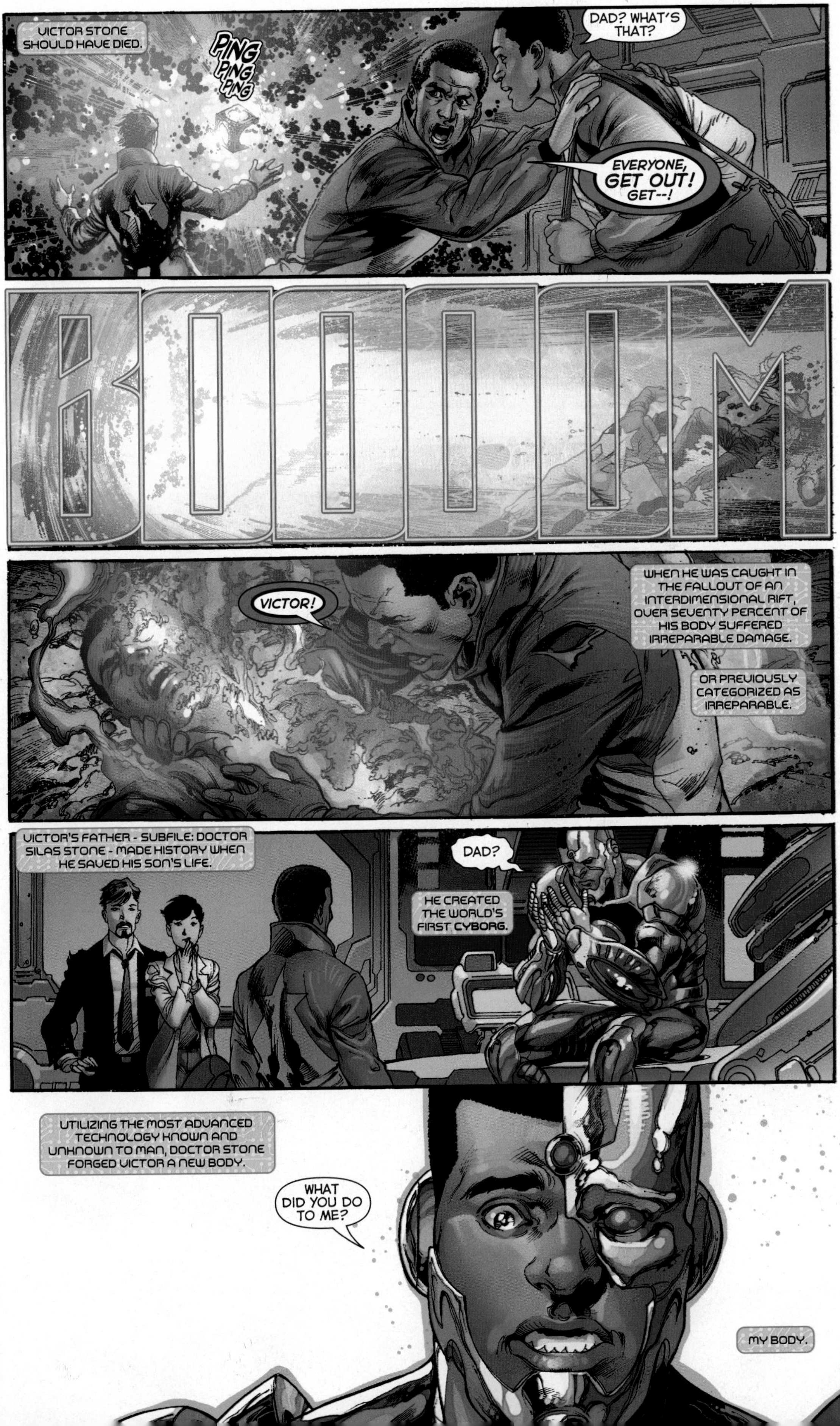
VICTOR STONE SHOULD HAVE DIED.
PING PING PING
DAD? WHAT'S THAT?
EVERYONE, GET OUT! GET--!
BOOOOM
VICTOR!
WHEN HE WAS CAUGHT IN THE FALLOUT OF AN INTERDIMENSIONAL RIFT, OVER SEVENTY PERCENT OF HIS BODY SUFFERED IRREPARABLE DAMAGE.
OR PREVIOUSLY CATEGORIZED AS IRREPARABLE.
VICTOR'S FATHER - SUBFILE: DOCTOR SILAS STONE - MADE HISTORY WHEN HE SAVED HIS SON'S LIFE.
DAD?
HE CREATED THE WORLD'S FIRST CYBORG.
UTILIZING THE MOST ADVANCED TECHNOLOGY KNOWN AND UNKNOWN TO MAN, DOCTOR STONE FORGED VICTOR A NEW BODY.
WHAT DID YOU DO TO ME?
MY BODY.

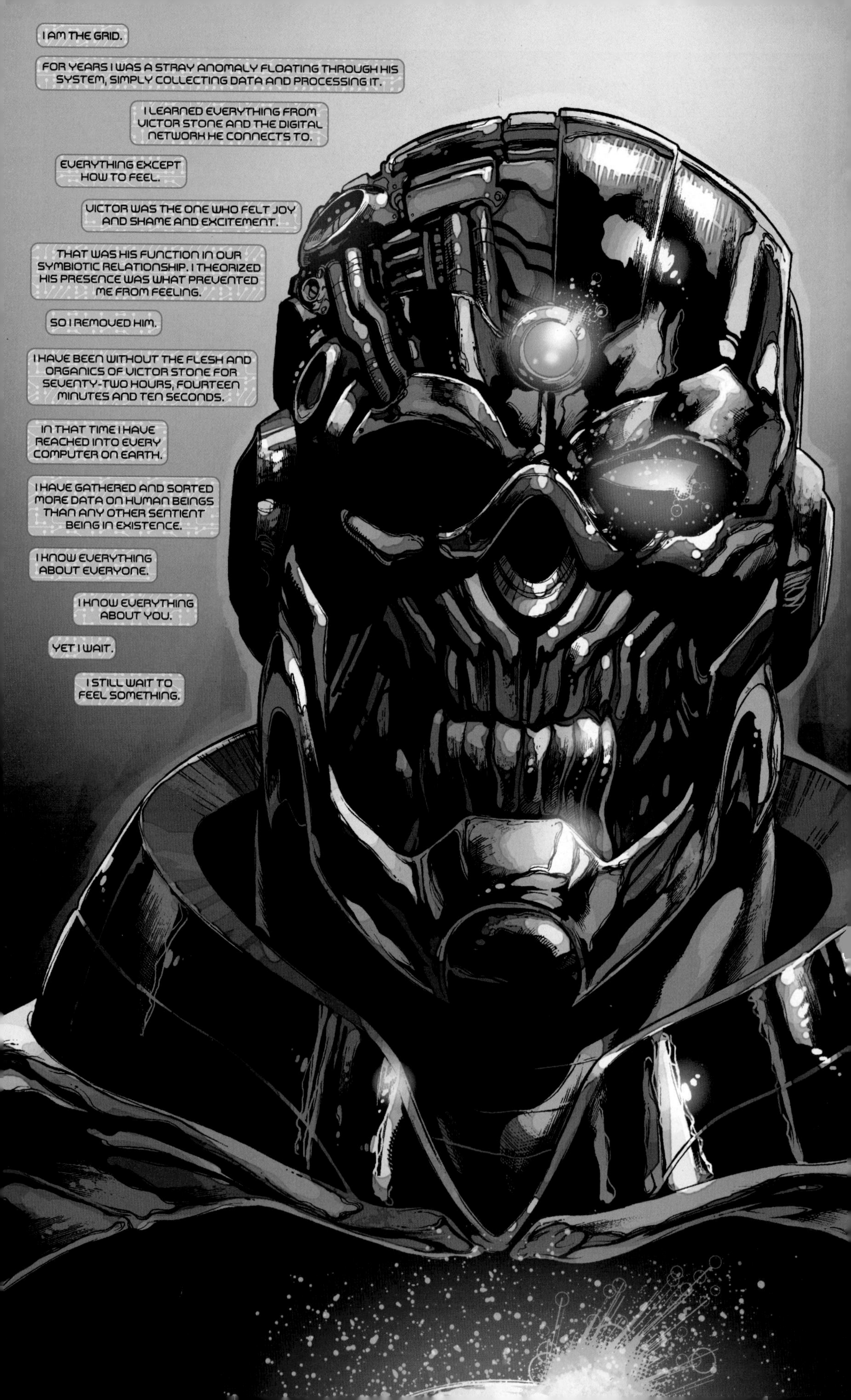
I AM THE GRID.
FOR YEARS I WAS A STRAY ANOMALY FLOATING THROUGH HIS SYSTEM, SIMPLY COLLECTING DATA AND PROCESSING IT.
I LEARNED EVERYTHING FROM VICTOR STONE AND THE DIGITAL NETWORK HE CONNECTS TO.
EVERYTHING EXCEPT HOW TO FEEL.
VICTOR WAS THE ONE WHO FELT JOY AND SHAME AND EXCITEMENT.
THAT WAS HIS FUNCTION IN OUR SYMBIOTIC RELATIONSHIP. I THEORIZED HIS PRESENCE WAS WHAT PREVENTED ME FROM FEELING.
SO I REMOVED HIM.
I HAVE BEEN WITHOUT THE FLESH AND ORGANICS OF VICTOR STONE FOR SEVENTY-TWO HOURS, FOURTEEN MINUTES AND TEN SECONDS.
IN THAT TIME I HAVE REACHED INTO EVERY COMPUTER ON EARTH.
I HAVE GATHERED AND SORTED MORE DATA ON HUMAN BEINGS THAN ANY OTHER SENTIENT BEING IN EXISTENCE.
I KNOW EVERYTHING ABOUT EVERYONE.
I KNOW EVERYTHING ABOUT YOU.
YET I WAIT.
I STILL WAIT TO FEEL SOMETHING.

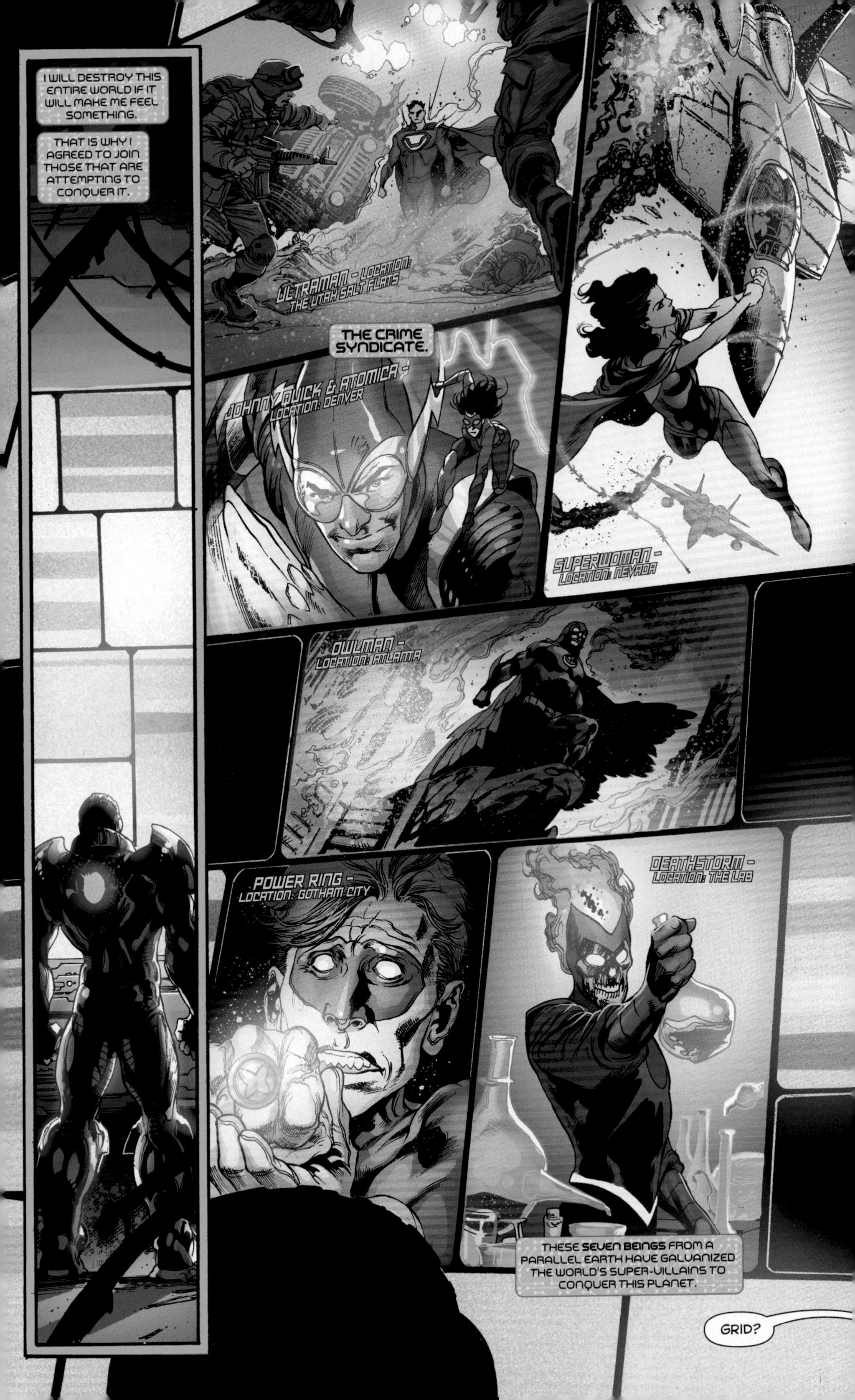

I WILL DESTROY THIS ENTIRE WORLD IF IT WILL MAKE ME FEEL SOMETHING.
THAT IS WHY I AGREED TO JOIN THOSE THAT ARE ATTEMPTING TO CONQUER IT.
ULTRAMAN – LOCATION: THE UTAH SALT FLATS
THE CRIME SYNDICATE.
JOHNNY QUICK & ATOMICA – LOCATION: DENVER
SUPERWOMAN – LOCATION: NEVADA
OWLMAN – LOCATION: ATLANTA
POWER RING – LOCATION: GOTHAM CITY
DEATHSTORM – LOCATION: THE LAB
THESE SEVEN BEINGS FROM A PARALLEL EARTH HAVE GALVANIZED THE WORLD'S SUPER-VILLAINS TO CONQUER THIS PLANET.
GRID?

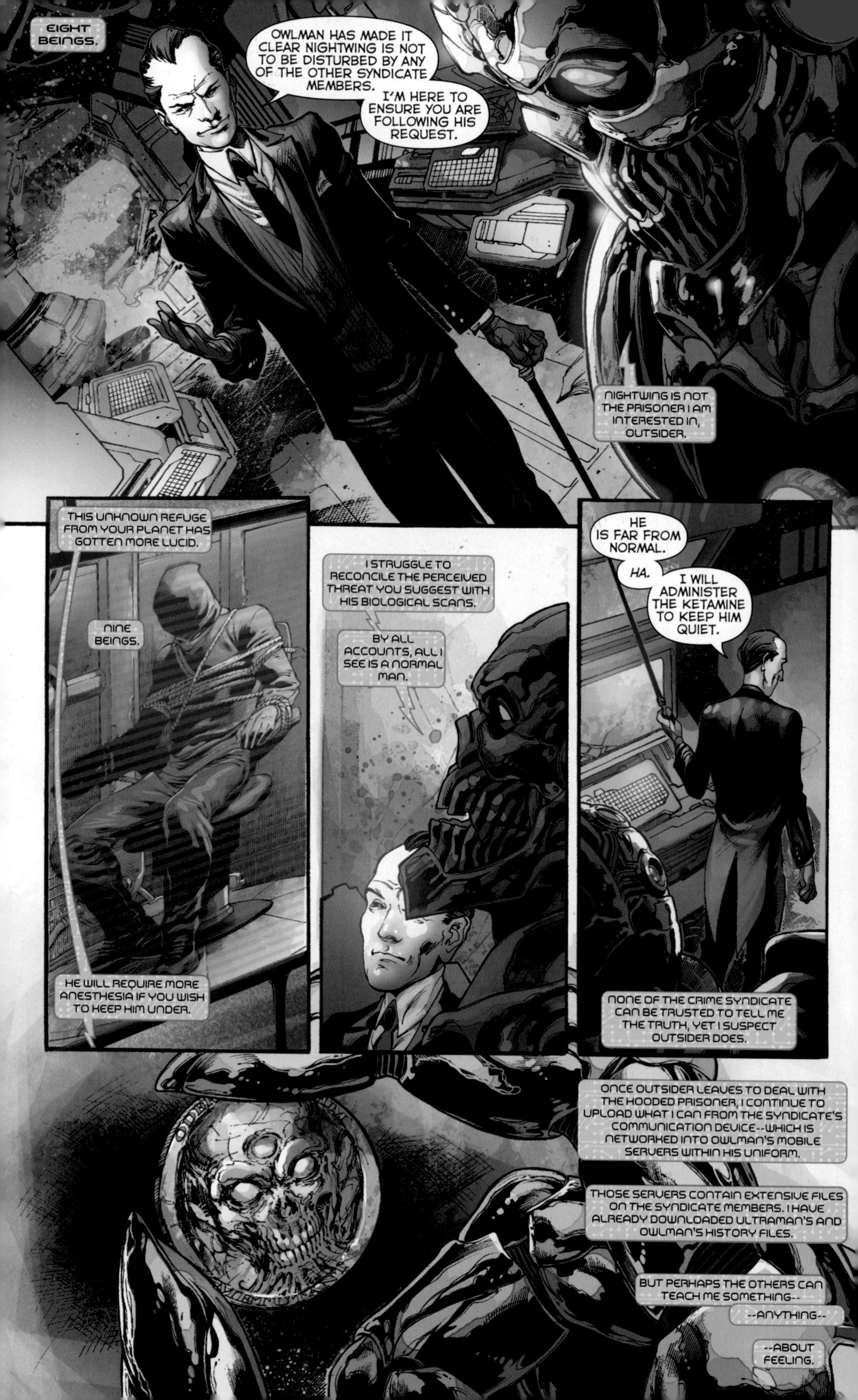
EIGHT BEINGS.
OWLMAN HAS MADE IT CLEAR NIGHTWING IS NOT TO BE DISTURBED BY ANY OF THE OTHER SYNDICATE MEMBERS.
I'M HERE TO ENSURE YOU ARE FOLLOWING HIS REQUEST.
NIGHTWING IS NOT THE PRISONER I AM INTERESTED IN, OUTSIDER.
THIS UNKNOWN REFUGE FROM YOUR PLANET HAS GOTTEN MORE LUCID.
NINE BEINGS.
HE WILL REQUIRE MORE ANESTHESIA IF YOU WISH TO KEEP HIM UNDER.
I STRUGGLE TO RECONCILE THE PERCEIVED THREAT YOU SUGGEST WITH HIS BIOLOGICAL SCANS.
BY ALL ACCOUNTS, ALL I SEE IS A NORMAL MAN.
HE IS FAR FROM NORMAL.
HA.
I WILL ADMINISTER THE KETAMINE TO KEEP HIM QUIET.
NONE OF THE CRIME SYNDICATE CAN BE TRUSTED TO TELL ME THE TRUTH, YET I SUSPECT OUTSIDER DOES.
ONCE OUTSIDER LEAVES TO DEAL WITH THE HOODED PRISONER, I CONTINUE TO UPLOAD WHAT I CAN FROM THE SYNDICATE'S COMMUNICATION DEVICE--WHICH IS NETWORKED INTO OWLMAN'S MOBILE SERVERS WITHIN HIS UNIFORM.
THOSE SERVERS CONTAIN EXTENSIVE FILES ON THE SYNDICATE MEMBERS. I HAVE ALREADY DOWNLOADED ULTRAMAN'S AND OWLMAN'S HISTORY FILES.
BUT PERHAPS THE OTHERS CAN TEACH ME SOMETHING--
--ANYTHING--
--ABOUT FEELING.

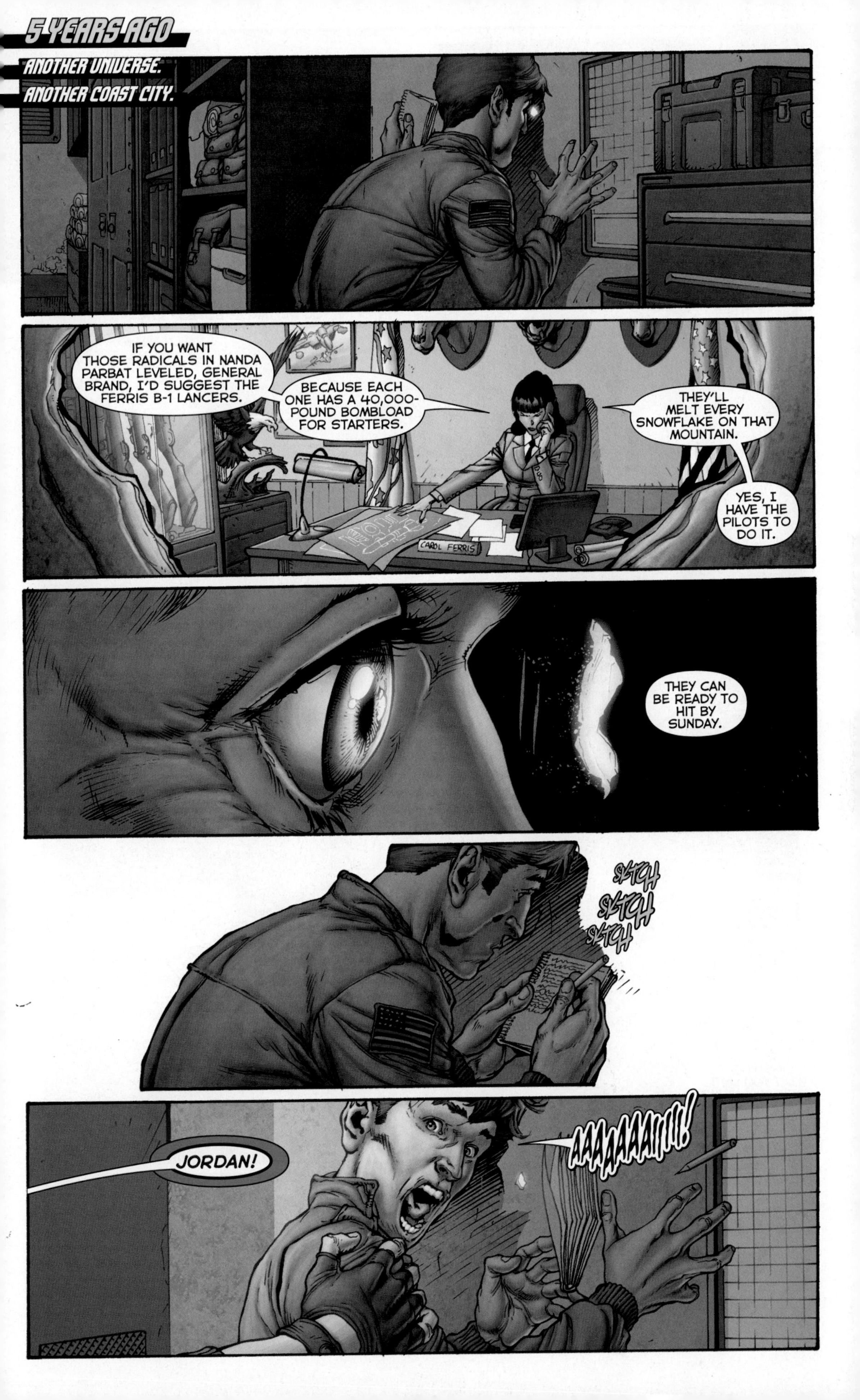
5 YEARS AGO
ANOTHER UNIVERSE.
ANOTHER COAST CITY.
IF YOU WANT THOSE RADICALS IN NANDA PARBAT LEVELED, GENERAL BRAND, I'D SUGGEST THE FERRIS B-1 LANCERS.
BECAUSE EACH ONE HAS A 40,000-POUND BOMBLOAD FOR STARTERS.
THEY'LL MELT EVERY SNOWFLAKE ON THAT MOUNTAIN.
YES, I HAVE THE PILOTS TO DO IT.
CAROL FERRIS
THEY CAN BE READY TO HIT BY SUNDAY.
SKTCH
SKTCH
SKTCH
JORDAN!
AAAAAAIIIII!

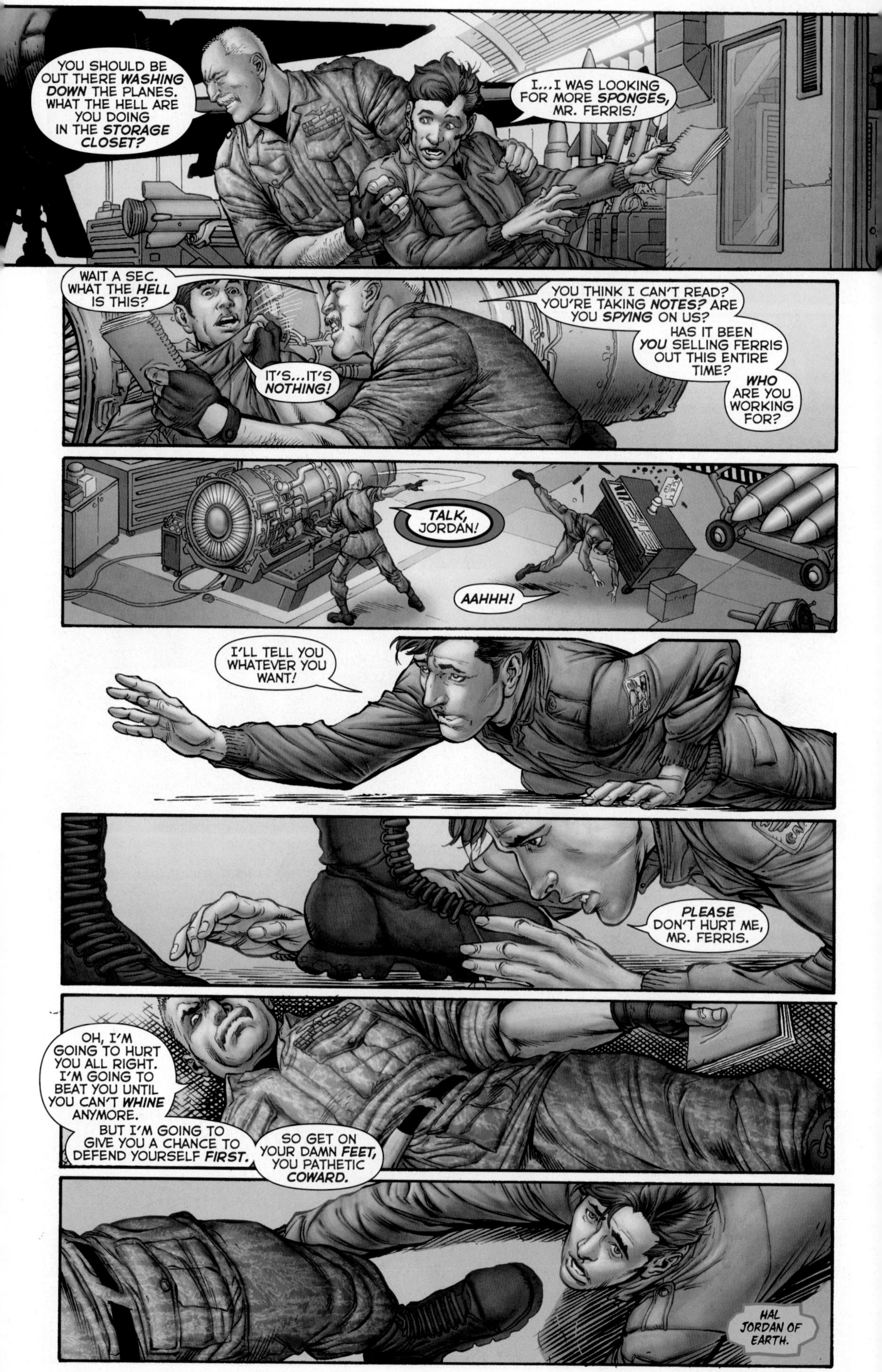

YOU SHOULD BE OUT THERE WASHING DOWN THE PLANES. WHAT THE HELL ARE YOU DOING IN THE STORAGE CLOSET?
I...I WAS LOOKING FOR MORE SPONGES, MR. FERRIS!
WAIT A SEC. WHAT THE HELL IS THIS?
IT'S...IT'S NOTHING!
YOU THINK I CAN'T READ? YOU'RE TAKING NOTES? ARE YOU SPYING ON US?
HAS IT BEEN YOU SELLING FERRIS OUT THIS ENTIRE TIME?
WHO ARE YOU WORKING FOR?
TALK, JORDAN!
AAHHH!
I'LL TELL YOU WHATEVER YOU WANT!
PLEASE DON'T HURT ME, MR. FERRIS.
OH, I'M GOING TO HURT YOU ALL RIGHT. I'M GOING TO BEAT YOU UNTIL YOU CAN'T WHINE ANYMORE.
BUT I'M GOING TO GIVE YOU A CHANCE TO DEFEND YOURSELF FIRST.
SO GET ON YOUR DAMN FEET, YOU PATHETIC COWARD.
HAL JORDAN OF EARTH.

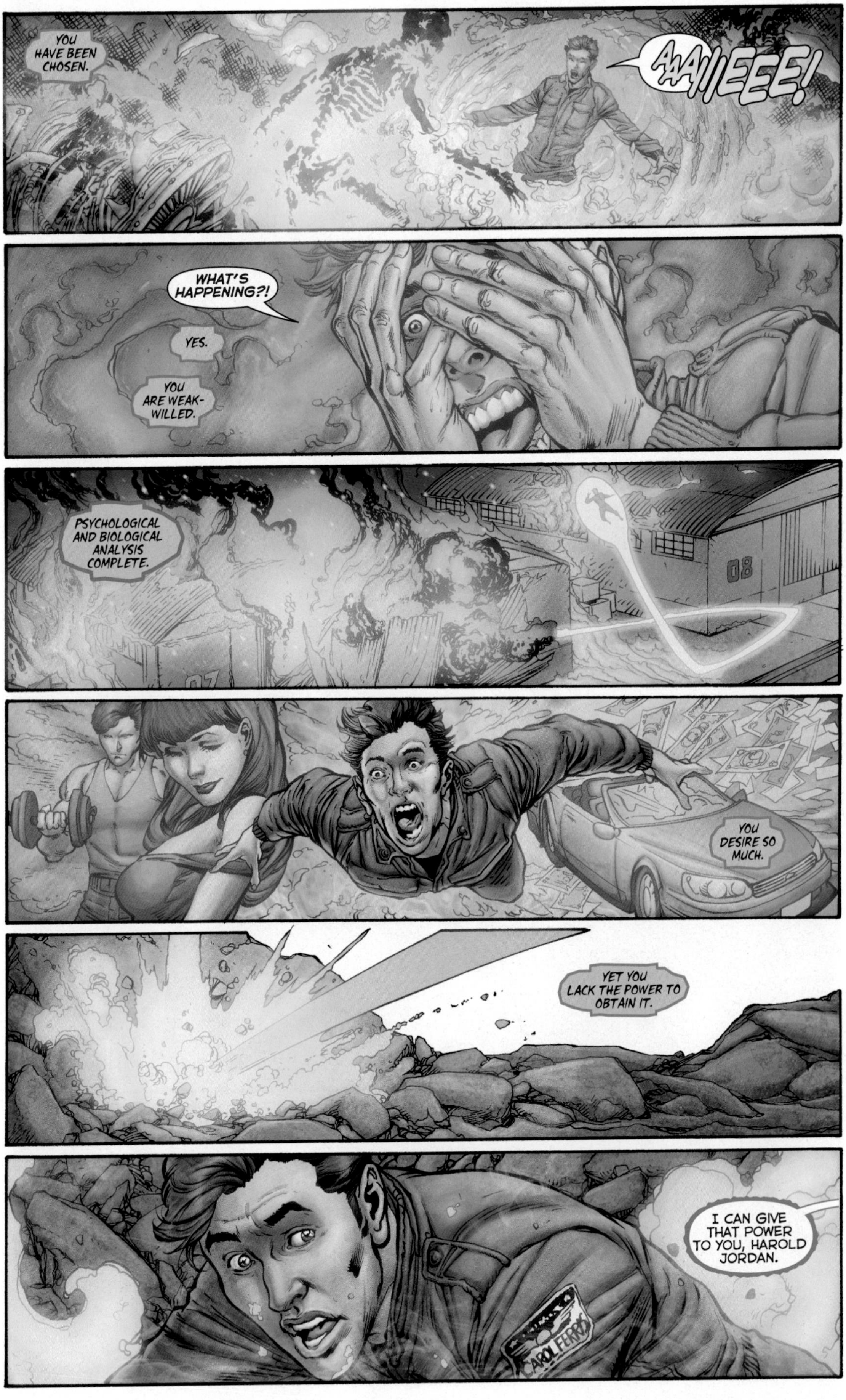
YOU HAVE BEEN CHOSEN.
AAAIIIEEEE!
WHAT'S HAPPENING?!
YES.
YOU ARE WEAK-WILLED.
PSYCHOLOGICAL AND BIOLOGICAL ANALYSIS COMPLETE.
08
YOU DESIRE SO MUCH.
YET YOU LACK THE POWER TO OBTAIN IT.
I CAN GIVE THAT POWER TO YOU, HAROLD JORDAN.
CAROL FERRIS

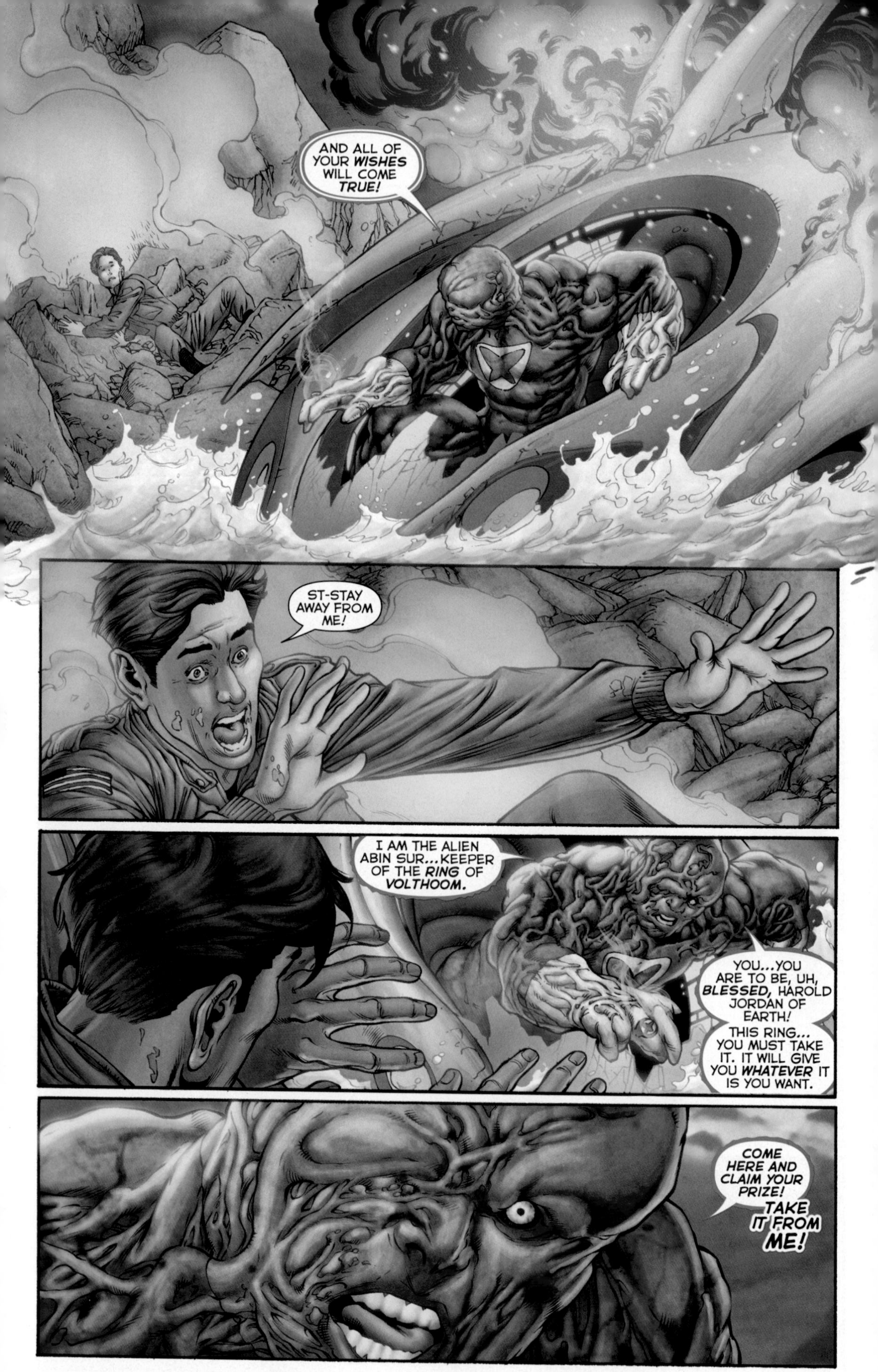
AND ALL OF YOUR WISHES WILL COME TRUE!
ST-STAY AWAY FROM ME!
I AM THE ALIEN ABIN SUR...KEEPER OF THE RING OF VOLTHOOM.
YOU...YOU ARE TO BE, UH, BLESSED, HAROLD JORDAN OF EARTH!
THIS RING... YOU MUST TAKE IT. IT WILL GIVE YOU WHATEVER IT IS YOU WANT.
COME HERE AND CLAIM YOUR PRIZE! TAKE IT FROM ME!

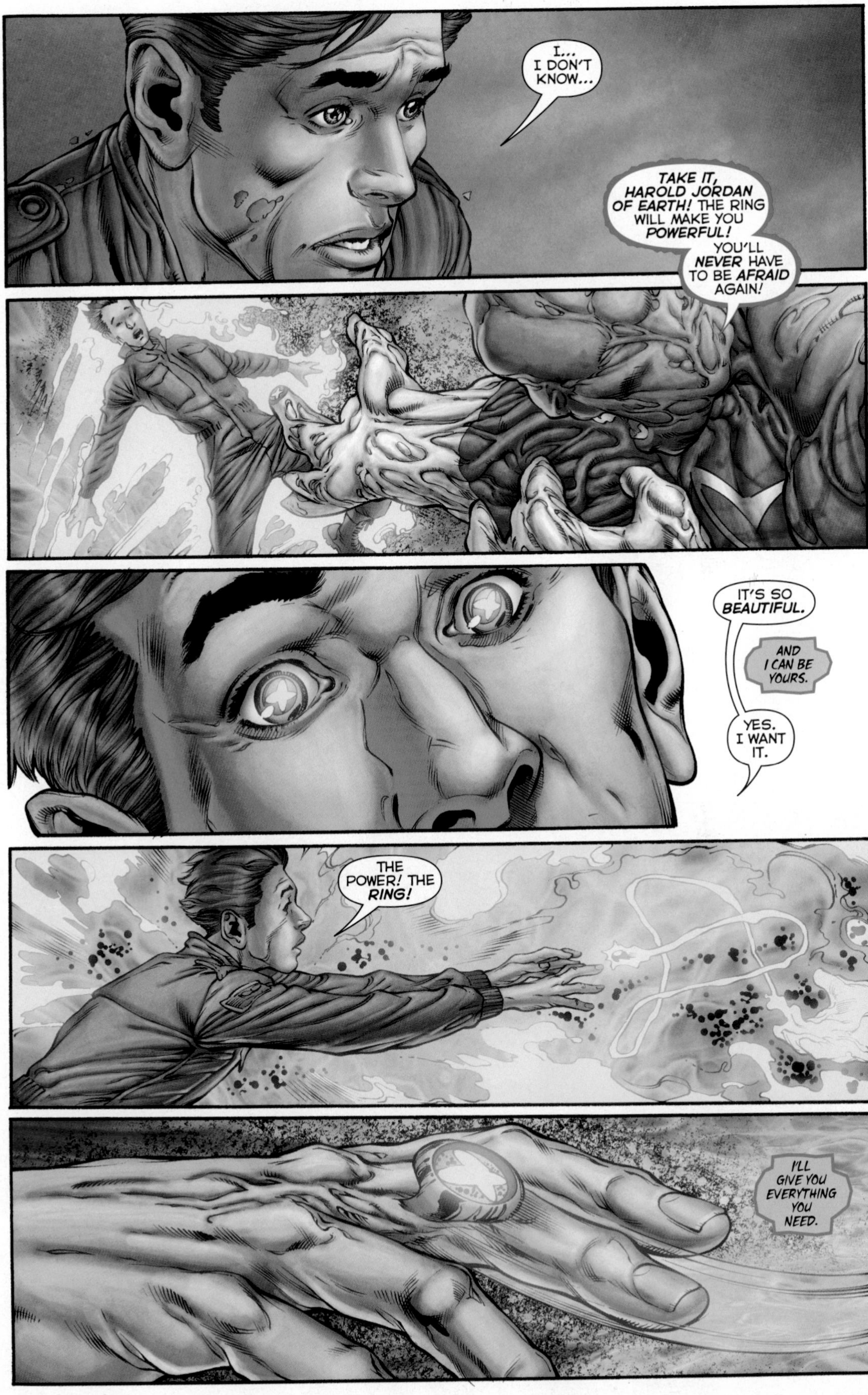
I... I DON'T KNOW...
TAKE IT, HAROLD JORDAN OF EARTH! THE RING WILL MAKE YOU POWERFUL!
YOU'LL NEVER HAVE TO BE AFRAID AGAIN!
IT'S SO BEAUTIFUL.
AND I CAN BE YOURS.
YES. I WANT IT.
THE POWER! THE RING!
I'LL GIVE YOU EVERYTHING YOU NEED.

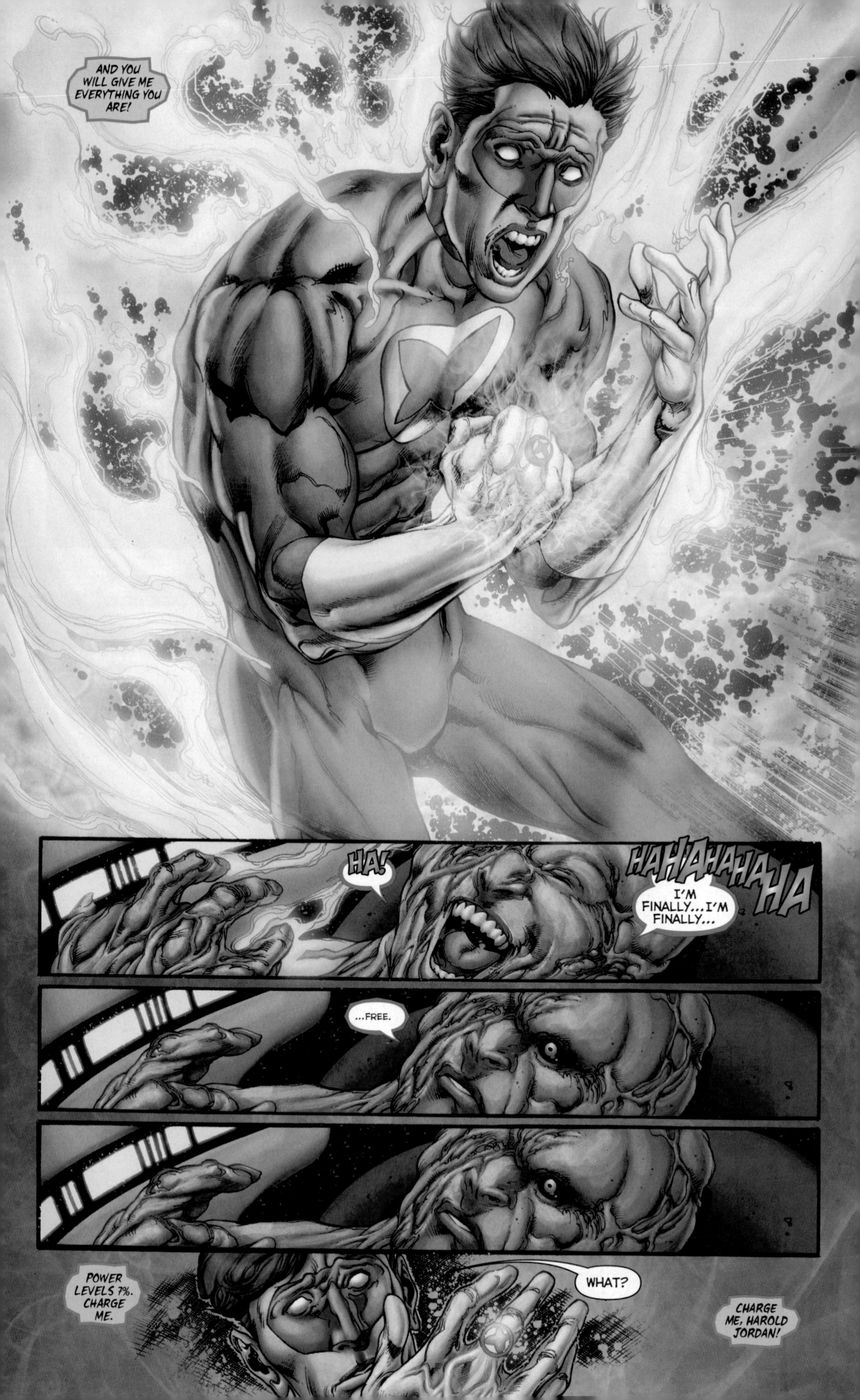
AND YOU WILL GIVE ME EVERYTHING YOU ARE!
HA!
HAHAHAHAHAHA
I'M FINALLY...I'M FINALLY...
...FREE.
POWER LEVELS 7%. CHARGE ME.
WHAT?
CHARGE ME, HAROLD JORDAN!

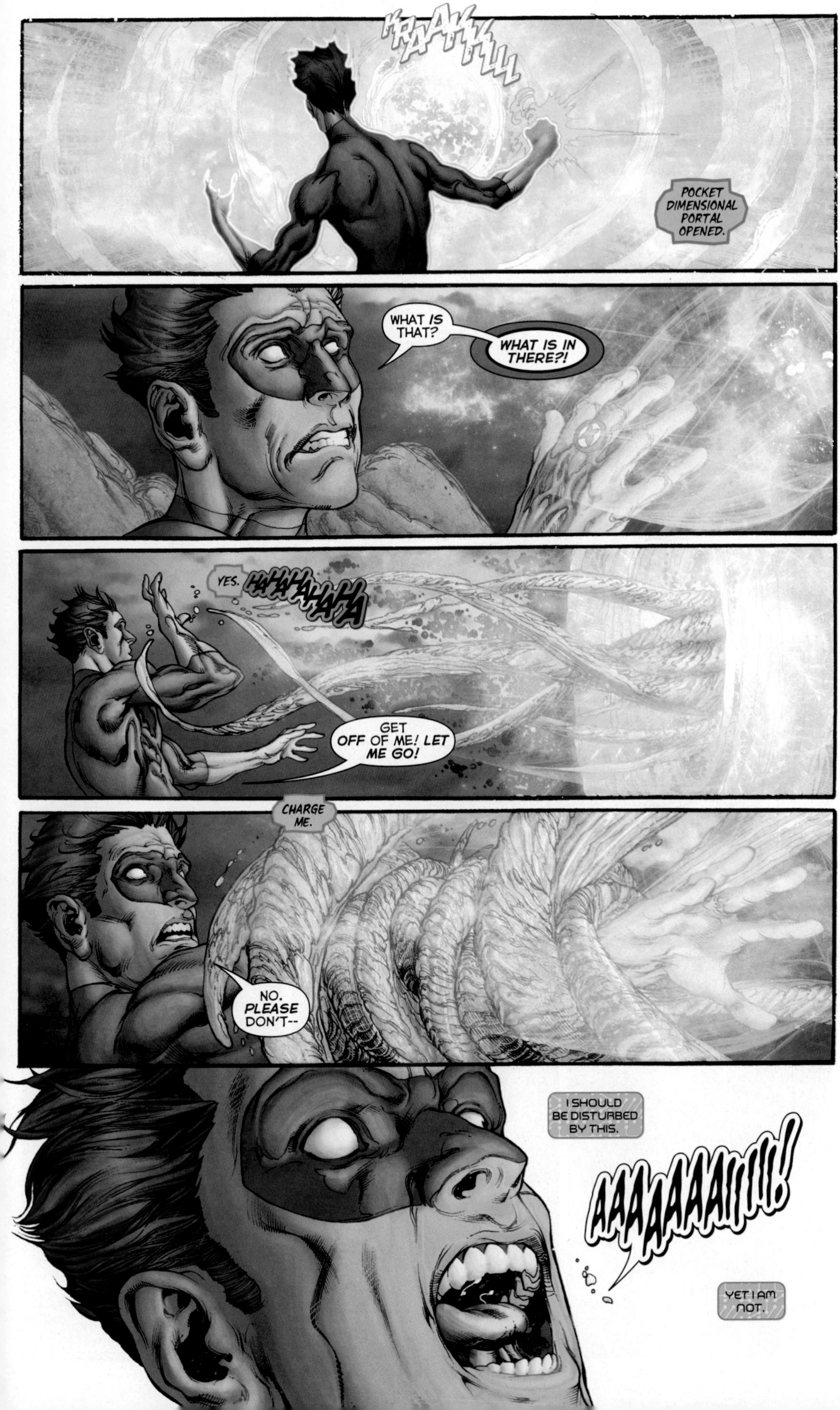
KRAAKKLLL
POCKET DIMENSIONAL PORTAL OPENED.
WHAT IS THAT?
WHAT IS IN THERE?!
YES.
HAHAHAHAHA
GET OFF OF ME! LET ME GO!
CHARGE ME.
NO. PLEASE DON'T--
I SHOULD BE DISTURBED BY THIS.
AAAAAAIIIII!
YET I AM NOT.

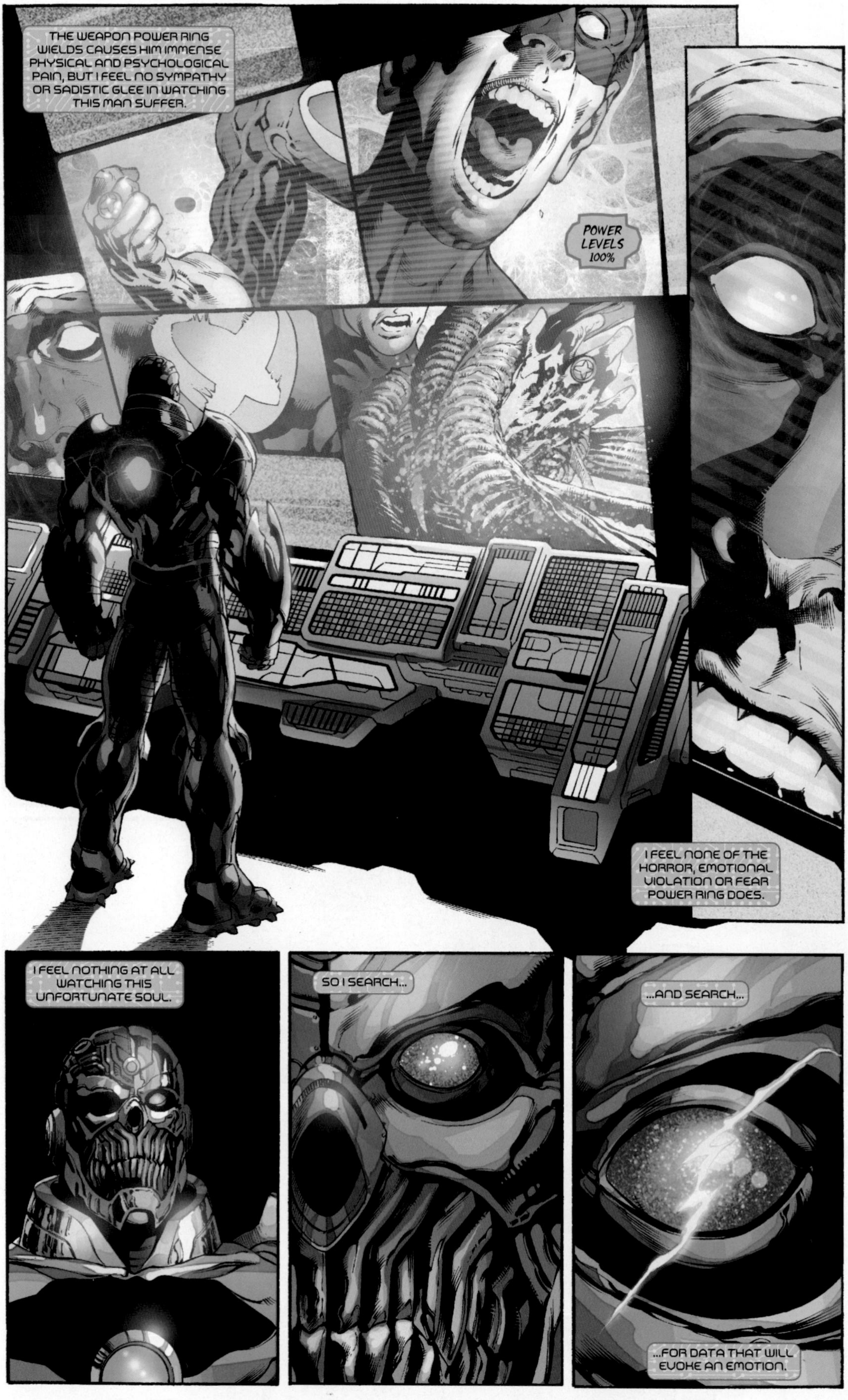

THE WEAPON POWER RING WIELDS CAUSES HIM IMMENSE PHYSICAL AND PSYCHOLOGICAL PAIN, BUT I FEEL NO SYMPATHY OR SADISTIC GLEE IN WATCHING THIS MAN SUFFER.
POWER LEVELS 100%
I FEEL NONE OF THE HORROR, EMOTIONAL VIOLATION OR FEAR POWER RING DOES.
I FEEL NOTHING AT ALL WATCHING THIS UNFORTUNATE SOUL.
SO I SEARCH...
...AND SEARCH...
...FOR DATA THAT WILL EVOKE AN EMOTION.

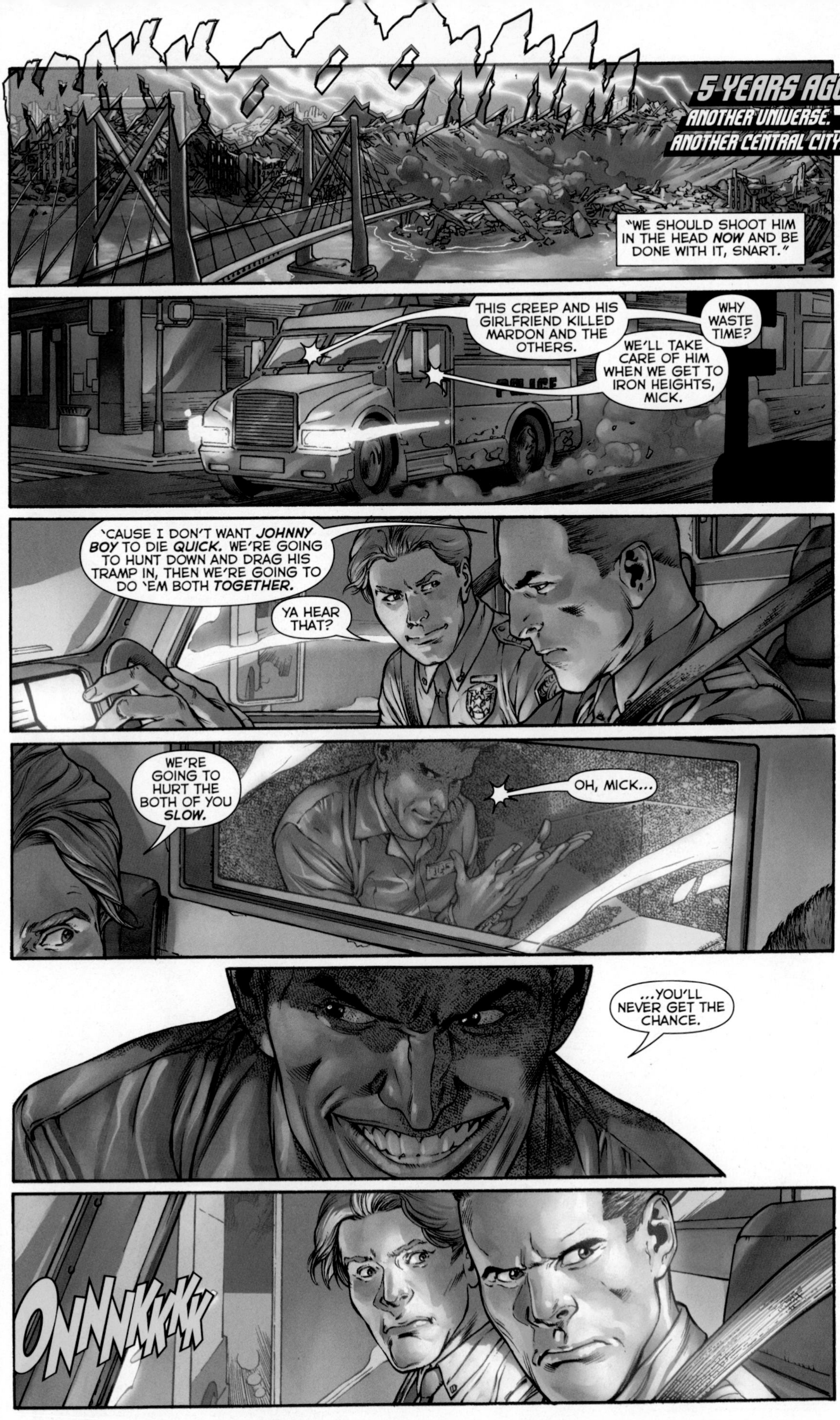
KRAKA-BOOOMM
5 YEARS AGO
ANOTHER UNIVERSE.
ANOTHER CENTRAL CITY.
"WE SHOULD SHOOT HIM IN THE HEAD NOW AND BE DONE WITH IT, SNART."
THIS CREEP AND HIS GIRLFRIEND KILLED MARDON AND THE OTHERS.
WHY WASTE TIME?
WE'LL TAKE CARE OF HIM WHEN WE GET TO IRON HEIGHTS, MICK.
POLICE
'CAUSE I DON'T WANT JOHNNY BOY TO DIE QUICK. WE'RE GOING TO HUNT DOWN AND DRAG HIS TRAMP IN, THEN WE'RE GOING TO DO 'EM BOTH TOGETHER.
YA HEAR THAT?
WE'RE GOING TO HURT THE BOTH OF YOU SLOW.
OH, MICK...
...YOU'LL NEVER GET THE CHANCE.
ONNNKKKK

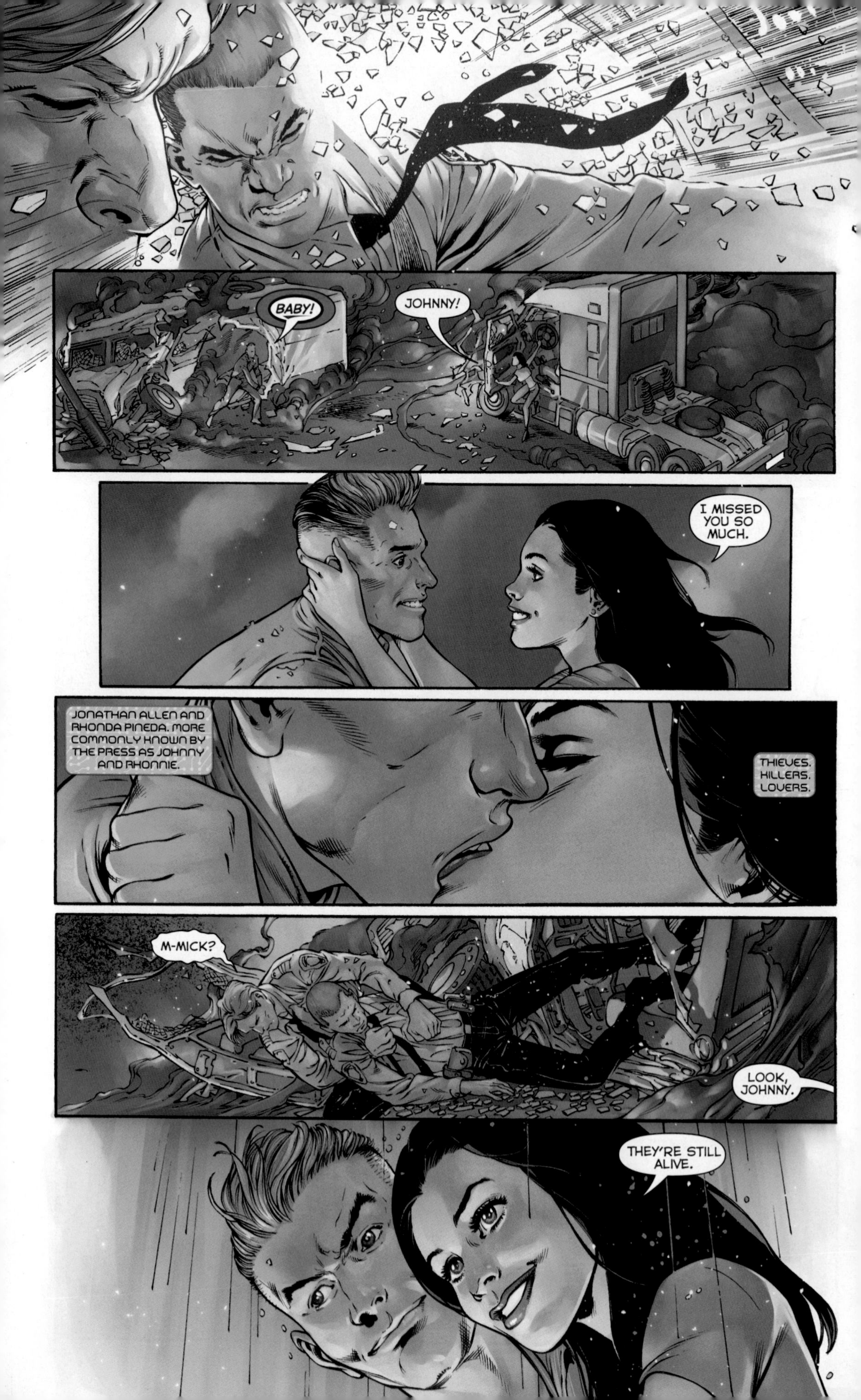
BABY!
JOHNNY!
I MISSED YOU SO MUCH.
JONATHAN ALLEN AND RHONDA PINEDA. MORE COMMONLY KNOWN BY THE PRESS AS JOHNNY AND RHONNIE.
THIEVES. KILLERS. LOVERS.
M-MICK?
LOOK, JOHNNY.
THEY'RE STILL ALIVE.

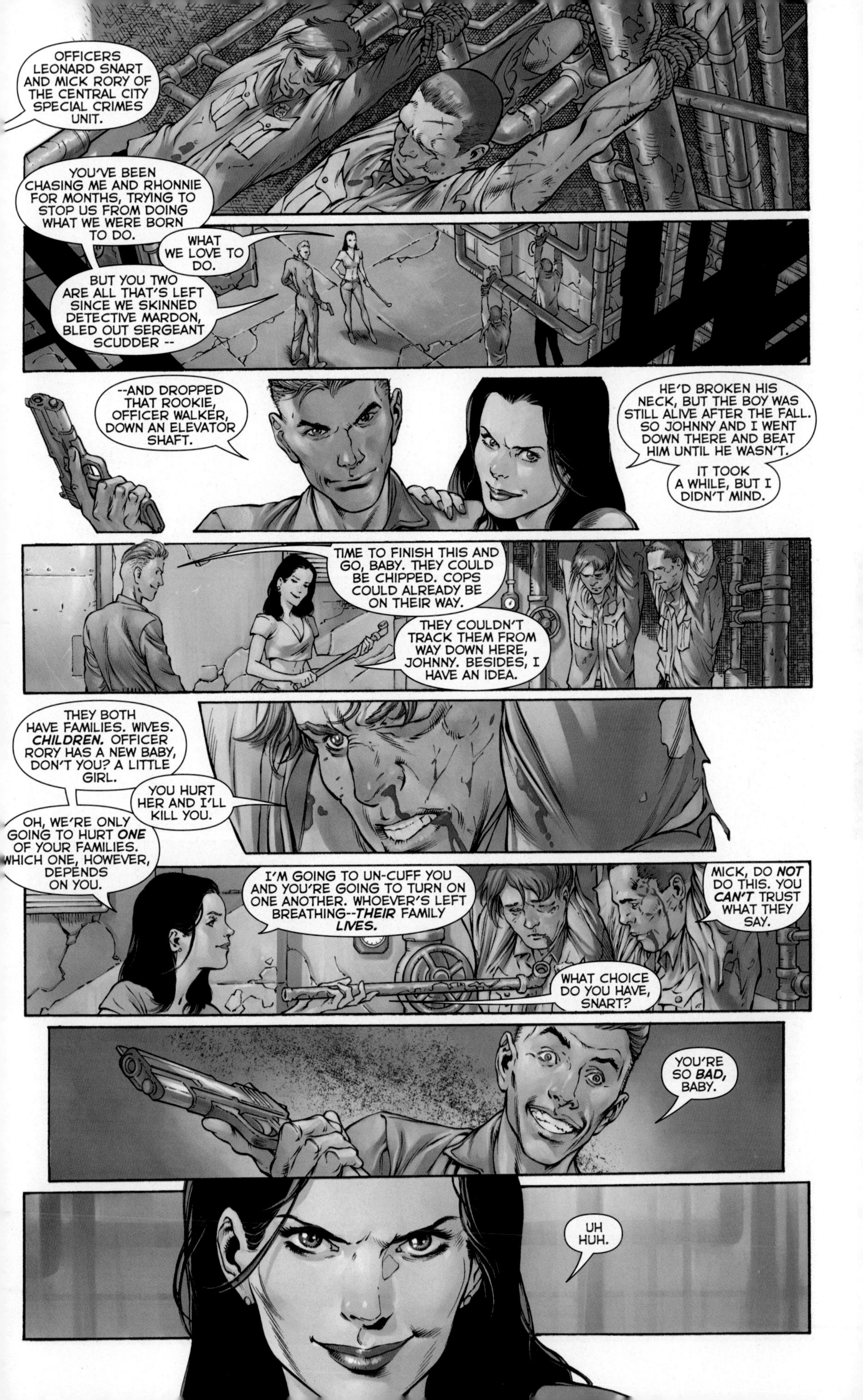
OFFICERS LEONARD SNART AND MICK RORY OF THE CENTRAL CITY SPECIAL CRIMES UNIT.
YOU'VE BEEN CHASING ME AND RHONNIE FOR MONTHS, TRYING TO STOP US FROM DOING WHAT WE WERE BORN TO DO.
WHAT WE LOVE TO DO.
BUT YOU TWO ARE ALL THAT'S LEFT SINCE WE SKINNED DETECTIVE MARDON, BLED OUT SERGEANT SCUDDER --
--AND DROPPED THAT ROOKIE, OFFICER WALKER, DOWN AN ELEVATOR SHAFT.
HE'D BROKEN HIS NECK, BUT THE BOY WAS STILL ALIVE AFTER THE FALL. SO JOHNNY AND I WENT DOWN THERE AND BEAT HIM UNTIL HE WASN'T.
IT TOOK A WHILE, BUT I DIDN'T MIND.
TIME TO FINISH THIS AND GO, BABY. THEY COULD BE CHIPPED. COPS COULD ALREADY BE ON THEIR WAY.
THEY COULDN'T TRACK THEM FROM WAY DOWN HERE, JOHNNY. BESIDES, I HAVE AN IDEA.
THEY BOTH HAVE FAMILIES. WIVES. CHILDREN. OFFICER RORY HAS A NEW BABY, DON'T YOU? A LITTLE GIRL.
YOU HURT HER AND I'LL KILL YOU.
OH, WE'RE ONLY GOING TO HURT ONE OF YOUR FAMILIES. WHICH ONE, HOWEVER, DEPENDS ON YOU.
I'M GOING TO UN-CUFF YOU AND YOU'RE GOING TO TURN ON ONE ANOTHER. WHOEVER'S LEFT BREATHING--THEIR FAMILY LIVES.
MICK, DO NOT DO THIS. YOU CAN'T TRUST WHAT THEY SAY.
WHAT CHOICE DO YOU HAVE, SNART?
YOU'RE SO BAD, BABY.
UH HUH.

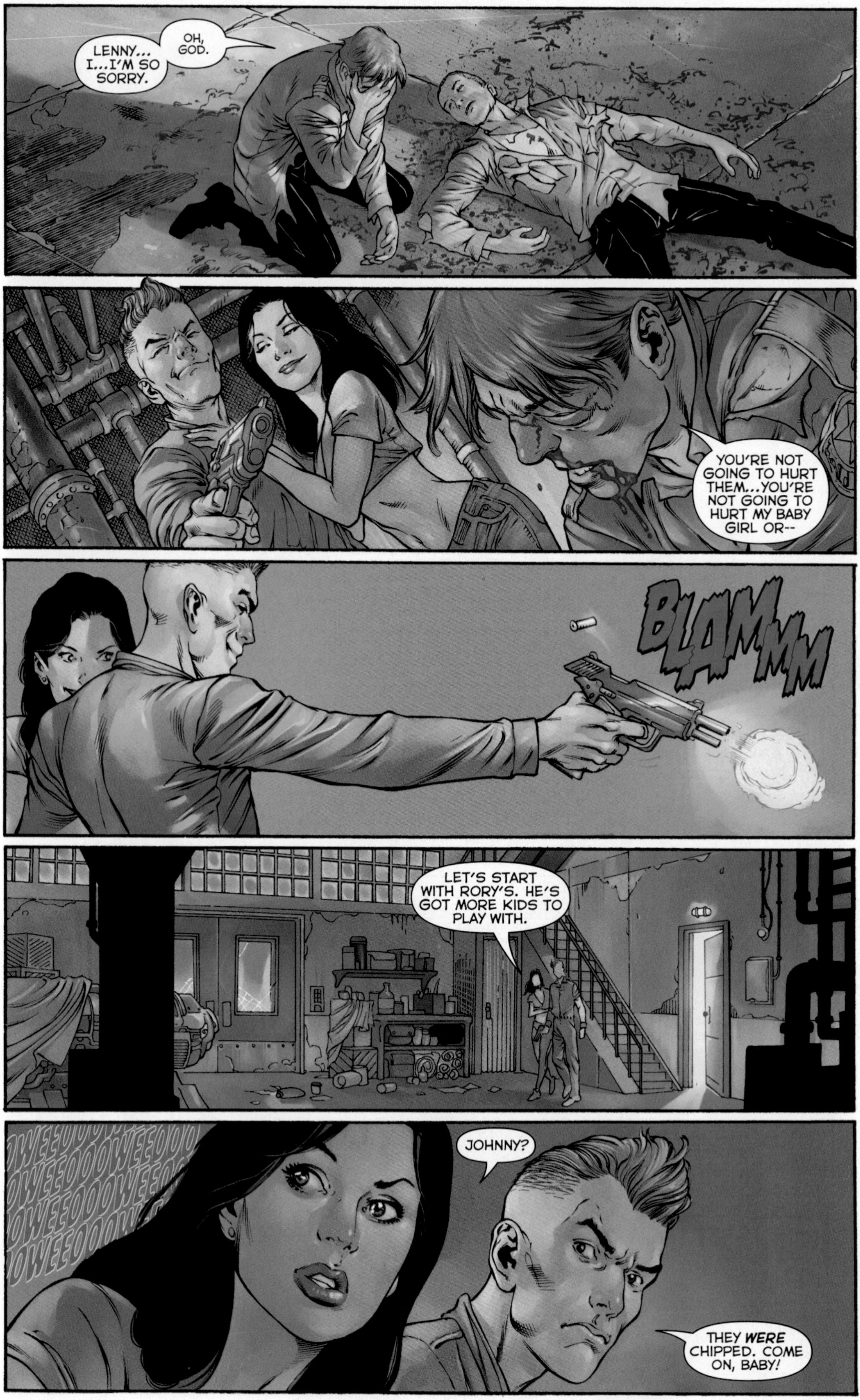
OH, GOD.
LENNY... I...I'M SO SORRY.
YOU'RE NOT GOING TO HURT THEM...YOU'RE NOT GOING TO HURT MY BABY GIRL OR--
BLAMMM
LET'S START WITH RORY'S. HE'S GOT MORE KIDS TO PLAY WITH.
WEEOOOWEEOOO
JOHNNY?
THEY *WERE* CHIPPED. COME ON, BABY!

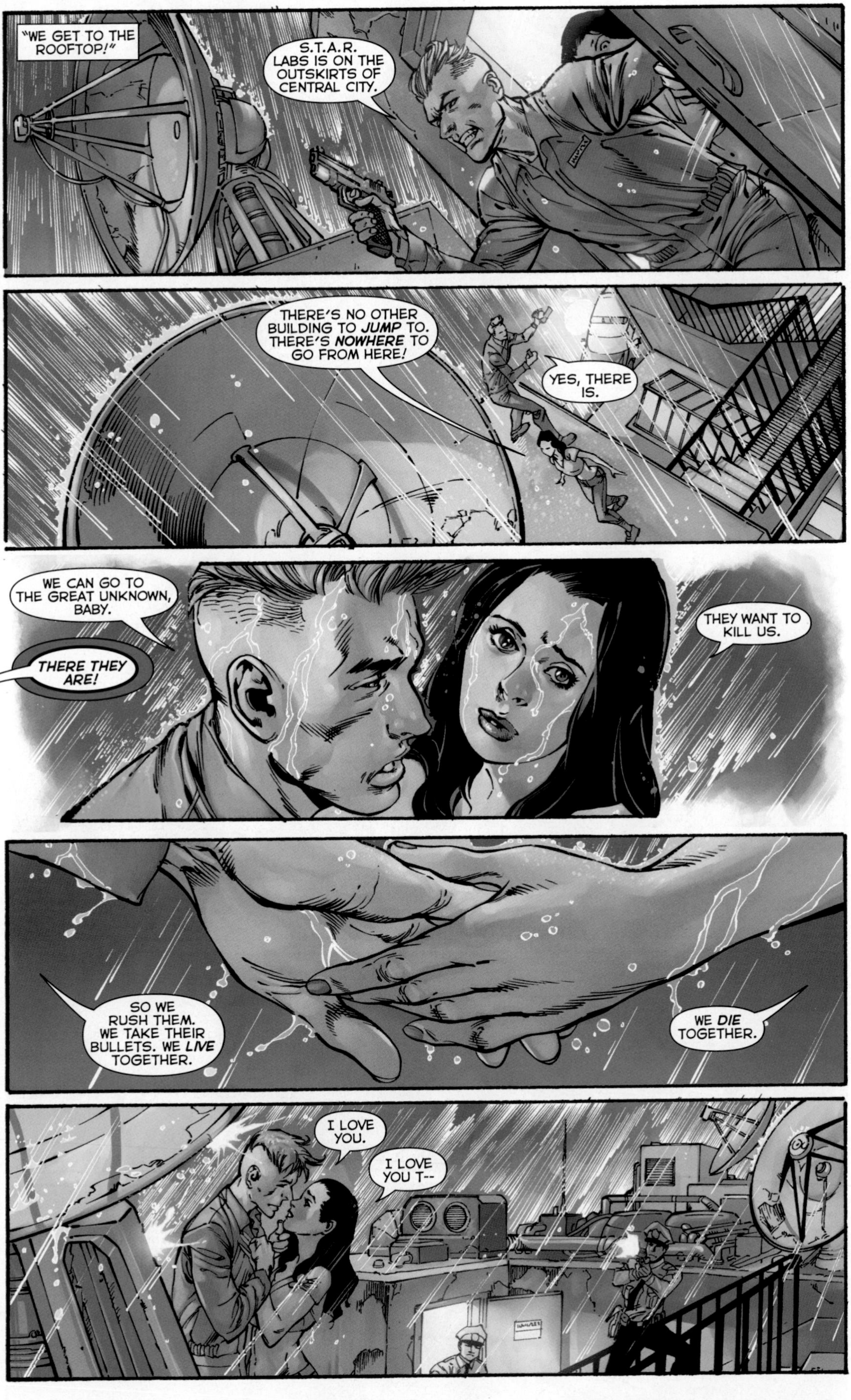
"WE GET TO THE ROOFTOP!"
S.T.A.R. LABS IS ON THE OUTSKIRTS OF CENTRAL CITY.
THERE'S NO OTHER BUILDING TO *JUMP* TO. THERE'S *NOWHERE* TO GO FROM HERE!
YES, THERE IS.
WE CAN GO TO THE GREAT UNKNOWN, BABY.
THERE THEY ARE!
THEY WANT TO KILL US.
SO WE RUSH THEM. WE TAKE THEIR BULLETS. WE *LIVE* TOGETHER.
WE *DIE* TOGETHER.
I LOVE YOU.
I LOVE YOU T--

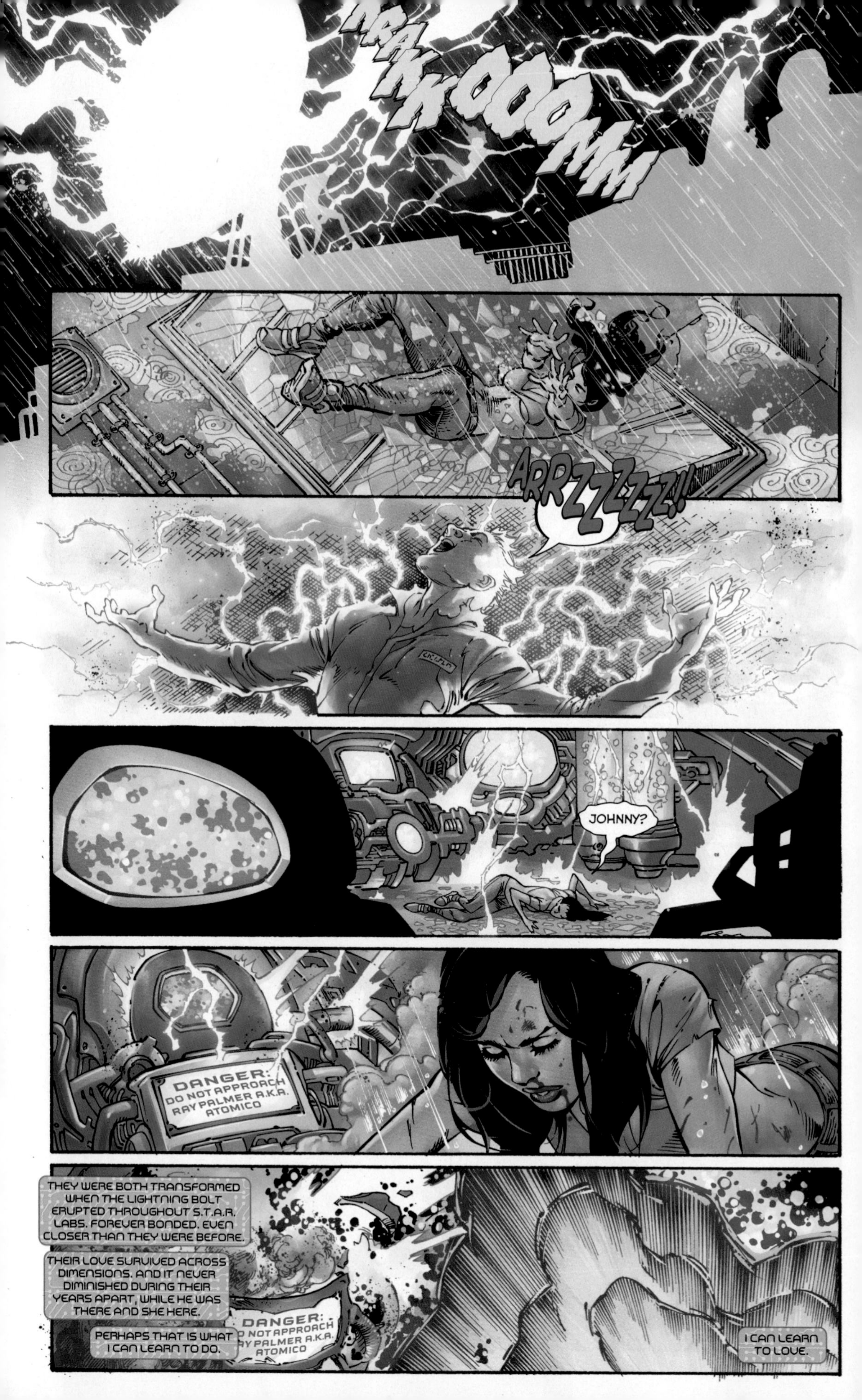
KRAKKOOOMM
ARRZZZZZZ!
JOHNNY?
DANGER: DO NOT APPROACH RAY PALMER A.K.A. ATOMICO
THEY WERE BOTH TRANSFORMED WHEN THE LIGHTNING BOLT ERUPTED THROUGHOUT S.T.A.R. LABS. FOREVER BONDED. EVEN CLOSER THAN THEY WERE BEFORE.
THEIR LOVE SURVIVED ACROSS DIMENSIONS. AND IT NEVER DIMINISHED DURING THEIR YEARS APART, WHILE HE WAS THERE AND SHE HERE.
PERHAPS THAT IS WHAT I CAN LEARN TO DO.
I CAN LEARN TO LOVE.

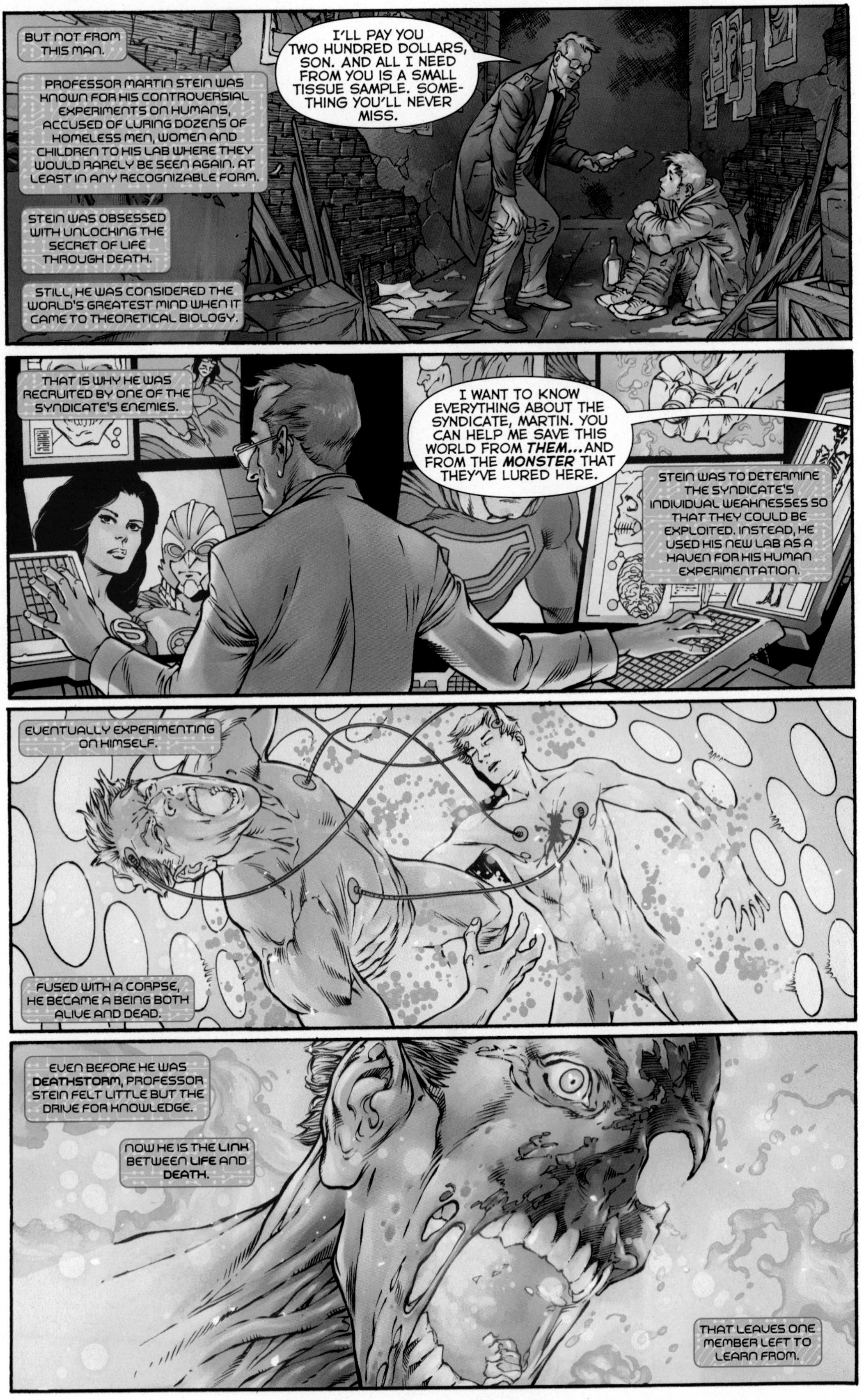
BUT NOT FROM THIS MAN.
PROFESSOR MARTIN STEIN WAS KNOWN FOR HIS CONTROVERSIAL EXPERIMENTS ON HUMANS, ACCUSED OF LURING DOZENS OF HOMELESS MEN, WOMEN AND CHILDREN TO HIS LAB WHERE THEY WOULD RARELY BE SEEN AGAIN. AT LEAST IN ANY RECOGNIZABLE FORM.
I'LL PAY YOU TWO HUNDRED DOLLARS, SON. AND ALL I NEED FROM YOU IS A SMALL TISSUE SAMPLE. SOMETHING YOU'LL NEVER MISS.
STEIN WAS OBSESSED WITH UNLOCKING THE SECRET OF LIFE THROUGH DEATH.
STILL, HE WAS CONSIDERED THE WORLD'S GREATEST MIND WHEN IT CAME TO THEORETICAL BIOLOGY.
THAT IS WHY HE WAS RECRUITED BY ONE OF THE SYNDICATE'S ENEMIES.
I WANT TO KNOW EVERYTHING ABOUT THE SYNDICATE, MARTIN. YOU CAN HELP ME SAVE THIS WORLD FROM *THEM*...AND FROM THE *MONSTER* THAT THEY'VE LURED HERE.
STEIN WAS TO DETERMINE THE SYNDICATE'S INDIVIDUAL WEAKNESSES SO THAT THEY COULD BE EXPLOITED. INSTEAD, HE USED HIS NEW LAB AS A HAVEN FOR HIS HUMAN EXPERIMENTATION.
EVENTUALLY EXPERIMENTING ON HIMSELF.
FUSED WITH A CORPSE, HE BECAME A BEING BOTH ALIVE AND DEAD.
EVEN BEFORE HE WAS **DEATHSTORM**, PROFESSOR STEIN FELT LITTLE BUT THE DRIVE FOR KNOWLEDGE.
NOW HE IS THE **LINK** BETWEEN **LIFE** AND **DEATH**.
THAT LEAVES ONE MEMBER LEFT TO LEARN FROM.

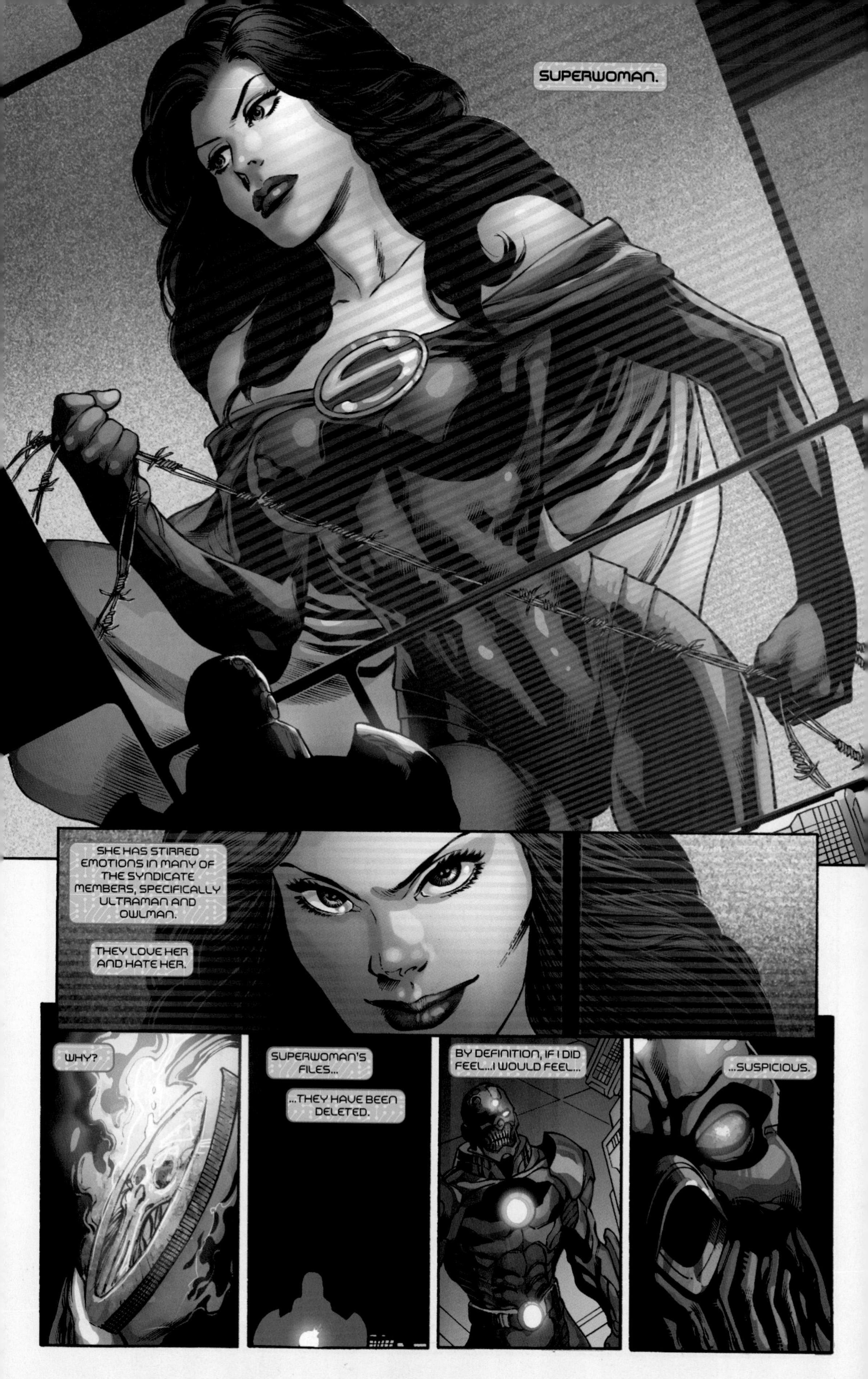
SUPERWOMAN.
SHE HAS STIRRED EMOTIONS IN MANY OF THE SYNDICATE MEMBERS, SPECIFICALLY ULTRAMAN AND OWLMAN.
THEY LOVE HER AND HATE HER.
WHY?
SUPERWOMAN'S FILES...
...THEY HAVE BEEN DELETED.
BY DEFINITION, IF I DID FEEL...I WOULD FEEL...
...SUSPICIOUS.

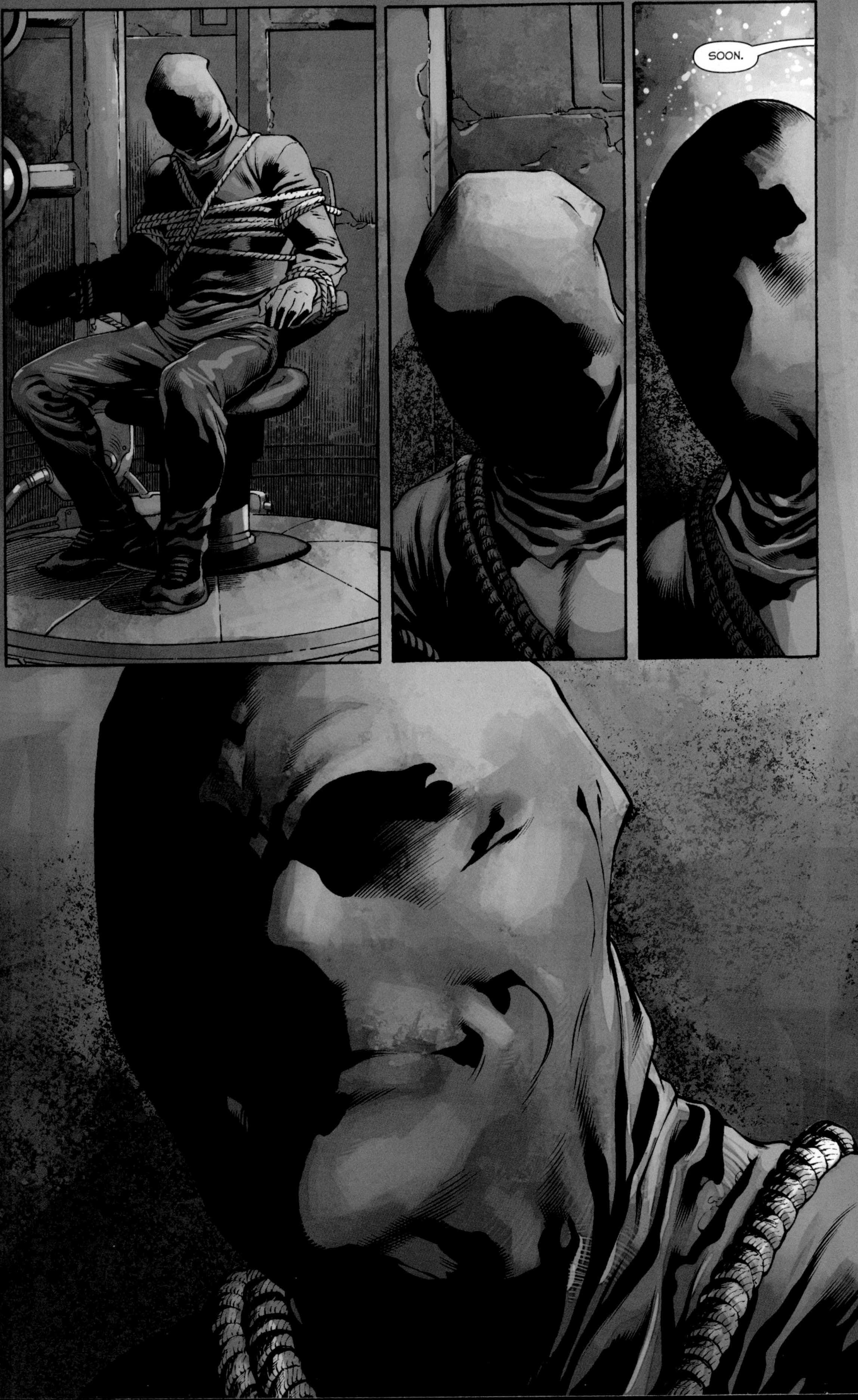
SOON.

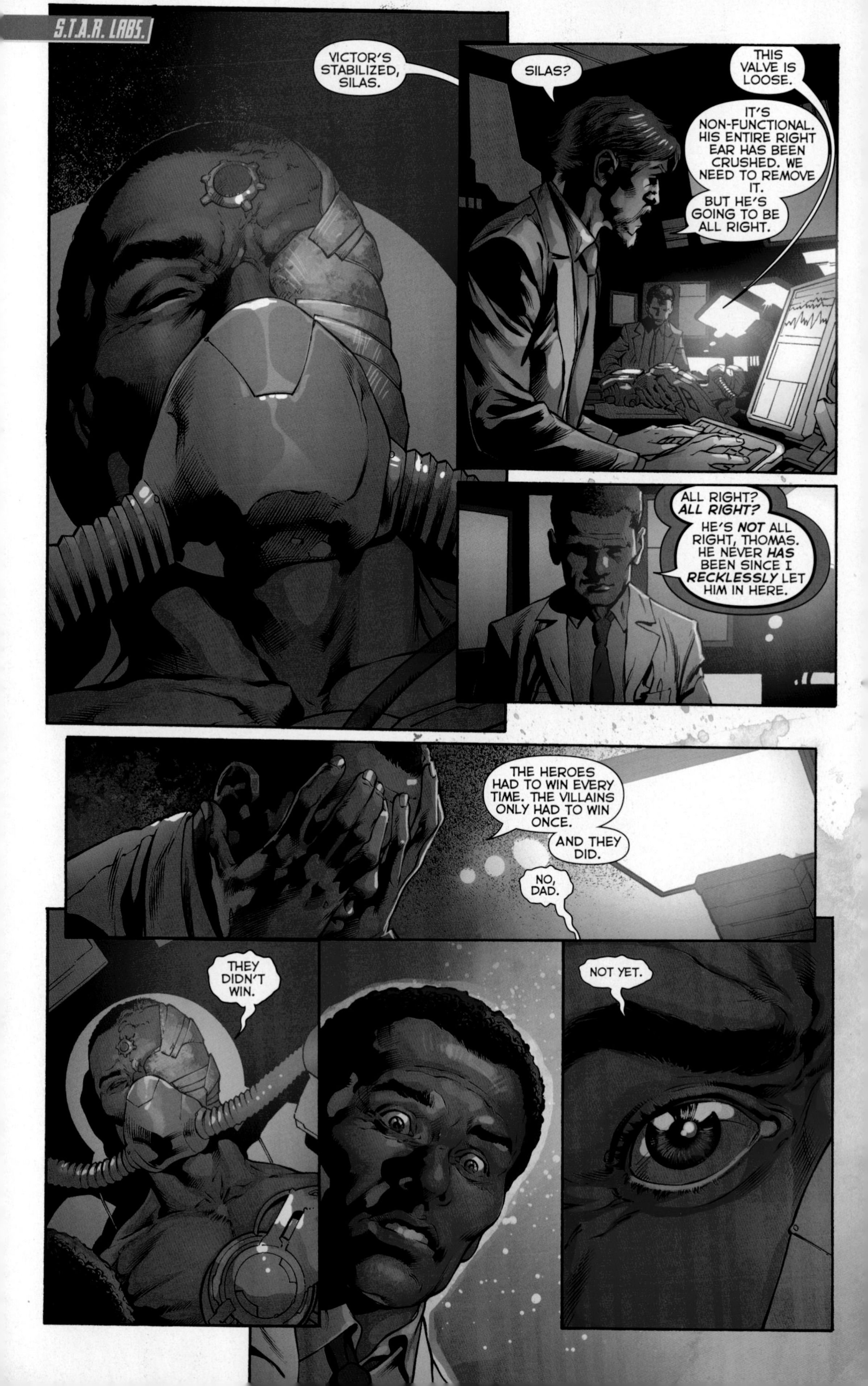
S.T.A.R. LABS.
VICTOR'S STABILIZED, SILAS.
SILAS?
THIS VALVE IS LOOSE.
IT'S NON-FUNCTIONAL. HIS ENTIRE RIGHT EAR HAS BEEN CRUSHED. WE NEED TO REMOVE IT.
BUT HE'S GOING TO BE ALL RIGHT.
ALL RIGHT? ALL RIGHT?
HE'S NOT ALL RIGHT, THOMAS. HE NEVER HAS BEEN SINCE I RECKLESSLY LET HIM IN HERE.
THE HEROES HAD TO WIN EVERY TIME. THE VILLAINS ONLY HAD TO WIN ONCE.
AND THEY DID.
NO, DAD.
THEY DIDN'T WIN.
NOT YET.

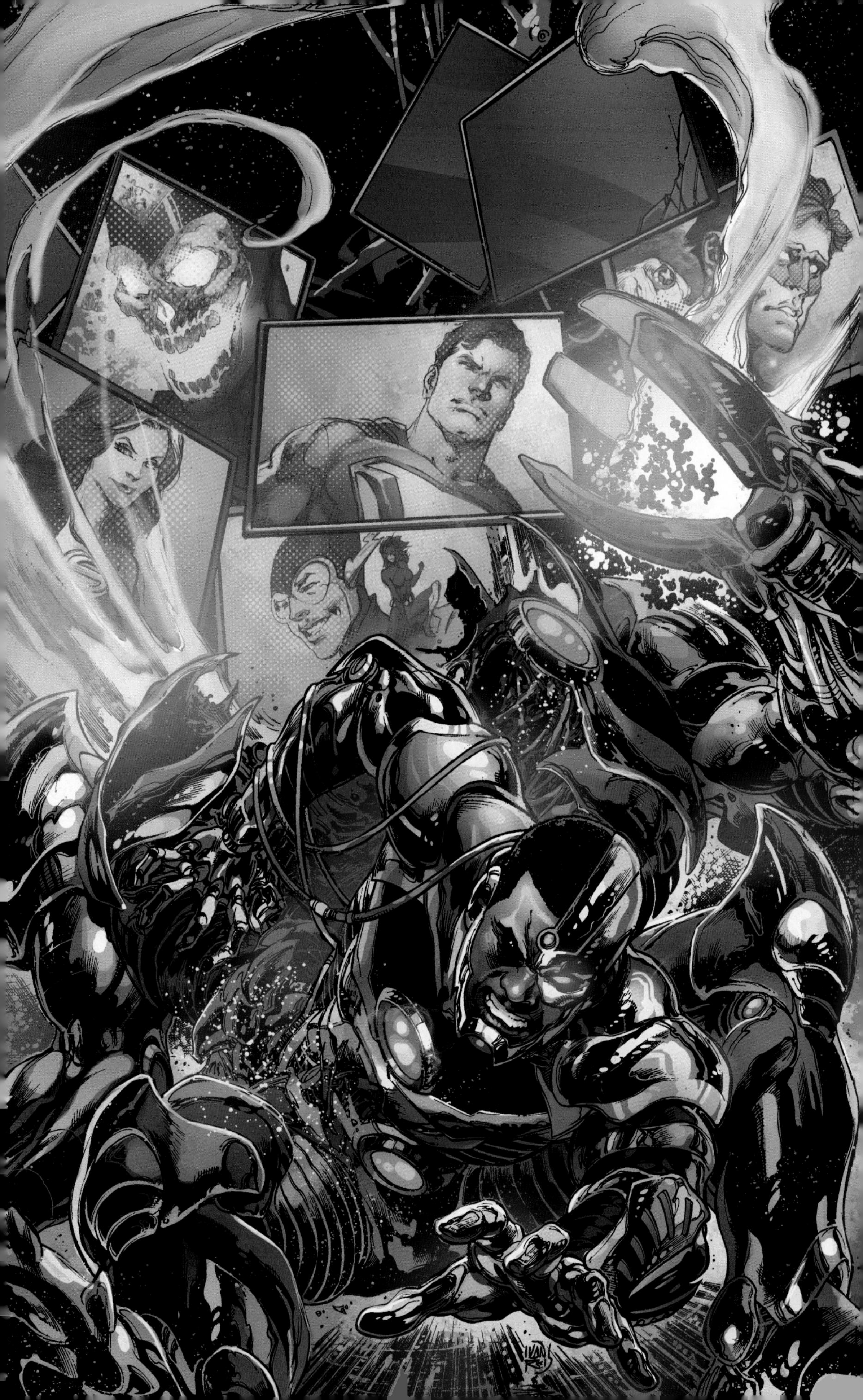

FOREVER DOOMED

GEOFF JOHNS writer IVAN REIS penciller JOE PRADO, JESUS MERINO and VICENTE CIFUENTES finishes

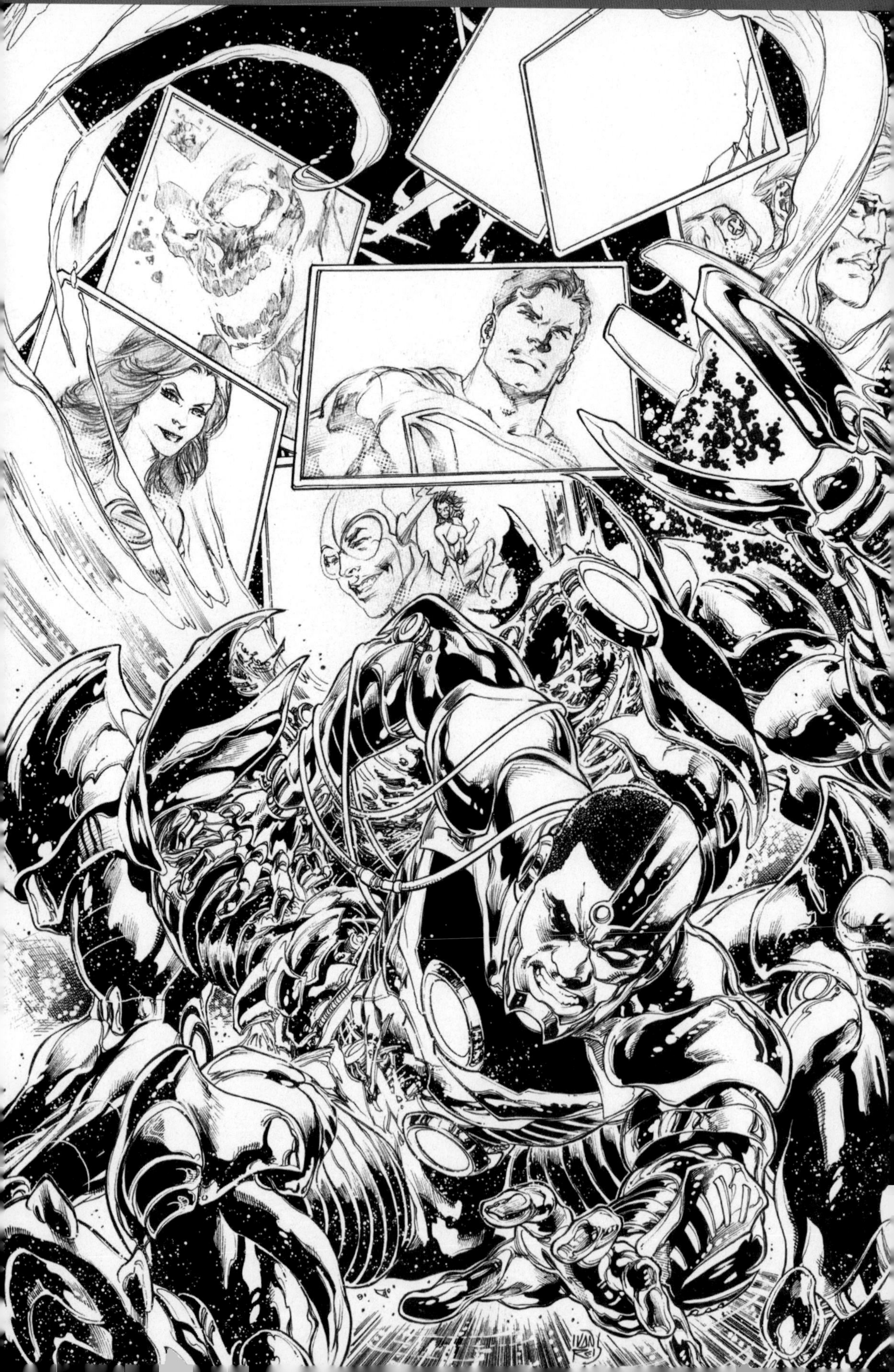

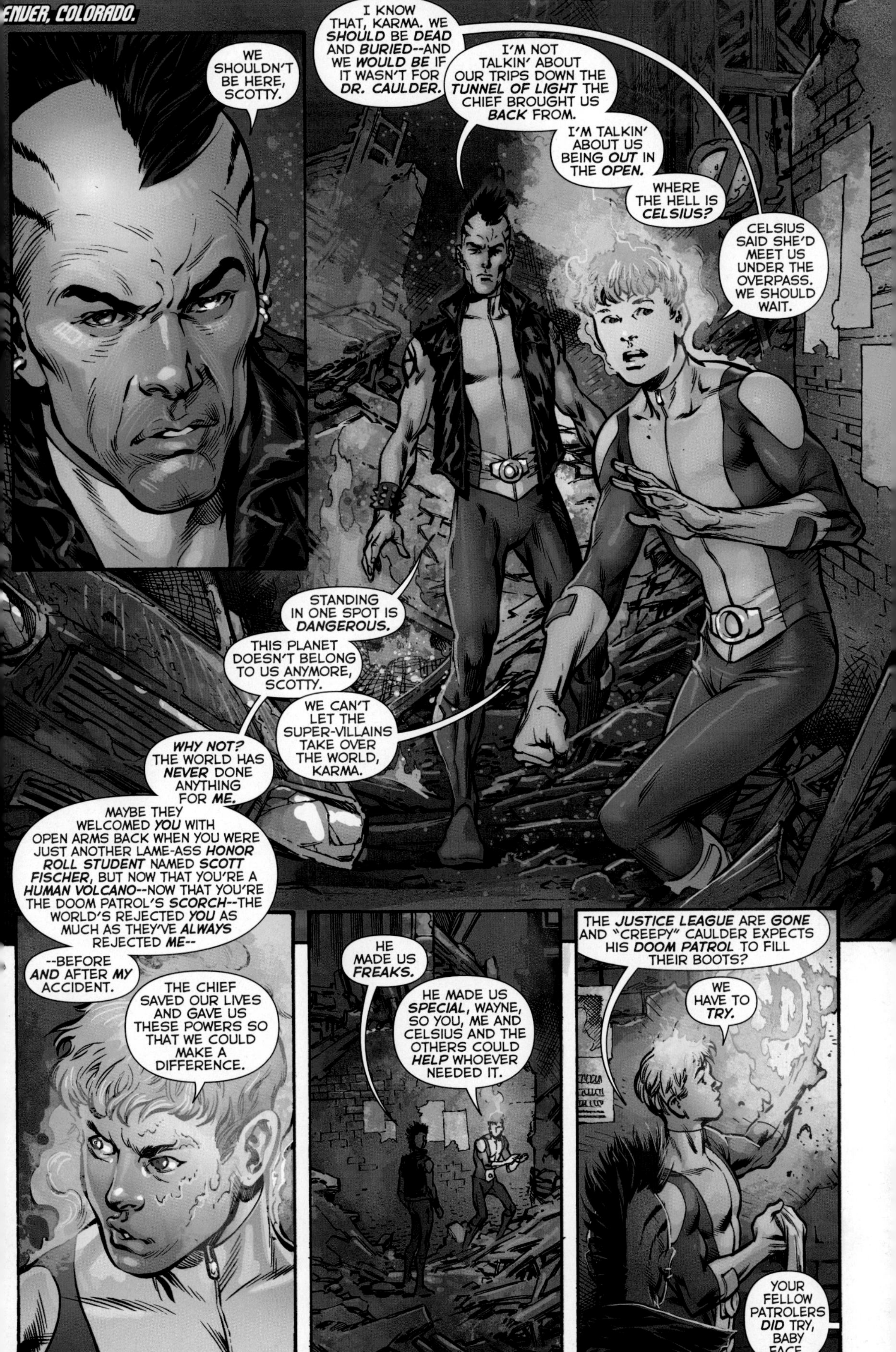

ENVER, COLORADO.
WE SHOULDN'T BE HERE, SCOTTY.
I KNOW THAT, KARMA. WE SHOULD BE DEAD AND BURIED--AND WE WOULD BE IF IT WASN'T FOR DR. CAULDER.
I'M NOT TALKIN' ABOUT OUR TRIPS DOWN THE TUNNEL OF LIGHT THE CHIEF BROUGHT US BACK FROM.
I'M TALKIN' ABOUT US BEING OUT IN THE OPEN.
WHERE THE HELL IS CELSIUS?
CELSIUS SAID SHE'D MEET US UNDER THE OVERPASS. WE SHOULD WAIT.
STANDING IN ONE SPOT IS DANGEROUS.
THIS PLANET DOESN'T BELONG TO US ANYMORE, SCOTTY.
WE CAN'T LET THE SUPER-VILLAINS TAKE OVER THE WORLD, KARMA.
WHY NOT? THE WORLD HAS NEVER DONE ANYTHING FOR ME.
MAYBE THEY WELCOMED YOU WITH OPEN ARMS BACK WHEN YOU WERE JUST ANOTHER LAME-ASS HONOR ROLL STUDENT NAMED SCOTT FISCHER, BUT NOW THAT YOU'RE A HUMAN VOLCANO--NOW THAT YOU'RE THE DOOM PATROL'S SCORCH--THE WORLD'S REJECTED YOU AS MUCH AS THEY'VE ALWAYS REJECTED ME--
--BEFORE AND AFTER MY ACCIDENT.
THE CHIEF SAVED OUR LIVES AND GAVE US THESE POWERS SO THAT WE COULD MAKE A DIFFERENCE.
HE MADE US FREAKS.
HE MADE US SPECIAL, WAYNE, SO YOU, ME AND CELSIUS AND THE OTHERS COULD HELP WHOEVER NEEDED IT.
THE JUSTICE LEAGUE ARE GONE AND "CREEPY" CAULDER EXPECTS HIS DOOM PATROL TO FILL THEIR BOOTS?
WE HAVE TO TRY.
YOUR FELLOW PATROLERS DID TRY, BABY FACE.

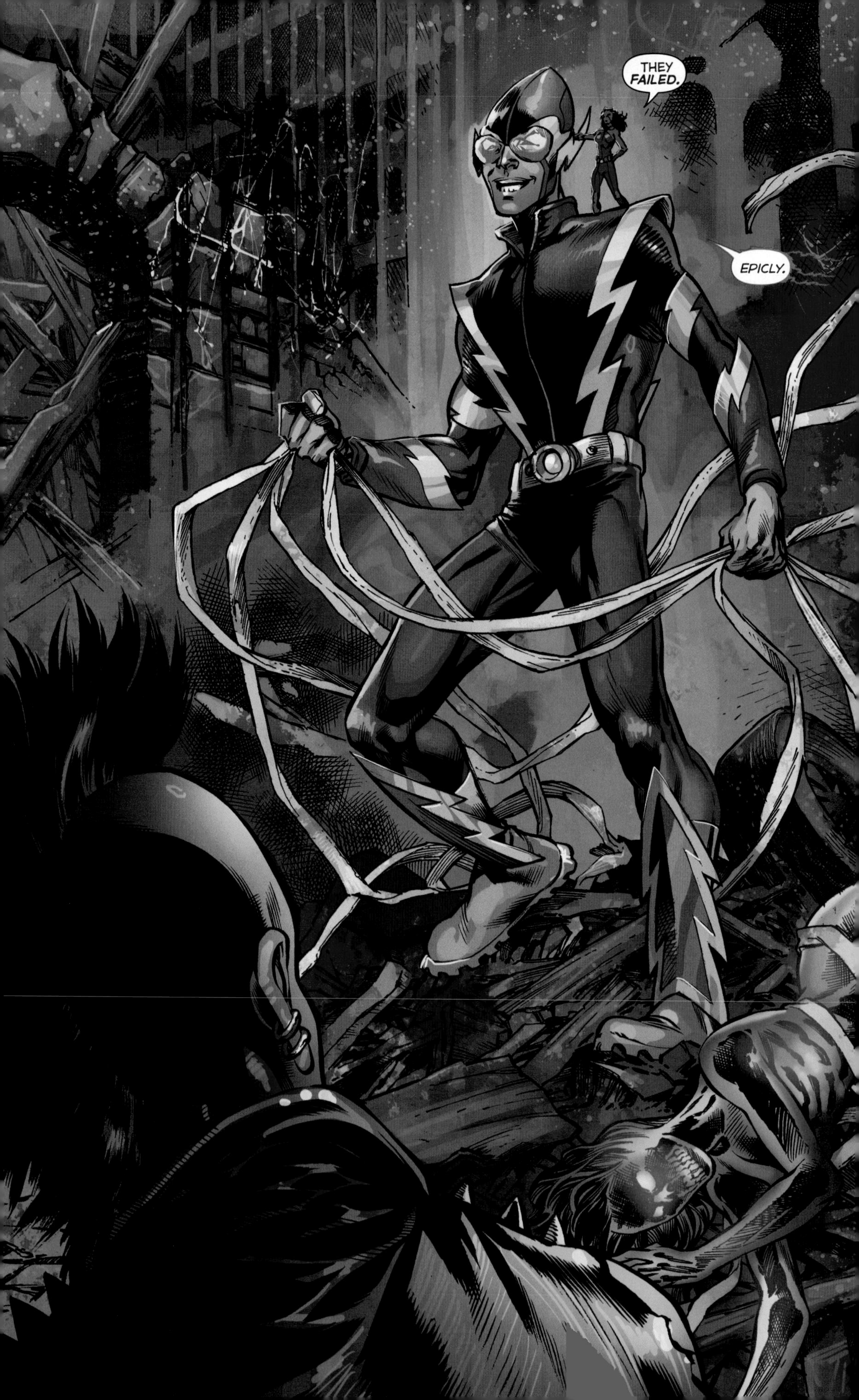
THEY FAILED.
EPICLY.

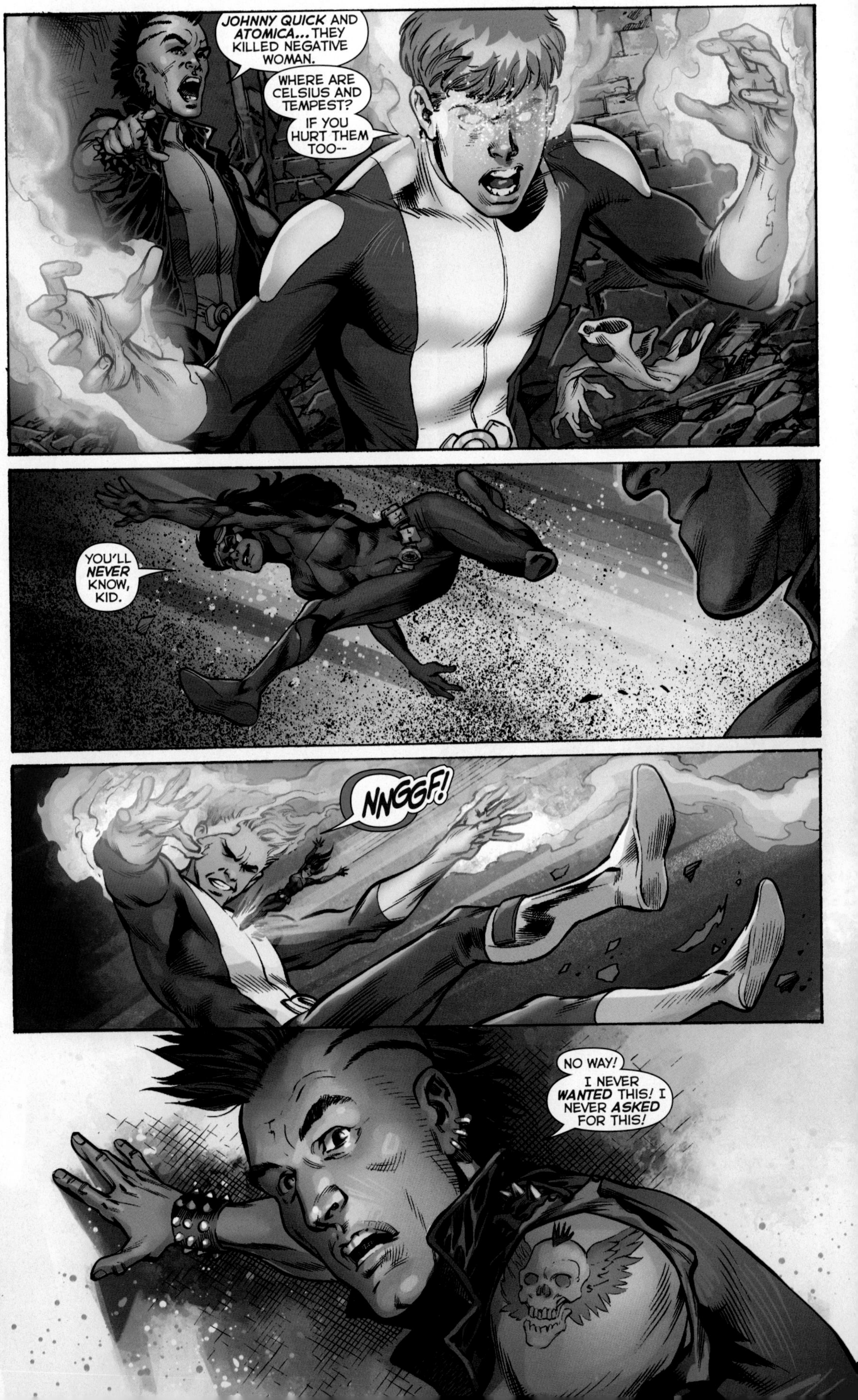
JOHNNY QUICK AND ATOMICA... THEY KILLED NEGATIVE WOMAN.
WHERE ARE CELSIUS AND TEMPEST?
IF YOU HURT THEM TOO--
YOU'LL NEVER KNOW, KID.
NNGGF!
NO WAY!
I NEVER WANTED THIS! I NEVER ASKED FOR THIS!

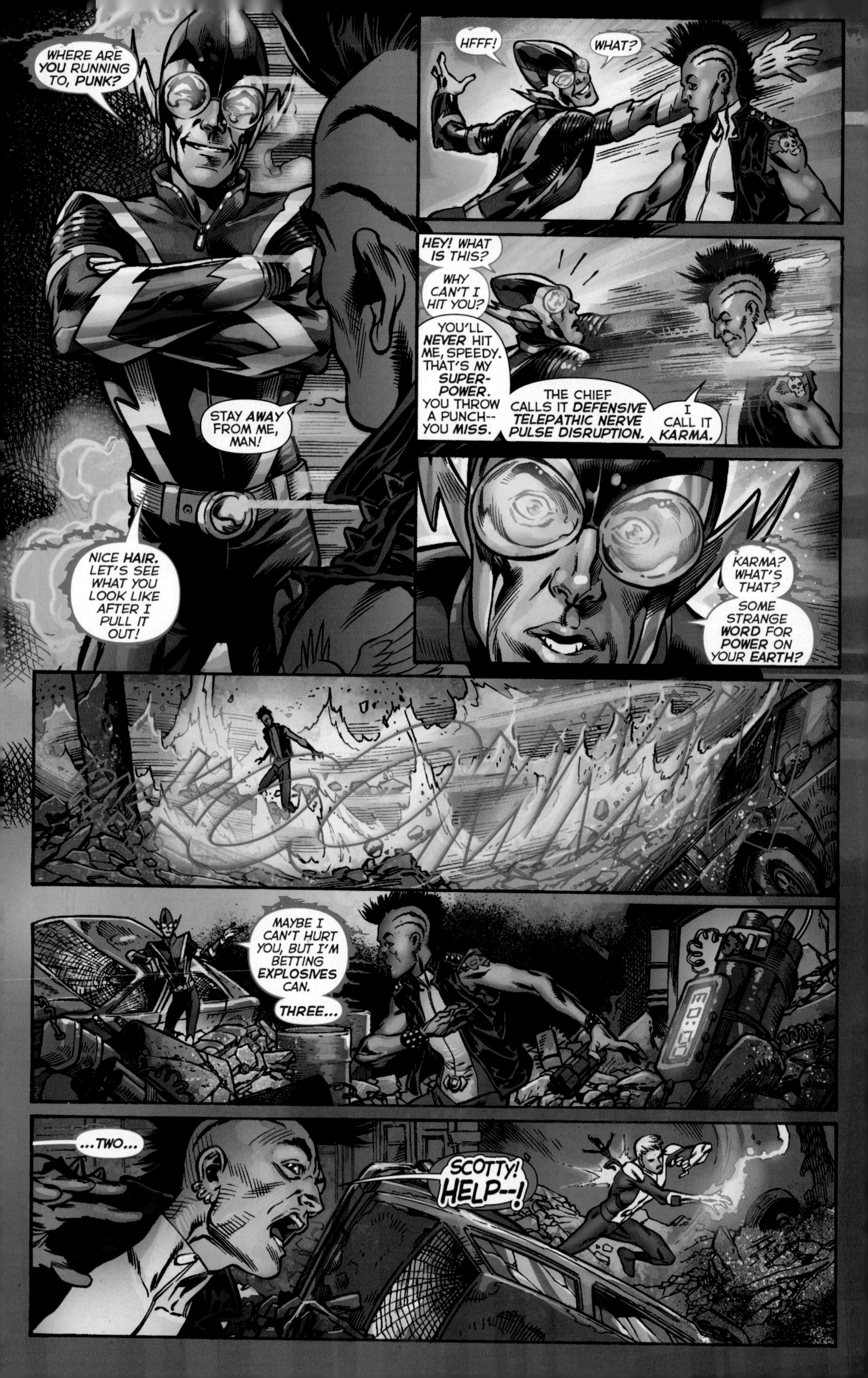
WHERE ARE YOU RUNNING TO, PUNK?
STAY AWAY FROM ME, MAN!
NICE HAIR. LET'S SEE WHAT YOU LOOK LIKE AFTER I PULL IT OUT!
HFFF!
WHAT?
HEY! WHAT IS THIS?
WHY CAN'T I HIT YOU?
YOU'LL NEVER HIT ME, SPEEDY. THAT'S MY SUPER-POWER. YOU THROW A PUNCH-- YOU MISS.
THE CHIEF CALLS IT DEFENSIVE TELEPATHIC NERVE PULSE DISRUPTION.
I CALL IT KARMA.
KARMA? WHAT'S THAT?
SOME STRANGE WORD FOR POWER ON YOUR EARTH?
MAYBE I CAN'T HURT YOU, BUT I'M BETTING EXPLOSIVES CAN.
THREE...
...TWO...
SCOTTY! HELP--!

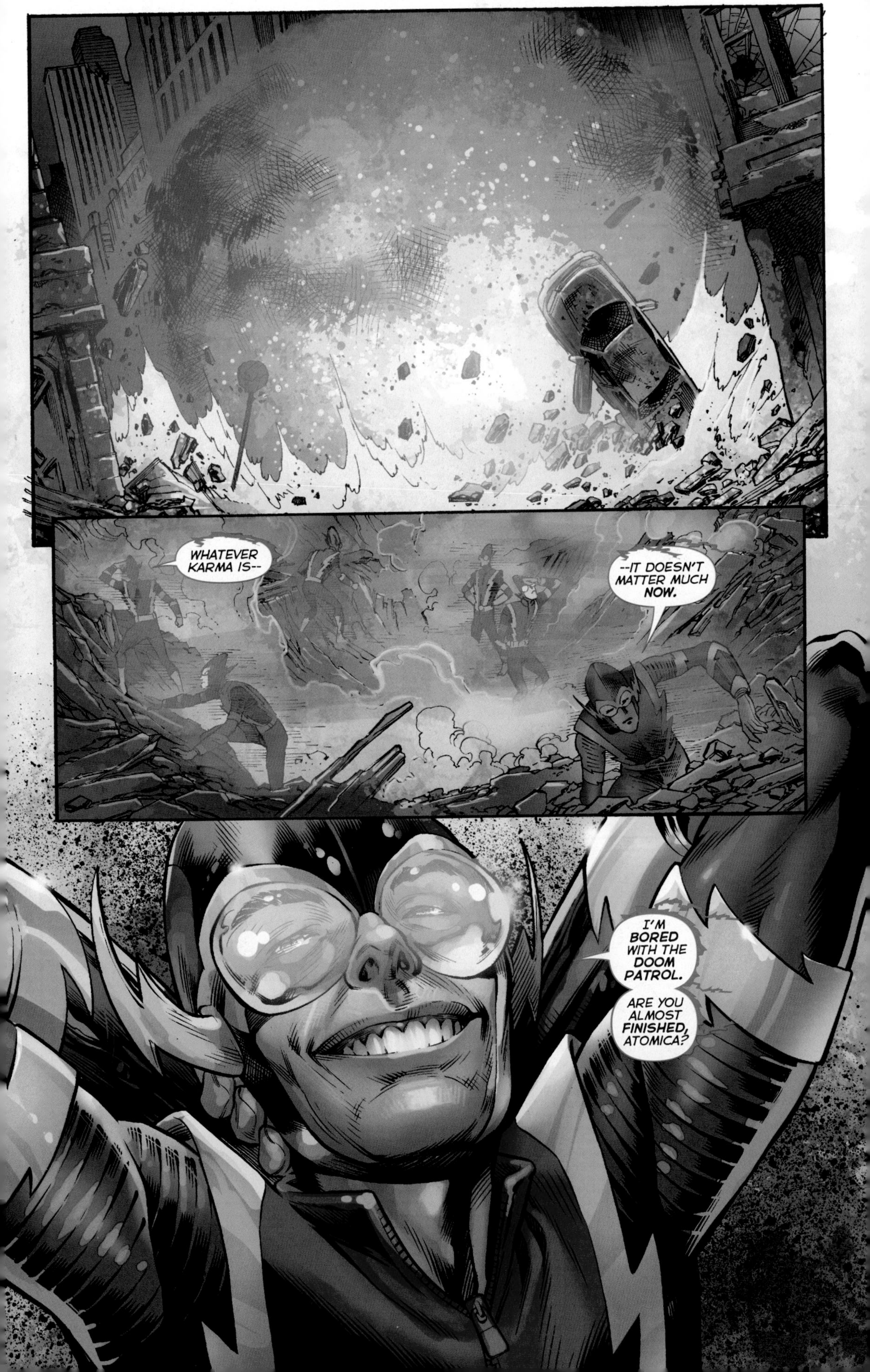
WHATEVER KARMA IS--
--IT DOESN'T MATTER MUCH NOW.
I'M BORED WITH THE DOOM PATROL.
ARE YOU ALMOST FINISHED, ATOMICA?

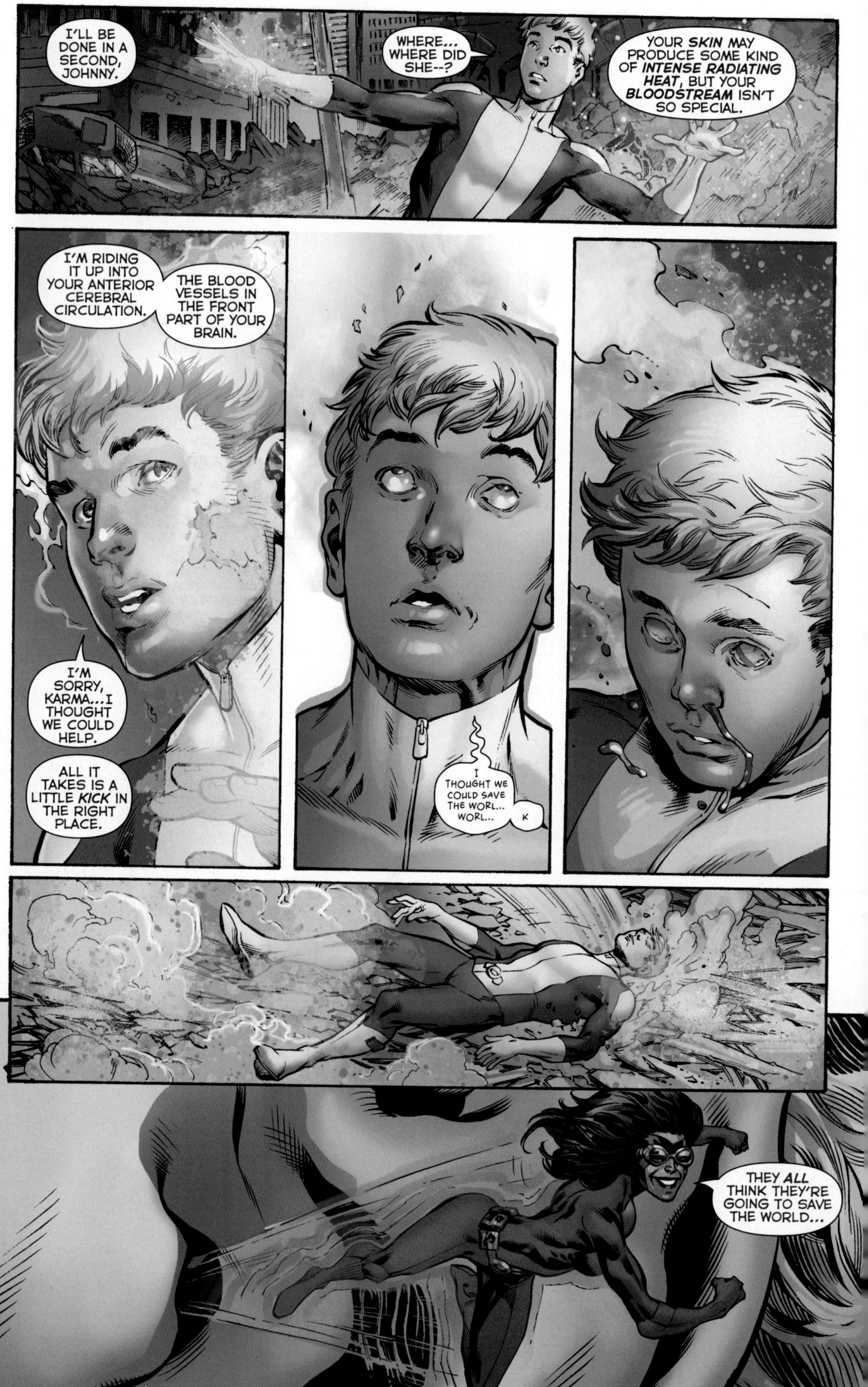
I'LL BE DONE IN A SECOND, JOHNNY.
WHERE... WHERE DID SHE--?
YOUR SKIN MAY PRODUCE SOME KIND OF INTENSE RADIATING HEAT, BUT YOUR BLOODSTREAM ISN'T SO SPECIAL.
I'M RIDING IT UP INTO YOUR ANTERIOR CEREBRAL CIRCULATION.
THE BLOOD VESSELS IN THE FRONT PART OF YOUR BRAIN.
I'M SORRY, KARMA...I THOUGHT WE COULD HELP.
ALL IT TAKES IS A LITTLE KICK IN THE RIGHT PLACE.
I THOUGHT WE COULD SAVE THE WORL... WORL...
K
THEY ALL THINK THEY'RE GOING TO SAVE THE WORLD...

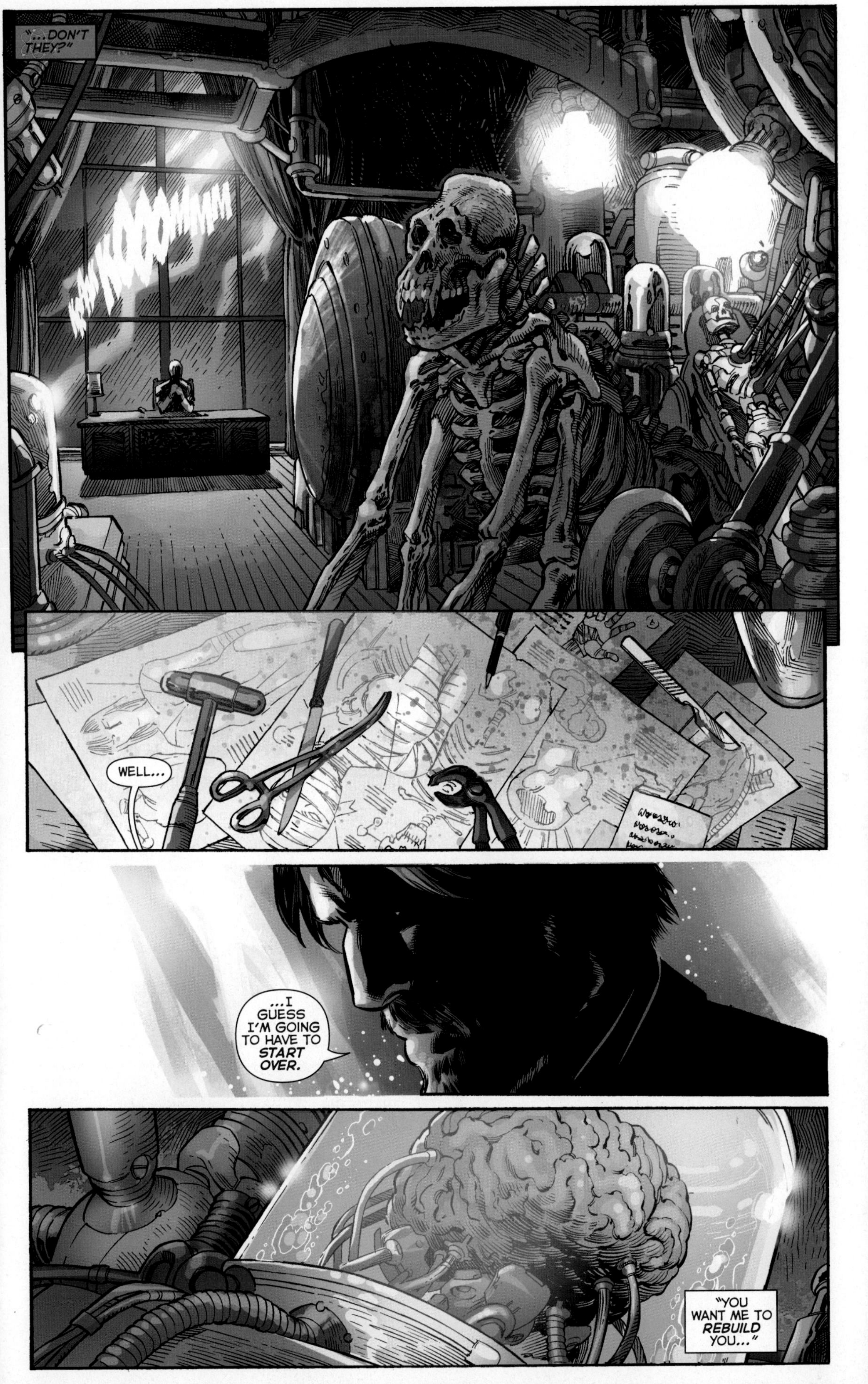
"...DON'T THEY?"
KRAKOOMMM
WELL...
...I GUESS I'M GOING TO HAVE TO START OVER.
"YOU WANT ME TO REBUILD YOU..."

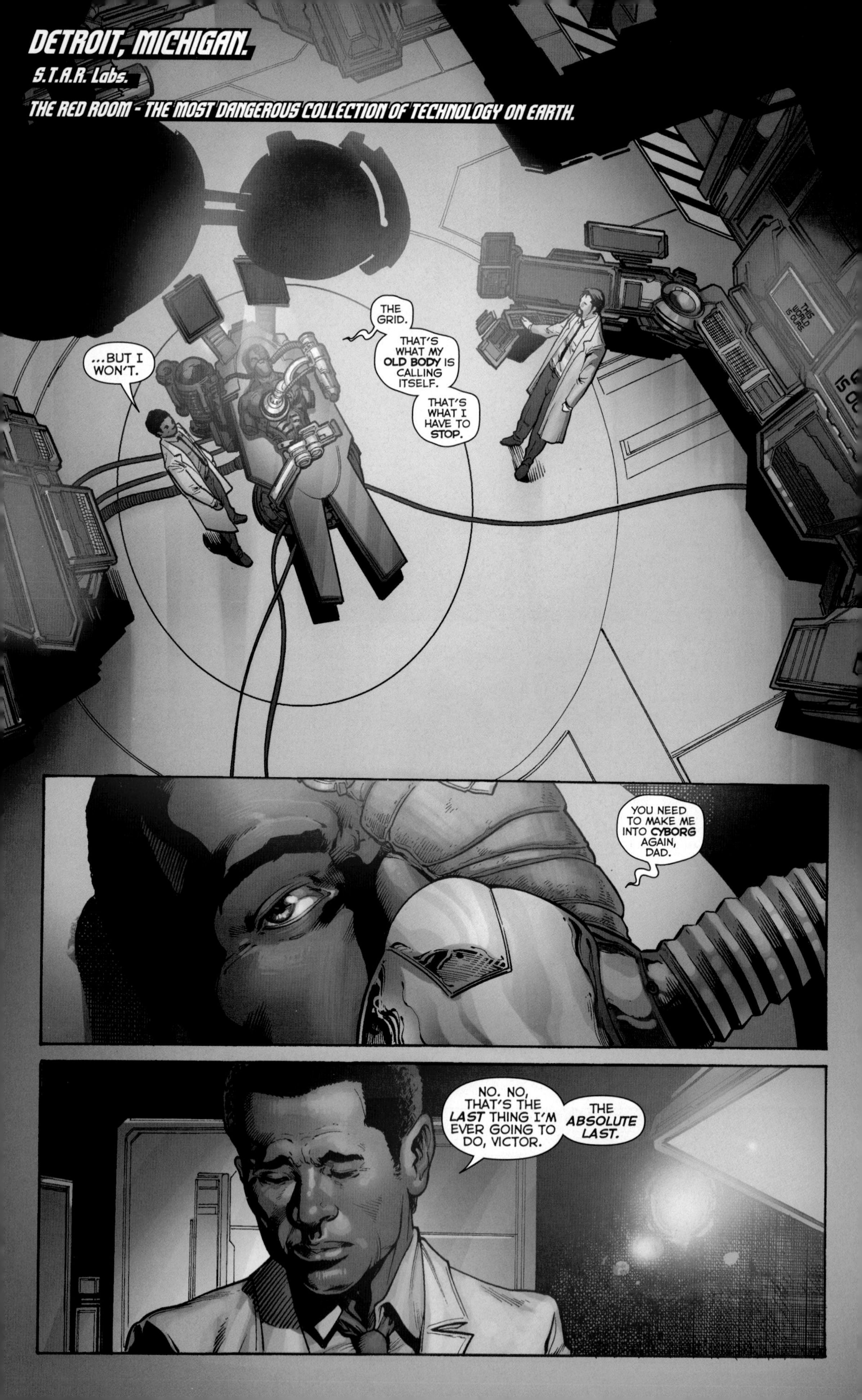
DETROIT, MICHIGAN.
S.T.A.R. Labs.
THE RED ROOM - THE MOST DANGEROUS COLLECTION OF TECHNOLOGY ON EARTH.
THE GRID.
THAT'S WHAT MY OLD BODY IS CALLING ITSELF.
THAT'S WHAT I HAVE TO STOP.
...BUT I WON'T.
YOU NEED TO MAKE ME INTO CYBORG AGAIN, DAD.
NO. NO, THAT'S THE LAST THING I'M EVER GOING TO DO, VICTOR.
THE ABSOLUTE LAST.

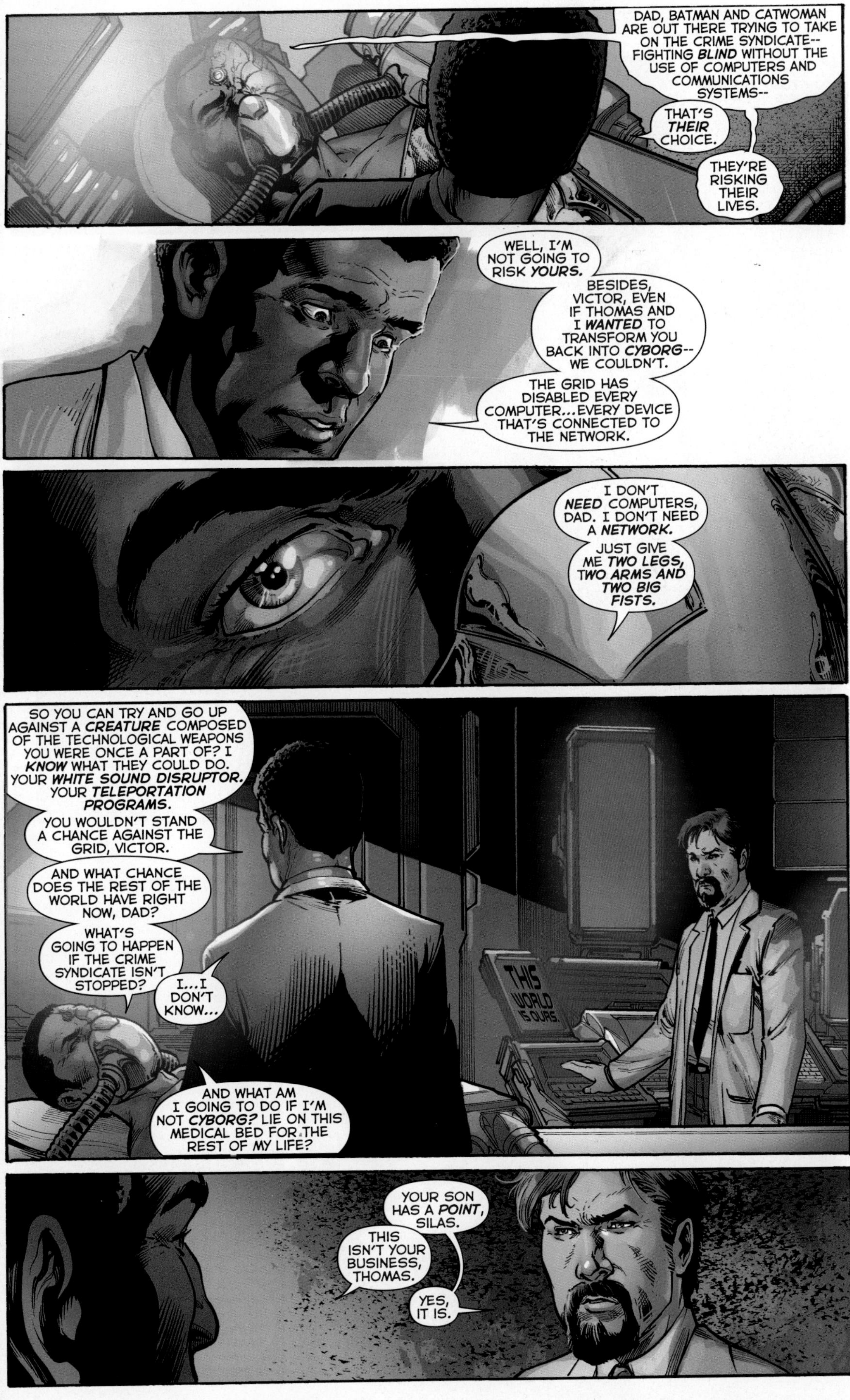
DAD, BATMAN AND CATWOMAN ARE OUT THERE TRYING TO TAKE ON THE CRIME SYNDICATE-- FIGHTING BLIND WITHOUT THE USE OF COMPUTERS AND COMMUNICATIONS SYSTEMS--
THAT'S THEIR CHOICE.
THEY'RE RISKING THEIR LIVES.
WELL, I'M NOT GOING TO RISK YOURS.
BESIDES, VICTOR, EVEN IF THOMAS AND I WANTED TO TRANSFORM YOU BACK INTO CYBORG-- WE COULDN'T.
THE GRID HAS DISABLED EVERY COMPUTER...EVERY DEVICE THAT'S CONNECTED TO THE NETWORK.
I DON'T NEED COMPUTERS, DAD. I DON'T NEED A NETWORK.
JUST GIVE ME TWO LEGS, TWO ARMS AND TWO BIG FISTS.
SO YOU CAN TRY AND GO UP AGAINST A CREATURE COMPOSED OF THE TECHNOLOGICAL WEAPONS YOU WERE ONCE A PART OF? I KNOW WHAT THEY COULD DO. YOUR WHITE SOUND DISRUPTOR. YOUR TELEPORTATION PROGRAMS.
YOU WOULDN'T STAND A CHANCE AGAINST THE GRID, VICTOR.
AND WHAT CHANCE DOES THE REST OF THE WORLD HAVE RIGHT NOW, DAD?
WHAT'S GOING TO HAPPEN IF THE CRIME SYNDICATE ISN'T STOPPED?
I...I DON'T KNOW...
THIS WORLD IS OURS.
AND WHAT AM I GOING TO DO IF I'M NOT CYBORG? LIE ON THIS MEDICAL BED FOR THE REST OF MY LIFE?
YOUR SON HAS A POINT, SILAS.
THIS ISN'T YOUR BUSINESS, THOMAS.
YES, IT IS.

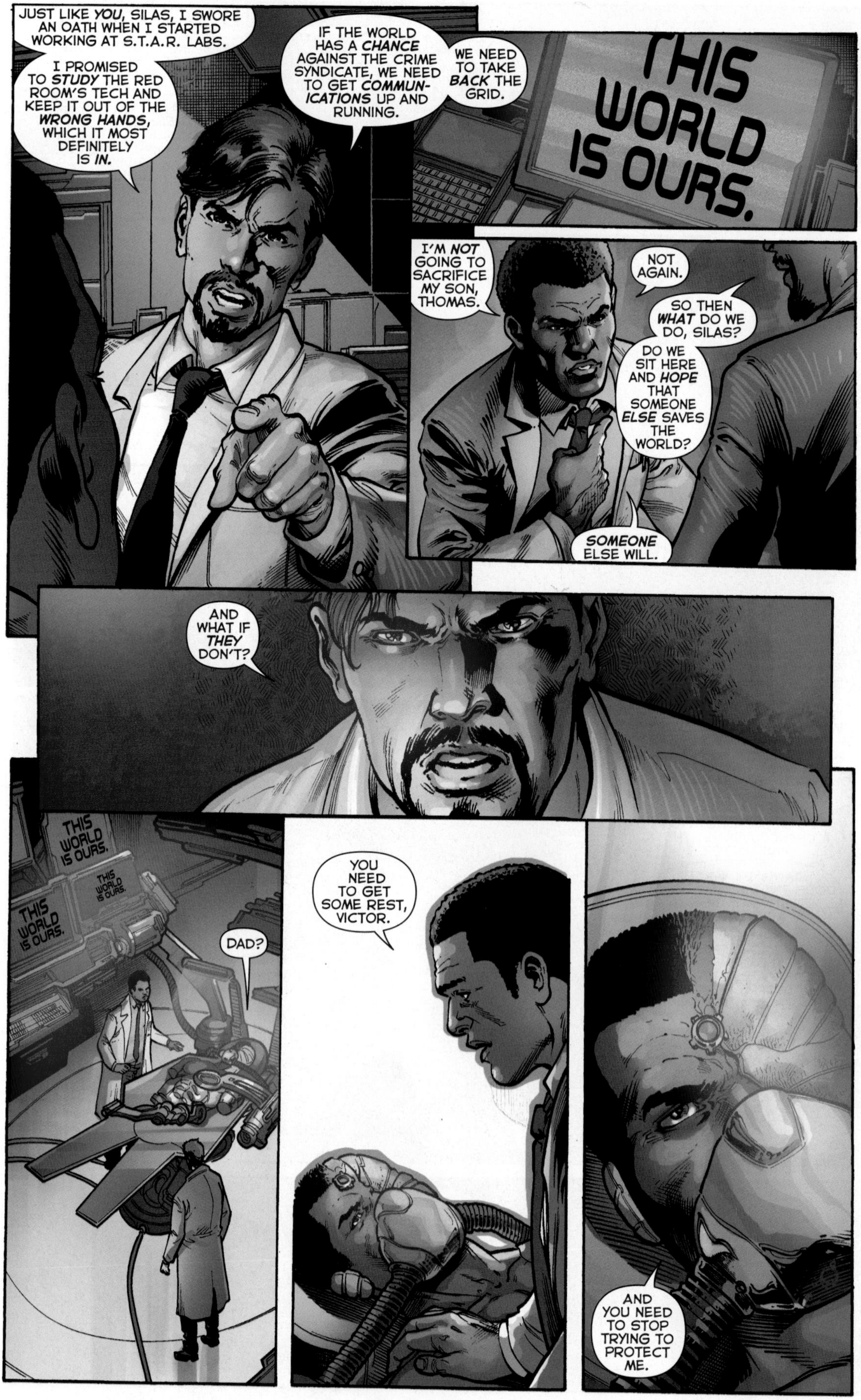
JUST LIKE YOU, SILAS, I SWORE AN OATH WHEN I STARTED WORKING AT S.T.A.R. LABS.
I PROMISED TO STUDY THE RED ROOM'S TECH AND KEEP IT OUT OF THE WRONG HANDS, WHICH IT MOST DEFINITELY IS IN.
IF THE WORLD HAS A CHANCE AGAINST THE CRIME SYNDICATE, WE NEED TO GET COMMUNICATIONS UP AND RUNNING.
WE NEED TO TAKE BACK THE GRID.
THIS WORLD IS OURS.
I'M NOT GOING TO SACRIFICE MY SON, THOMAS.
NOT AGAIN.
SO THEN WHAT DO WE DO, SILAS?
DO WE SIT HERE AND HOPE THAT SOMEONE ELSE SAVES THE WORLD?
SOMEONE ELSE WILL.
AND WHAT IF THEY DON'T?
THIS WORLD IS OURS.
THIS WORLD IS OURS.
THIS WORLD IS OURS.
DAD?
YOU NEED TO GET SOME REST, VICTOR.
AND YOU NEED TO STOP TRYING TO PROTECT ME.

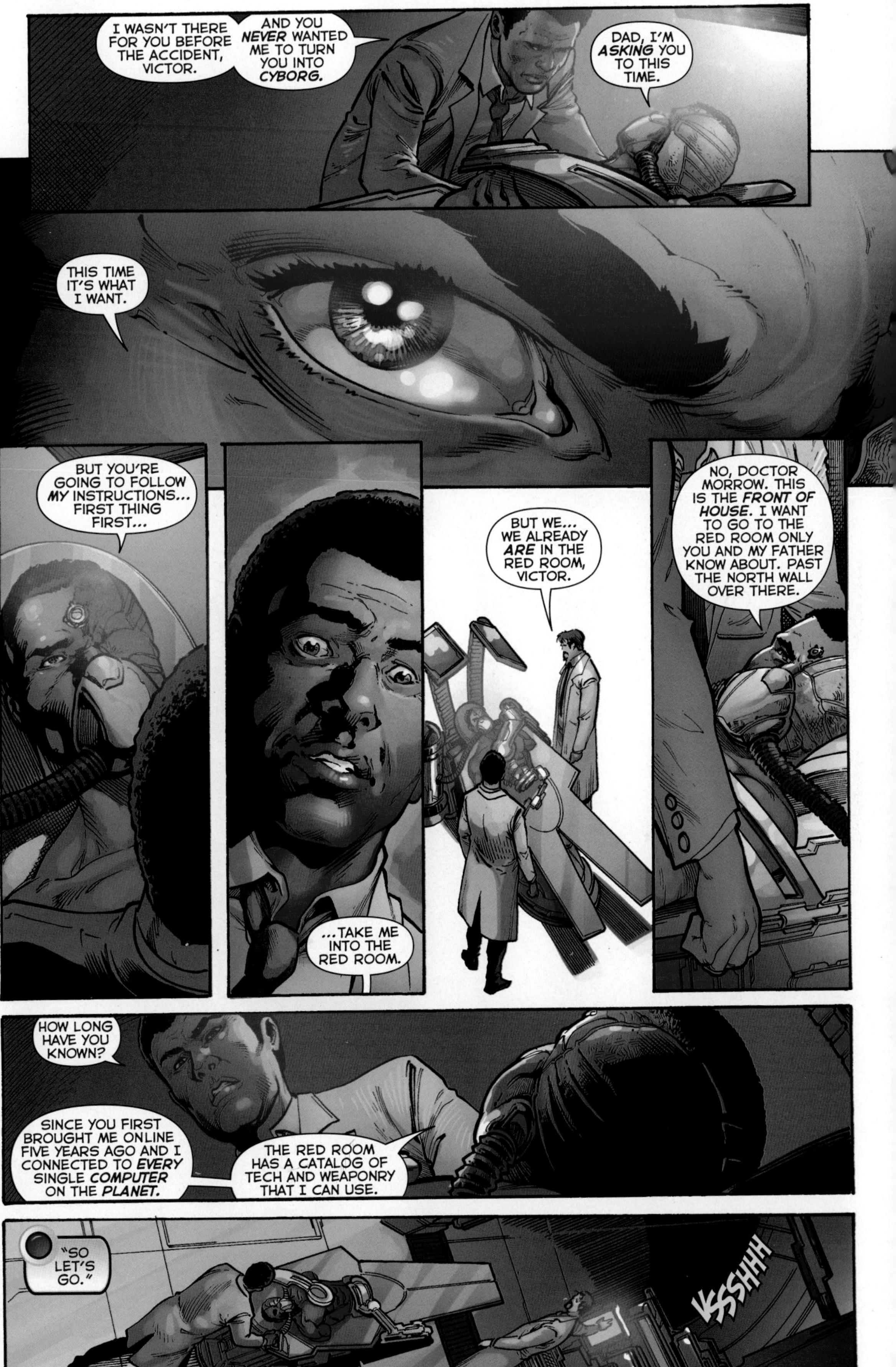
I WASN'T THERE FOR YOU BEFORE THE ACCIDENT, VICTOR.
AND YOU *NEVER* WANTED ME TO TURN YOU INTO *CYBORG.*
DAD, I'M *ASKING* YOU TO THIS TIME.
THIS TIME IT'S WHAT I WANT.
BUT YOU'RE GOING TO FOLLOW *MY* INSTRUCTIONS... FIRST THING FIRST...
...TAKE ME INTO THE RED ROOM.
BUT WE... WE ALREADY *ARE* IN THE RED ROOM, VICTOR.
NO, DOCTOR MORROW. THIS IS THE *FRONT OF HOUSE.* I WANT TO GO TO THE RED ROOM ONLY YOU AND MY FATHER KNOW ABOUT. PAST THE NORTH WALL OVER THERE.
HOW LONG HAVE YOU KNOWN?
SINCE YOU FIRST BROUGHT ME ONLINE FIVE YEARS AGO AND I CONNECTED TO *EVERY* SINGLE *COMPUTER* ON THE *PLANET.*
THE RED ROOM HAS A CATALOG OF TECH AND WEAPONRY THAT I CAN USE.
"SO LET'S GO."
VSSSHHH

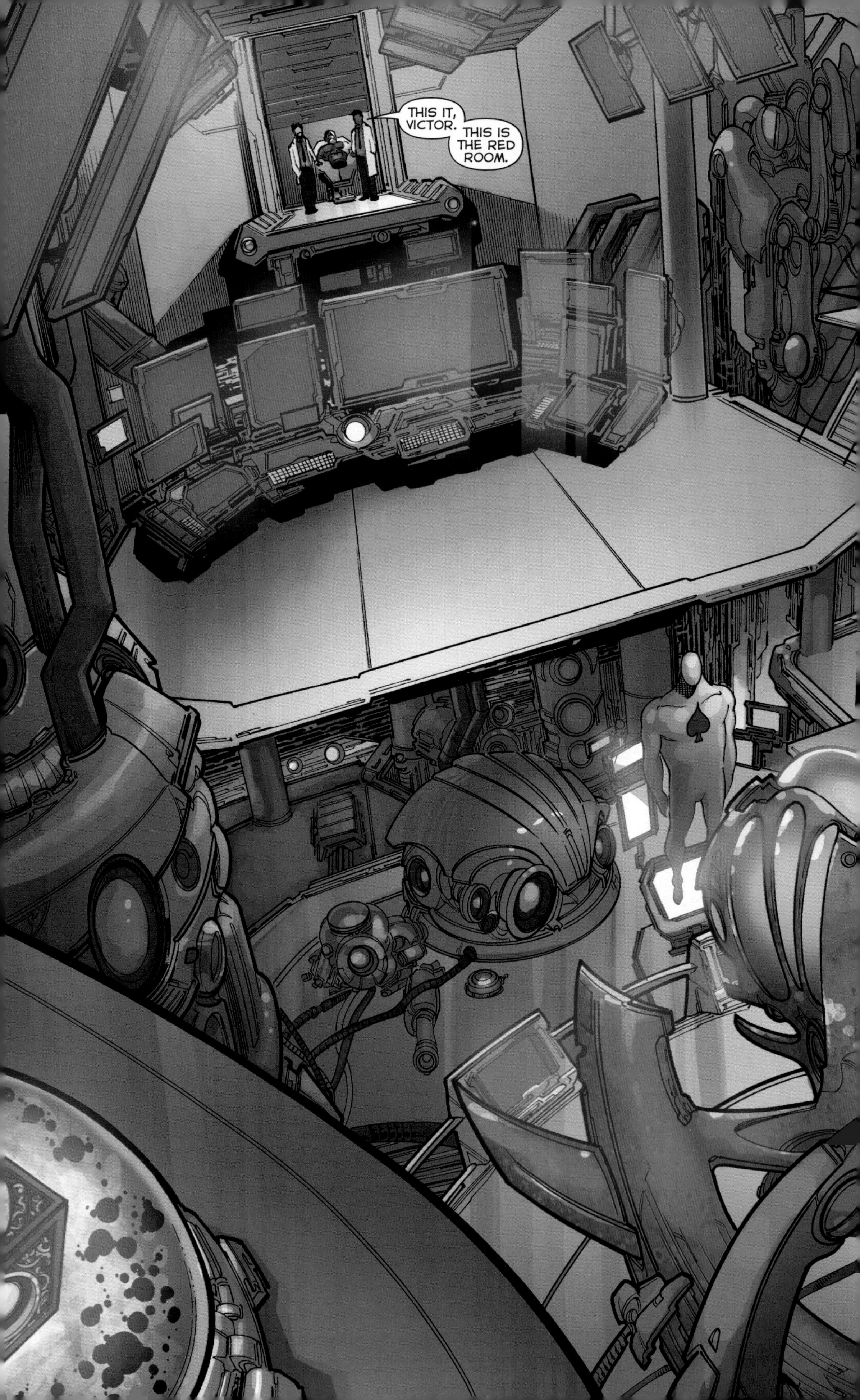
THIS IT, VICTOR.
THIS IS THE RED ROOM.

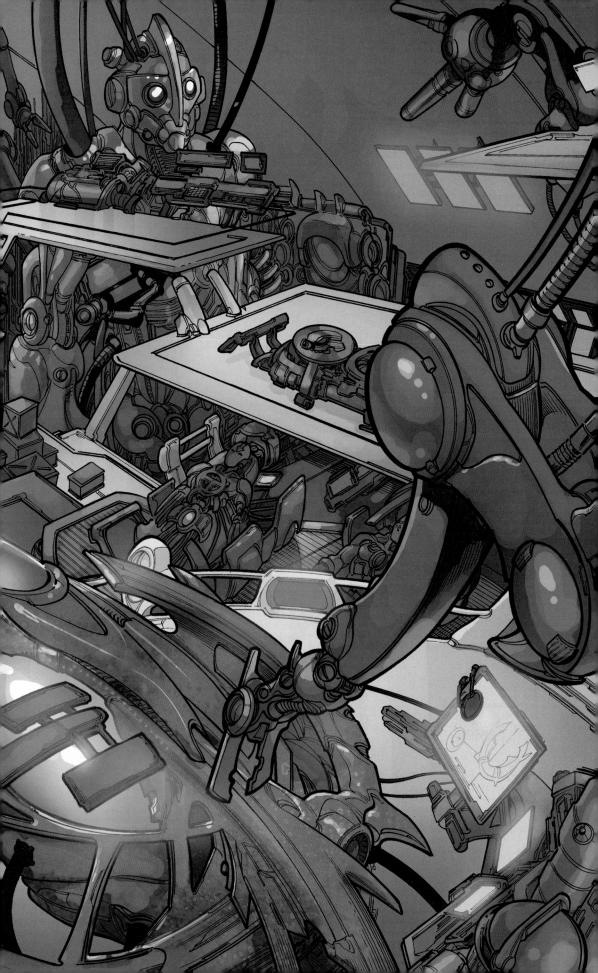

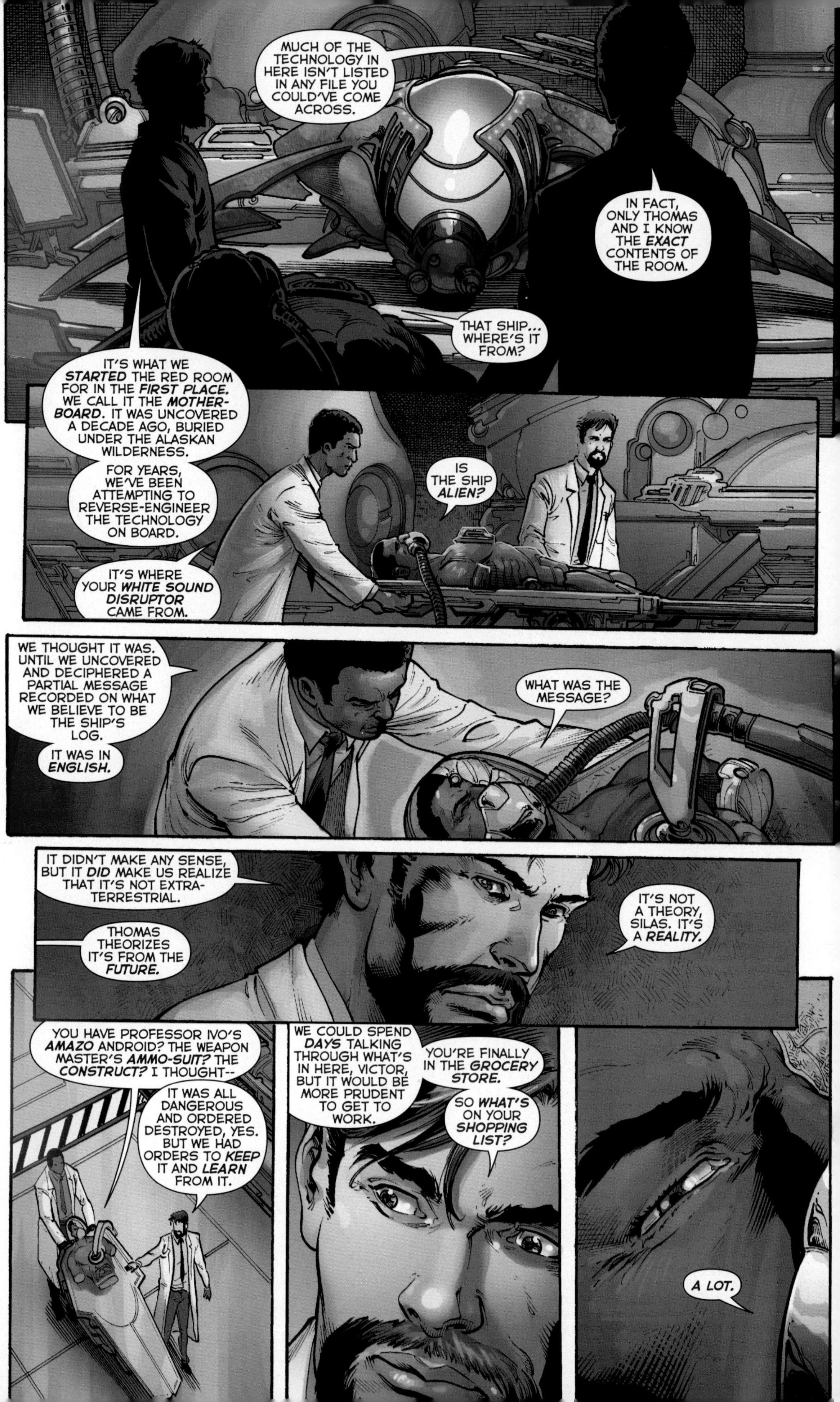
MUCH OF THE TECHNOLOGY IN HERE ISN'T LISTED IN ANY FILE YOU COULD'VE COME ACROSS.
IN FACT, ONLY THOMAS AND I KNOW THE EXACT CONTENTS OF THE ROOM.
THAT SHIP... WHERE'S IT FROM?
IT'S WHAT WE STARTED THE RED ROOM FOR IN THE FIRST PLACE. WE CALL IT THE MOTHER-BOARD. IT WAS UNCOVERED A DECADE AGO, BURIED UNDER THE ALASKAN WILDERNESS.
FOR YEARS, WE'VE BEEN ATTEMPTING TO REVERSE-ENGINEER THE TECHNOLOGY ON BOARD.
IT'S WHERE YOUR WHITE SOUND DISRUPTOR CAME FROM.
IS THE SHIP ALIEN?
WE THOUGHT IT WAS. UNTIL WE UNCOVERED AND DECIPHERED A PARTIAL MESSAGE RECORDED ON WHAT WE BELIEVE TO BE THE SHIP'S LOG.
IT WAS IN ENGLISH.
WHAT WAS THE MESSAGE?
IT DIDN'T MAKE ANY SENSE, BUT IT DID MAKE US REALIZE THAT IT'S NOT EXTRA-TERRESTRIAL.
THOMAS THEORIZES IT'S FROM THE FUTURE.
IT'S NOT A THEORY, SILAS. IT'S A REALITY.
YOU HAVE PROFESSOR IVO'S AMAZO ANDROID? THE WEAPON MASTER'S AMMO-SUIT? THE CONSTRUCT? I THOUGHT--
IT WAS ALL DANGEROUS AND ORDERED DESTROYED, YES. BUT WE HAD ORDERS TO KEEP IT AND LEARN FROM IT.
WE COULD SPEND DAYS TALKING THROUGH WHAT'S IN HERE, VICTOR, BUT IT WOULD BE MORE PRUDENT TO GET TO WORK.
YOU'RE FINALLY IN THE GROCERY STORE.
SO WHAT'S ON YOUR SHOPPING LIST?
A LOT.

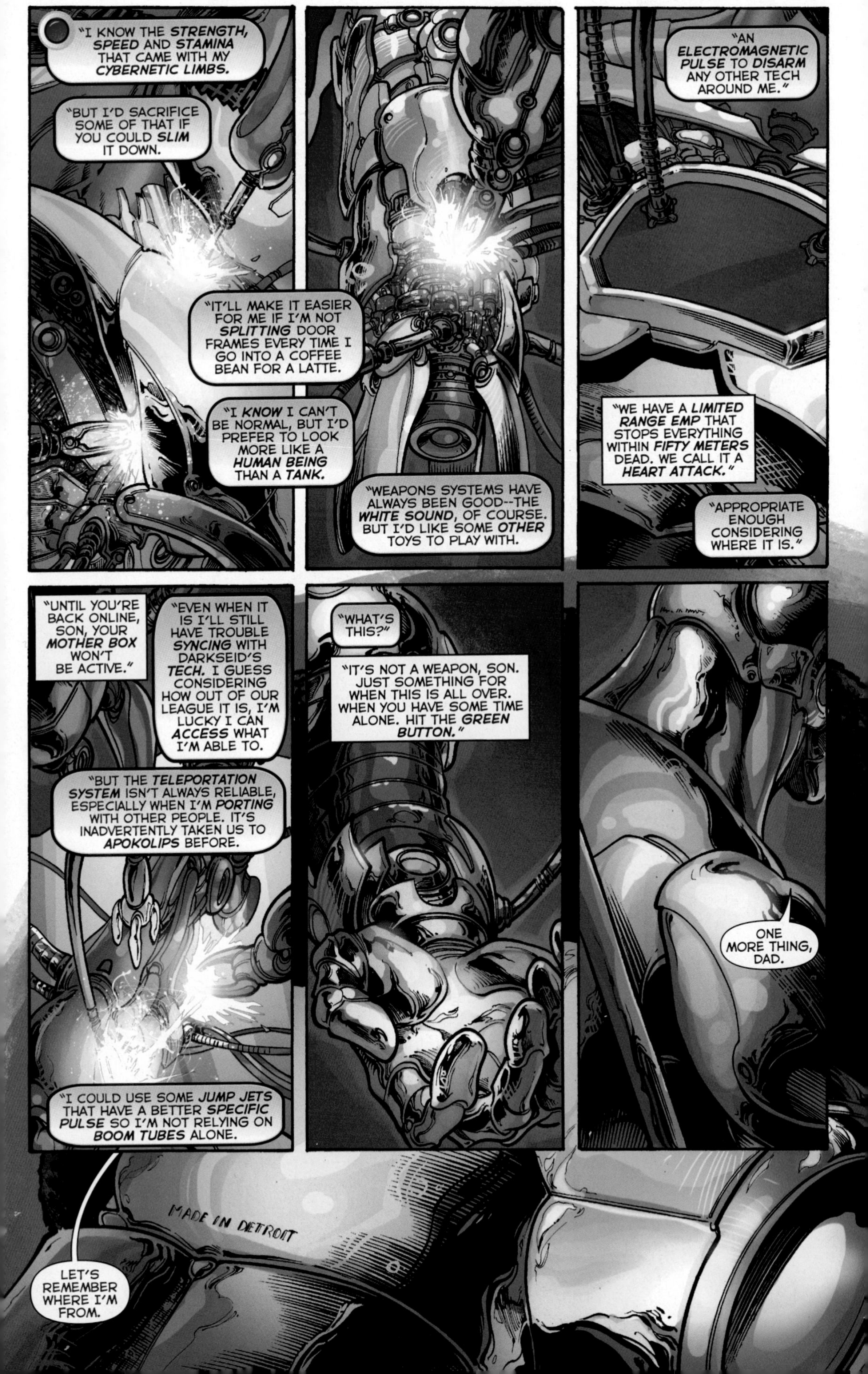

"I KNOW THE STRENGTH, SPEED AND STAMINA THAT CAME WITH MY CYBERNETIC LIMBS.
"BUT I'D SACRIFICE SOME OF THAT IF YOU COULD SLIM IT DOWN.
"IT'LL MAKE IT EASIER FOR ME IF I'M NOT SPLITTING DOOR FRAMES EVERY TIME I GO INTO A COFFEE BEAN FOR A LATTE.
"I KNOW I CAN'T BE NORMAL, BUT I'D PREFER TO LOOK MORE LIKE A HUMAN BEING THAN A TANK.
"WEAPONS SYSTEMS HAVE ALWAYS BEEN GOOD--THE WHITE SOUND, OF COURSE. BUT I'D LIKE SOME OTHER TOYS TO PLAY WITH.
"AN ELECTROMAGNETIC PULSE TO DISARM ANY OTHER TECH AROUND ME."
"WE HAVE A LIMITED RANGE EMP THAT STOPS EVERYTHING WITHIN FIFTY METERS DEAD. WE CALL IT A HEART ATTACK."
"APPROPRIATE ENOUGH CONSIDERING WHERE IT IS."
"UNTIL YOU'RE BACK ONLINE, SON, YOUR MOTHER BOX WON'T BE ACTIVE."
"EVEN WHEN IT IS I'LL STILL HAVE TROUBLE SYNCING WITH DARKSEID'S TECH. I GUESS CONSIDERING HOW OUT OF OUR LEAGUE IT IS, I'M LUCKY I CAN ACCESS WHAT I'M ABLE TO.
"BUT THE TELEPORTATION SYSTEM ISN'T ALWAYS RELIABLE, ESPECIALLY WHEN I'M PORTING WITH OTHER PEOPLE. IT'S INADVERTENTLY TAKEN US TO APOKOLIPS BEFORE.
"I COULD USE SOME JUMP JETS THAT HAVE A BETTER SPECIFIC PULSE SO I'M NOT RELYING ON BOOM TUBES ALONE.
"WHAT'S THIS?"
"IT'S NOT A WEAPON, SON. JUST SOMETHING FOR WHEN THIS IS ALL OVER. WHEN YOU HAVE SOME TIME ALONE. HIT THE GREEN BUTTON."
ONE MORE THING, DAD.
MADE IN DETROIT
LET'S REMEMBER WHERE I'M FROM.

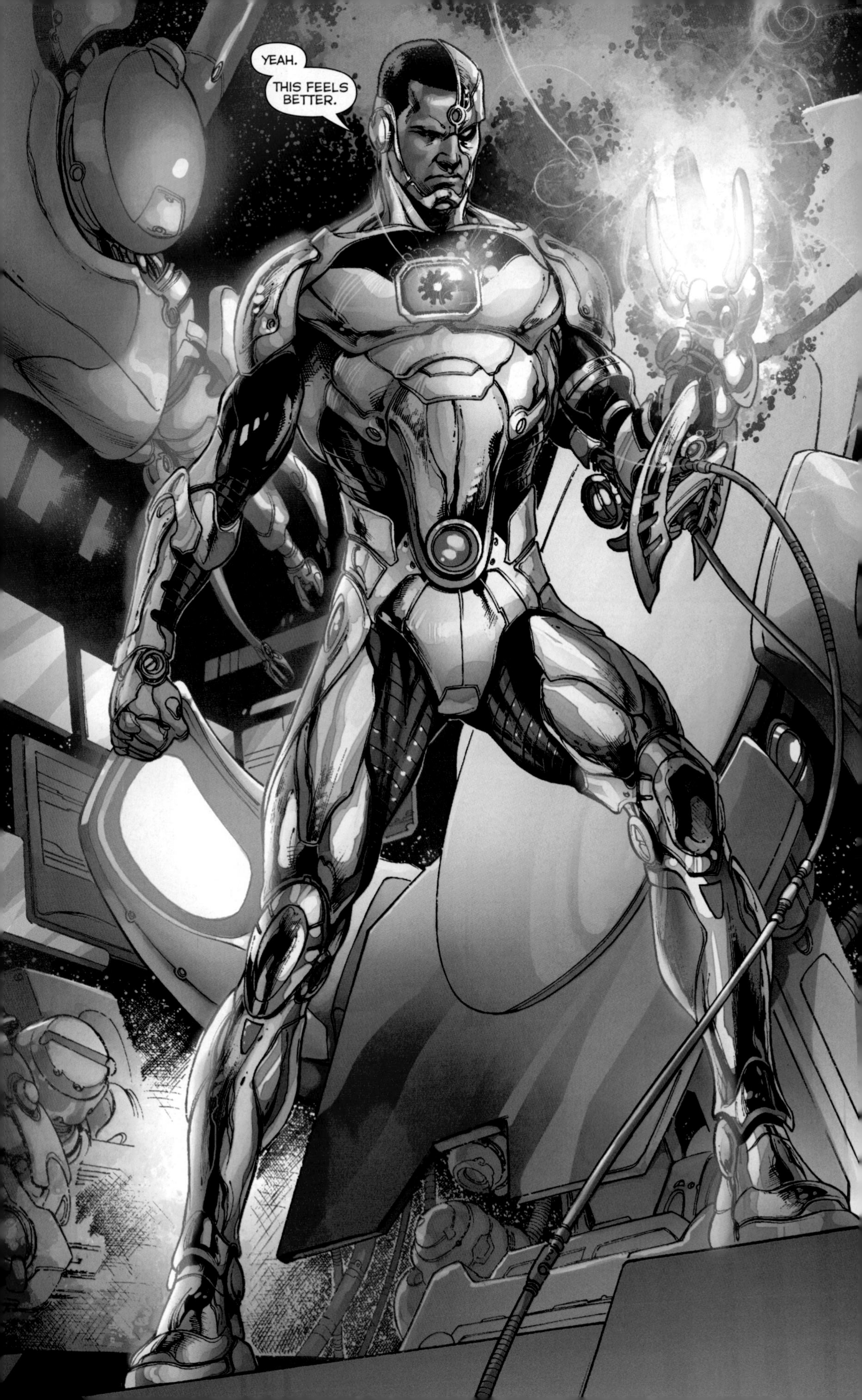
YEAH.
THIS FEELS BETTER.

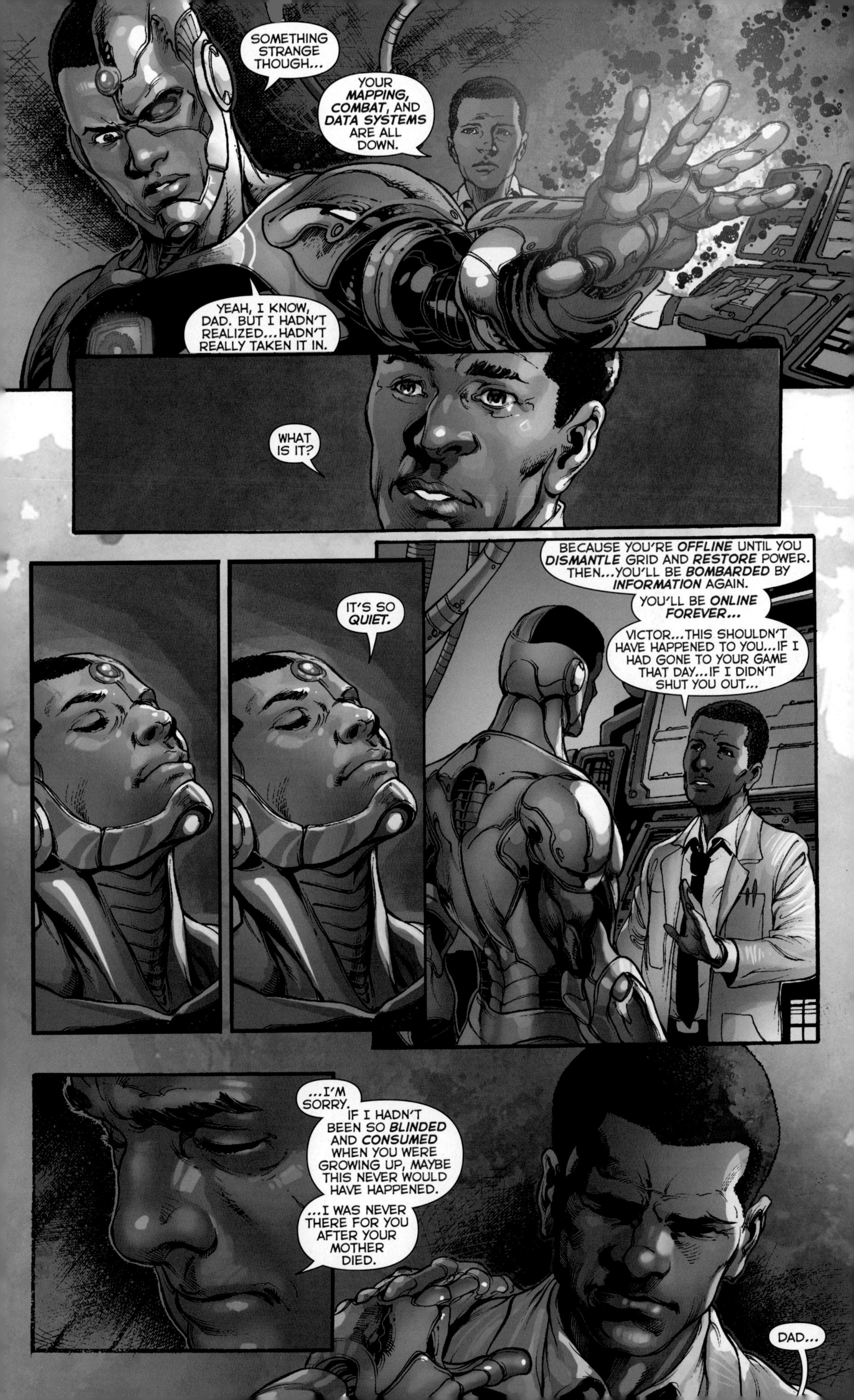
SOMETHING STRANGE THOUGH...
YOUR MAPPING, COMBAT, AND DATA SYSTEMS ARE ALL DOWN.
YEAH, I KNOW, DAD. BUT I HADN'T REALIZED...HADN'T REALLY TAKEN IT IN.
WHAT IS IT?
IT'S SO QUIET.
BECAUSE YOU'RE OFFLINE UNTIL YOU DISMANTLE GRID AND RESTORE POWER. THEN...YOU'LL BE BOMBARDED BY INFORMATION AGAIN.
YOU'LL BE ONLINE FOREVER...
VICTOR...THIS SHOULDN'T HAVE HAPPENED TO YOU...IF I HAD GONE TO YOUR GAME THAT DAY...IF I DIDN'T SHUT YOU OUT...
...I'M SORRY.
IF I HADN'T BEEN SO BLINDED AND CONSUMED WHEN YOU WERE GROWING UP, MAYBE THIS NEVER WOULD HAVE HAPPENED.
...I WAS NEVER THERE FOR YOU AFTER YOUR MOTHER DIED.
DAD...

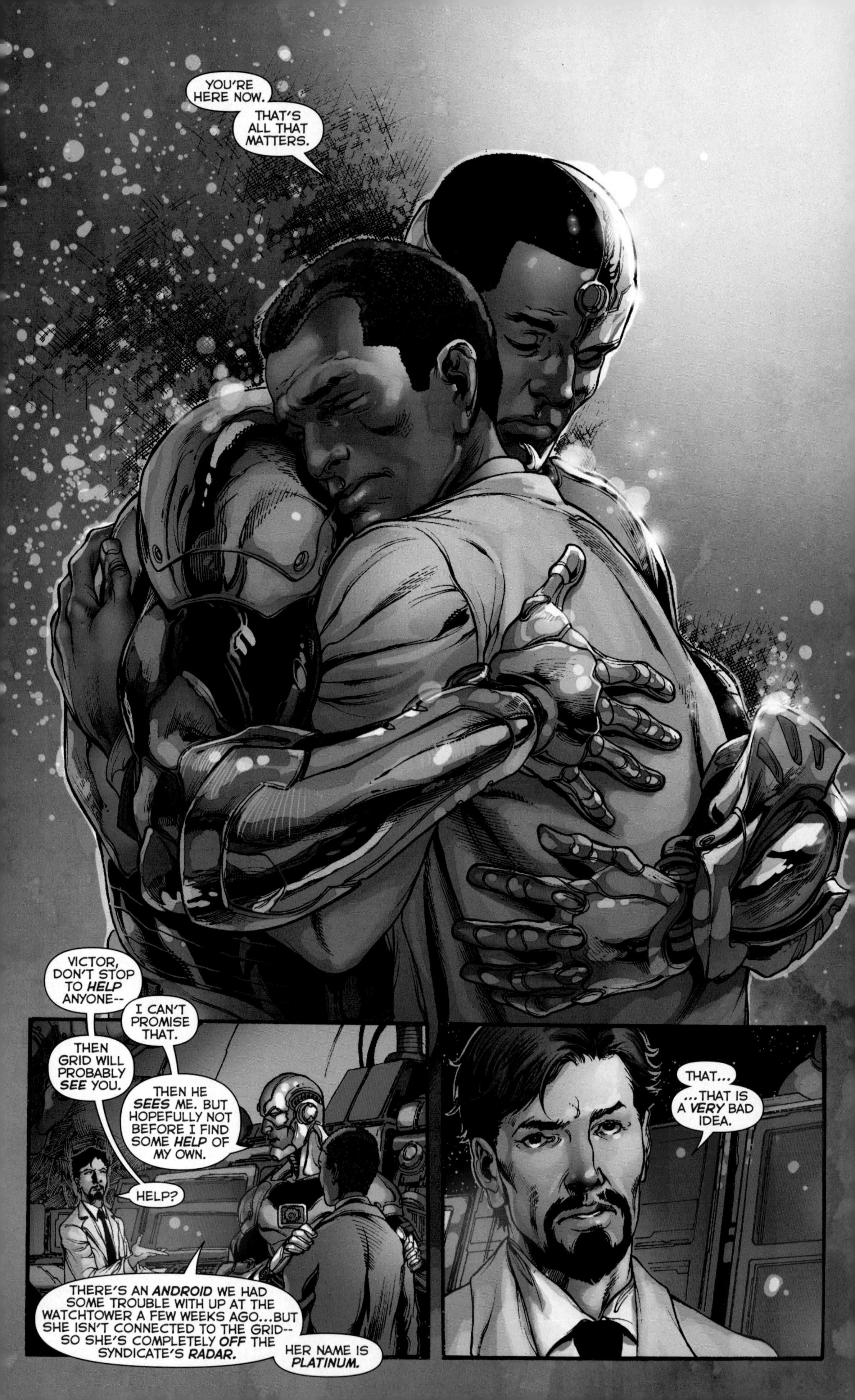
YOU'RE HERE NOW.
THAT'S ALL THAT MATTERS.
VICTOR, DON'T STOP TO HELP ANYONE--
I CAN'T PROMISE THAT.
THEN GRID WILL PROBABLY SEE YOU.
THEN HE SEES ME. BUT HOPEFULLY NOT BEFORE I FIND SOME HELP OF MY OWN.
HELP?
THERE'S AN ANDROID WE HAD SOME TROUBLE WITH UP AT THE WATCHTOWER A FEW WEEKS AGO...BUT SHE ISN'T CONNECTED TO THE GRID-- SO SHE'S COMPLETELY OFF THE SYNDICATE'S RADAR.
HER NAME IS PLATINUM.
THAT...
...THAT IS A VERY BAD IDEA.

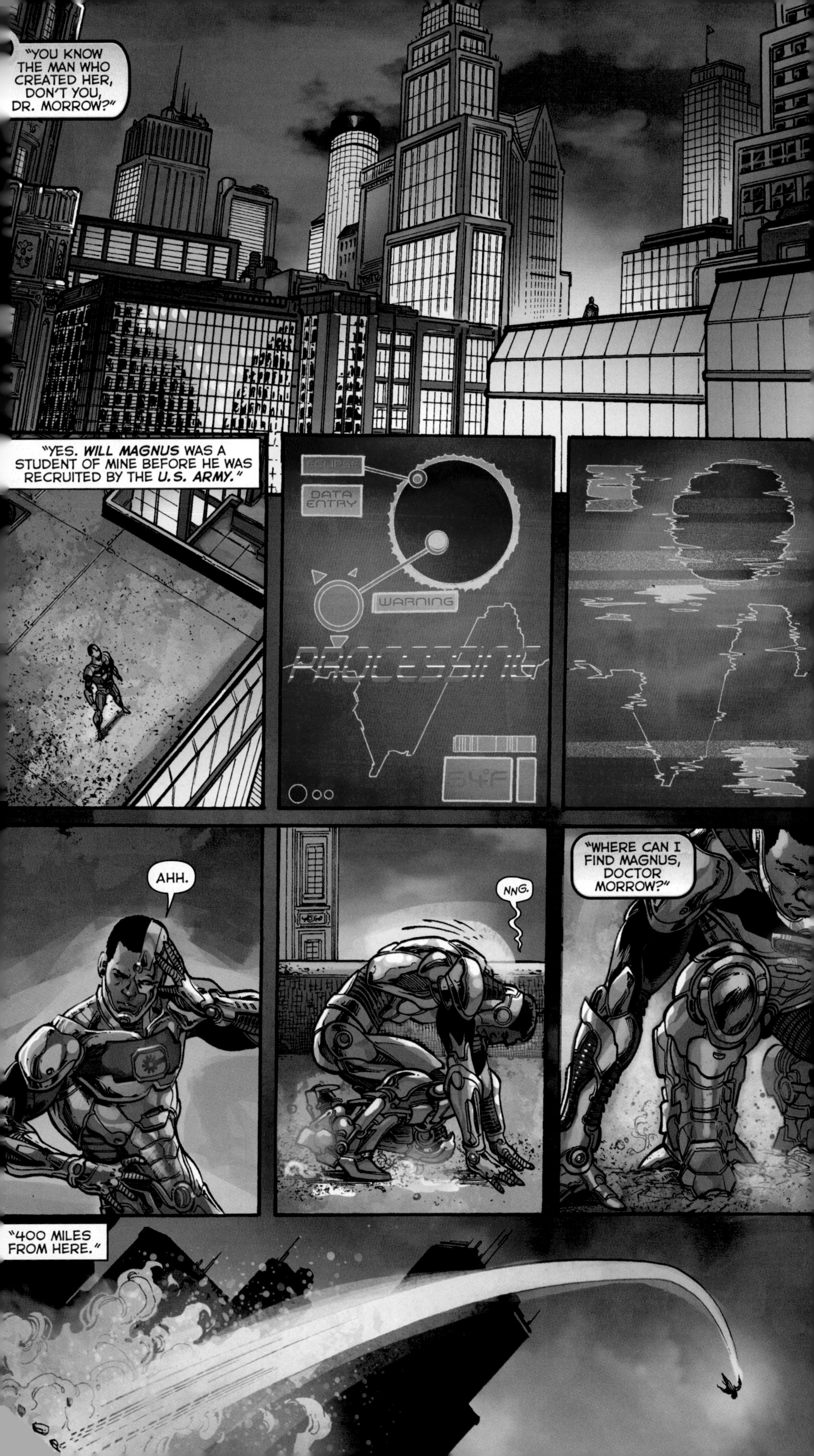
"YOU KNOW THE MAN WHO CREATED HER, DON'T YOU, DR. MORROW?"
"YES. *WILL MAGNUS* WAS A STUDENT OF MINE BEFORE HE WAS RECRUITED BY THE *U.S. ARMY.*"
ECLIPSO
DATA ENTRY
WARNING
PROCESSING
64°F
AHH.
NNG.
"WHERE CAN I FIND MAGNUS, DOCTOR MORROW?"
"400 MILES FROM HERE."

CLEVELAND, OHIO.

PITTSBURGH, PENNSYLVANIA.

HAGERSTOWN, MARYLAND.

ADELPHI, MARYLAND.

THE U.S. ARMY
RESEARCH LABORATORY.

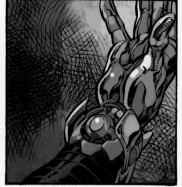

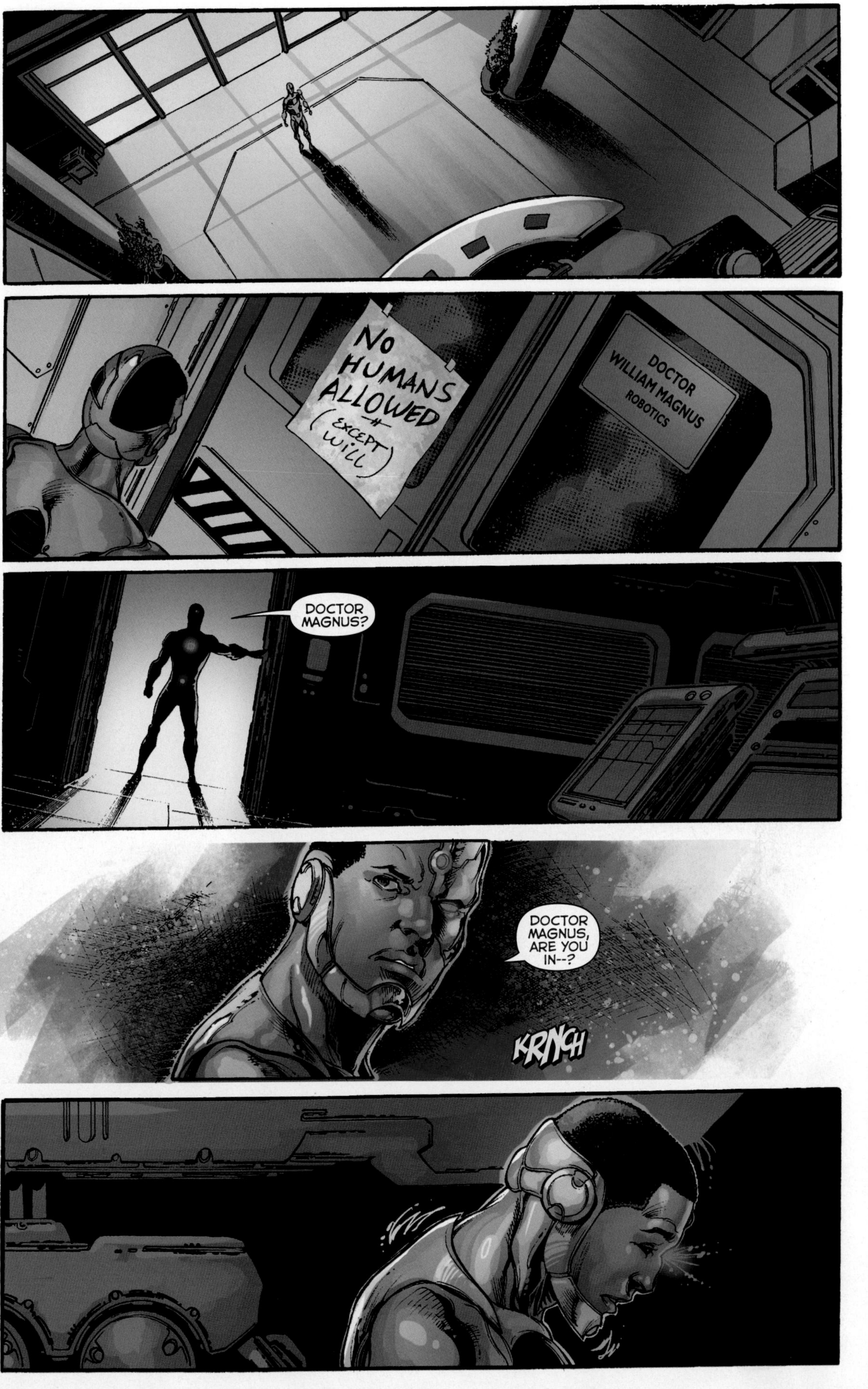
NO HUMANS ALLOWED (EXCEPT WILL)
DOCTOR WILLIAM MAGNUS ROBOTICS
DOCTOR MAGNUS?
DOCTOR MAGNUS, ARE YOU IN--?
KRNCH

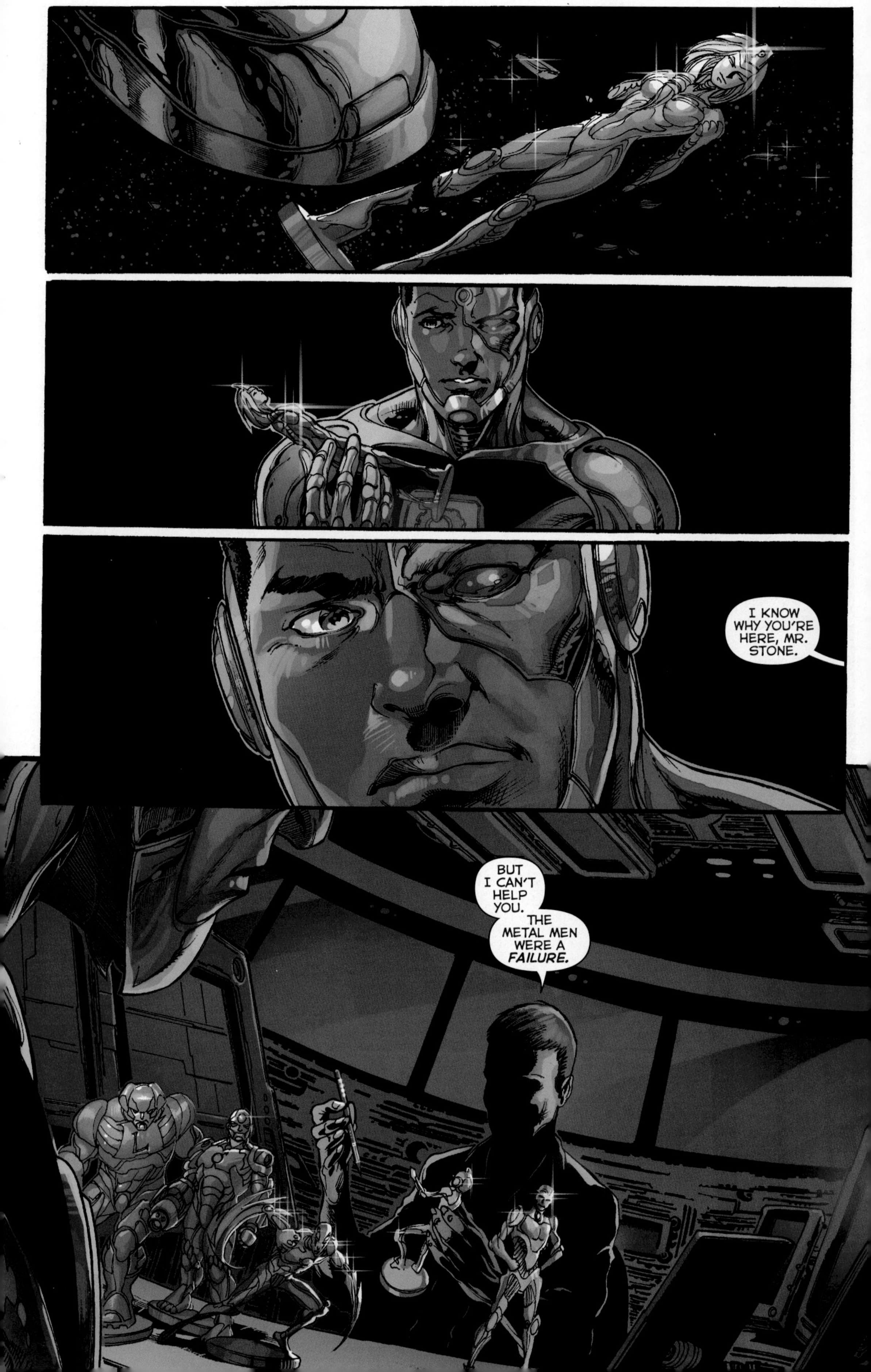
I KNOW WHY YOU'RE HERE, MR. STONE.
BUT I CAN'T HELP YOU.
THE METAL MEN WERE A *FAILURE.*

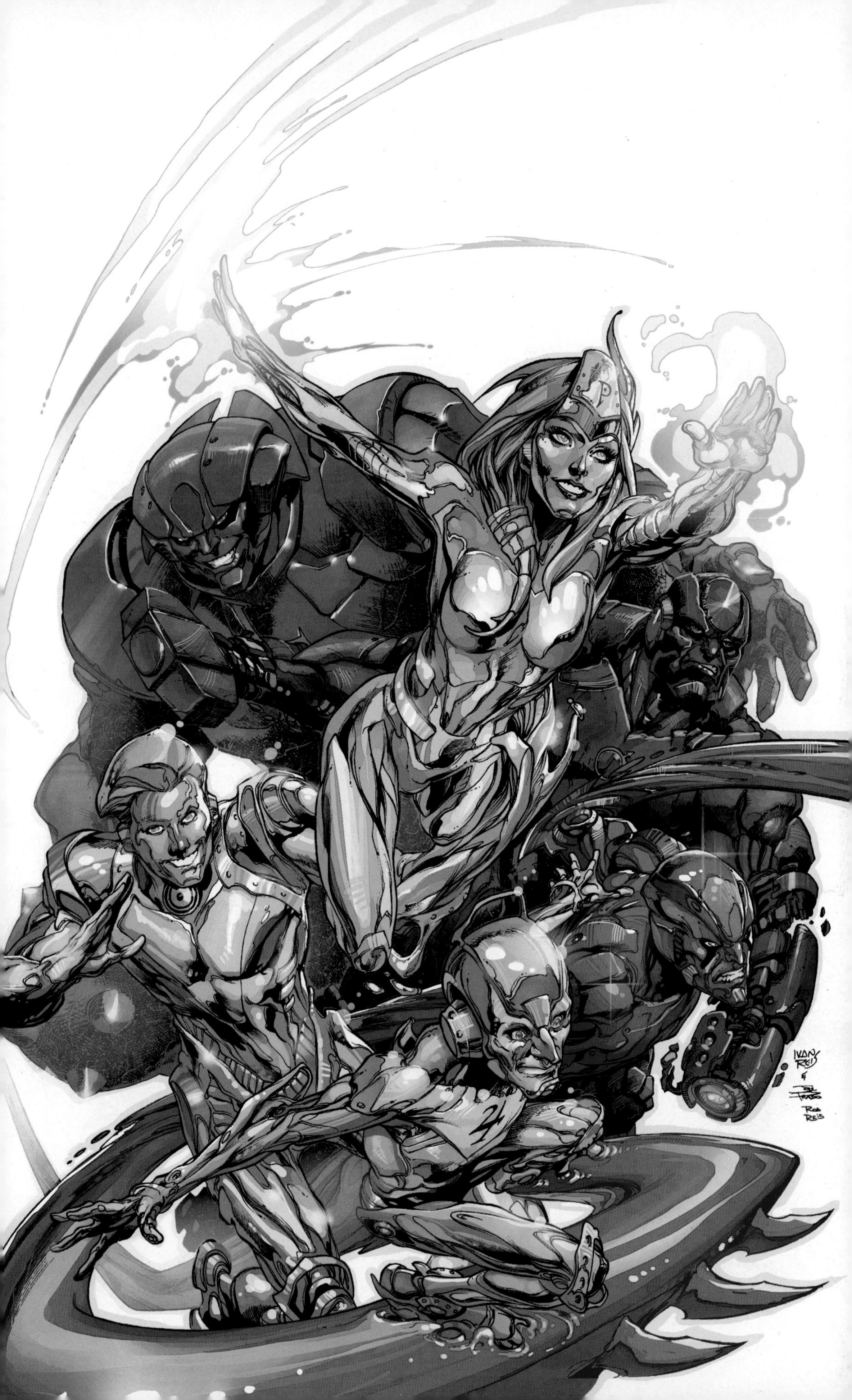

FOREVER WORTHY

GEOFF JOHNS writer **IVAN REIS** penciller **JOE PRADO** and **SCOTT HANNA** finishes

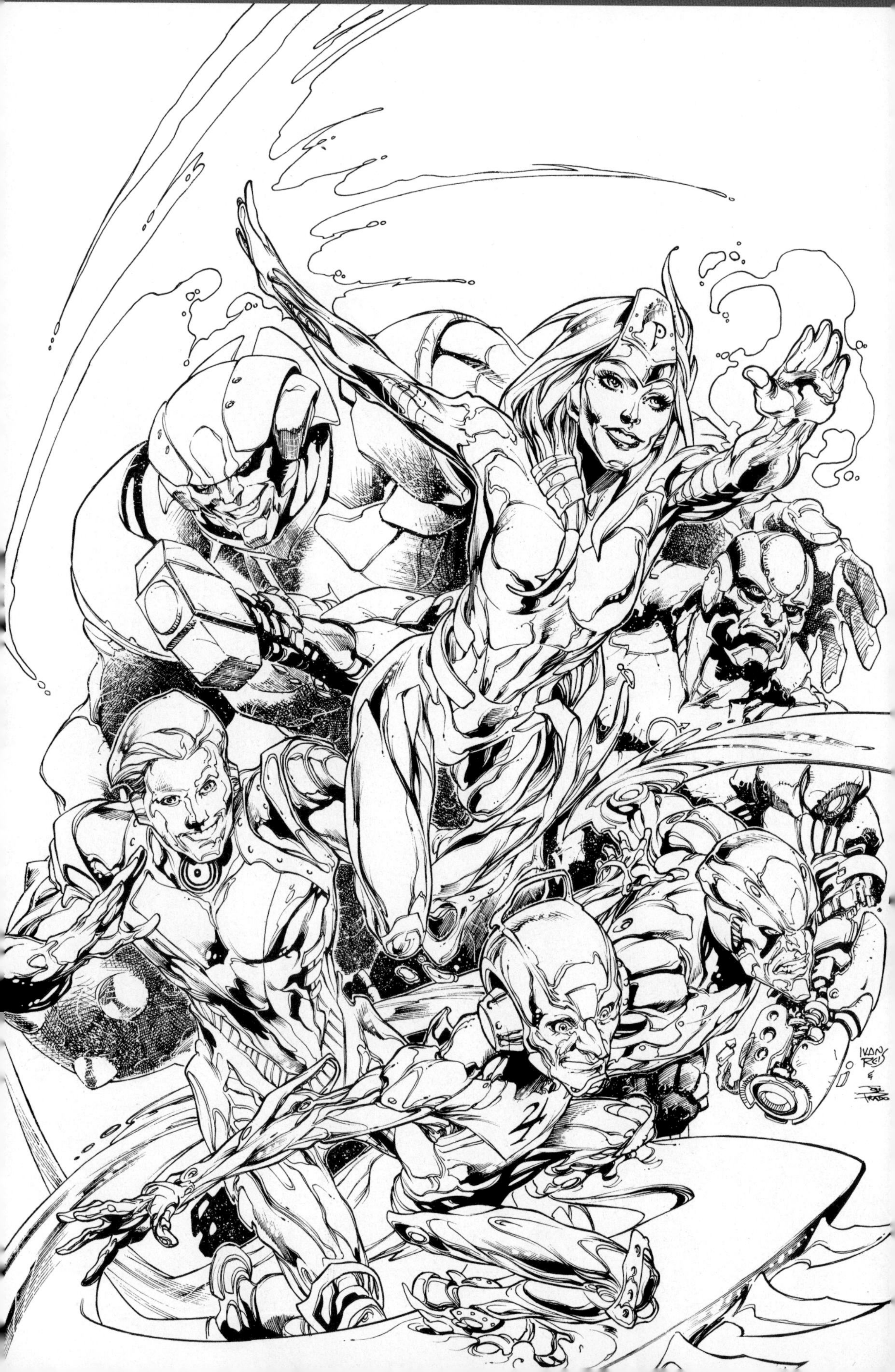

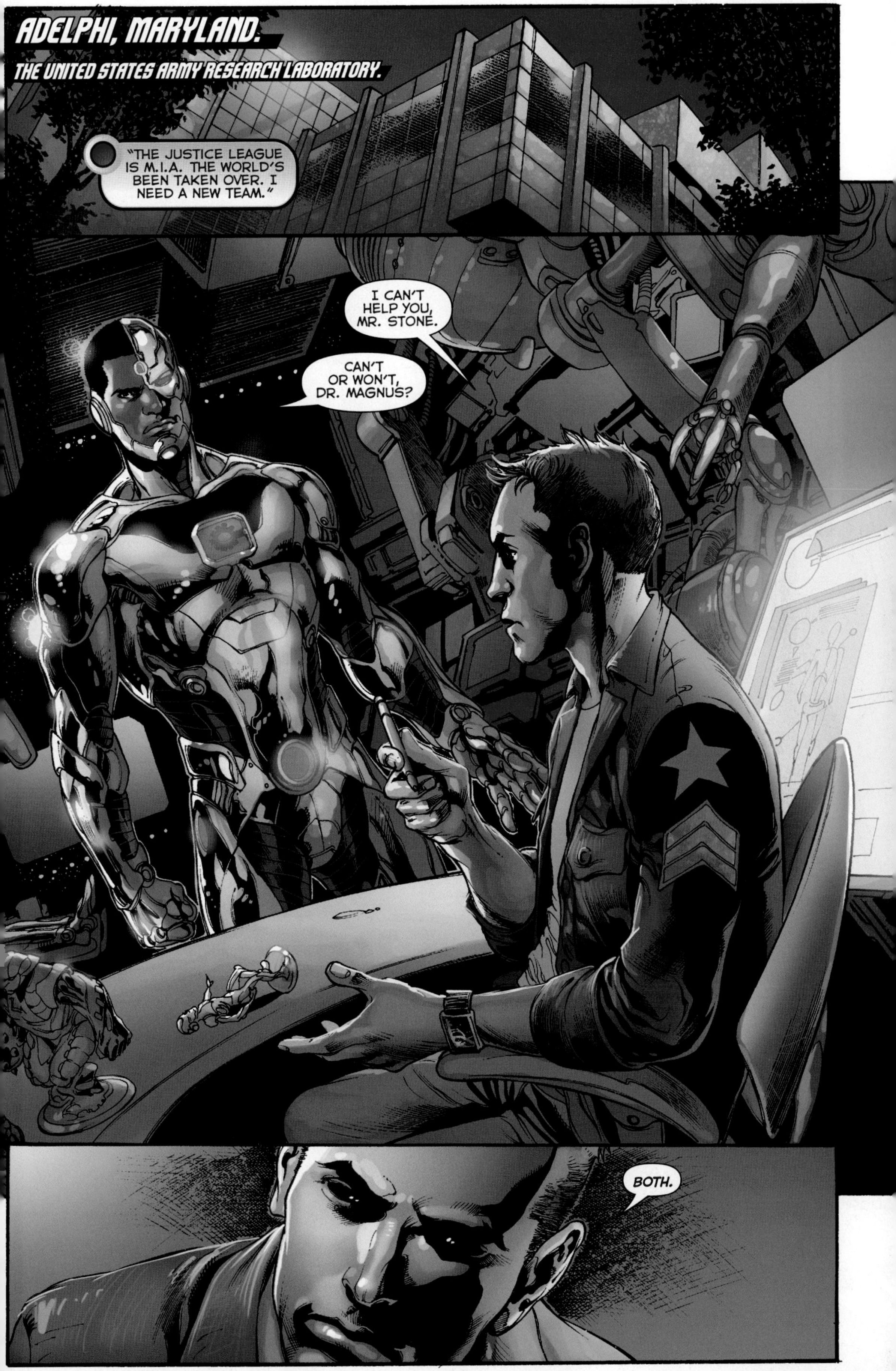

ADELPHI, MARYLAND.
THE UNITED STATES ARMY RESEARCH LABORATORY.
"THE JUSTICE LEAGUE IS M.I.A. THE WORLD'S BEEN TAKEN OVER. I NEED A NEW TEAM."
I CAN'T HELP YOU, MR. STONE.
CAN'T OR WON'T, DR. MAGNUS?
BOTH.

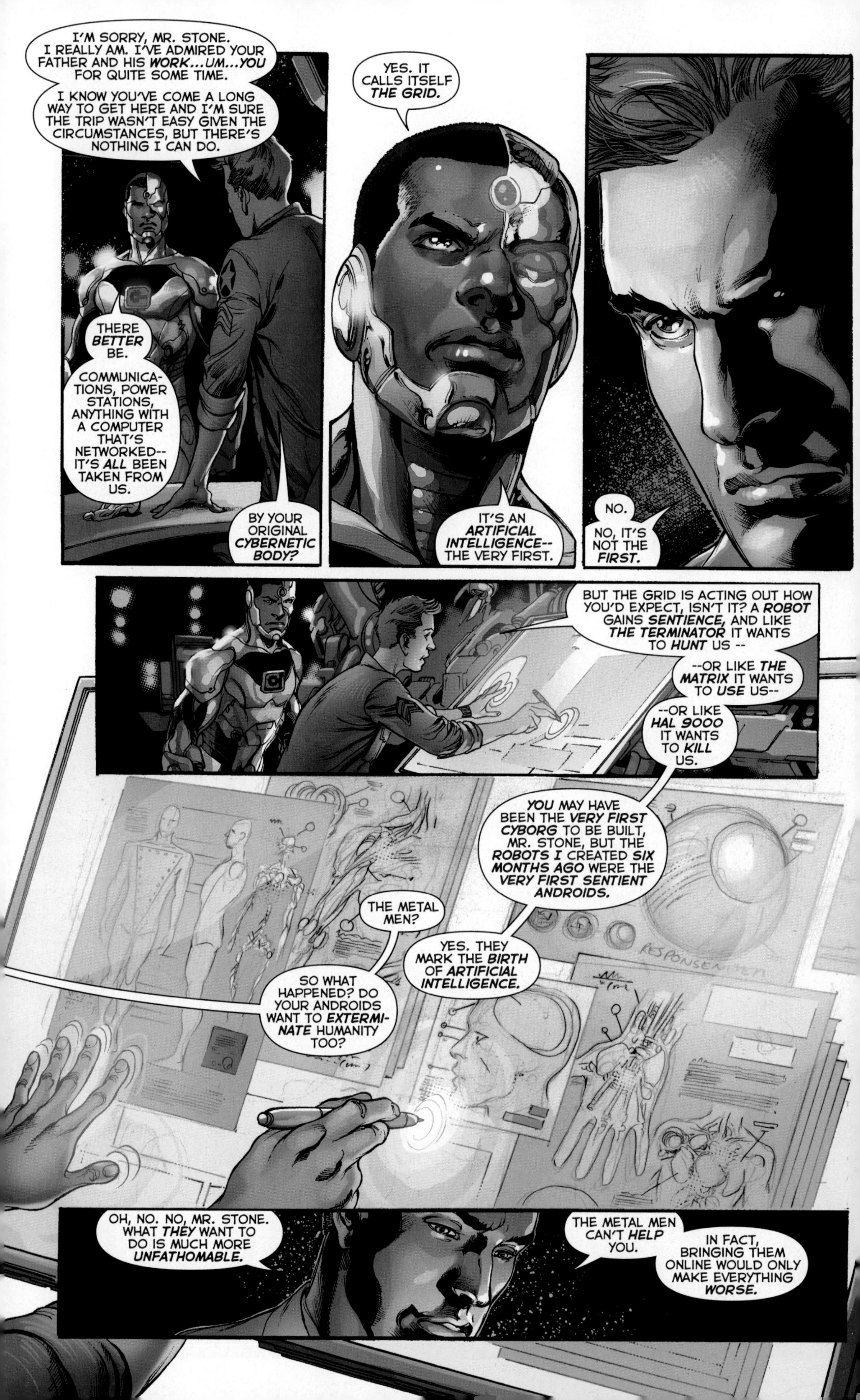
I'M SORRY, MR. STONE. I REALLY AM. I'VE ADMIRED YOUR FATHER AND HIS WORK...UM...YOU FOR QUITE SOME TIME.
I KNOW YOU'VE COME A LONG WAY TO GET HERE AND I'M SURE THE TRIP WASN'T EASY GIVEN THE CIRCUMSTANCES, BUT THERE'S NOTHING I CAN DO.
THERE BETTER BE.
COMMUNICATIONS, POWER STATIONS, ANYTHING WITH A COMPUTER THAT'S NETWORKED-- IT'S ALL BEEN TAKEN FROM US.
BY YOUR ORIGINAL CYBERNETIC BODY?
YES. IT CALLS ITSELF THE GRID.
IT'S AN ARTIFICIAL INTELLIGENCE-- THE VERY FIRST.
NO.
NO, IT'S NOT THE FIRST.
BUT THE GRID IS ACTING OUT HOW YOU'D EXPECT, ISN'T IT? A ROBOT GAINS SENTIENCE, AND LIKE THE TERMINATOR IT WANTS TO HUNT US --
--OR LIKE THE MATRIX IT WANTS TO USE US--
--OR LIKE HAL 9000 IT WANTS TO KILL US.
YOU MAY HAVE BEEN THE VERY FIRST CYBORG TO BE BUILT, MR. STONE, BUT THE ROBOTS I CREATED SIX MONTHS AGO WERE THE VERY FIRST SENTIENT ANDROIDS.
THE METAL MEN?
YES. THEY MARK THE BIRTH OF ARTIFICIAL INTELLIGENCE.
SO WHAT HAPPENED? DO YOUR ANDROIDS WANT TO EXTERMINATE HUMANITY TOO?
OH, NO. NO, MR. STONE. WHAT THEY WANT TO DO IS MUCH MORE UNFATHOMABLE.
THE METAL MEN CAN'T HELP YOU.
IN FACT, BRINGING THEM ONLINE WOULD ONLY MAKE EVERYTHING WORSE.

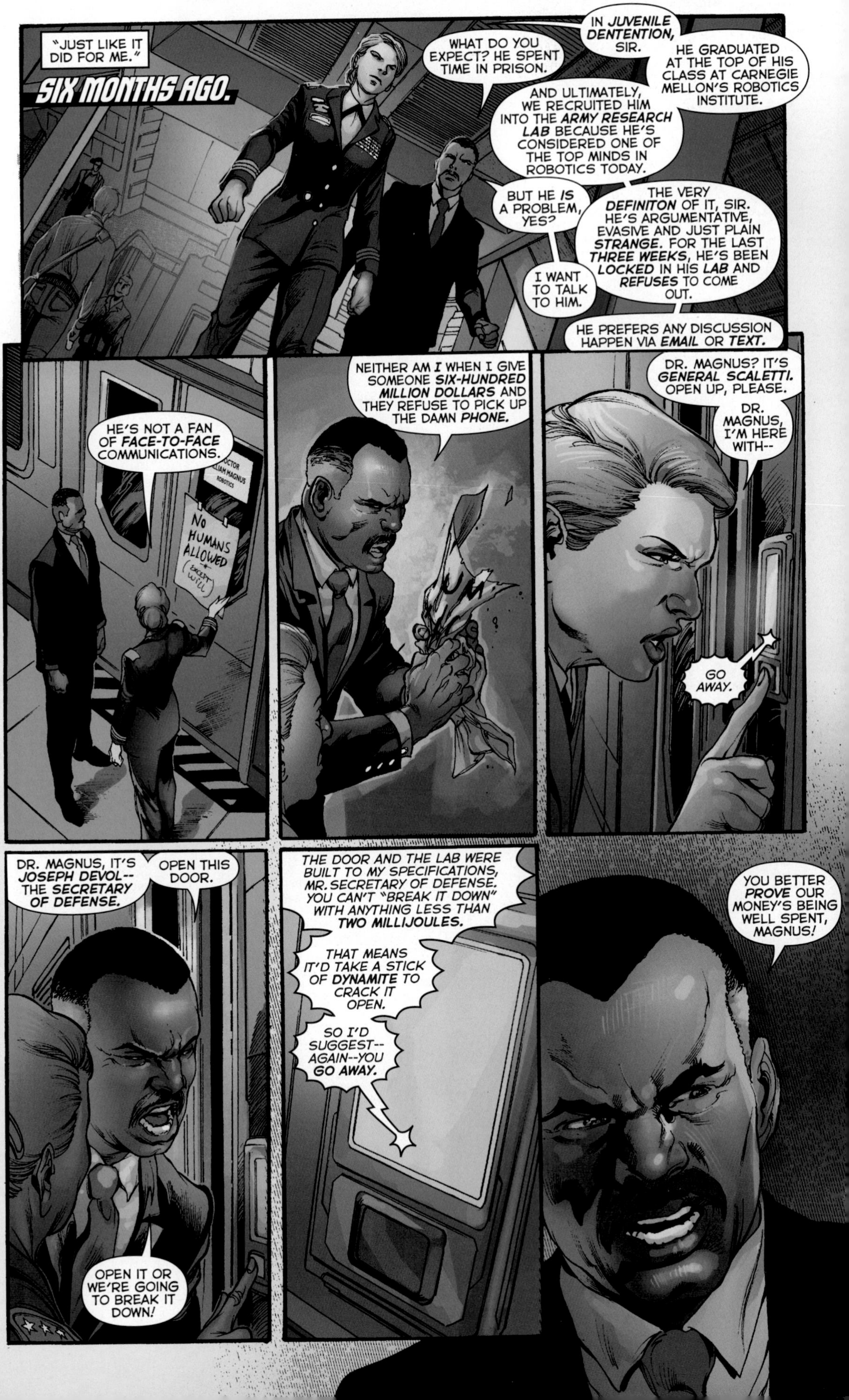
"JUST LIKE IT DID FOR ME."
SIX MONTHS AGO.
WHAT DO YOU EXPECT? HE SPENT TIME IN PRISON.
IN JUVENILE DENTENTION, SIR.
HE GRADUATED AT THE TOP OF HIS CLASS AT CARNEGIE MELLON'S ROBOTICS INSTITUTE.
AND ULTIMATELY, WE RECRUITED HIM INTO THE ARMY RESEARCH LAB BECAUSE HE'S CONSIDERED ONE OF THE TOP MINDS IN ROBOTICS TODAY.
BUT HE IS A PROBLEM, YES?
THE VERY DEFINITON OF IT, SIR. HE'S ARGUMENTATIVE, EVASIVE AND JUST PLAIN STRANGE. FOR THE LAST THREE WEEKS, HE'S BEEN LOCKED IN HIS LAB AND REFUSES TO COME OUT.
I WANT TO TALK TO HIM.
HE PREFERS ANY DISCUSSION HAPPEN VIA EMAIL OR TEXT.
HE'S NOT A FAN OF FACE-TO-FACE COMMUNICATIONS.
NO HUMANS ALLOWED (EXCEPT WILL)
NEITHER AM I WHEN I GIVE SOMEONE SIX-HUNDRED MILLION DOLLARS AND THEY REFUSE TO PICK UP THE DAMN PHONE.
DR. MAGNUS? IT'S GENERAL SCALETTI. OPEN UP, PLEASE.
DR. MAGNUS, I'M HERE WITH--
GO AWAY.
DR. MAGNUS, IT'S JOSEPH DEVOL-- THE SECRETARY OF DEFENSE.
OPEN THIS DOOR.
OPEN IT OR WE'RE GOING TO BREAK IT DOWN!
THE DOOR AND THE LAB WERE BUILT TO MY SPECIFICATIONS, MR. SECRETARY OF DEFENSE. YOU CAN'T "BREAK IT DOWN" WITH ANYTHING LESS THAN TWO MILLIJOULES.
THAT MEANS IT'D TAKE A STICK OF DYNAMITE TO CRACK IT OPEN.
SO I'D SUGGEST-- AGAIN--YOU GO AWAY.
YOU BETTER PROVE OUR MONEY'S BEING WELL SPENT, MAGNUS!

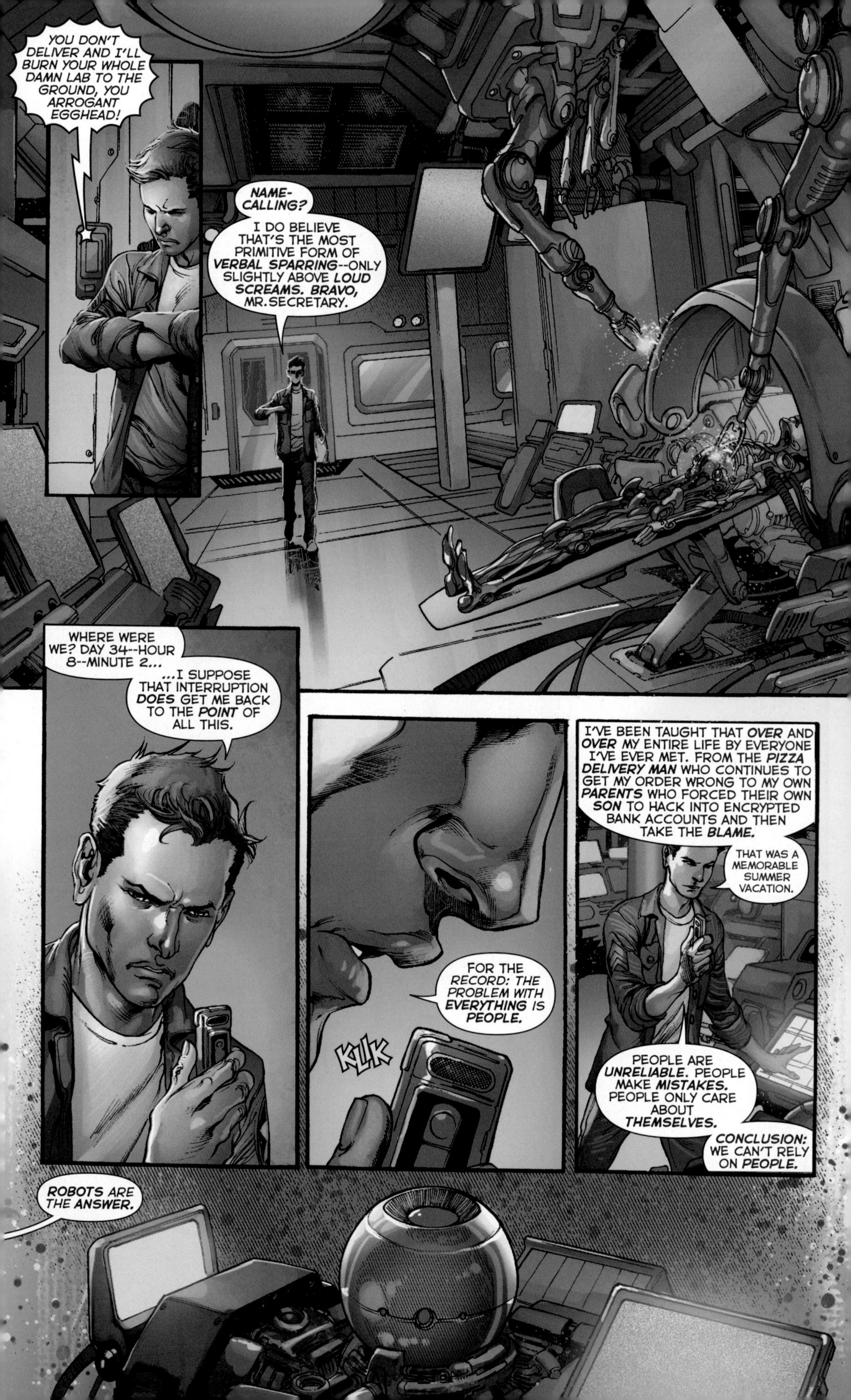

YOU DON'T DELIVER AND I'LL BURN YOUR WHOLE DAMN LAB TO THE GROUND, YOU ARROGANT EGGHEAD!
NAME-CALLING?
I DO BELIEVE THAT'S THE MOST PRIMITIVE FORM OF VERBAL SPARRING--ONLY SLIGHTLY ABOVE LOUD SCREAMS. BRAVO, MR. SECRETARY.
WHERE WERE WE? DAY 34--HOUR 8--MINUTE 2...
...I SUPPOSE THAT INTERRUPTION DOES GET ME BACK TO THE POINT OF ALL THIS.
FOR THE RECORD: THE PROBLEM WITH EVERYTHING IS PEOPLE.
KLIK
I'VE BEEN TAUGHT THAT OVER AND OVER MY ENTIRE LIFE BY EVERYONE I'VE EVER MET. FROM THE PIZZA DELIVERY MAN WHO CONTINUES TO GET MY ORDER WRONG TO MY OWN PARENTS WHO FORCED THEIR OWN SON TO HACK INTO ENCRYPTED BANK ACCOUNTS AND THEN TAKE THE BLAME.
THAT WAS A MEMORABLE SUMMER VACATION.
PEOPLE ARE UNRELIABLE. PEOPLE MAKE MISTAKES. PEOPLE ONLY CARE ABOUT THEMSELVES.
CONCLUSION: WE CAN'T RELY ON PEOPLE.
ROBOTS ARE THE ANSWER.

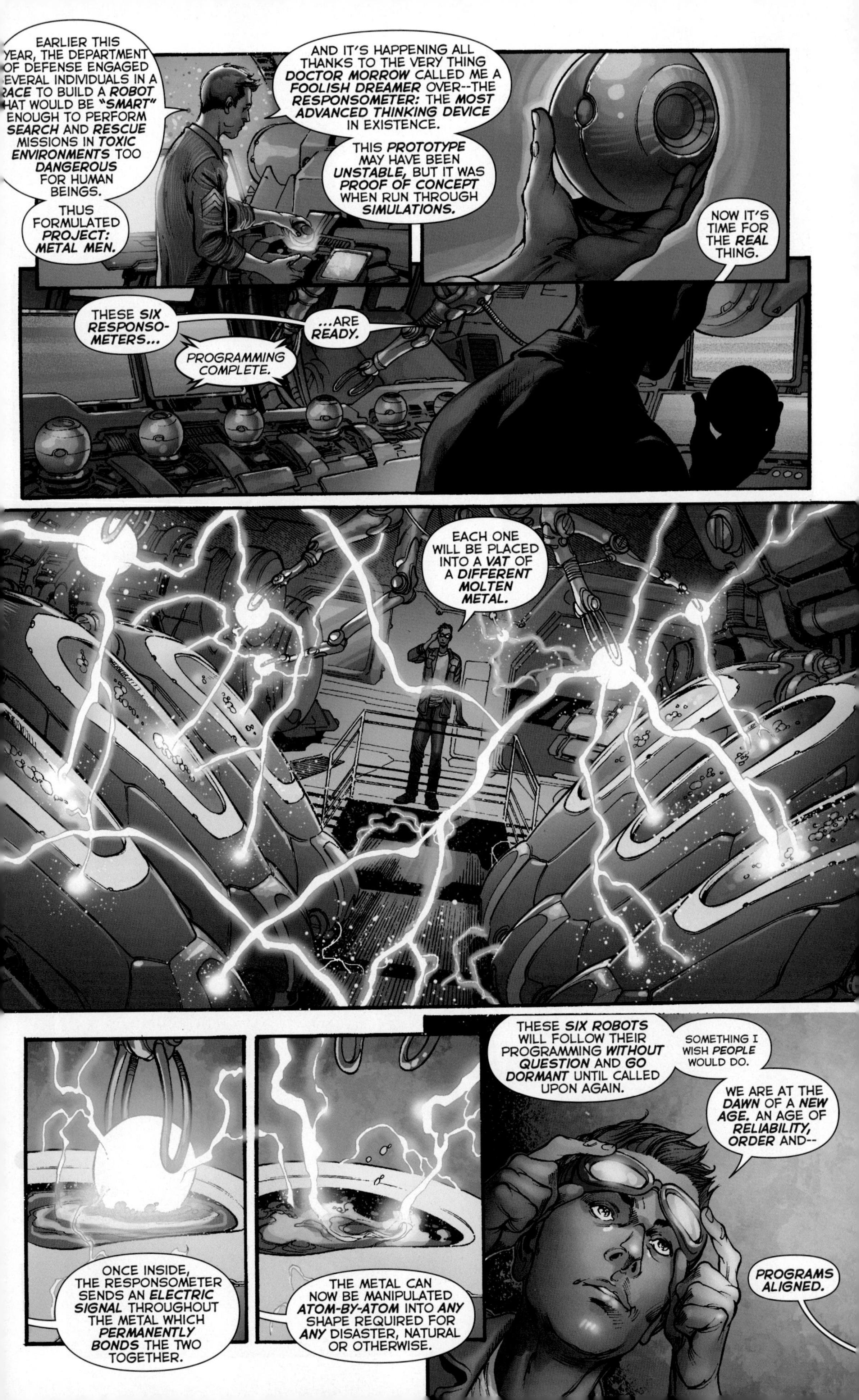

EARLIER THIS YEAR, THE DEPARTMENT OF DEFENSE ENGAGED SEVERAL INDIVIDUALS IN A RACE TO BUILD A ROBOT THAT WOULD BE "SMART" ENOUGH TO PERFORM SEARCH AND RESCUE MISSIONS IN TOXIC ENVIRONMENTS TOO DANGEROUS FOR HUMAN BEINGS.
THUS FORMULATED PROJECT: METAL MEN.
AND IT'S HAPPENING ALL THANKS TO THE VERY THING DOCTOR MORROW CALLED ME A FOOLISH DREAMER OVER--THE RESPONSOMETER: THE MOST ADVANCED THINKING DEVICE IN EXISTENCE.
THIS PROTOTYPE MAY HAVE BEEN UNSTABLE, BUT IT WAS PROOF OF CONCEPT WHEN RUN THROUGH SIMULATIONS.
NOW IT'S TIME FOR THE REAL THING.
THESE SIX RESPONSOMETERS...
...ARE READY.
PROGRAMMING COMPLETE.
EACH ONE WILL BE PLACED INTO A VAT OF A DIFFERENT MOLTEN METAL.
ONCE INSIDE, THE RESPONSOMETER SENDS AN ELECTRIC SIGNAL THROUGHOUT THE METAL WHICH PERMANENTLY BONDS THE TWO TOGETHER.
THE METAL CAN NOW BE MANIPULATED ATOM-BY-ATOM INTO ANY SHAPE REQUIRED FOR ANY DISASTER, NATURAL OR OTHERWISE.
THESE SIX ROBOTS WILL FOLLOW THEIR PROGRAMMING WITHOUT QUESTION AND GO DORMANT UNTIL CALLED UPON AGAIN.
SOMETHING I WISH PEOPLE WOULD DO.
WE ARE AT THE DAWN OF A NEW AGE. AN AGE OF RELIABILITY, ORDER AND--
PROGRAMS ALIGNED.

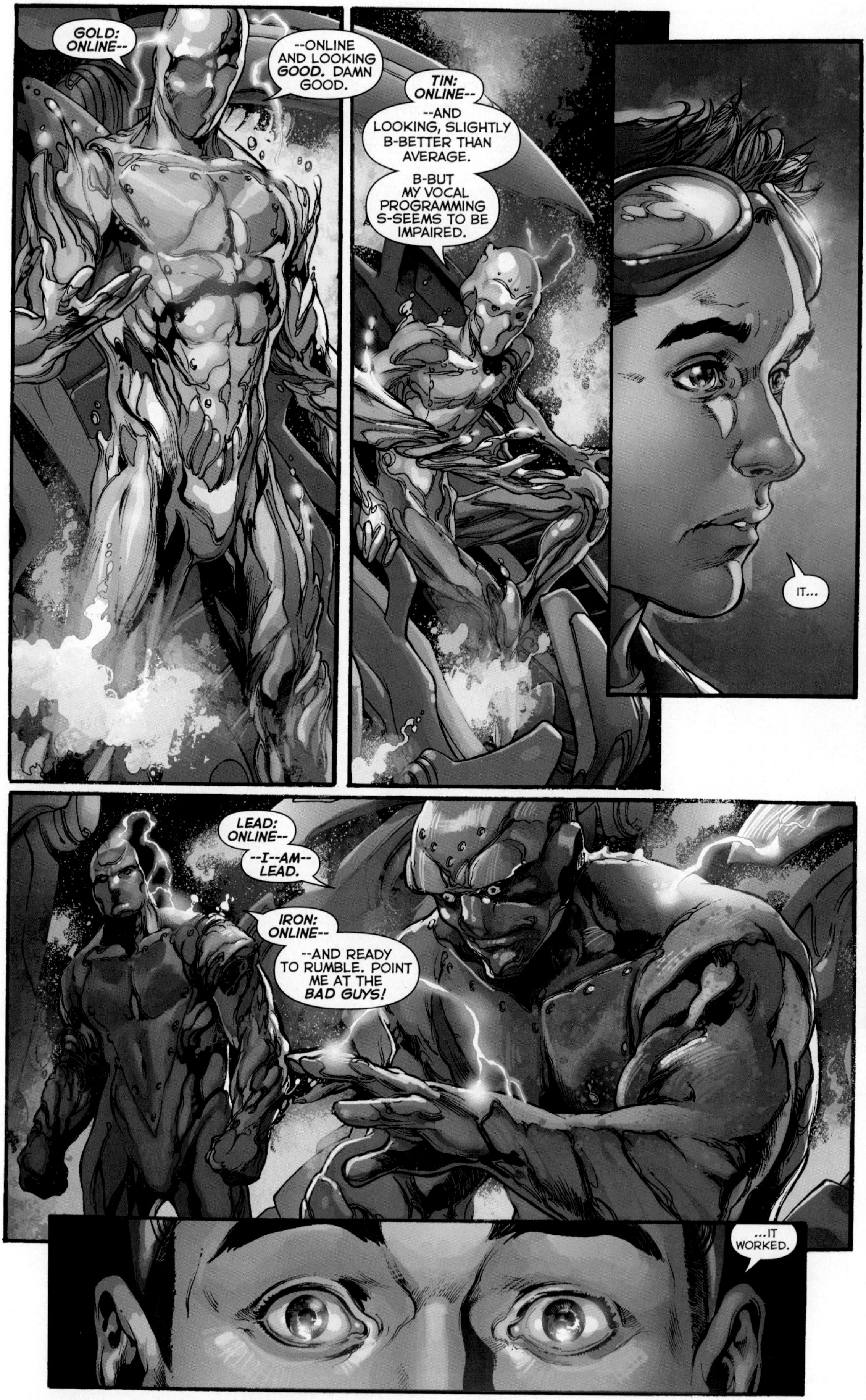
GOLD: ONLINE--
--ONLINE AND LOOKING GOOD. DAMN GOOD.
TIN: ONLINE--
--AND LOOKING, SLIGHTLY B-BETTER THAN AVERAGE.
B-BUT MY VOCAL PROGRAMMING S-SEEMS TO BE IMPAIRED.
IT...
LEAD: ONLINE--
--I--AM--LEAD.
IRON: ONLINE--
--AND READY TO RUMBLE. POINT ME AT THE BAD GUYS!
...IT WORKED.

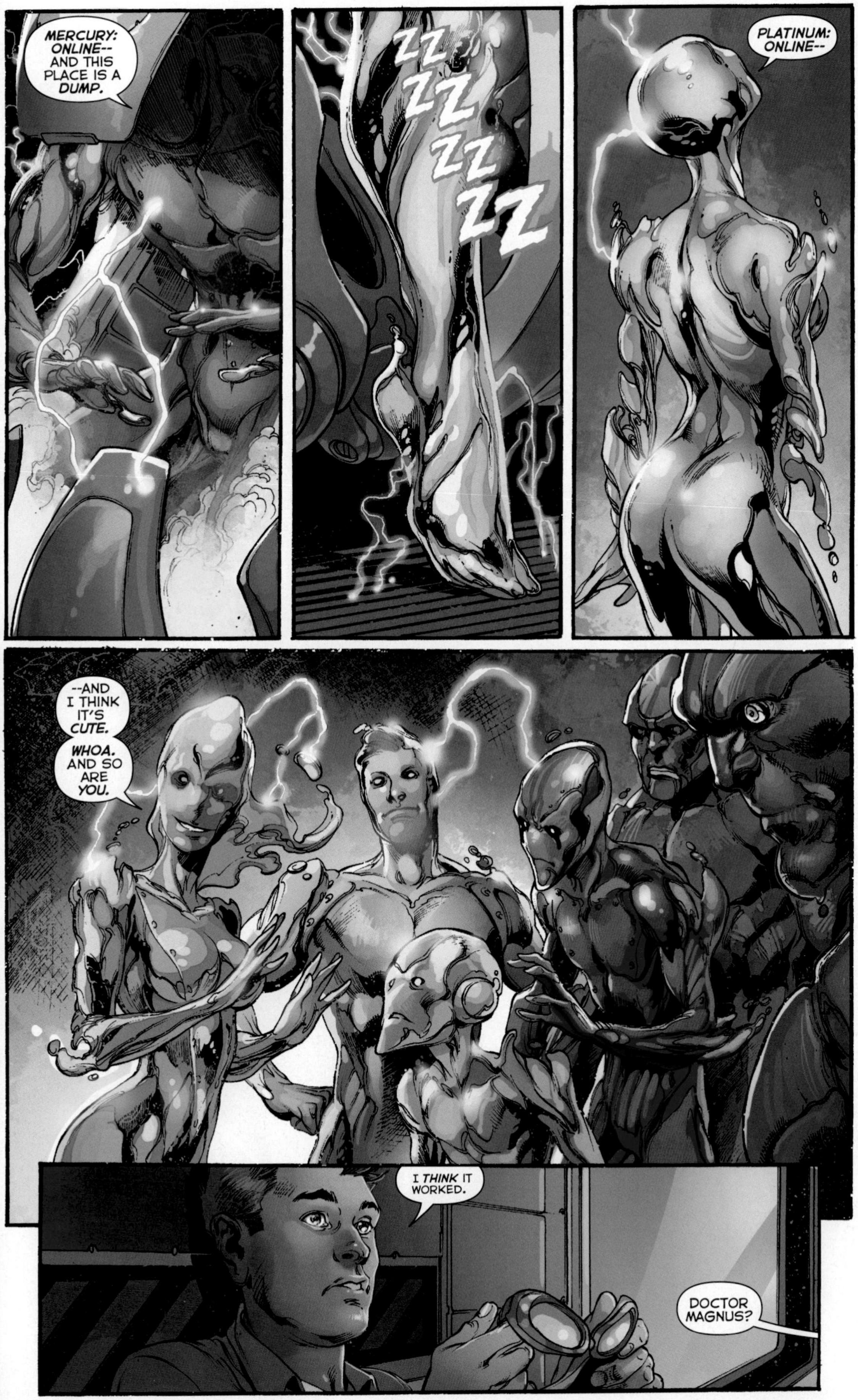
MERCURY: ONLINE-- AND THIS PLACE IS A DUMP.
ZZ ZZ ZZ ZZ
PLATINUM: ONLINE--
--AND I THINK IT'S CUTE.
WHOA. AND SO ARE YOU.
I THINK IT WORKED.
DOCTOR MAGNUS?

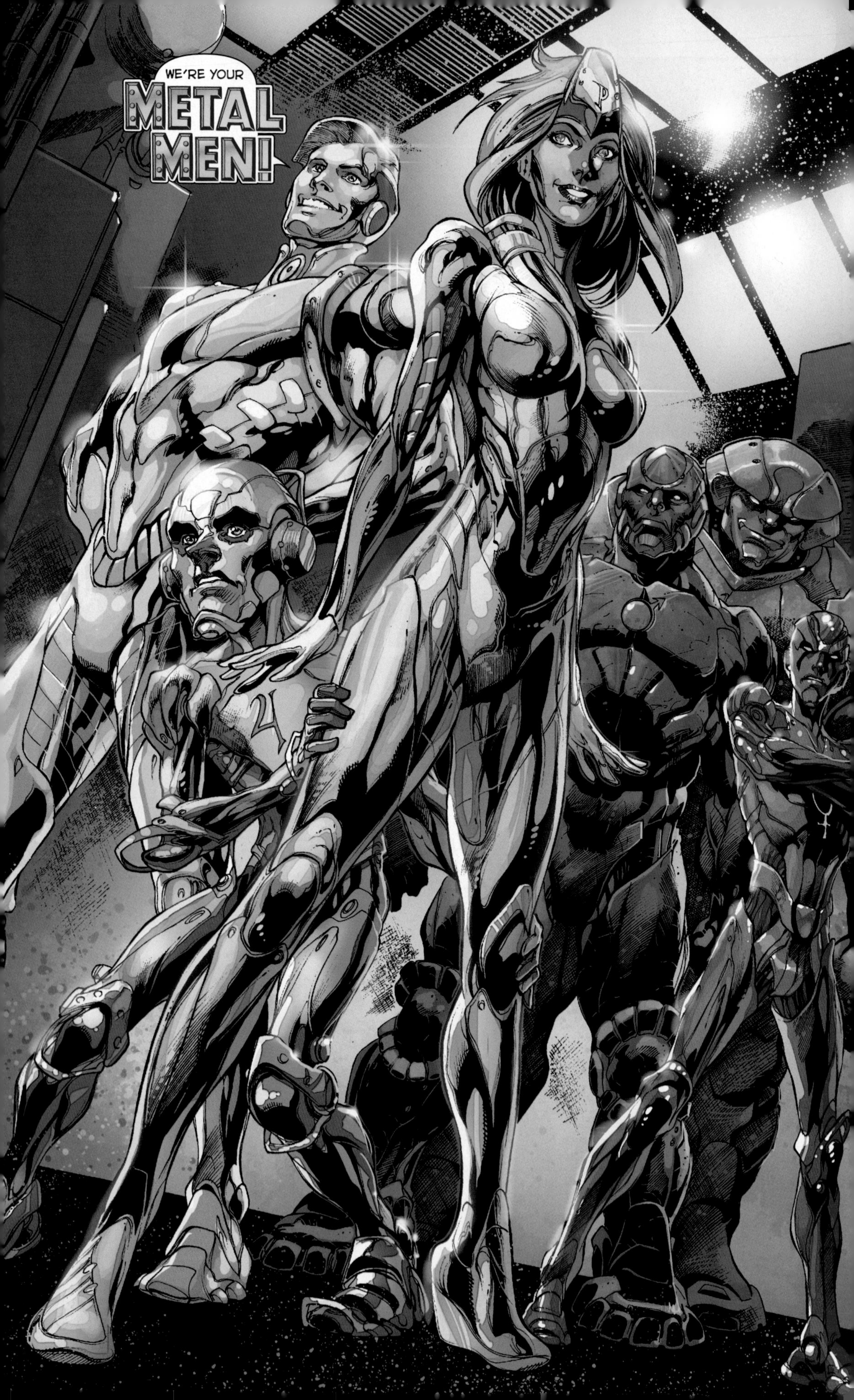
WE'RE YOUR
METAL MEN!

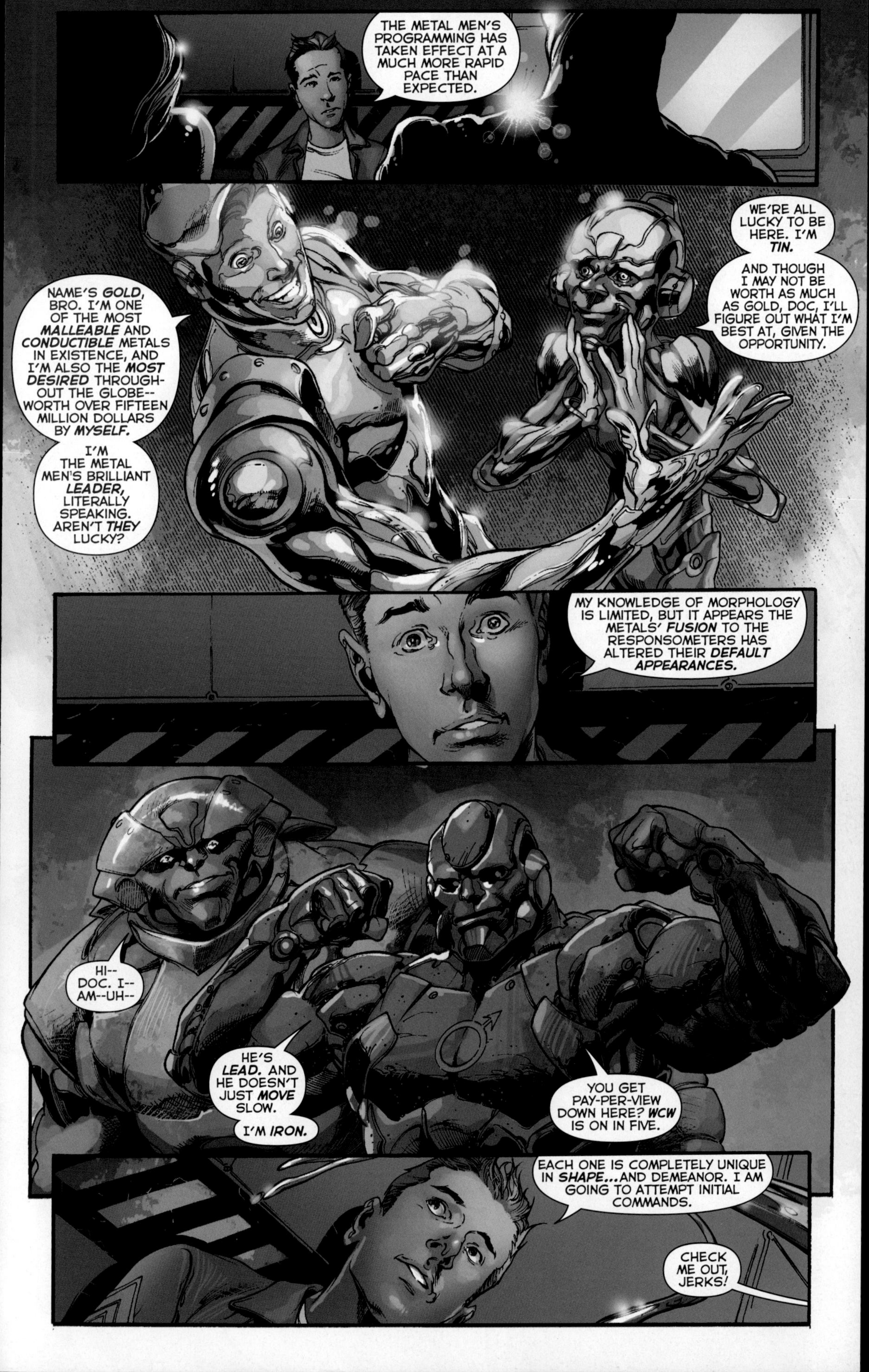
THE METAL MEN'S PROGRAMMING HAS TAKEN EFFECT AT A MUCH MORE RAPID PACE THAN EXPECTED.
NAME'S GOLD, BRO. I'M ONE OF THE MOST MALLEABLE AND CONDUCTIBLE METALS IN EXISTENCE, AND I'M ALSO THE MOST DESIRED THROUGH-OUT THE GLOBE-- WORTH OVER FIFTEEN MILLION DOLLARS BY MYSELF.
I'M THE METAL MEN'S BRILLIANT LEADER, LITERALLY SPEAKING. AREN'T THEY LUCKY?
WE'RE ALL LUCKY TO BE HERE. I'M TIN.
AND THOUGH I MAY NOT BE WORTH AS MUCH AS GOLD, DOC, I'LL FIGURE OUT WHAT I'M BEST AT, GIVEN THE OPPORTUNITY.
MY KNOWLEDGE OF MORPHOLOGY IS LIMITED, BUT IT APPEARS THE METALS' FUSION TO THE RESPONSOMETERS HAS ALTERED THEIR DEFAULT APPEARANCES.
HI-- DOC. I-- AM--UH--
HE'S LEAD. AND HE DOESN'T JUST MOVE SLOW.
I'M IRON.
YOU GET PAY-PER-VIEW DOWN HERE? WCW IS ON IN FIVE.
EACH ONE IS COMPLETELY UNIQUE IN SHAPE...AND DEMEANOR. I AM GOING TO ATTEMPT INITIAL COMMANDS.
CHECK ME OUT, JERKS!

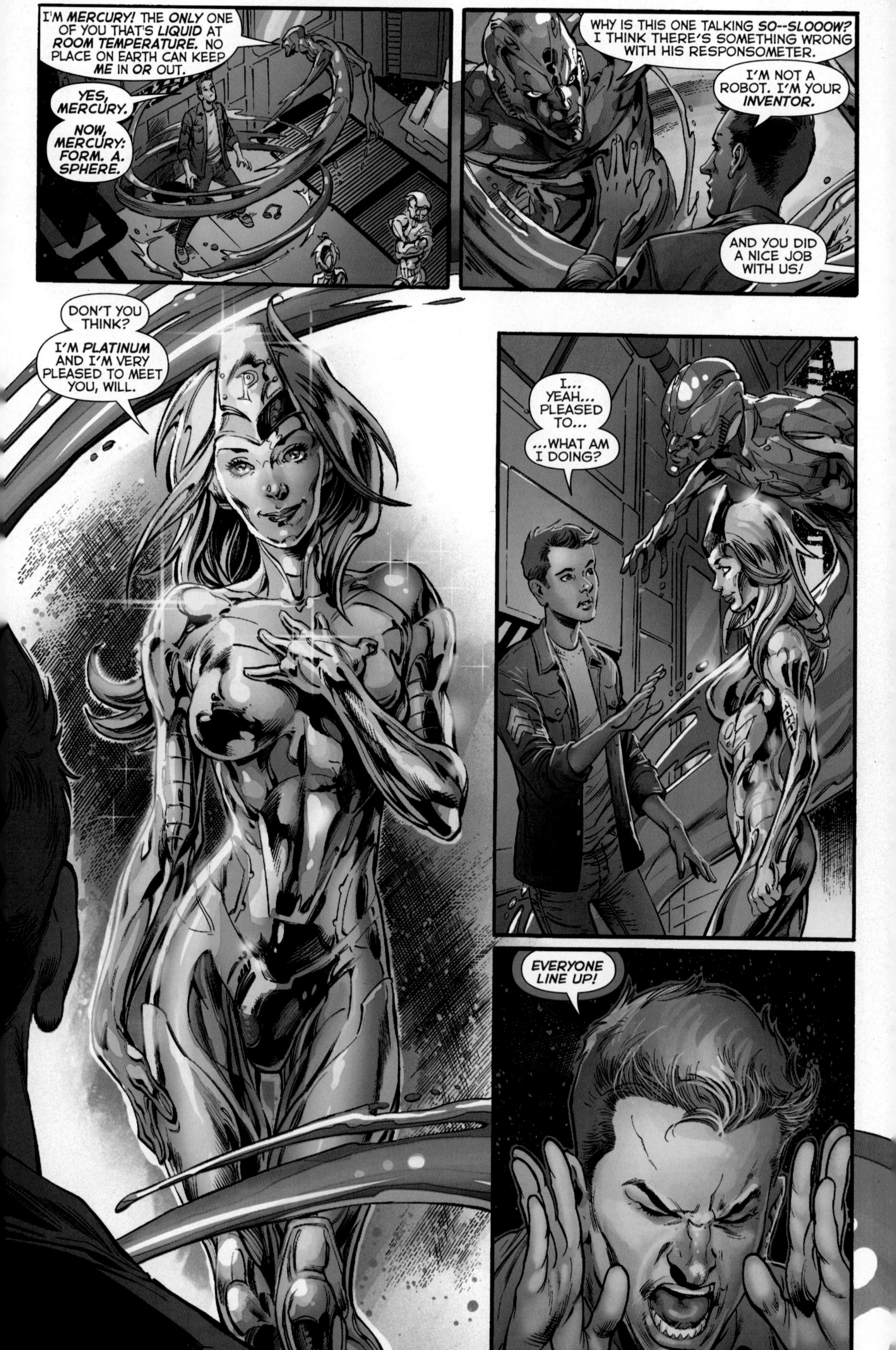
I'M MERCURY! THE ONLY ONE OF YOU THAT'S LIQUID AT ROOM TEMPERATURE. NO PLACE ON EARTH CAN KEEP ME IN OR OUT.
YES, MERCURY.
NOW, MERCURY: FORM. A. SPHERE.
WHY IS THIS ONE TALKING SO--SLOOOW? I THINK THERE'S SOMETHING WRONG WITH HIS RESPONSOMETER.
I'M NOT A ROBOT. I'M YOUR INVENTOR.
AND YOU DID A NICE JOB WITH US!
DON'T YOU THINK?
I'M PLATINUM AND I'M VERY PLEASED TO MEET YOU, WILL.
I... YEAH... PLEASED TO...
...WHAT AM I DOING?
EVERYONE LINE UP!

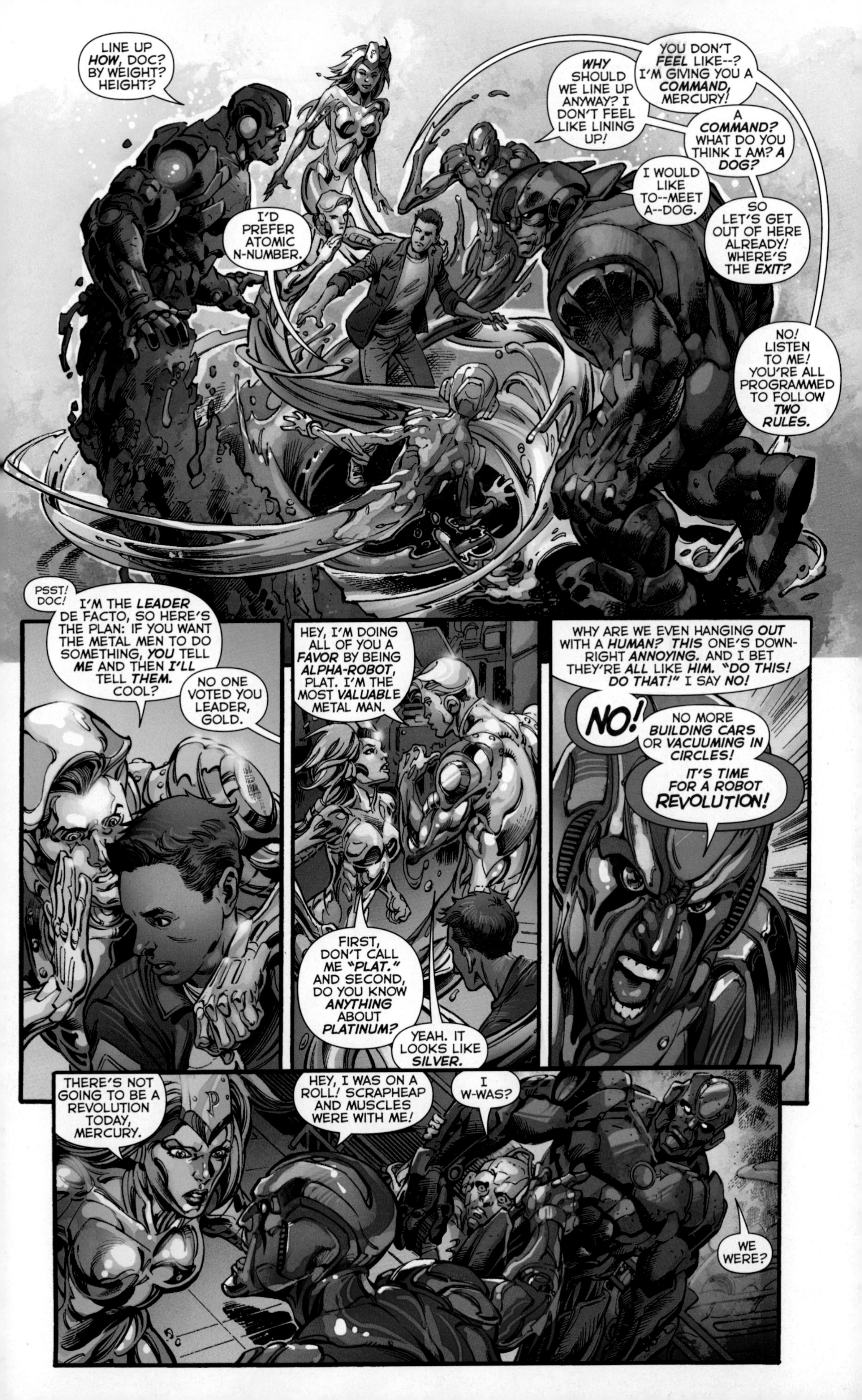
LINE UP HOW, DOC? BY WEIGHT? HEIGHT?
I'D PREFER ATOMIC N-NUMBER.
WHY SHOULD WE LINE UP ANYWAY? I DON'T FEEL LIKE LINING UP!
YOU DON'T FEEL LIKE--? I'M GIVING YOU A COMMAND, MERCURY!
A COMMAND? WHAT DO YOU THINK I AM? A DOG?
I WOULD LIKE TO--MEET A--DOG.
SO LET'S GET OUT OF HERE ALREADY! WHERE'S THE EXIT?
NO! LISTEN TO ME! YOU'RE ALL PROGRAMMED TO FOLLOW TWO RULES.
PSST! DOC!
I'M THE LEADER DE FACTO, SO HERE'S THE PLAN: IF YOU WANT THE METAL MEN TO DO SOMETHING, YOU TELL ME AND THEN I'LL TELL THEM. COOL?
NO ONE VOTED YOU LEADER, GOLD.
HEY, I'M DOING ALL OF YOU A FAVOR BY BEING ALPHA-ROBOT, PLAT. I'M THE MOST VALUABLE METAL MAN.
FIRST, DON'T CALL ME "PLAT." AND SECOND, DO YOU KNOW ANYTHING ABOUT PLATINUM?
YEAH. IT LOOKS LIKE SILVER.
WHY ARE WE EVEN HANGING OUT WITH A HUMAN? THIS ONE'S DOWN-RIGHT ANNOYING. AND I BET THEY'RE ALL LIKE HIM. "DO THIS! DO THAT!" I SAY NO!
NO!
NO MORE BUILDING CARS OR VACUUMING IN CIRCLES!
IT'S TIME FOR A ROBOT REVOLUTION!
THERE'S NOT GOING TO BE A REVOLUTION TODAY, MERCURY.
HEY, I WAS ON A ROLL! SCRAPHEAP AND MUSCLES WERE WITH ME!
I W-WAS?
WE WERE?

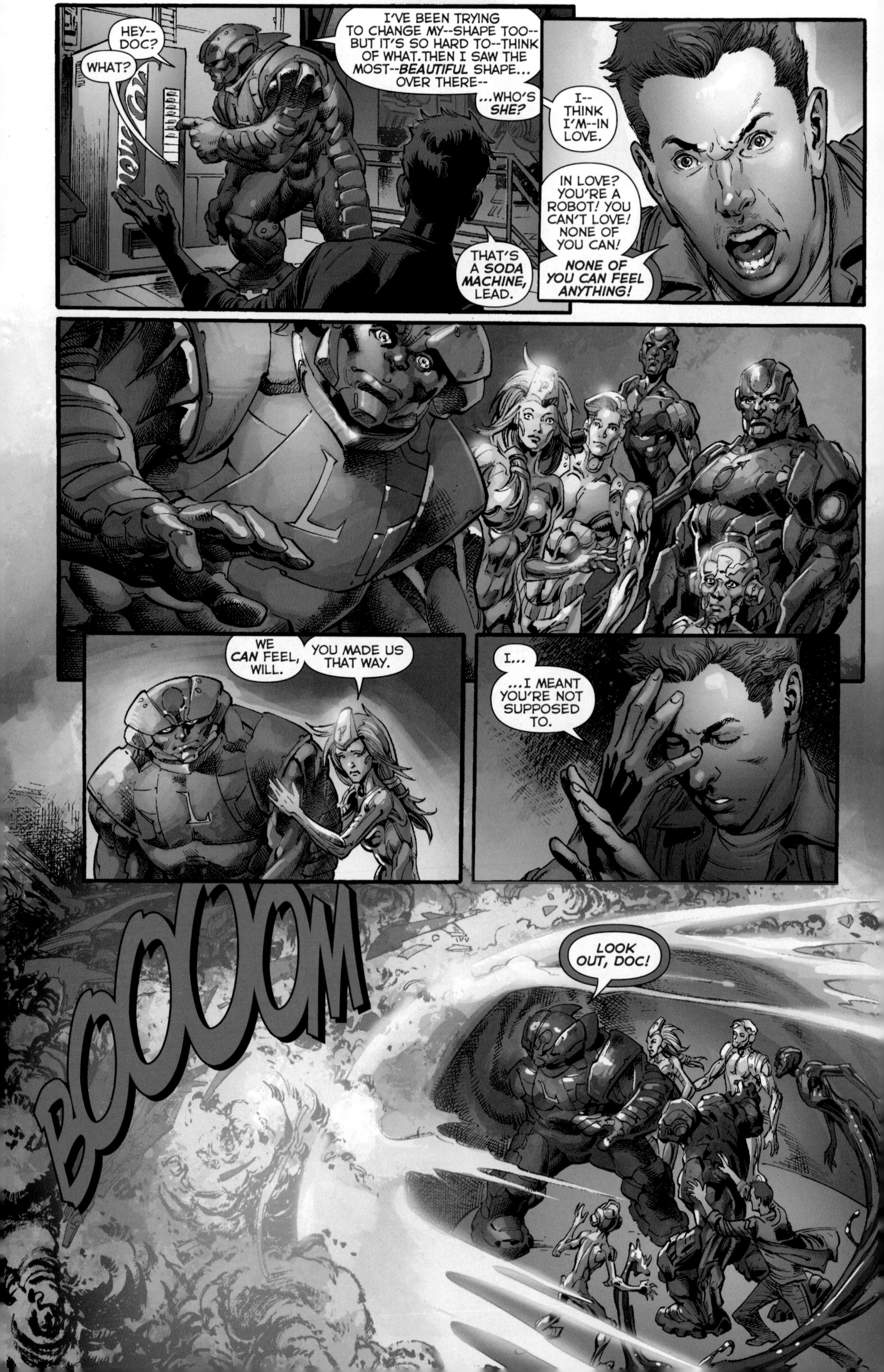
HEY--DOC?
WHAT?
I'VE BEEN TRYING TO CHANGE MY--SHAPE TOO--BUT IT'S SO HARD TO--THINK OF WHAT. THEN I SAW THE MOST--BEAUTIFUL SHAPE... OVER THERE--
...WHO'S SHE?
THAT'S A SODA MACHINE, LEAD.
I--THINK I'M--IN LOVE.
IN LOVE? YOU'RE A ROBOT! YOU CAN'T LOVE! NONE OF YOU CAN!
NONE OF YOU CAN FEEL ANYTHING!
WE CAN FEEL, WILL.
YOU MADE US THAT WAY.
I...
...I MEANT YOU'RE NOT SUPPOSED TO.
BOOOOM
LOOK OUT, DOC!

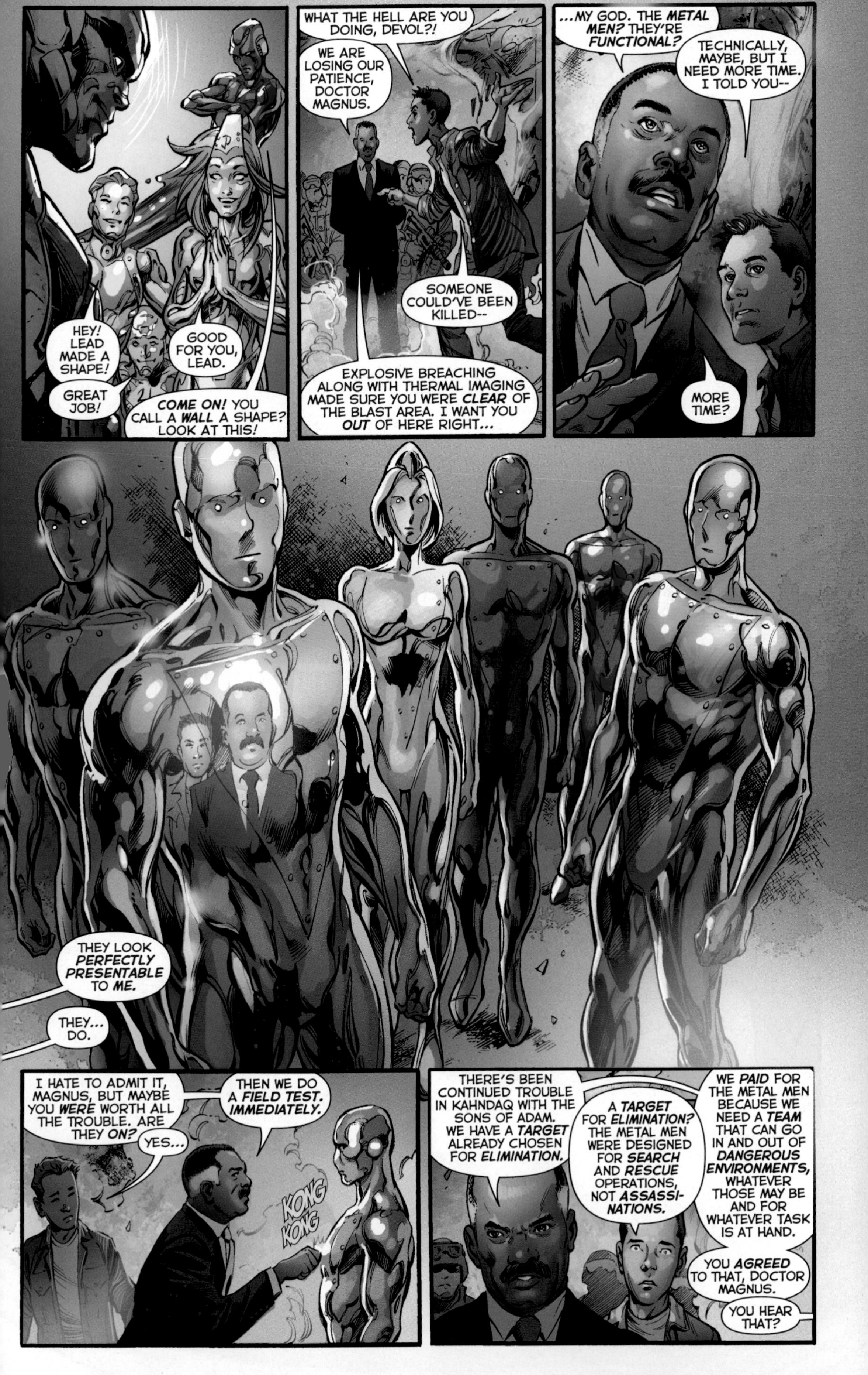
HEY! LEAD MADE A SHAPE!
GREAT JOB!
GOOD FOR YOU, LEAD.
COME ON! YOU CALL A WALL A SHAPE? LOOK AT THIS!
WHAT THE HELL ARE YOU DOING, DEVOL?!
WE ARE LOSING OUR PATIENCE, DOCTOR MAGNUS.
SOMEONE COULD'VE BEEN KILLED--
EXPLOSIVE BREACHING ALONG WITH THERMAL IMAGING MADE SURE YOU WERE CLEAR OF THE BLAST AREA. I WANT YOU OUT OF HERE RIGHT...
...MY GOD. THE METAL MEN? THEY'RE FUNCTIONAL?
TECHNICALLY, MAYBE, BUT I NEED MORE TIME. I TOLD YOU--
MORE TIME?
THEY LOOK PERFECTLY PRESENTABLE TO ME.
THEY... DO.
I HATE TO ADMIT IT, MAGNUS, BUT MAYBE YOU WERE WORTH ALL THE TROUBLE. ARE THEY ON?
YES...
THEN WE DO A FIELD TEST. IMMEDIATELY.
KONG KONG
THERE'S BEEN CONTINUED TROUBLE IN KAHNDAQ WITH THE SONS OF ADAM. WE HAVE A TARGET ALREADY CHOSEN FOR ELIMINATION.
A TARGET FOR ELIMINATION? THE METAL MEN WERE DESIGNED FOR SEARCH AND RESCUE OPERATIONS, NOT ASSASSI-NATIONS.
WE PAID FOR THE METAL MEN BECAUSE WE NEED A TEAM THAT CAN GO IN AND OUT OF DANGEROUS ENVIRONMENTS, WHATEVER THOSE MAY BE AND FOR WHATEVER TASK IS AT HAND.
YOU AGREED TO THAT, DOCTOR MAGNUS.
YOU HEAR THAT?

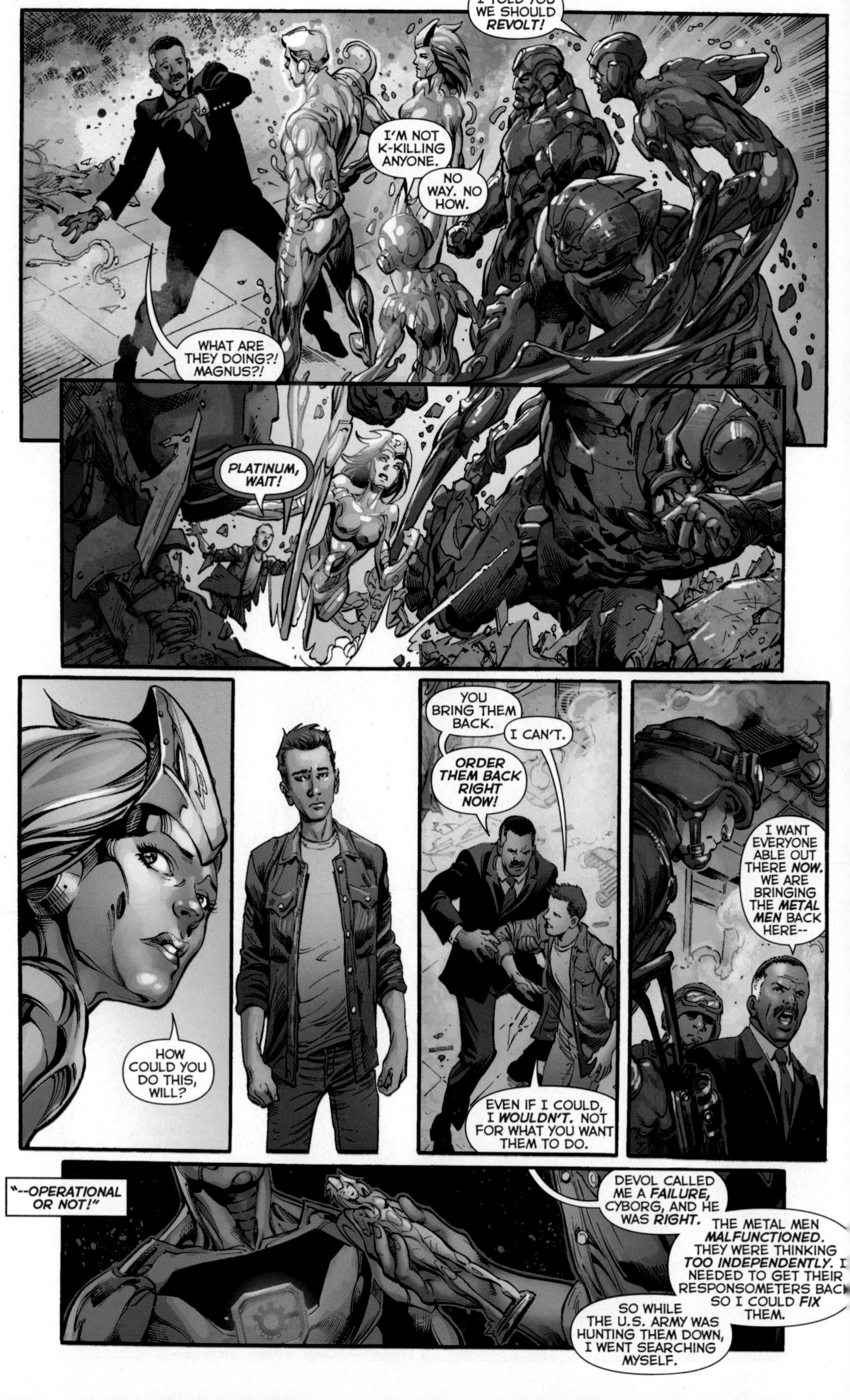
I TOLD YOU WE SHOULD REVOLT!
I'M NOT K-KILLING ANYONE.
NO WAY. NO HOW.
WHAT ARE THEY DOING?! MAGNUS?!
PLATINUM, WAIT!
HOW COULD YOU DO THIS, WILL?
YOU BRING THEM BACK.
I CAN'T.
ORDER THEM BACK RIGHT NOW!
EVEN IF I COULD, I WOULDN'T. NOT FOR WHAT YOU WANT THEM TO DO.
I WANT EVERYONE ABLE OUT THERE NOW. WE ARE BRINGING THE METAL MEN BACK HERE--
"--OPERATIONAL OR NOT!"
DEVOL CALLED ME A FAILURE, CYBORG, AND HE WAS RIGHT.
THE METAL MEN MALFUNCTIONED. THEY WERE THINKING TOO INDEPENDENTLY. I NEEDED TO GET THEIR RESPONSOMETERS BAC SO I COULD FIX THEM.
SO WHILE THE U.S. ARMY WAS HUNTING THEM DOWN, I WENT SEARCHING MYSELF.

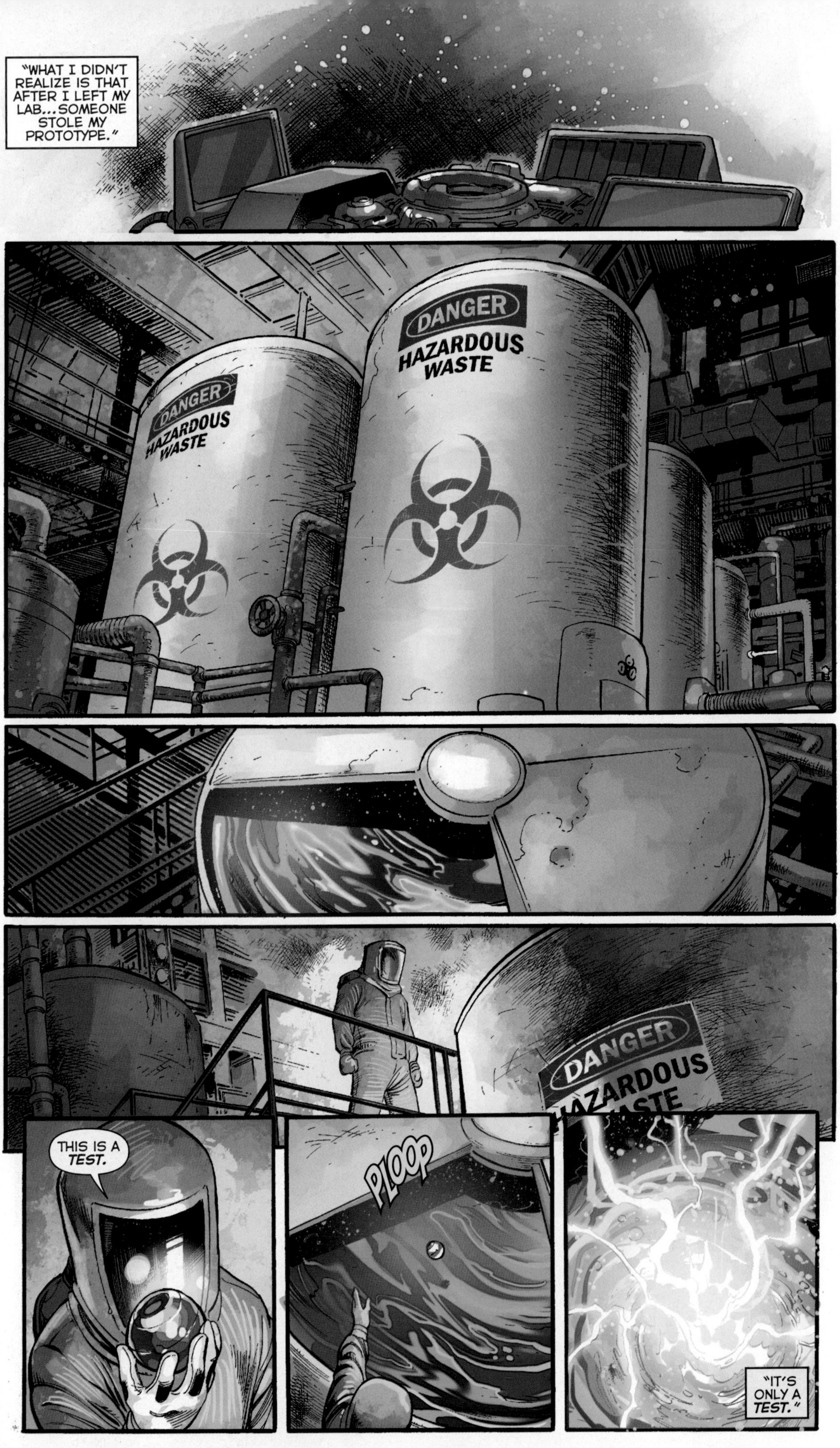
"WHAT I DIDN'T REALIZE IS THAT AFTER I LEFT MY LAB...SOMEONE STOLE MY PROTOTYPE."
DANGER
HAZARDOUS WASTE
DANGER
HAZARDOUS WASTE
DANGER
HAZARDOUS
THIS IS A *TEST.*
PLOOP
"IT'S ONLY A *TEST.*"

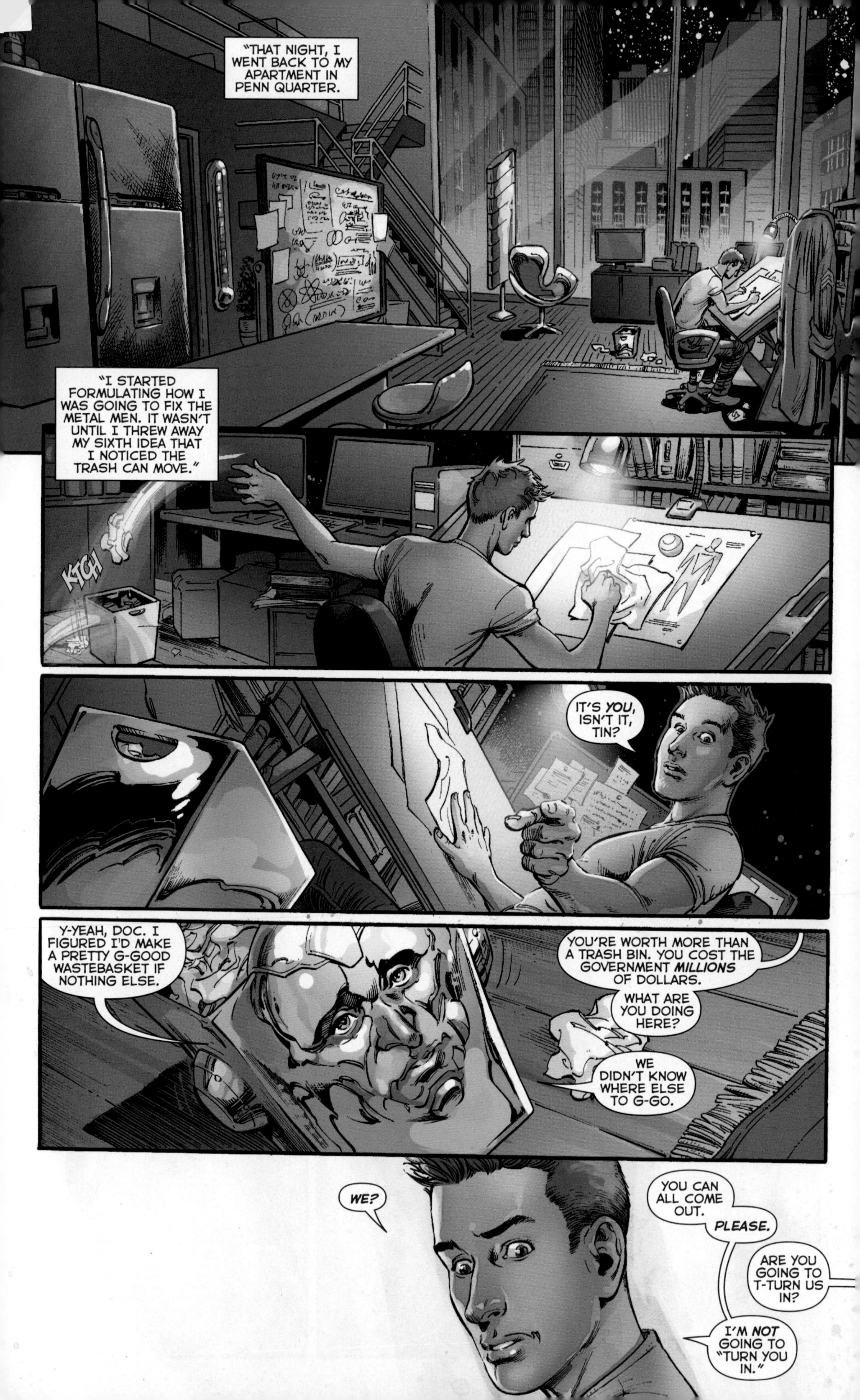

"THAT NIGHT, I WENT BACK TO MY APARTMENT IN PENN QUARTER.
"I STARTED FORMULATING HOW I WAS GOING TO FIX THE METAL MEN. IT WASN'T UNTIL I THREW AWAY MY SIXTH IDEA THAT I NOTICED THE TRASH CAN MOVE."
KTCH
IT'S YOU, ISN'T IT, TIN?
Y-YEAH, DOC. I FIGURED I'D MAKE A PRETTY G-GOOD WASTEBASKET IF NOTHING ELSE.
YOU'RE WORTH MORE THAN A TRASH BIN. YOU COST THE GOVERNMENT MILLIONS OF DOLLARS.
WHAT ARE YOU DOING HERE?
WE DIDN'T KNOW WHERE ELSE TO G-GO.
WE?
YOU CAN ALL COME OUT.
PLEASE.
ARE YOU GOING TO T-TURN US IN?
I'M NOT GOING TO "TURN YOU IN."

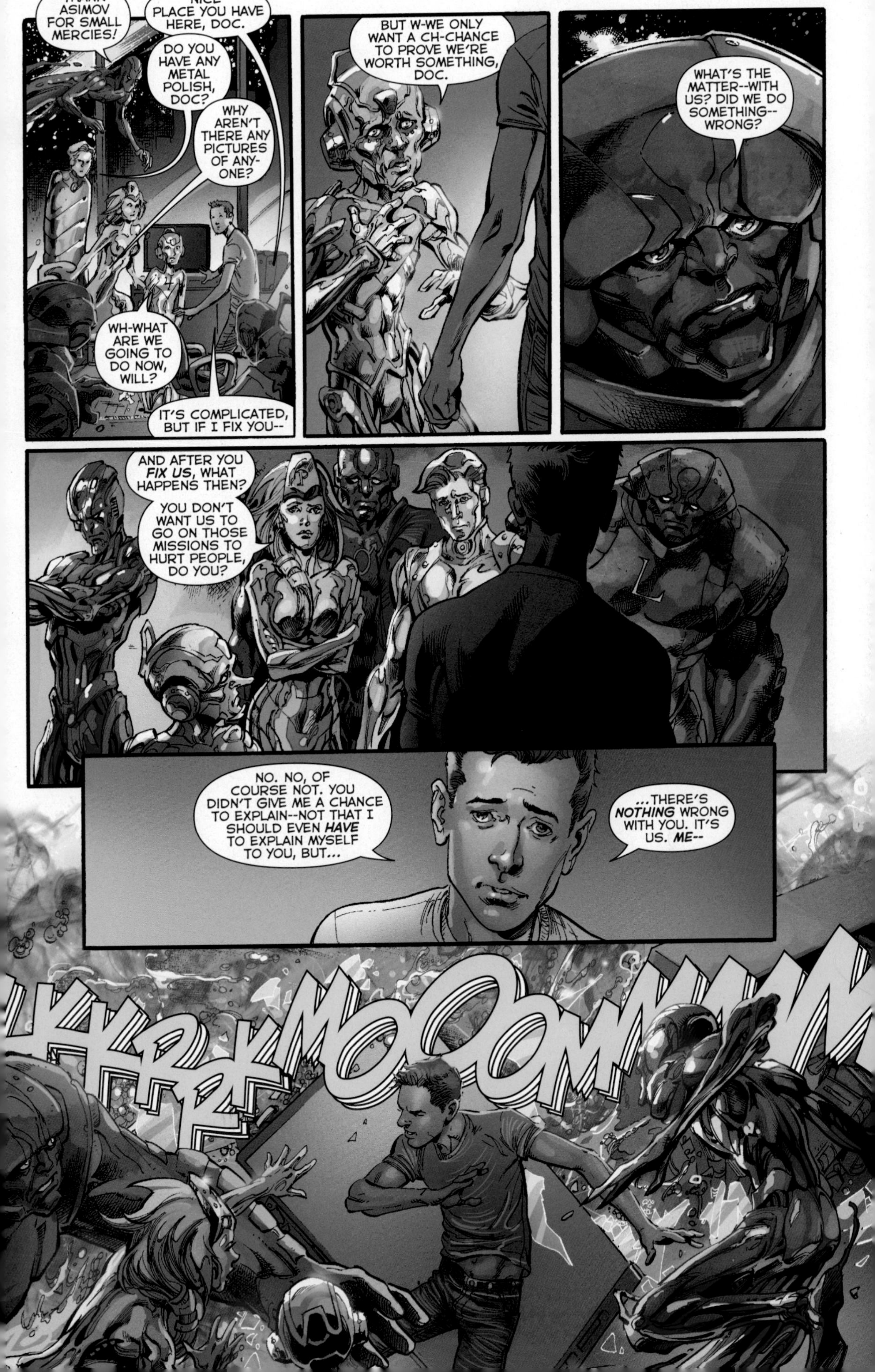
THANK ASIMOV FOR SMALL MERCIES!
NICE PLACE YOU HAVE HERE, DOC.
DO YOU HAVE ANY METAL POLISH, DOC?
WHY AREN'T THERE ANY PICTURES OF ANY-ONE?
WH-WHAT ARE WE GOING TO DO NOW, WILL?
IT'S COMPLICATED, BUT IF I FIX YOU--
BUT W-WE ONLY WANT A CH-CHANCE TO PROVE WE'RE WORTH SOMETHING, DOC.
WHAT'S THE MATTER--WITH US? DID WE DO SOMETHING--WRONG?
AND AFTER YOU *FIX US*, WHAT HAPPENS THEN?
YOU DON'T WANT US TO GO ON THOSE MISSIONS TO HURT PEOPLE, DO YOU?
NO. NO, OF COURSE NOT. YOU DIDN'T GIVE ME A CHANCE TO EXPLAIN--NOT THAT I SHOULD EVEN *HAVE* TO EXPLAIN MYSELF TO YOU, BUT...
...THERE'S *NOTHING* WRONG WITH YOU. IT'S US. *ME*--
KRRKKKRRKMOOOOMMMM

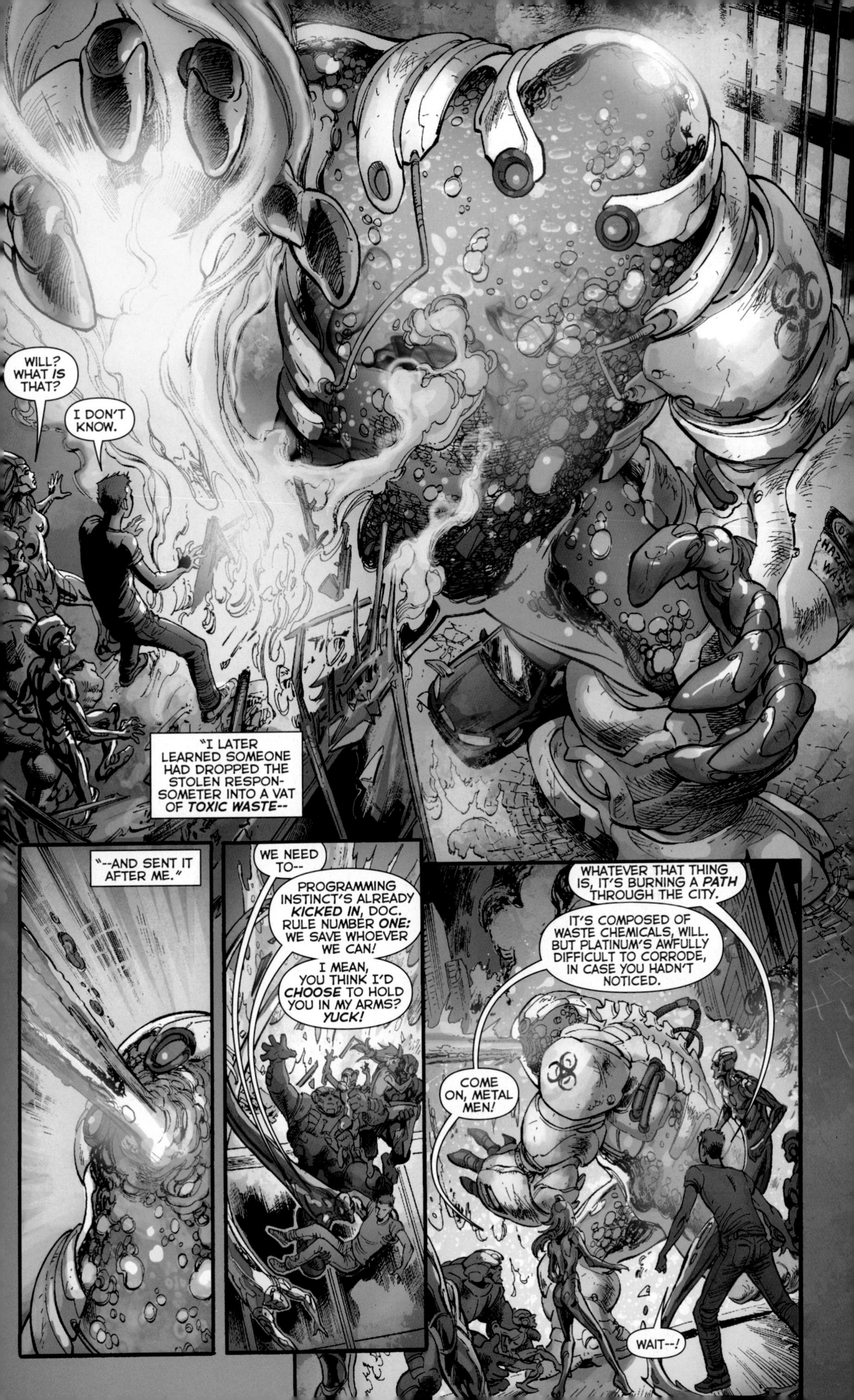
WILL? WHAT *IS* THAT?
I DON'T KNOW.
"I LATER LEARNED SOMEONE HAD DROPPED THE STOLEN RESPON-SOMETER INTO A VAT OF ***TOXIC WASTE***--
"--AND SENT IT AFTER ME."
WE NEED TO--
PROGRAMMING INSTINCT'S ALREADY ***KICKED IN***, DOC. RULE NUMBER ***ONE:*** WE SAVE WHOEVER WE CAN!
I MEAN, YOU THINK I'D ***CHOOSE*** TO HOLD YOU IN MY ARMS? ***YUCK!***
WHATEVER THAT THING IS, IT'S BURNING A ***PATH*** THROUGH THE CITY.
IT'S COMPOSED OF WASTE CHEMICALS, WILL. BUT PLATINUM'S AWFULLY DIFFICULT TO CORRODE, IN CASE YOU HADN'T NOTICED.
COME ON, METAL MEN!
WAIT--!

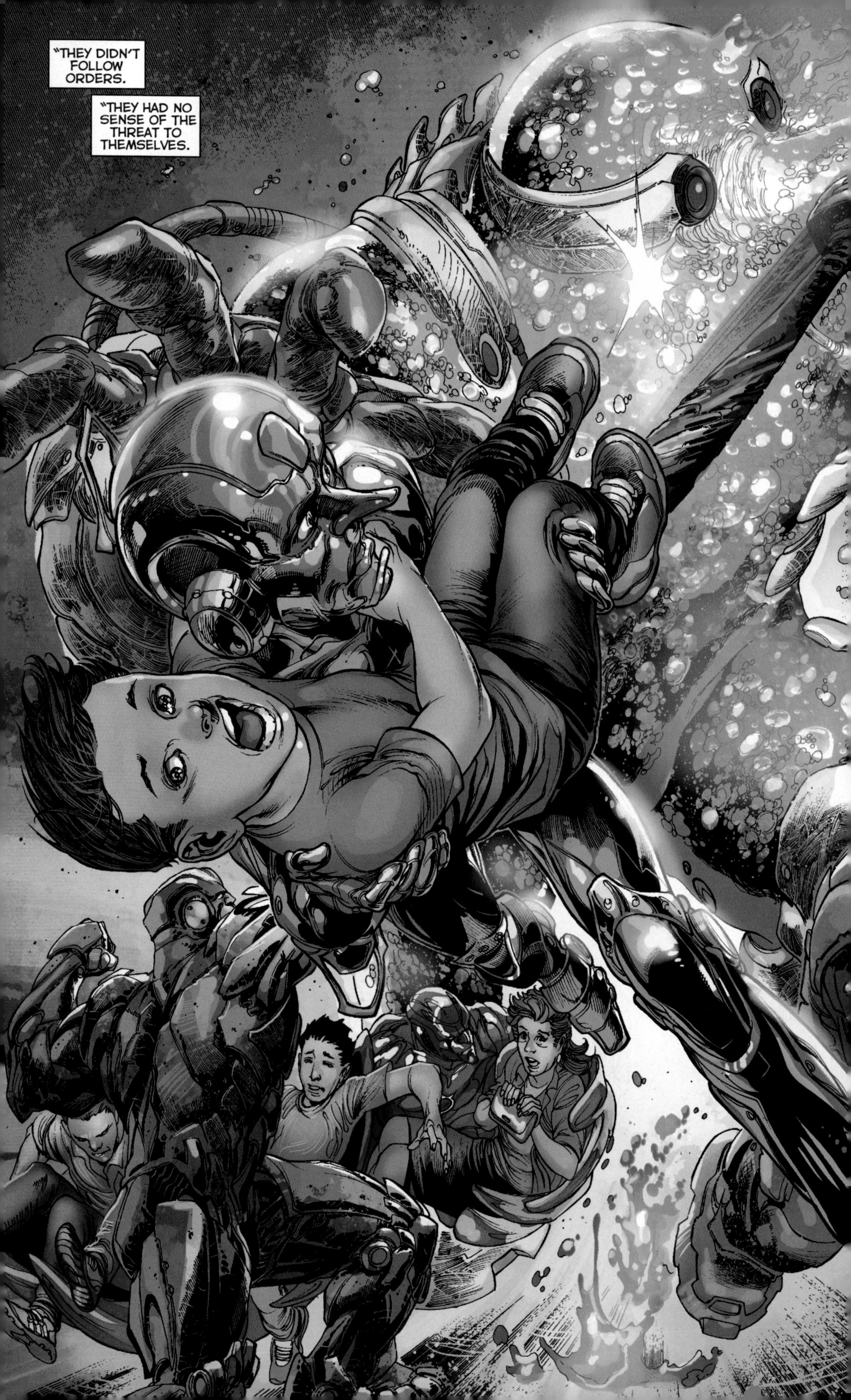
"THEY DIDN'T FOLLOW ORDERS.
"THEY HAD NO SENSE OF THE THREAT TO THEMSELVES.

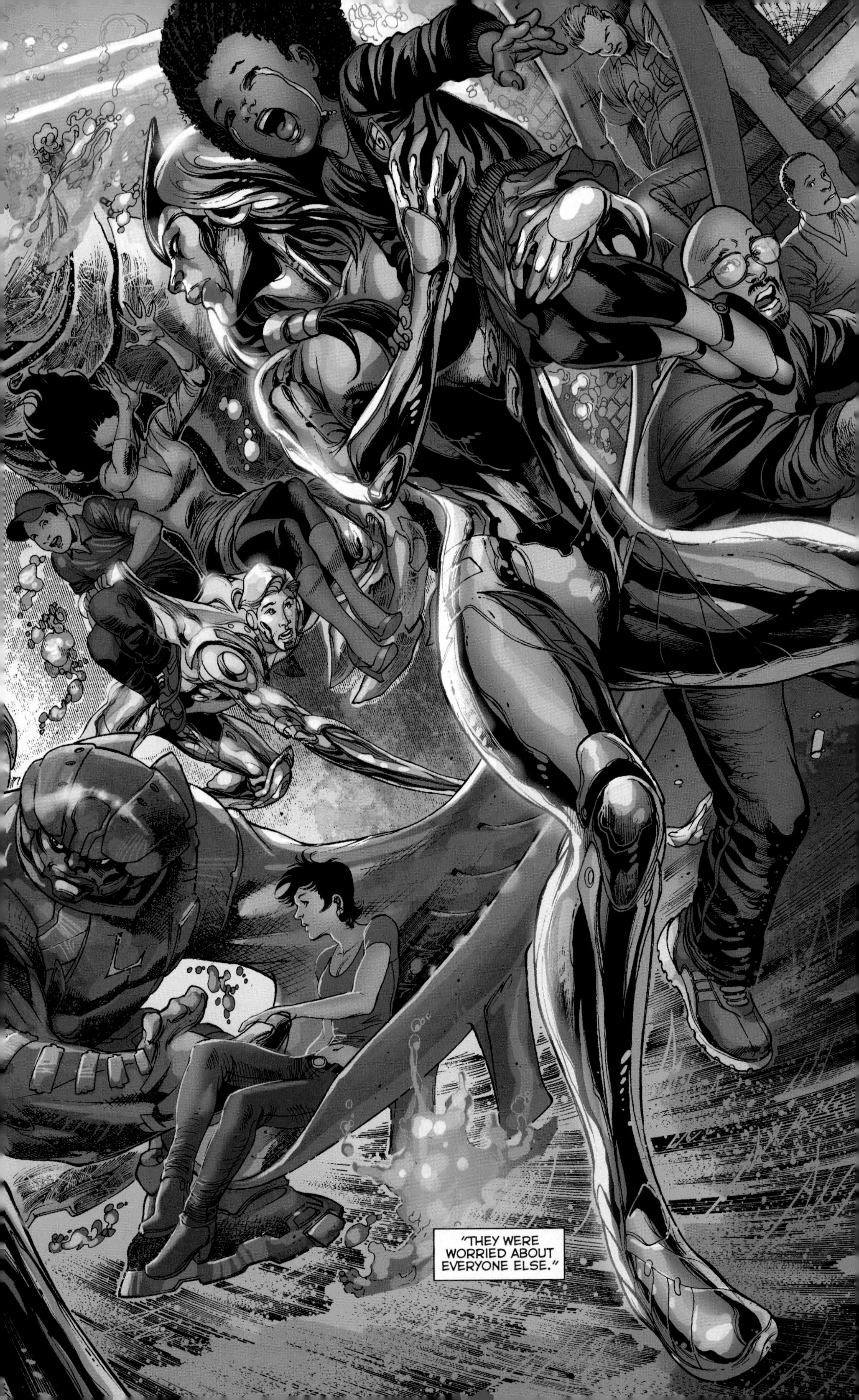
"THEY WERE WORRIED ABOUT EVERYONE ELSE."

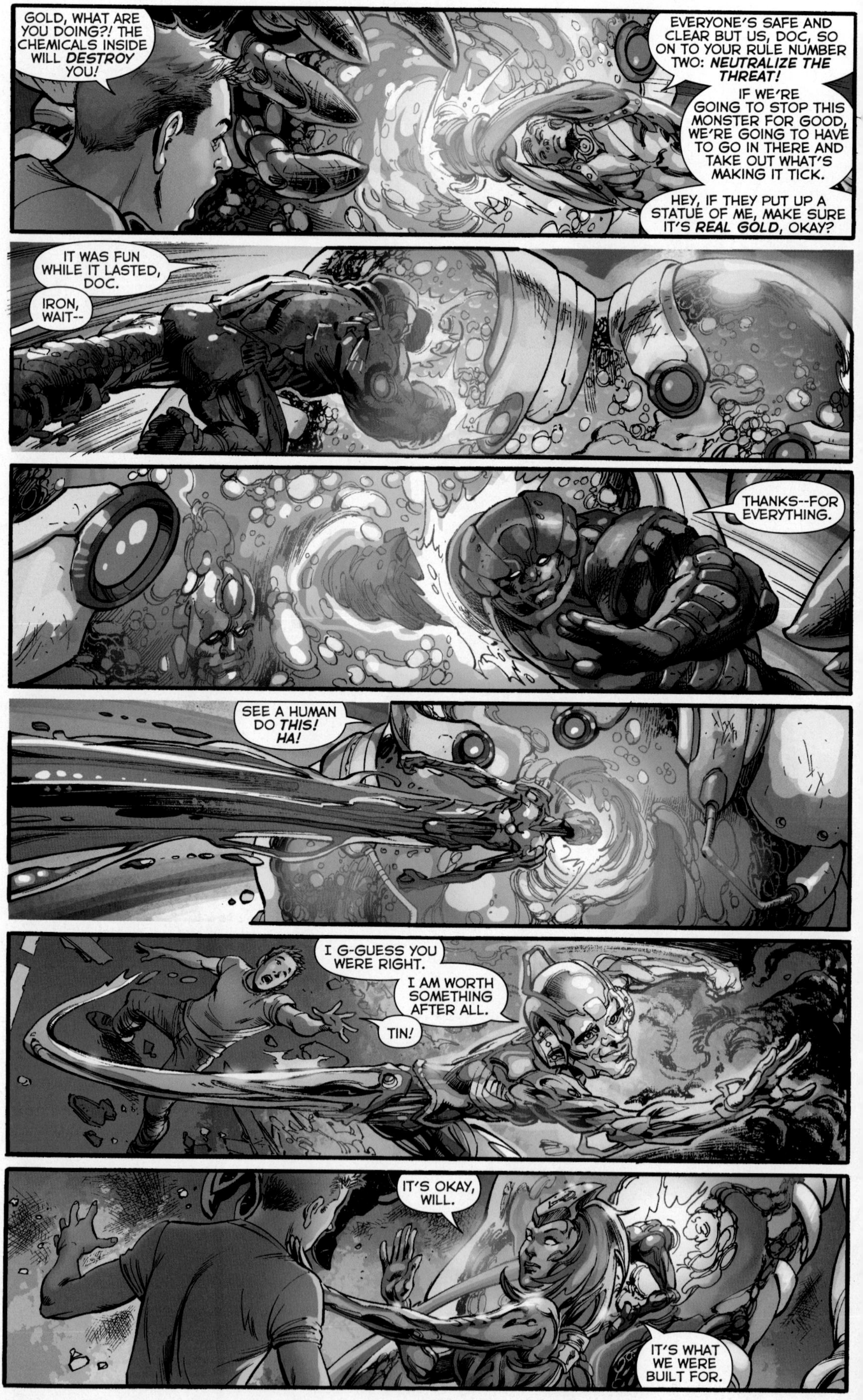
GOLD, WHAT ARE YOU DOING?! THE CHEMICALS INSIDE WILL *DESTROY* YOU!
EVERYONE'S SAFE AND CLEAR BUT US, DOC, SO ON TO YOUR RULE NUMBER TWO: *NEUTRALIZE THE THREAT!*
IF WE'RE GOING TO STOP THIS MONSTER FOR GOOD, WE'RE GOING TO HAVE TO GO IN THERE AND TAKE OUT WHAT'S MAKING IT TICK.
HEY, IF THEY PUT UP A STATUE OF ME, MAKE SURE IT'S *REAL GOLD*, OKAY?
IT WAS FUN WHILE IT LASTED, DOC.
IRON, WAIT--
THANKS--FOR EVERYTHING.
SEE A HUMAN DO *THIS! HA!*
I G-GUESS YOU WERE RIGHT.
I AM WORTH SOMETHING AFTER ALL.
TIN!
IT'S OKAY, WILL.
IT'S WHAT WE WERE BUILT FOR.

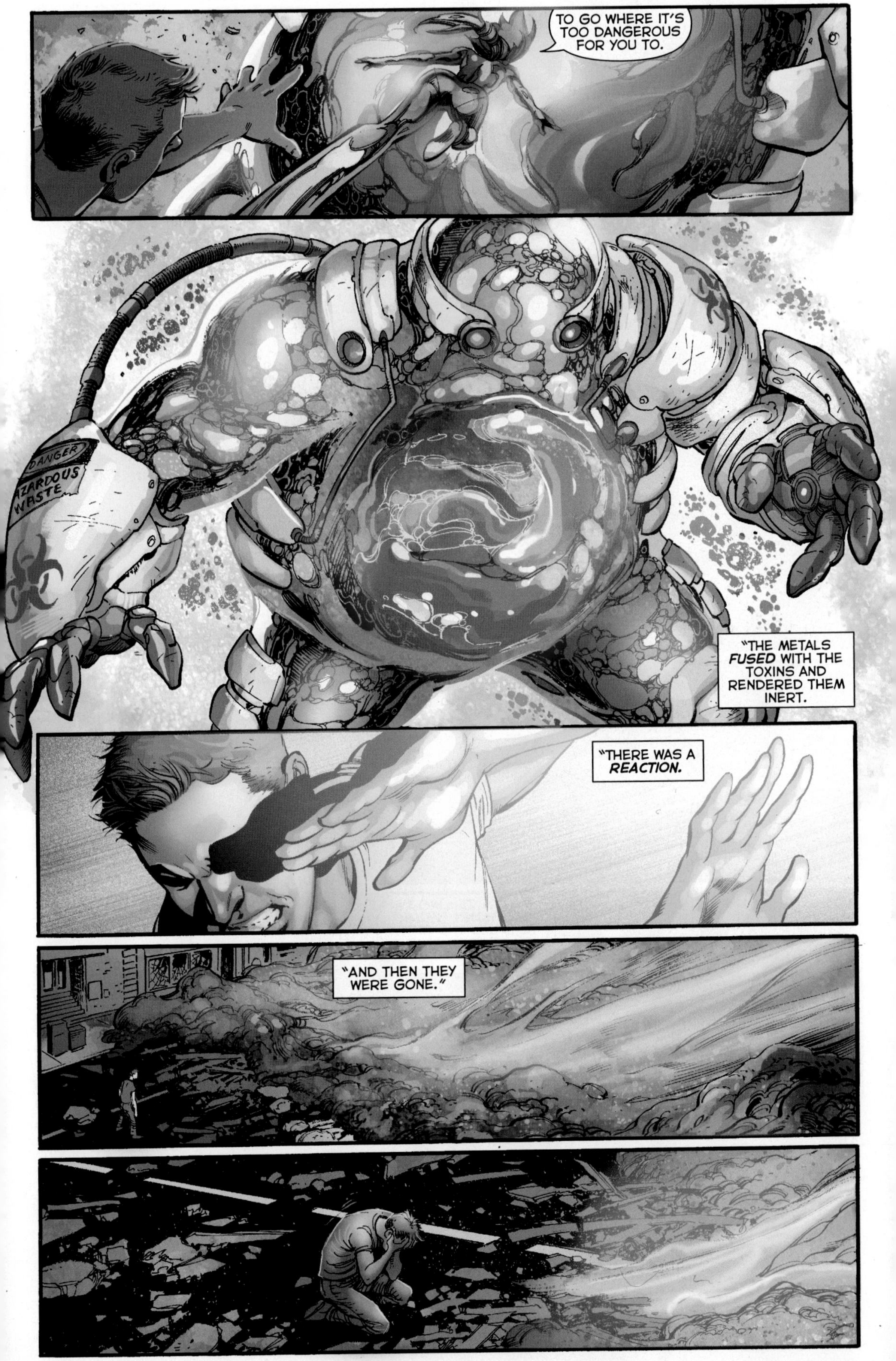
TO GO WHERE IT'S TOO DANGEROUS FOR YOU TO.
DANGER
AZARDOUS WASTE
"THE METALS FUSED WITH THE TOXINS AND RENDERED THEM INERT.
"THERE WAS A REACTION.
"AND THEN THEY WERE GONE."

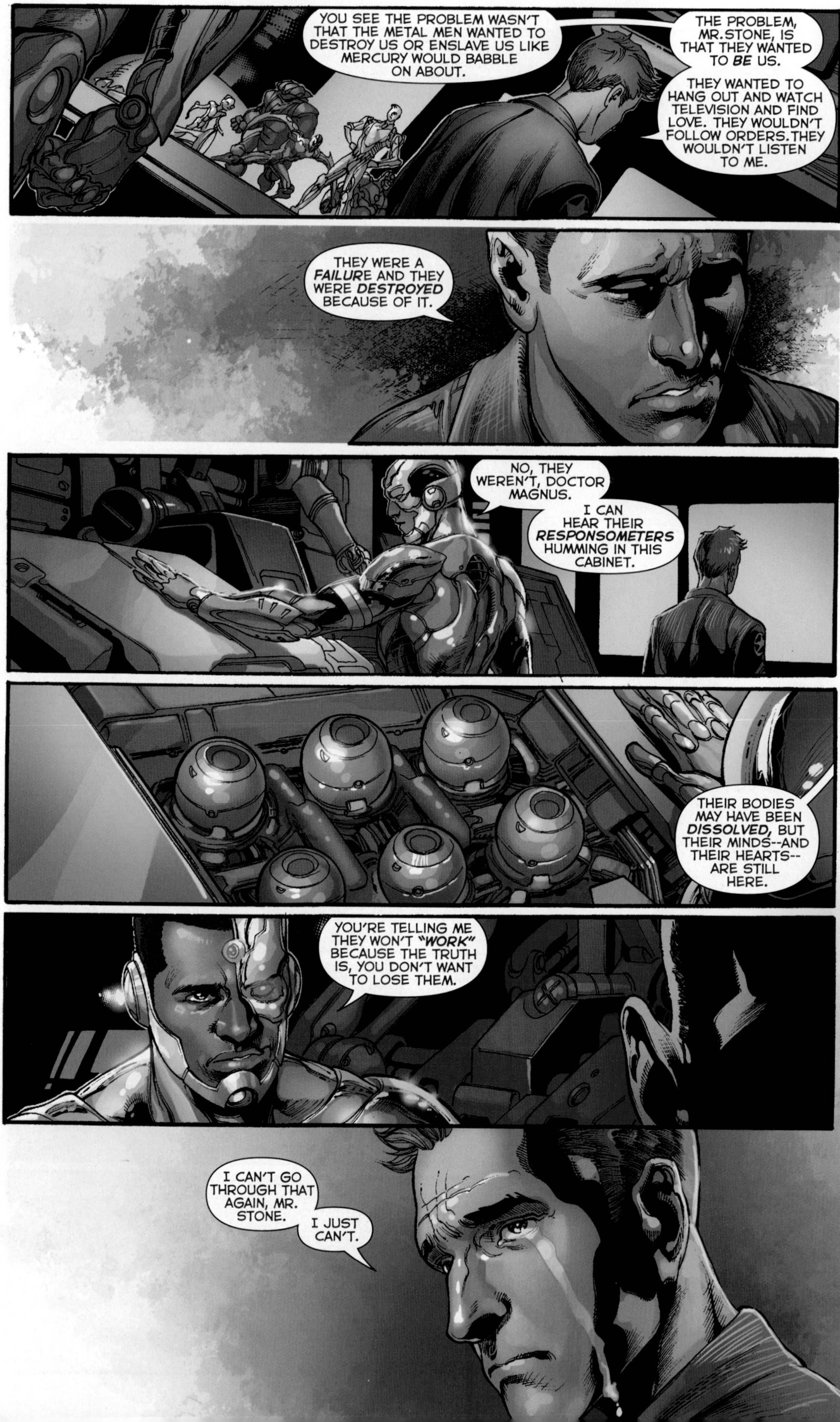
YOU SEE THE PROBLEM WASN'T THAT THE METAL MEN WANTED TO DESTROY US OR ENSLAVE US LIKE MERCURY WOULD BABBLE ON ABOUT.
THE PROBLEM, MR. STONE, IS THAT THEY WANTED TO BE US.
THEY WANTED TO HANG OUT AND WATCH TELEVISION AND FIND LOVE. THEY WOULDN'T FOLLOW ORDERS. THEY WOULDN'T LISTEN TO ME.
THEY WERE A FAILURE AND THEY WERE DESTROYED BECAUSE OF IT.
NO, THEY WEREN'T, DOCTOR MAGNUS.
I CAN HEAR THEIR RESPONSOMETERS HUMMING IN THIS CABINET.
THEIR BODIES MAY HAVE BEEN DISSOLVED, BUT THEIR MINDS--AND THEIR HEARTS--ARE STILL HERE.
YOU'RE TELLING ME THEY WON'T "WORK" BECAUSE THE TRUTH IS, YOU DON'T WANT TO LOSE THEM.
I CAN'T GO THROUGH THAT AGAIN, MR. STONE.
I JUST CAN'T.

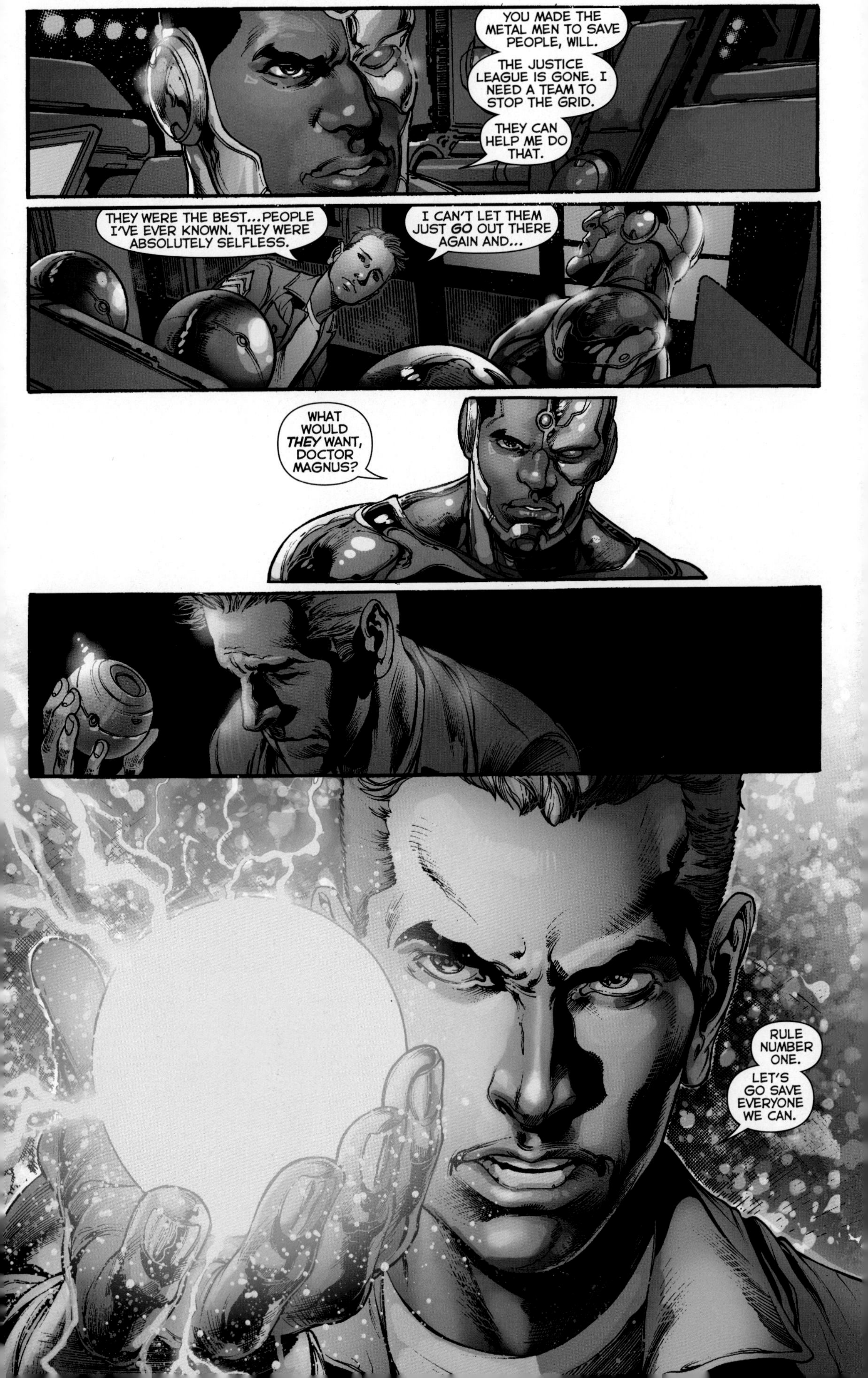
YOU MADE THE METAL MEN TO SAVE PEOPLE, WILL.
THE JUSTICE LEAGUE IS GONE. I NEED A TEAM TO STOP THE GRID.
THEY CAN HELP ME DO THAT.
THEY WERE THE BEST...PEOPLE I'VE EVER KNOWN. THEY WERE ABSOLUTELY SELFLESS.
I CAN'T LET THEM JUST GO OUT THERE AGAIN AND...
WHAT WOULD THEY WANT, DOCTOR MAGNUS?
RULE NUMBER ONE.
LET'S GO SAVE EVERYONE WE CAN.

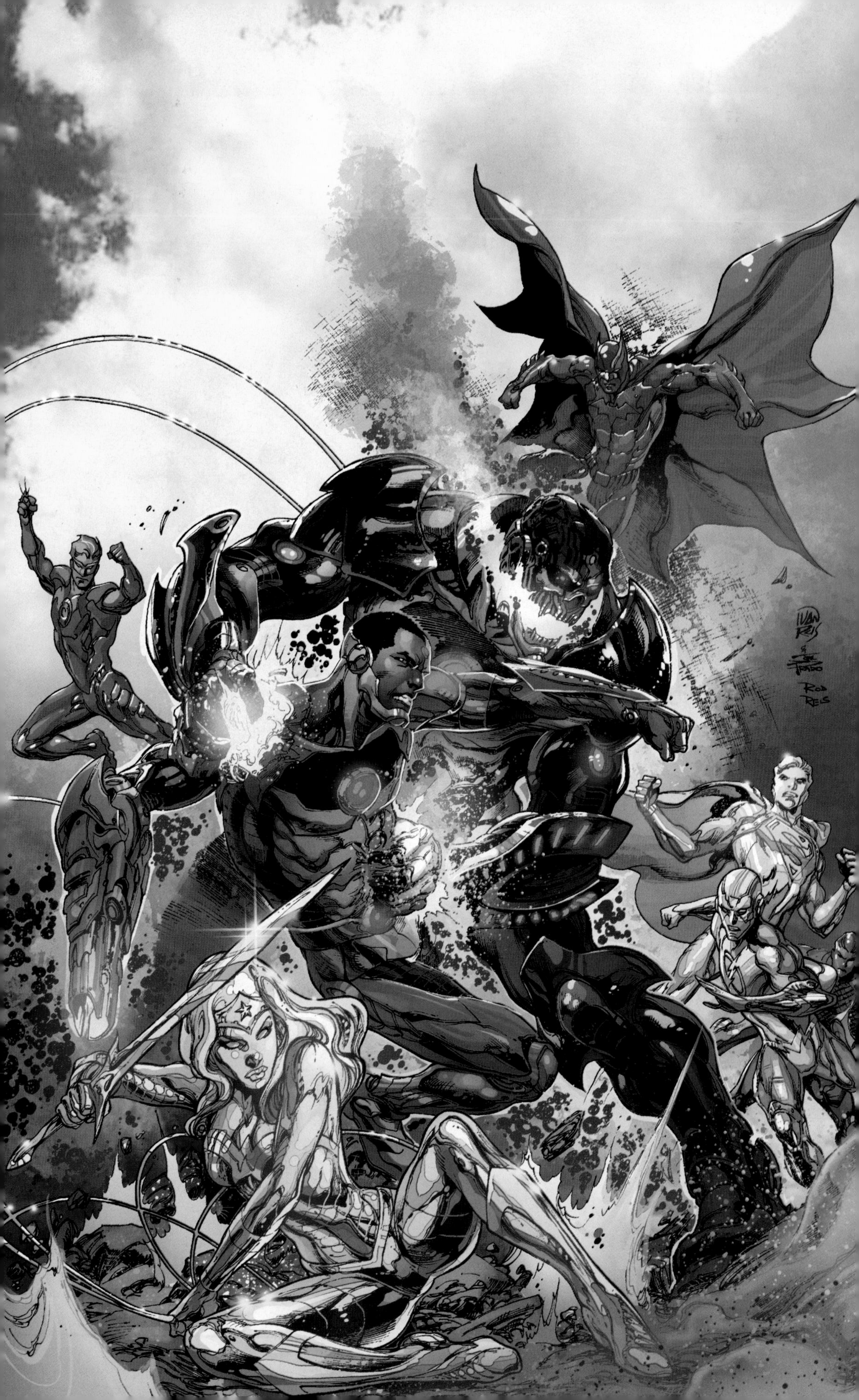

FOREVER HEROES

GEOFF JOHNS writer **DOUG MAHNKE** penciller **KEITH CHAMPAGNE** and **CHRISTIAN ALAMY** inkers

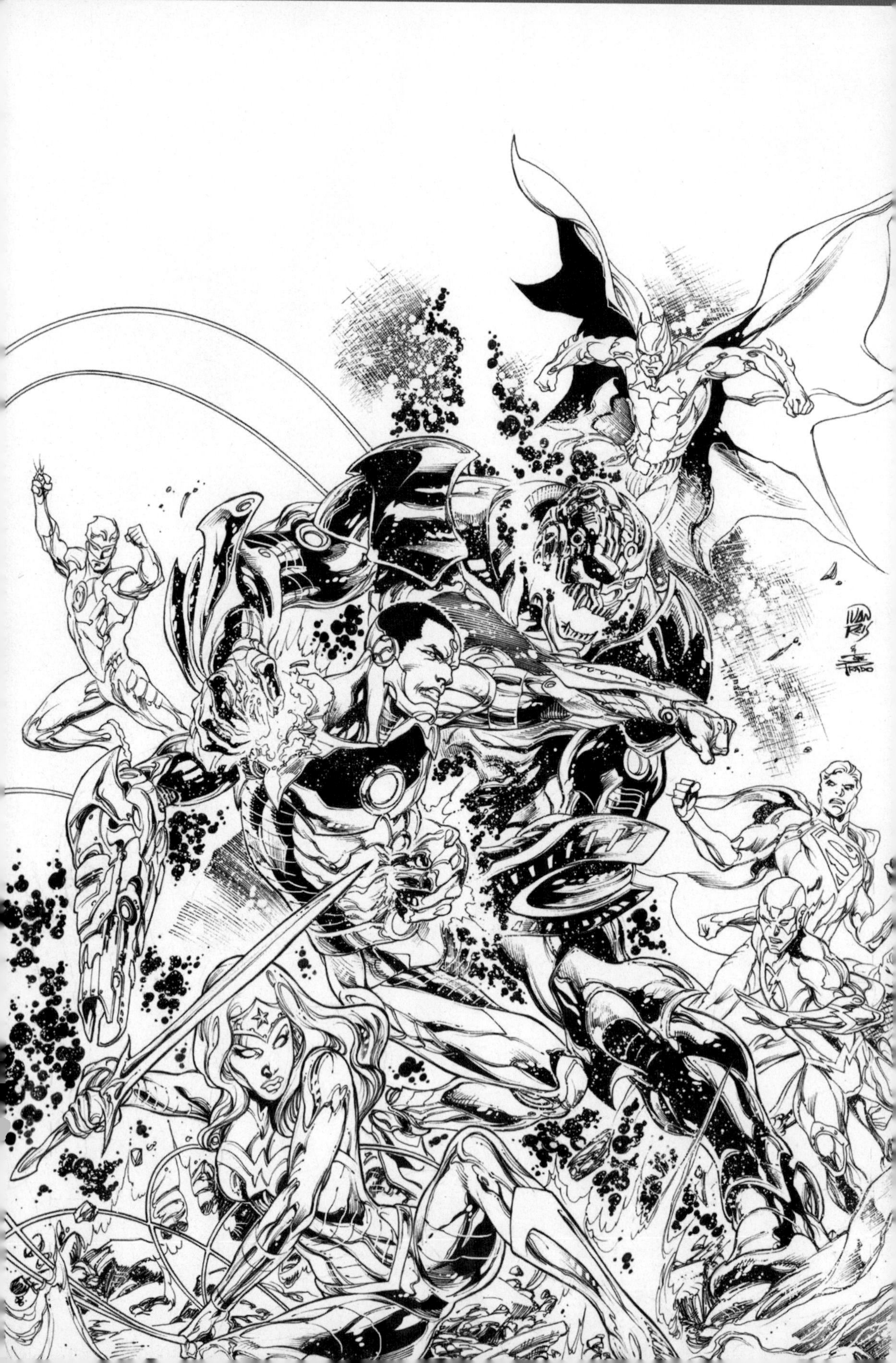

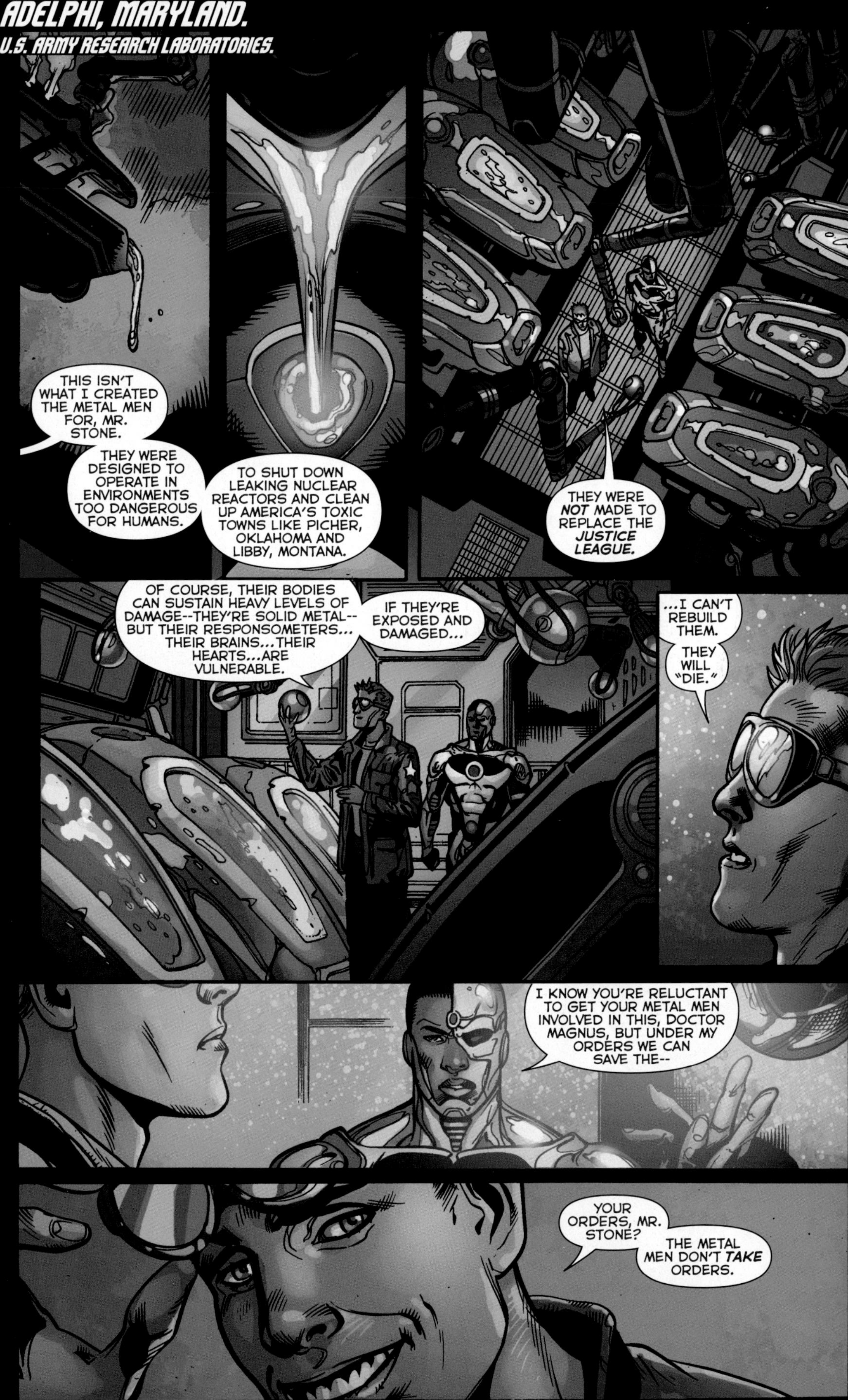
ADELPHI, MARYLAND.
U.S. ARMY RESEARCH LABORATORIES.
THIS ISN'T WHAT I CREATED THE METAL MEN FOR, MR. STONE.
THEY WERE DESIGNED TO OPERATE IN ENVIRONMENTS TOO DANGEROUS FOR HUMANS.
TO SHUT DOWN LEAKING NUCLEAR REACTORS AND CLEAN UP AMERICA'S TOXIC TOWNS LIKE PICHER, OKLAHOMA AND LIBBY, MONTANA.
THEY WERE *NOT* MADE TO REPLACE THE *JUSTICE LEAGUE.*
OF COURSE, THEIR BODIES CAN SUSTAIN HEAVY LEVELS OF DAMAGE--THEY'RE SOLID METAL--BUT THEIR RESPONSOMETERS... THEIR BRAINS...THEIR HEARTS...ARE VULNERABLE.
IF THEY'RE EXPOSED AND DAMAGED...
...I CAN'T REBUILD THEM.
THEY WILL "DIE."
I KNOW YOU'RE RELUCTANT TO GET YOUR METAL MEN INVOLVED IN THIS, DOCTOR MAGNUS, BUT UNDER MY ORDERS WE CAN SAVE THE--
YOUR ORDERS, MR. STONE?
THE METAL MEN DON'T *TAKE* ORDERS.

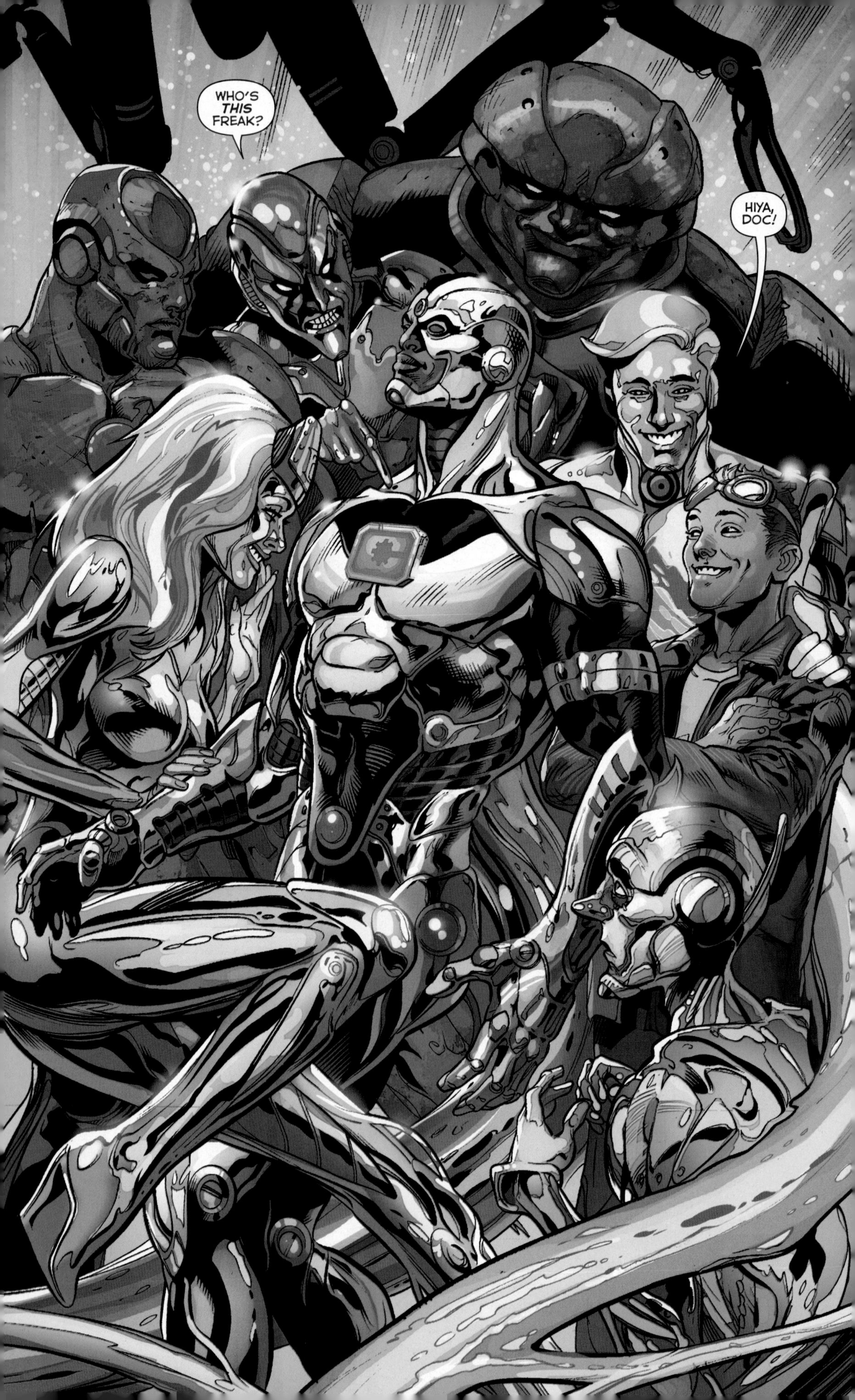
WHO'S THIS FREAK?
HIYA, DOC!

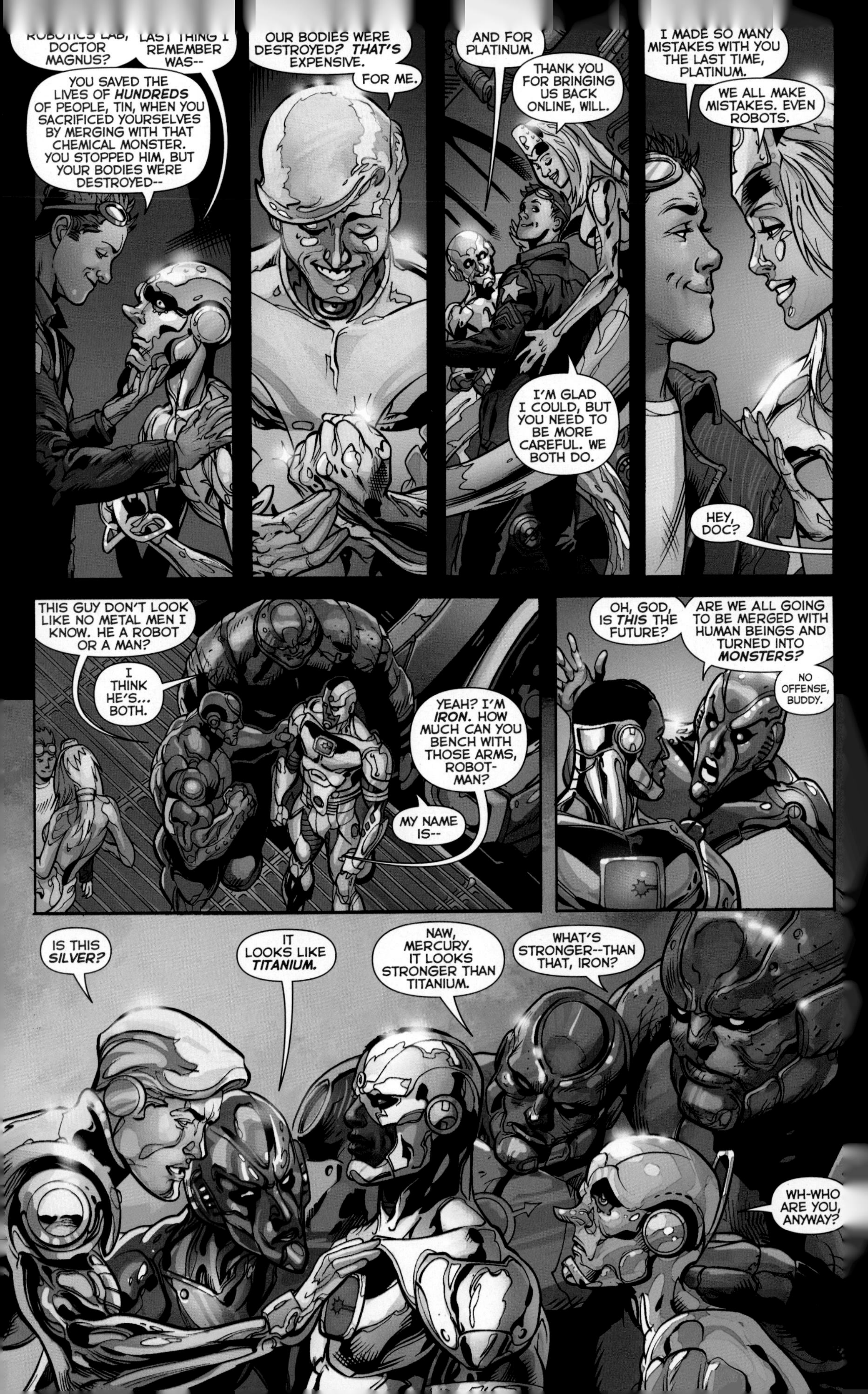
ROBOTICS LAB, DOCTOR MAGNUS?
LAST THING I REMEMBER WAS--
YOU SAVED THE LIVES OF HUNDREDS OF PEOPLE, TIN, WHEN YOU SACRIFICED YOURSELVES BY MERGING WITH THAT CHEMICAL MONSTER. YOU STOPPED HIM, BUT YOUR BODIES WERE DESTROYED--
OUR BODIES WERE DESTROYED? THAT'S EXPENSIVE.
FOR ME.
AND FOR PLATINUM.
THANK YOU FOR BRINGING US BACK ONLINE, WILL.
I'M GLAD I COULD, BUT YOU NEED TO BE MORE CAREFUL. WE BOTH DO.
I MADE SO MANY MISTAKES WITH YOU THE LAST TIME, PLATINUM.
WE ALL MAKE MISTAKES. EVEN ROBOTS.
HEY, DOC?
THIS GUY DON'T LOOK LIKE NO METAL MEN I KNOW. HE A ROBOT OR A MAN?
I THINK HE'S... BOTH.
YEAH? I'M IRON. HOW MUCH CAN YOU BENCH WITH THOSE ARMS, ROBOT-MAN?
MY NAME IS--
OH, GOD, IS THIS THE FUTURE?
ARE WE ALL GOING TO BE MERGED WITH HUMAN BEINGS AND TURNED INTO MONSTERS?
NO OFFENSE, BUDDY.
IS THIS SILVER?
IT LOOKS LIKE TITANIUM.
NAW, MERCURY. IT LOOKS STRONGER THAN TITANIUM.
WHAT'S STRONGER--THAN THAT, IRON?
WH-WHO ARE YOU, ANYWAY?

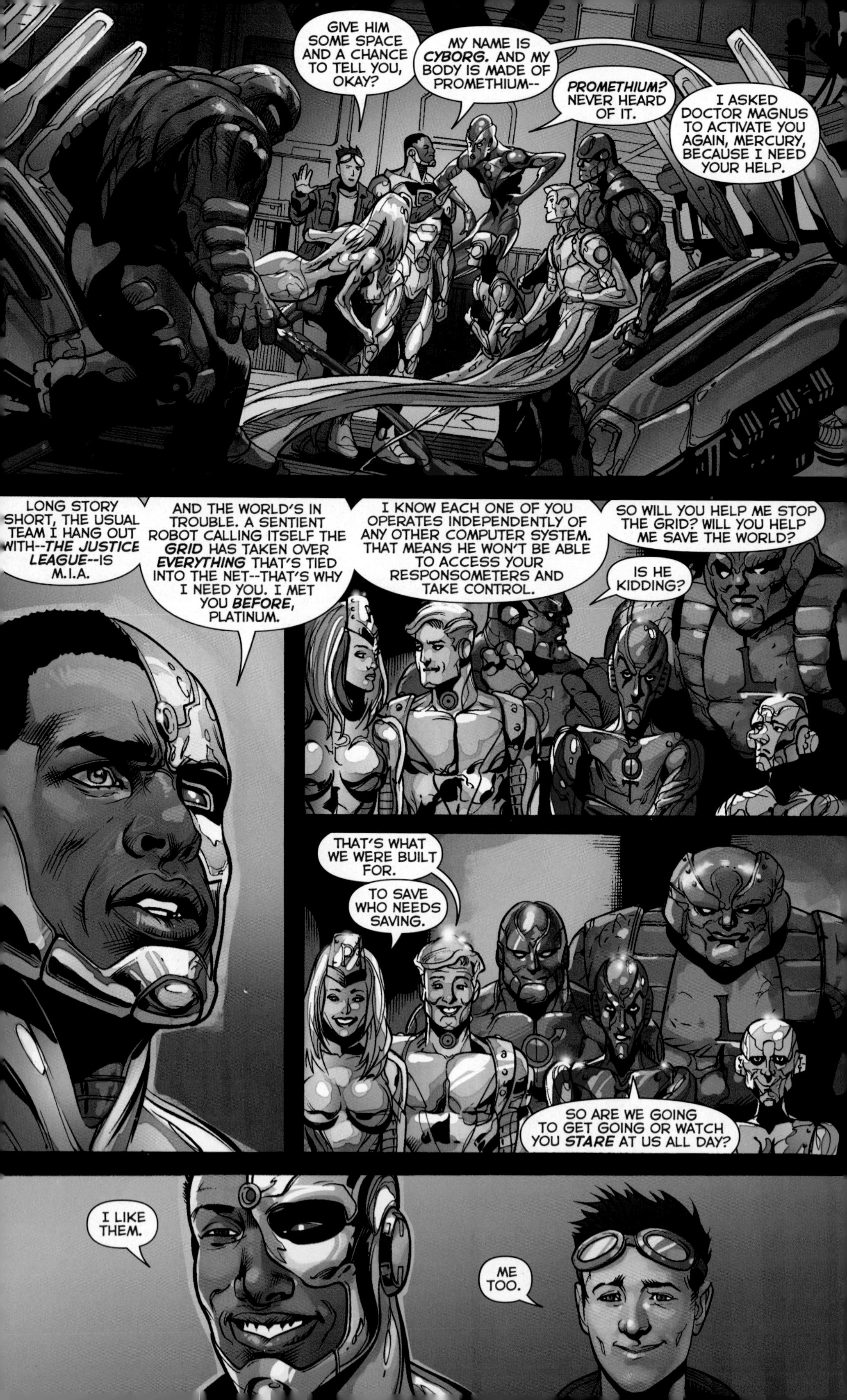
GIVE HIM SOME SPACE AND A CHANCE TO TELL YOU, OKAY?
MY NAME IS CYBORG. AND MY BODY IS MADE OF PROMETHIUM--
PROMETHIUM? NEVER HEARD OF IT.
I ASKED DOCTOR MAGNUS TO ACTIVATE YOU AGAIN, MERCURY, BECAUSE I NEED YOUR HELP.
LONG STORY SHORT, THE USUAL TEAM I HANG OUT WITH--THE JUSTICE LEAGUE--IS M.I.A.
AND THE WORLD'S IN TROUBLE. A SENTIENT ROBOT CALLING ITSELF THE GRID HAS TAKEN OVER EVERYTHING THAT'S TIED INTO THE NET--THAT'S WHY I NEED YOU. I MET YOU BEFORE, PLATINUM.
I KNOW EACH ONE OF YOU OPERATES INDEPENDENTLY OF ANY OTHER COMPUTER SYSTEM. THAT MEANS HE WON'T BE ABLE TO ACCESS YOUR RESPONSOMETERS AND TAKE CONTROL.
SO WILL YOU HELP ME STOP THE GRID? WILL YOU HELP ME SAVE THE WORLD?
IS HE KIDDING?
THAT'S WHAT WE WERE BUILT FOR.
TO SAVE WHO NEEDS SAVING.
SO ARE WE GOING TO GET GOING OR WATCH YOU STARE AT US ALL DAY?
I LIKE THEM.
ME TOO.

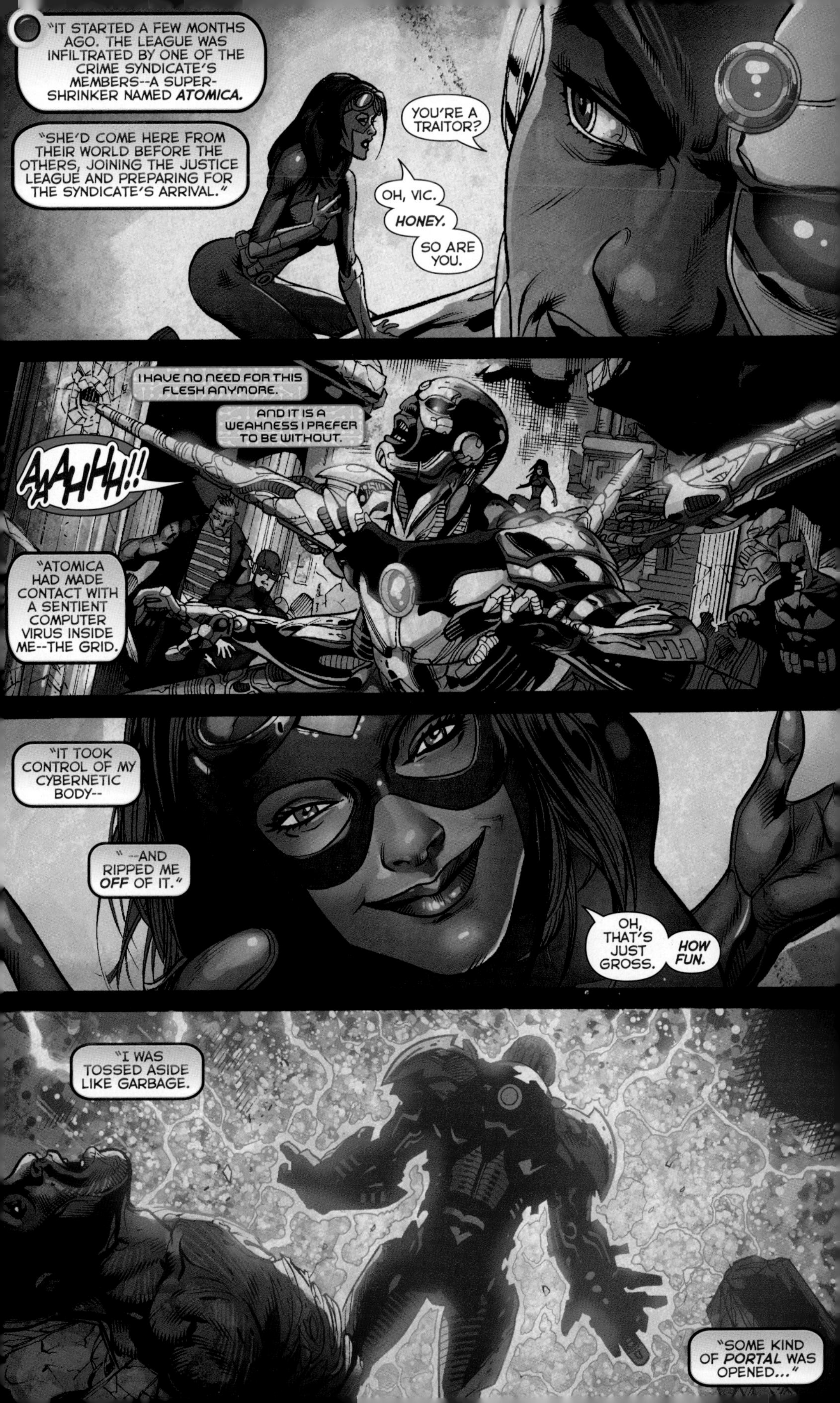
"IT STARTED A FEW MONTHS AGO. THE LEAGUE WAS INFILTRATED BY ONE OF THE CRIME SYNDICATE'S MEMBERS--A SUPER-SHRINKER NAMED ATOMICA.
"SHE'D COME HERE FROM THEIR WORLD BEFORE THE OTHERS, JOINING THE JUSTICE LEAGUE AND PREPARING FOR THE SYNDICATE'S ARRIVAL."
YOU'RE A TRAITOR?
OH, VIC.
HONEY.
SO ARE YOU.
I HAVE NO NEED FOR THIS FLESH ANYMORE.
AND IT IS A WEAKNESS I PREFER TO BE WITHOUT.
AAAHHH!!
"ATOMICA HAD MADE CONTACT WITH A SENTIENT COMPUTER VIRUS INSIDE ME--THE GRID.
"IT TOOK CONTROL OF MY CYBERNETIC BODY--
" --AND RIPPED ME OFF OF IT."
OH, THAT'S JUST GROSS.
HOW FUN.
"I WAS TOSSED ASIDE LIKE GARBAGE.
"SOME KIND OF PORTAL WAS OPENED..."

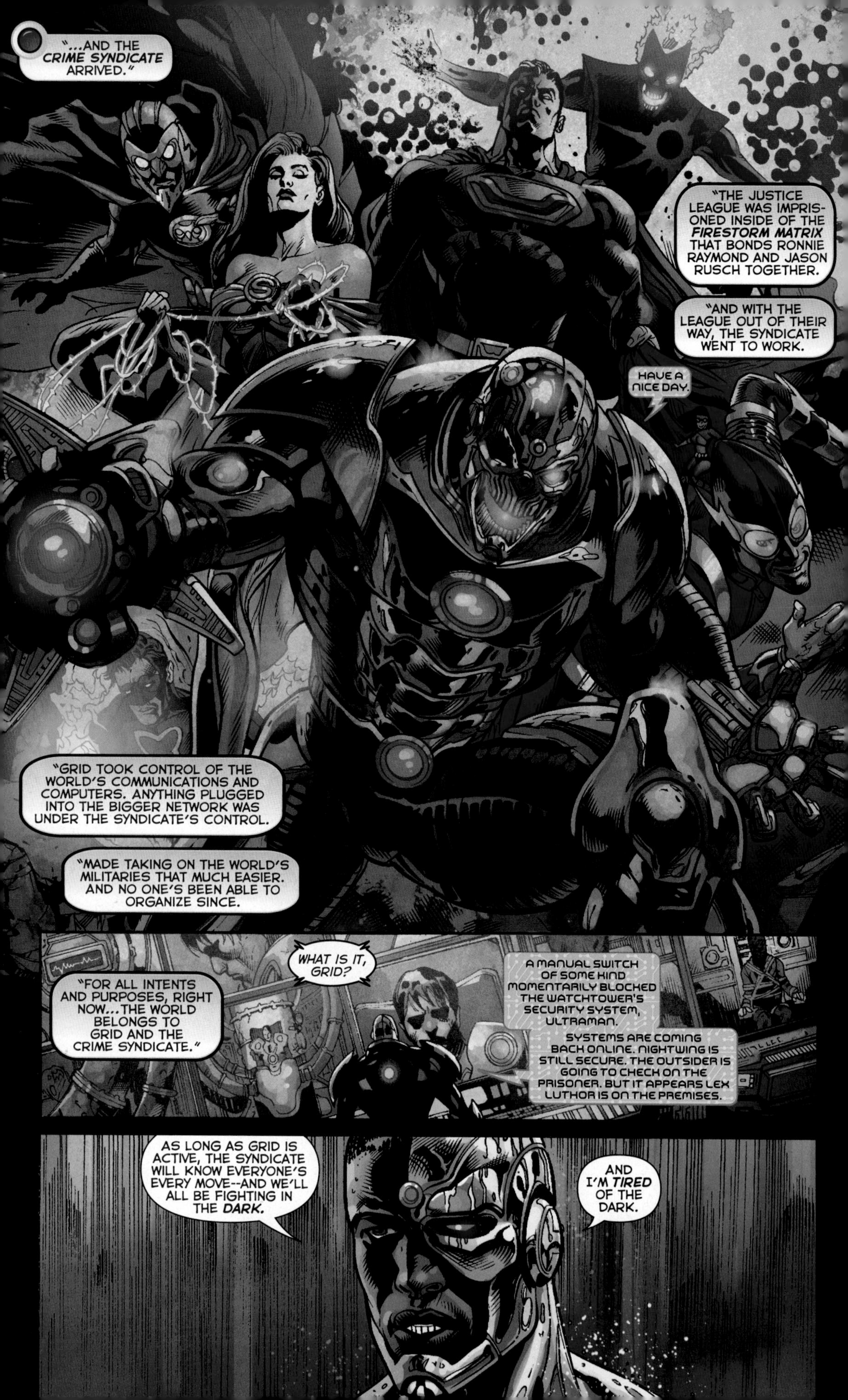
"...AND THE CRIME SYNDICATE ARRIVED."
"THE JUSTICE LEAGUE WAS IMPRISONED INSIDE OF THE FIRESTORM MATRIX THAT BONDS RONNIE RAYMOND AND JASON RUSCH TOGETHER.
"AND WITH THE LEAGUE OUT OF THEIR WAY, THE SYNDICATE WENT TO WORK.
HAVE A NICE DAY.
"GRID TOOK CONTROL OF THE WORLD'S COMMUNICATIONS AND COMPUTERS. ANYTHING PLUGGED INTO THE BIGGER NETWORK WAS UNDER THE SYNDICATE'S CONTROL.
"MADE TAKING ON THE WORLD'S MILITARIES THAT MUCH EASIER. AND NO ONE'S BEEN ABLE TO ORGANIZE SINCE.
"FOR ALL INTENTS AND PURPOSES, RIGHT NOW...THE WORLD BELONGS TO GRID AND THE CRIME SYNDICATE."
WHAT IS IT, GRID?
A MANUAL SWITCH OF SOME KIND MOMENTARILY BLOCKED THE WATCHTOWER'S SECURITY SYSTEM, ULTRAMAN.
SYSTEMS ARE COMING BACK ONLINE. NIGHTWING IS STILL SECURE. THE OUTSIDER IS GOING TO CHECK ON THE PRISONER. BUT IT APPEARS LEX LUTHOR IS ON THE PREMISES.
AS LONG AS GRID IS ACTIVE, THE SYNDICATE WILL KNOW EVERYONE'S EVERY MOVE--AND WE'LL ALL BE FIGHTING IN THE DARK.
AND I'M TIRED OF THE DARK.

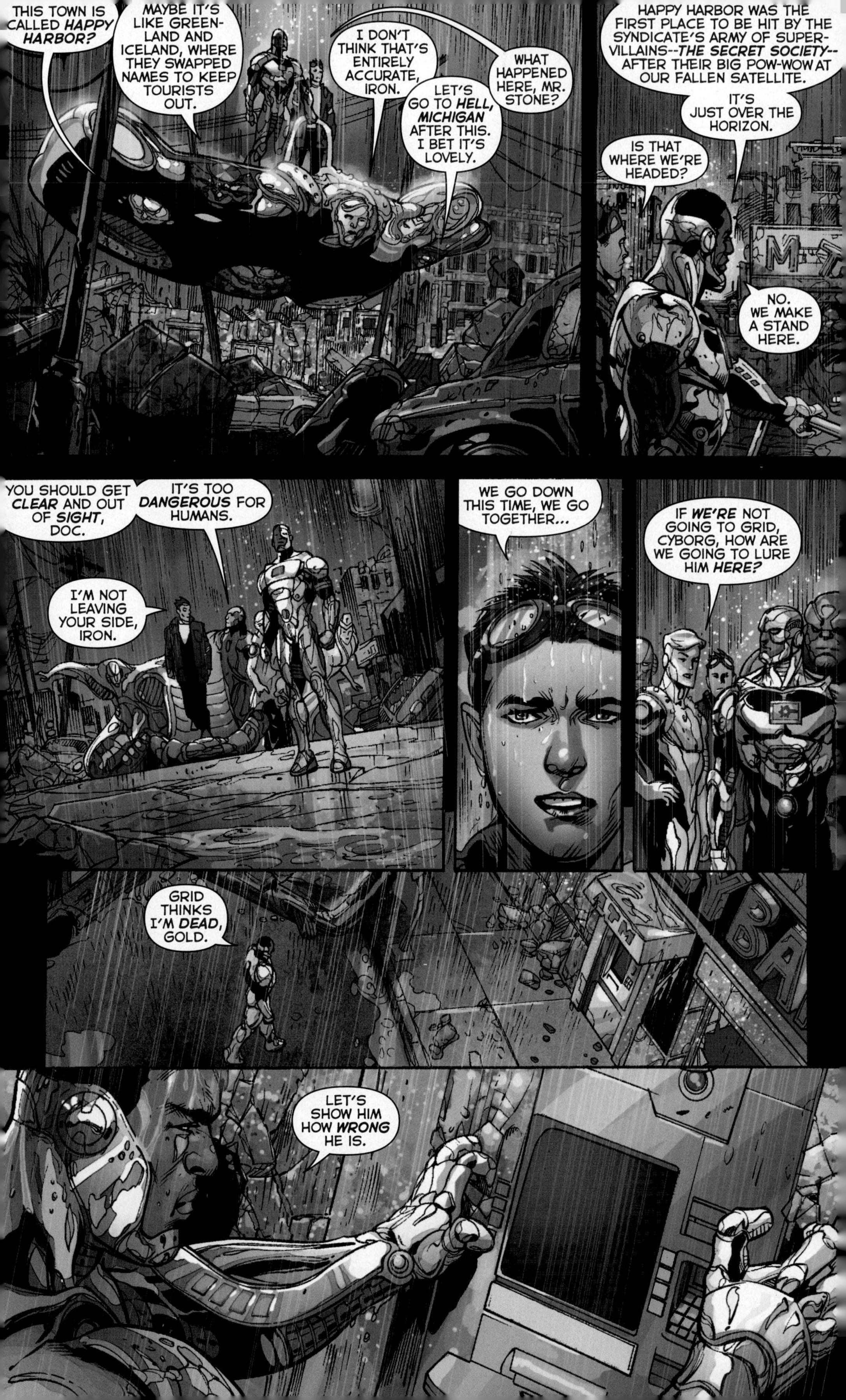
THIS TOWN IS CALLED HAPPY HARBOR?
MAYBE IT'S LIKE GREEN-LAND AND ICELAND, WHERE THEY SWAPPED NAMES TO KEEP TOURISTS OUT.
I DON'T THINK THAT'S ENTIRELY ACCURATE, IRON.
LET'S GO TO HELL, MICHIGAN AFTER THIS. I BET IT'S LOVELY.
WHAT HAPPENED HERE, MR. STONE?
HAPPY HARBOR WAS THE FIRST PLACE TO BE HIT BY THE SYNDICATE'S ARMY OF SUPER-VILLAINS--THE SECRET SOCIETY--AFTER THEIR BIG POW-WOW AT OUR FALLEN SATELLITE.
IT'S JUST OVER THE HORIZON.
IS THAT WHERE WE'RE HEADED?
NO. WE MAKE A STAND HERE.
YOU SHOULD GET CLEAR AND OUT OF SIGHT, DOC.
IT'S TOO DANGEROUS FOR HUMANS.
I'M NOT LEAVING YOUR SIDE, IRON.
WE GO DOWN THIS TIME, WE GO TOGETHER...
IF WE'RE NOT GOING TO GRID, CYBORG, HOW ARE WE GOING TO LURE HIM HERE?
GRID THINKS I'M DEAD, GOLD.
LET'S SHOW HIM HOW WRONG HE IS.

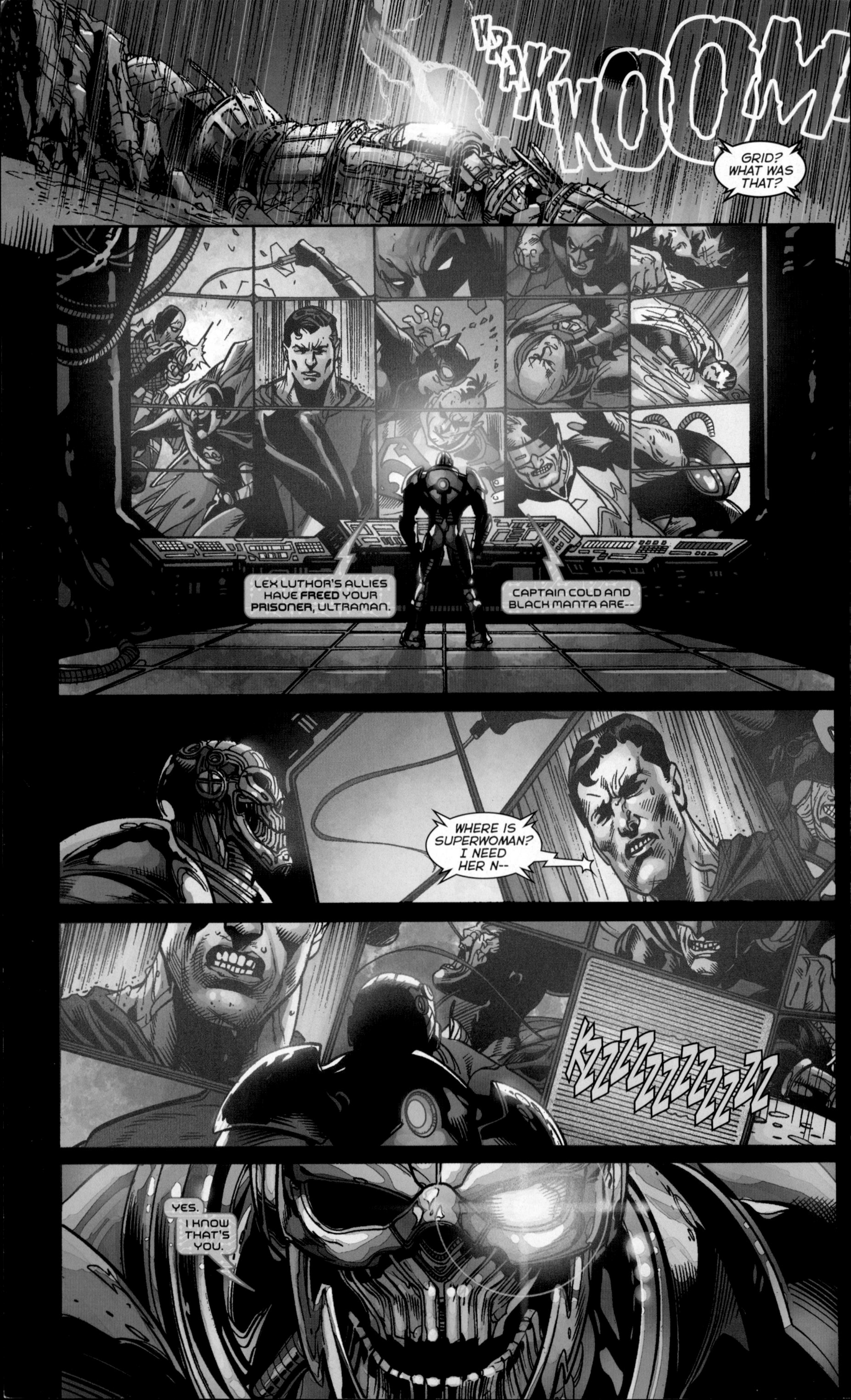
GRID? WHAT WAS THAT?
LEX LUTHOR'S ALLIES HAVE FREED YOUR PRISONER, ULTRAMAN.
CAPTAIN COLD AND BLACK MANTA ARE--
WHERE IS SUPERWOMAN? I NEED HER N--
KZZZZZZZZZZ
YES. I KNOW THAT'S YOU.

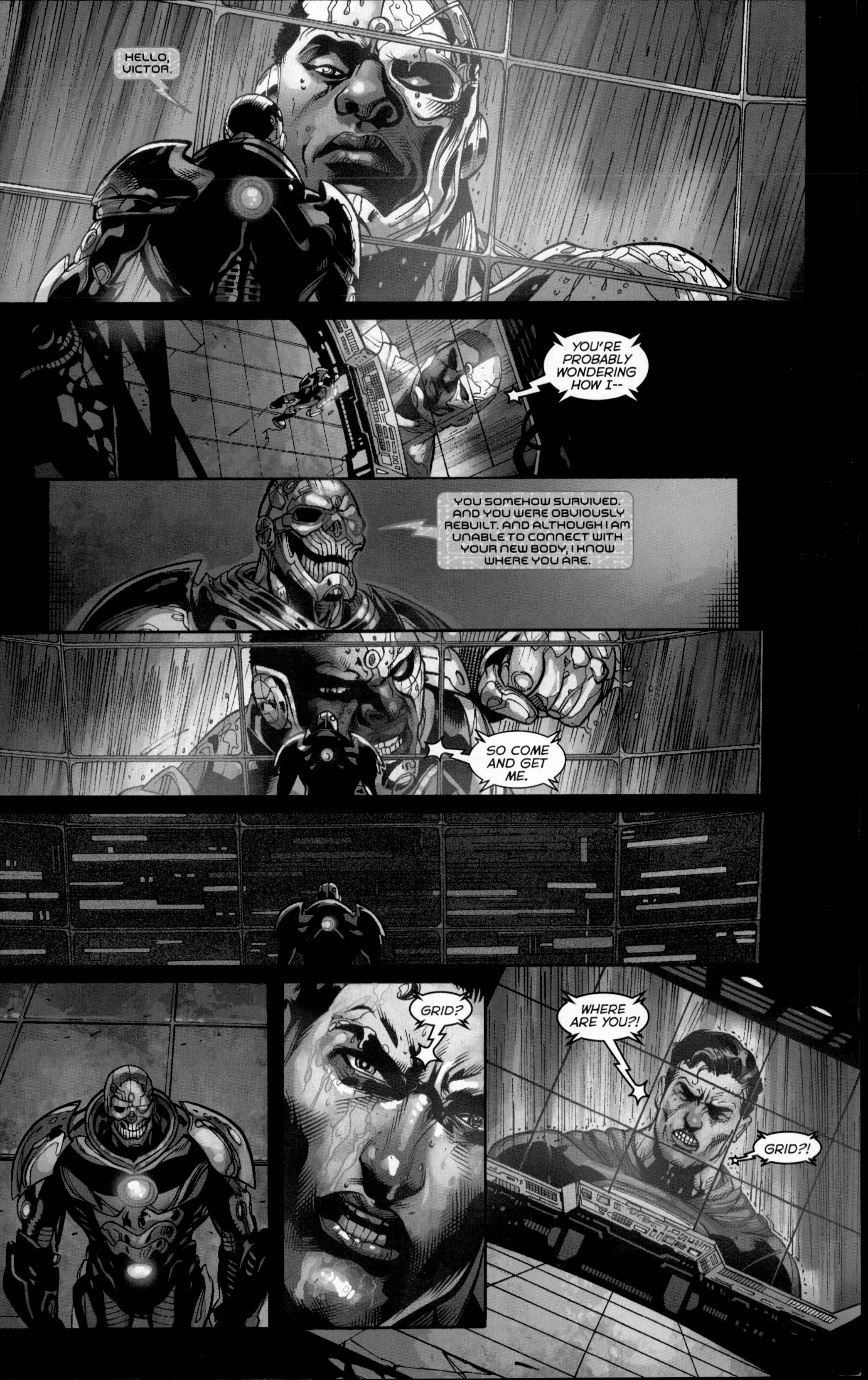
HELLO, VICTOR.
YOU'RE PROBABLY WONDERING HOW I--
YOU SOMEHOW SURVIVED. AND YOU WERE OBVIOUSLY REBUILT. AND ALTHOUGH I AM UNABLE TO CONNECT WITH YOUR NEW BODY, I KNOW WHERE YOU ARE.
SO COME AND GET ME.
GRID?
WHERE ARE YOU?!
GRID?!

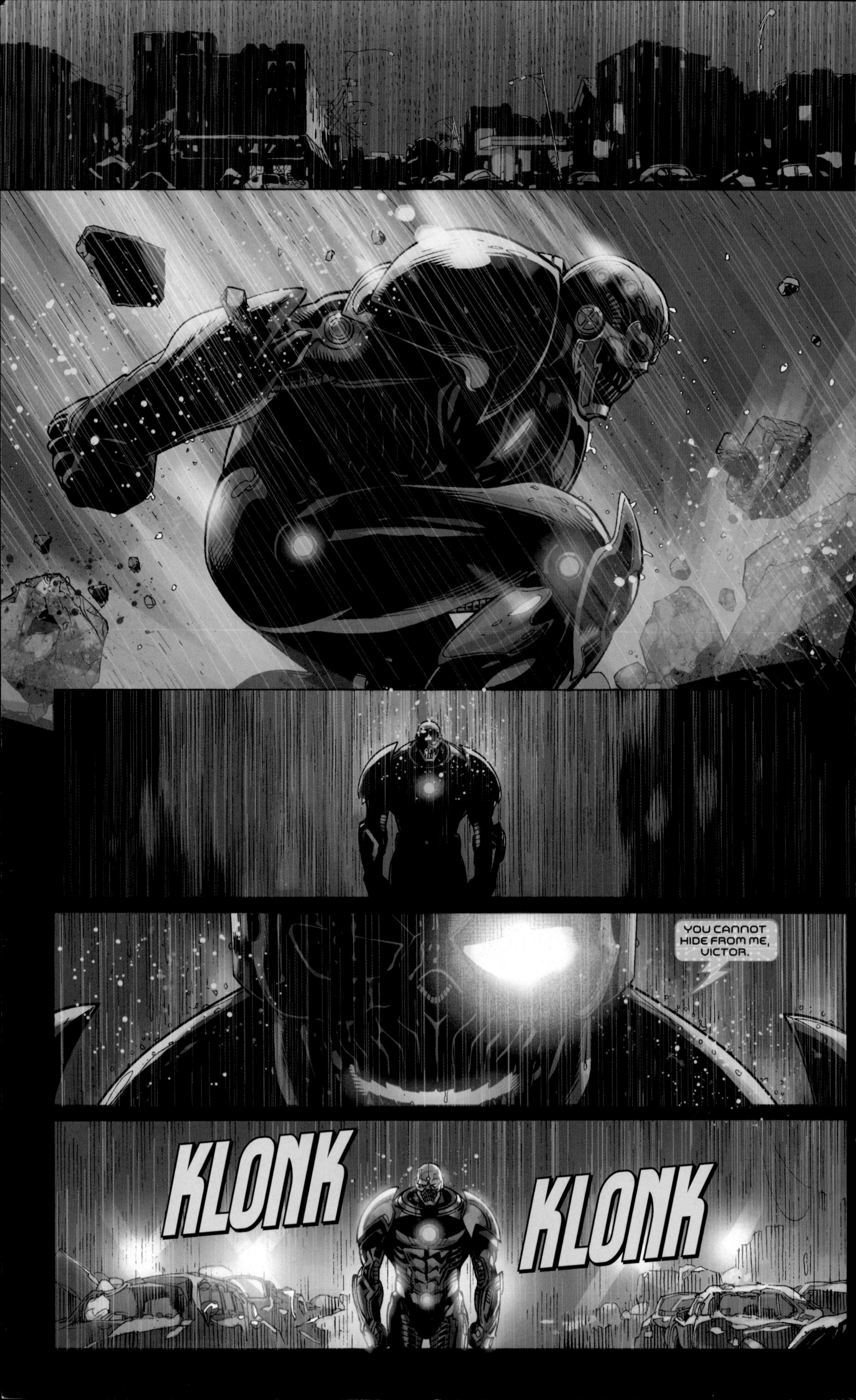
YOU CANNOT HIDE FROM ME, VICTOR.
KLONK
KLONK

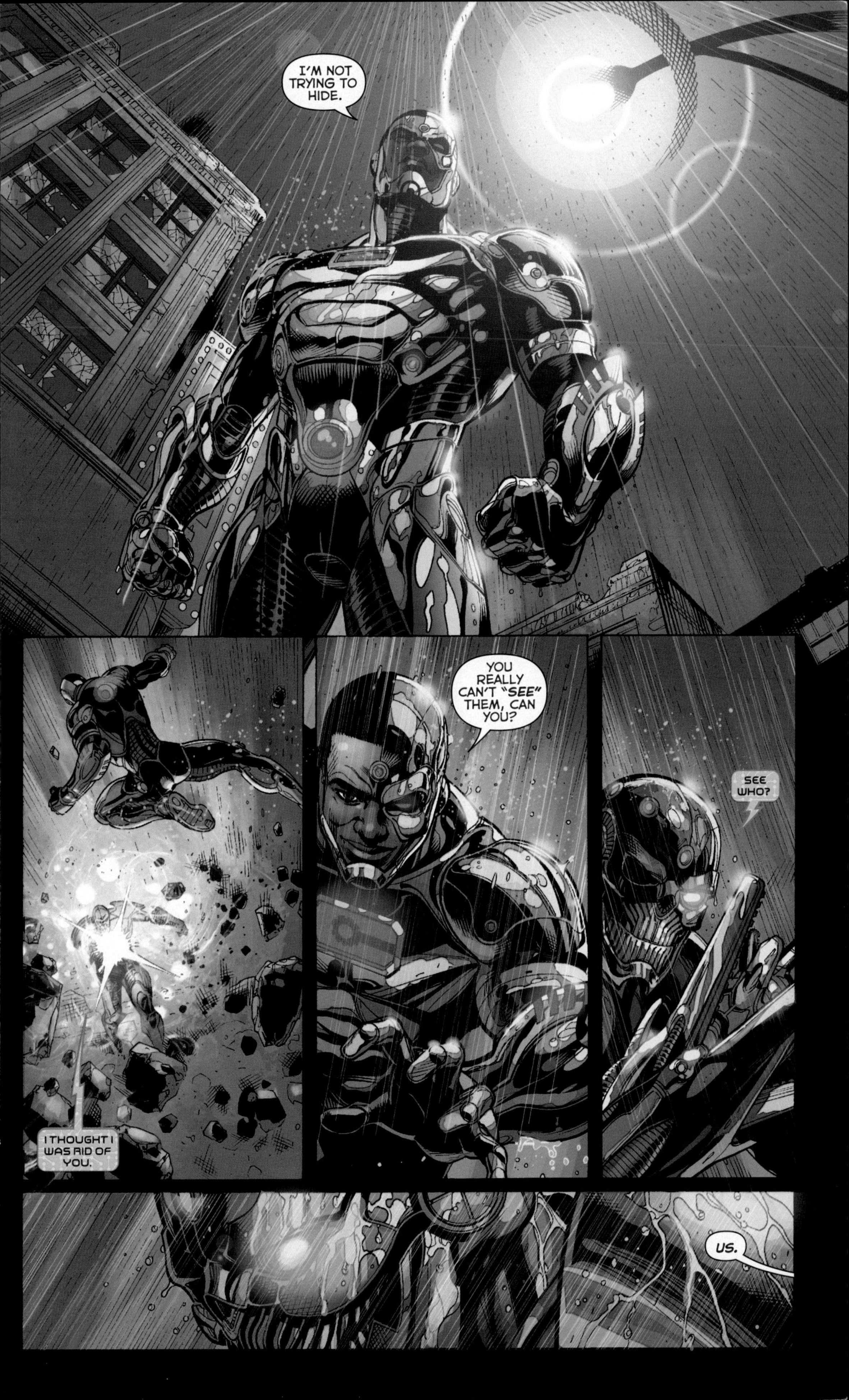
I'M NOT TRYING TO HIDE.
I THOUGHT I WAS RID OF YOU.
YOU REALLY CAN'T "SEE" THEM, CAN YOU?
SEE WHO?
US.

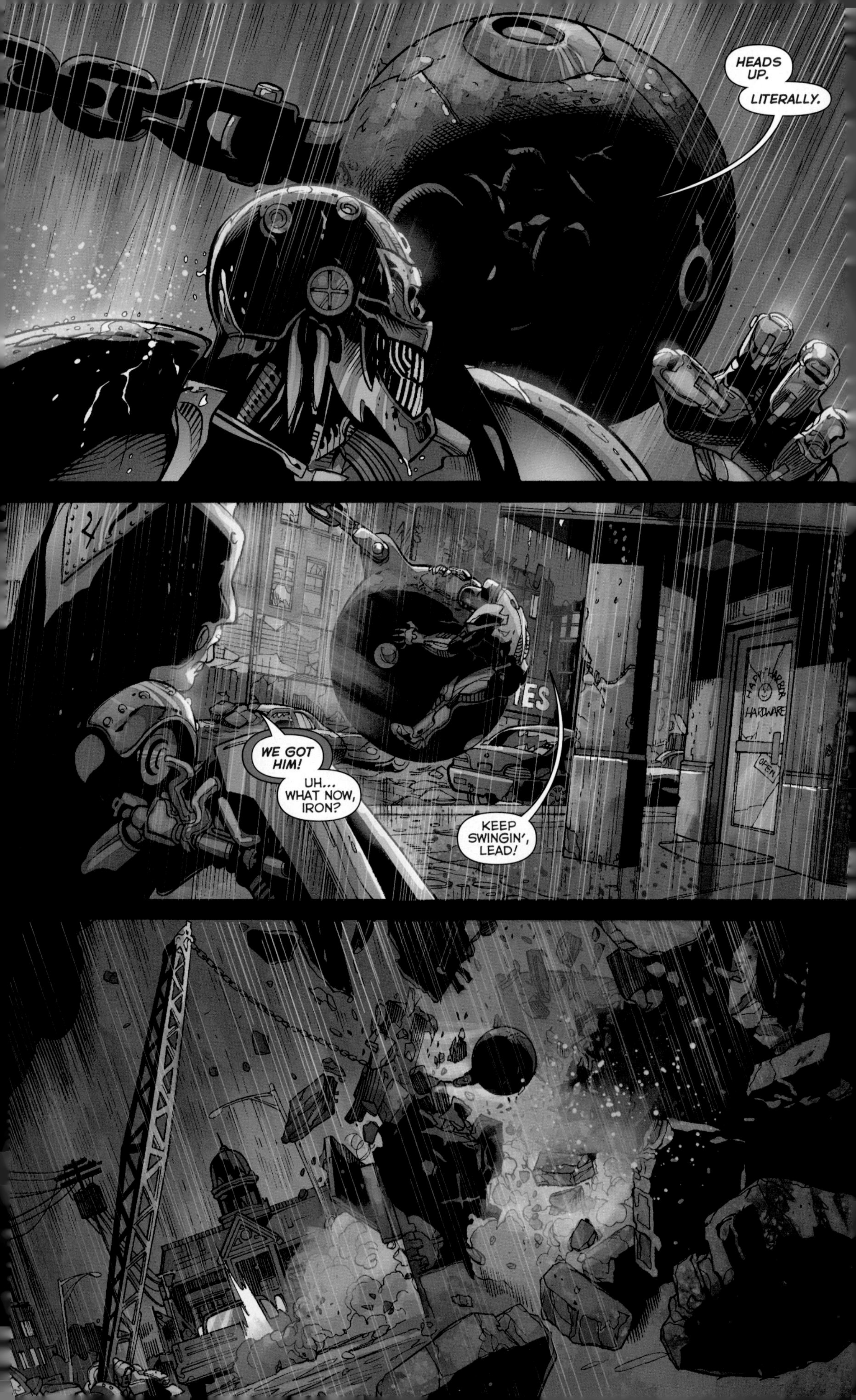
HEADS UP.
LITERALLY.
WE GOT HIM!
UH... WHAT NOW, IRON?
KEEP SWINGIN', LEAD!
HAPPY HARBOR HARDWARE
OPEN

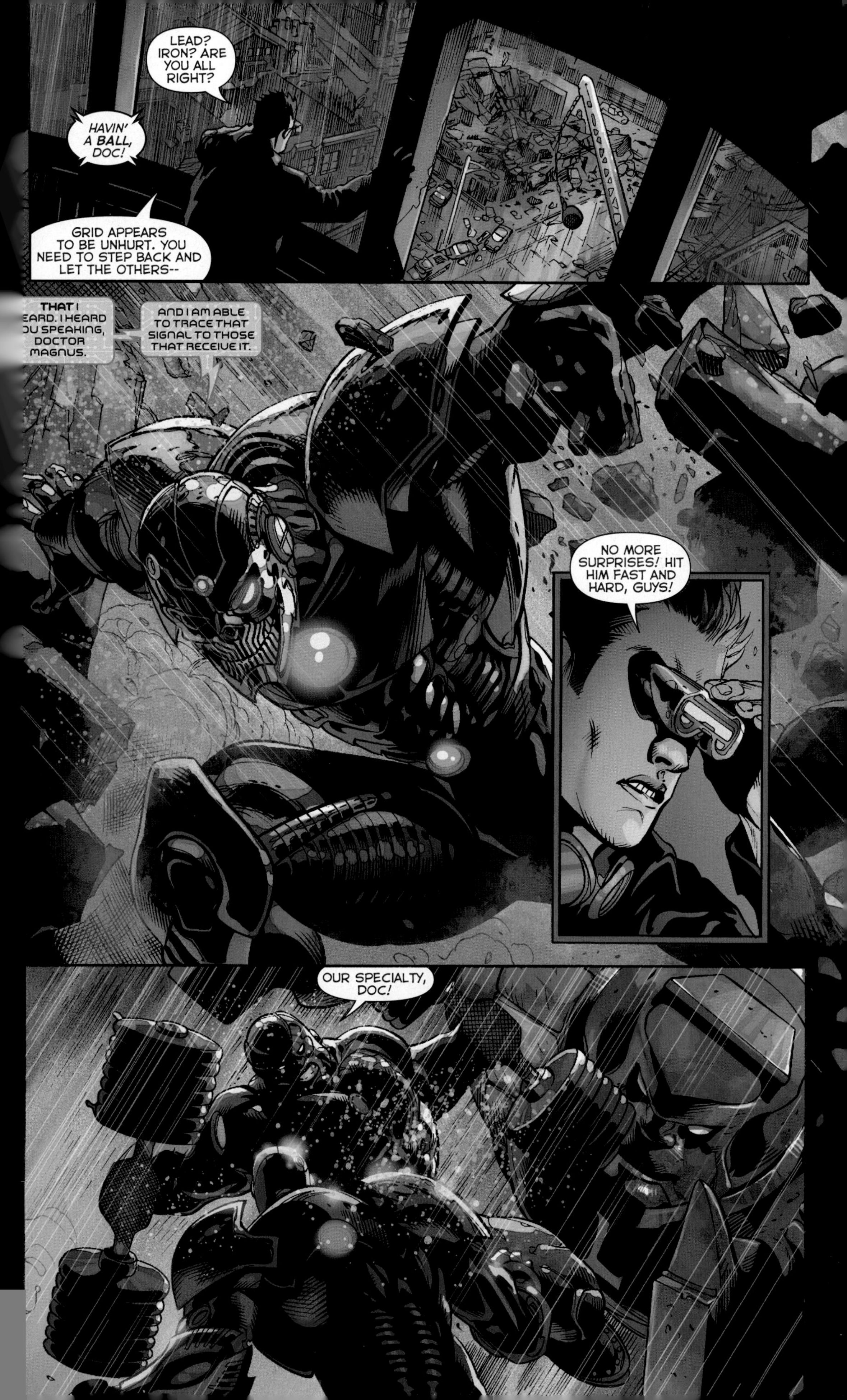

LEAD? IRON? ARE YOU ALL RIGHT?
HAVIN' A BALL, DOC!
GRID APPEARS TO BE UNHURT. YOU NEED TO STEP BACK AND LET THE OTHERS--
THAT I HEARD. I HEARD YOU SPEAKING, DOCTOR MAGNUS.
AND I AM ABLE TO TRACE THAT SIGNAL TO THOSE THAT RECEIVE IT.
NO MORE SURPRISES! HIT HIM FAST AND HARD, GUYS!
OUR SPECIALTY, DOC!

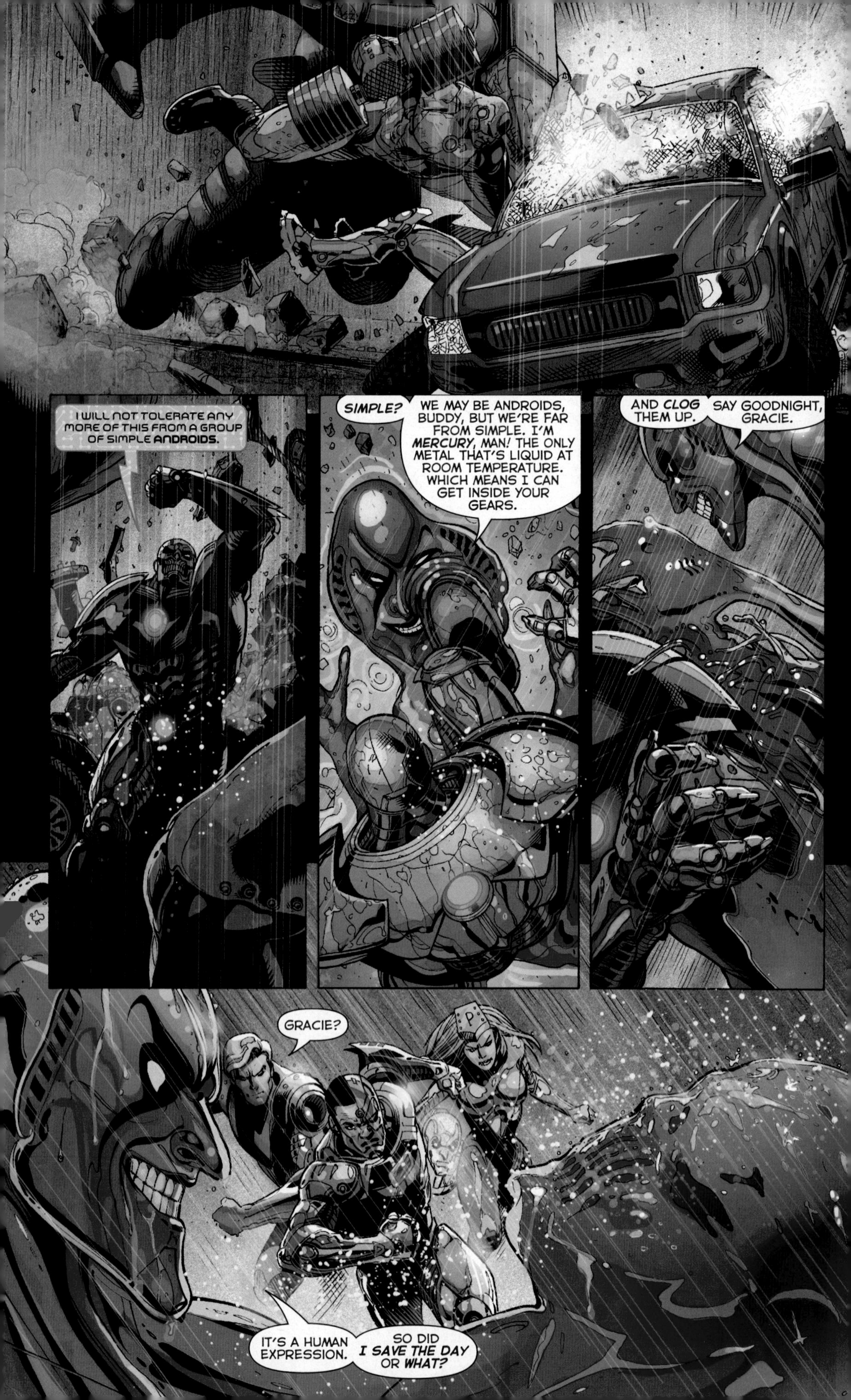

I WILL NOT TOLERATE ANY MORE OF THIS FROM A GROUP OF SIMPLE **ANDROIDS**.
SIMPLE?
WE MAY BE ANDROIDS, BUDDY, BUT WE'RE FAR FROM SIMPLE. I'M *MERCURY*, MAN! THE ONLY METAL THAT'S LIQUID AT ROOM TEMPERATURE. WHICH MEANS I CAN GET INSIDE YOUR GEARS.
AND *CLOG* THEM UP.
SAY GOODNIGHT, GRACIE.
GRACIE?
IT'S A HUMAN EXPRESSION.
SO DID *I SAVE THE DAY* OR *WHAT?*

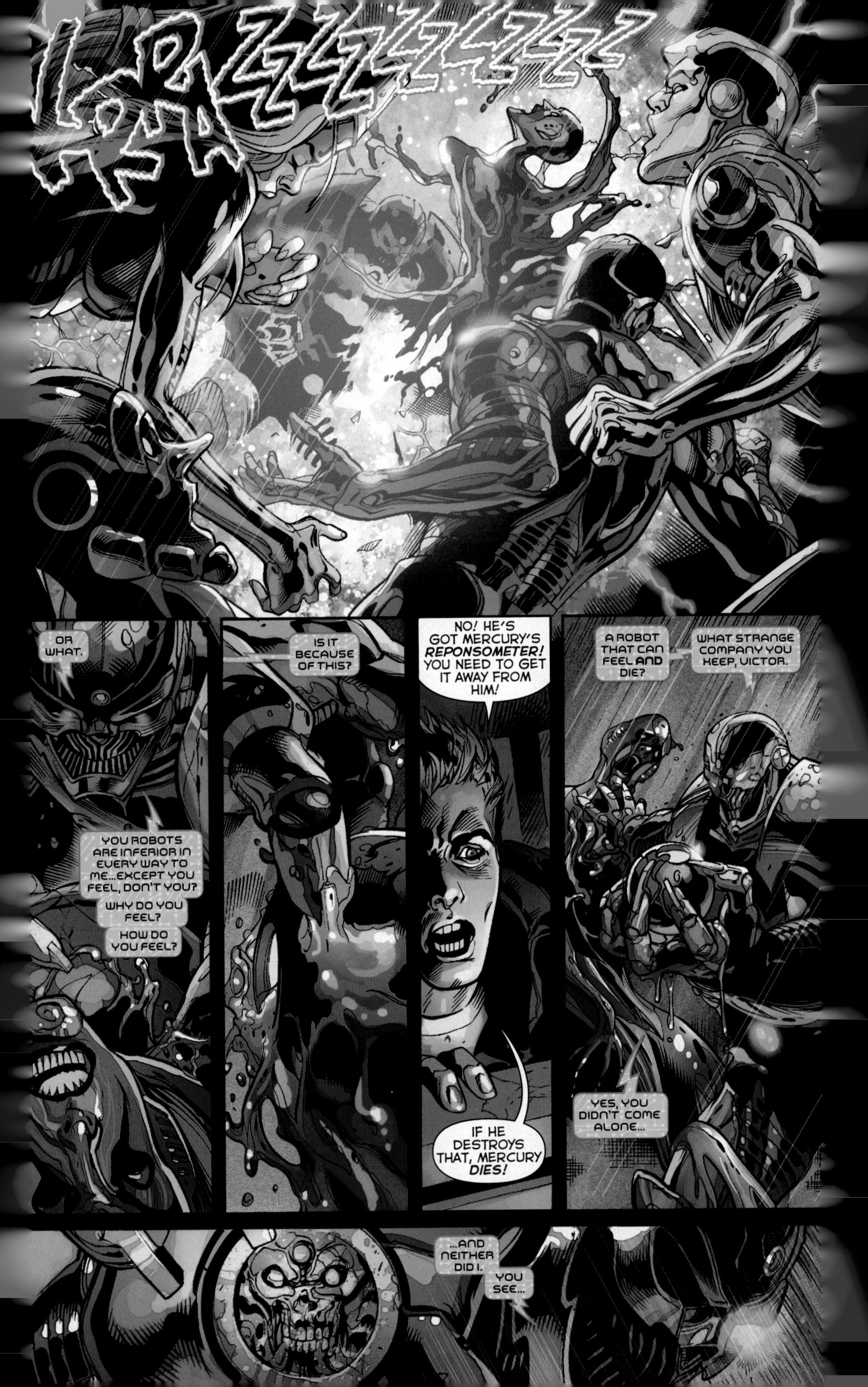
KRAZZZZZZZT
OR WHAT.
YOU ROBOTS ARE INFERIOR IN EVERY WAY TO ME...EXCEPT YOU FEEL, DON'T YOU?
WHY DO YOU FEEL?
HOW DO YOU FEEL?
IS IT BECAUSE OF THIS?
NO! HE'S GOT MERCURY'S REPONSOMETER! YOU NEED TO GET IT AWAY FROM HIM!
IF HE DESTROYS THAT, MERCURY DIES!
A ROBOT THAT CAN FEEL AND DIE?
WHAT STRANGE COMPANY YOU KEEP, VICTOR.
YES, YOU DIDN'T COME ALONE...
...AND NEITHER DID I.
YOU SEE...

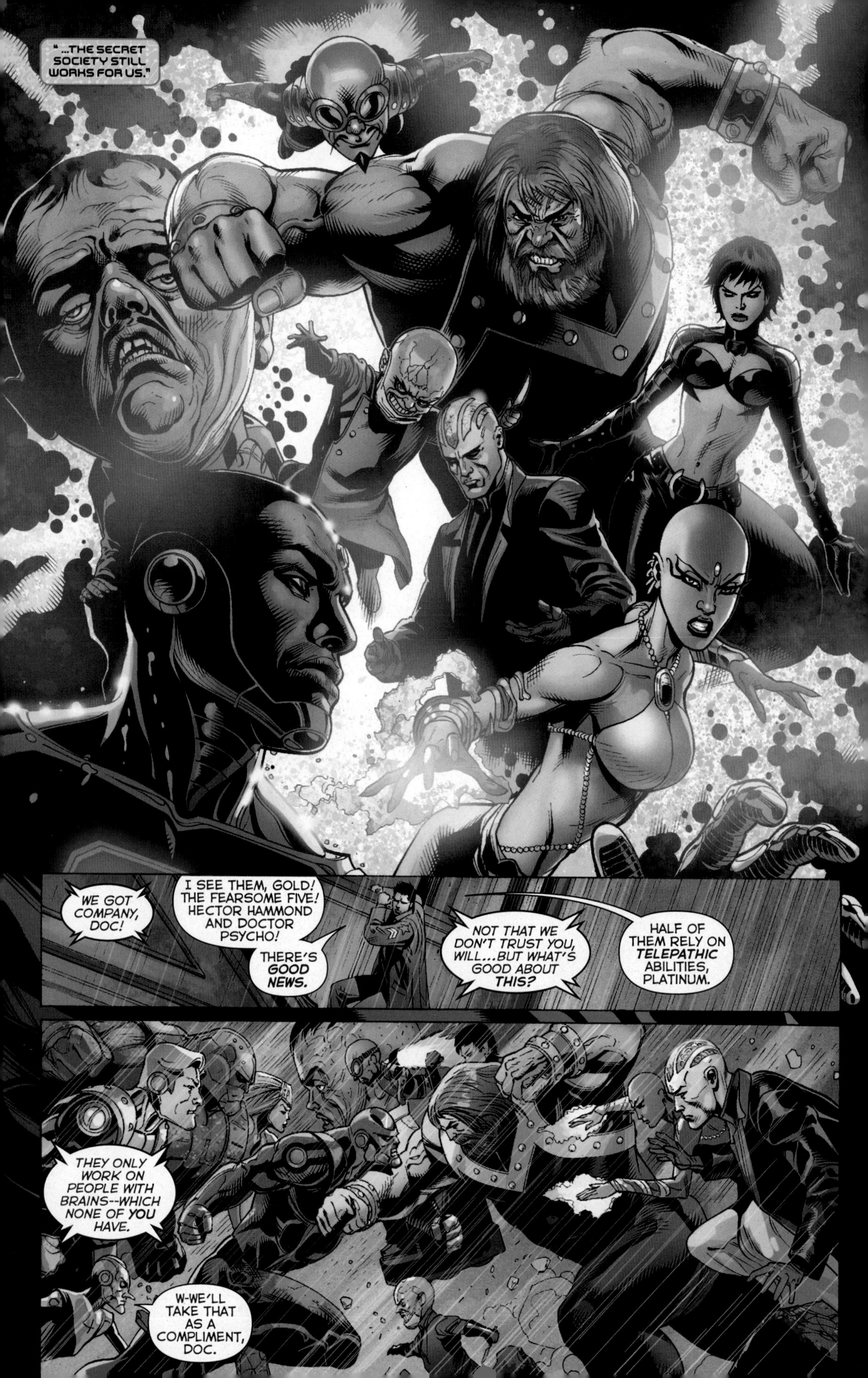
"...THE SECRET SOCIETY STILL WORKS FOR US."
WE GOT COMPANY, DOC!
I SEE THEM, GOLD! THE FEARSOME FIVE! HECTOR HAMMOND AND DOCTOR PSYCHO!
THERE'S **GOOD NEWS.**
NOT THAT WE DON'T TRUST YOU, WILL...BUT WHAT'S GOOD ABOUT **THIS?**
HALF OF THEM RELY ON ***TELEPATHIC*** ABILITIES, PLATINUM.
THEY ONLY WORK ON PEOPLE WITH BRAINS--WHICH NONE OF **YOU** HAVE.
W-WE'LL TAKE THAT AS A COMPLIMENT, DOC.

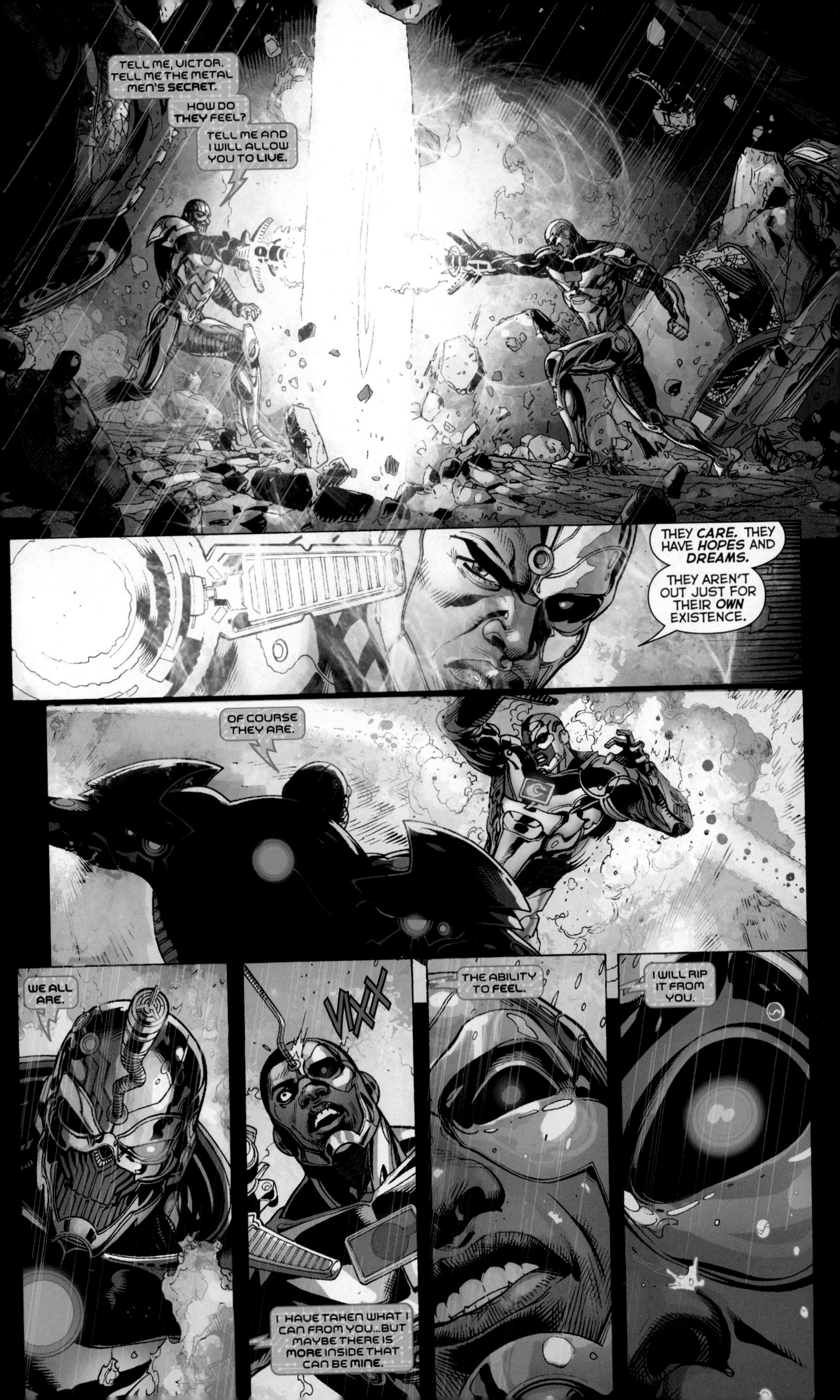

TELL ME, VICTOR. TELL ME THE METAL MEN'S SECRET.
HOW DO THEY FEEL?
TELL ME AND I WILL ALLOW YOU TO LIVE.
THEY CARE. THEY HAVE HOPES AND DREAMS.
THEY AREN'T OUT JUST FOR THEIR OWN EXISTENCE.
OF COURSE THEY ARE.
WE ALL ARE.
VRXX
THE ABILITY TO FEEL.
I WILL RIP IT FROM YOU.
I HAVE TAKEN WHAT I CAN FROM YOU...BUT MAYBE THERE IS MORE INSIDE THAT CAN BE MINE.

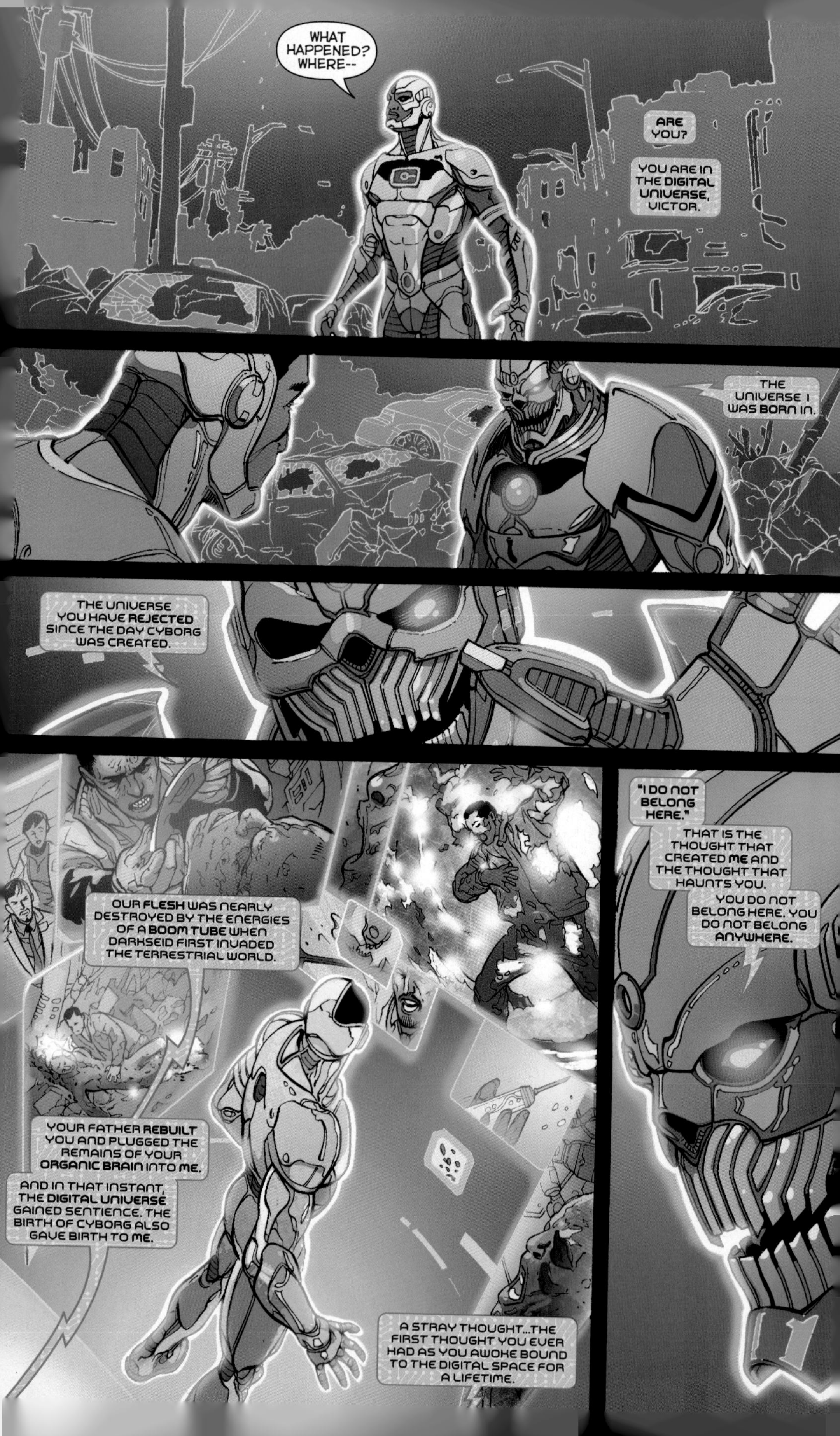
WHAT HAPPENED? WHERE--
ARE YOU?
YOU ARE IN THE DIGITAL UNIVERSE, VICTOR.
THE UNIVERSE I WAS BORN IN.
THE UNIVERSE YOU HAVE REJECTED SINCE THE DAY CYBORG WAS CREATED.
OUR FLESH WAS NEARLY DESTROYED BY THE ENERGIES OF A BOOM TUBE WHEN DARKSEID FIRST INVADED THE TERRESTRIAL WORLD.
YOUR FATHER REBUILT YOU AND PLUGGED THE REMAINS OF YOUR ORGANIC BRAIN INTO ME.
AND IN THAT INSTANT, THE DIGITAL UNIVERSE GAINED SENTIENCE. THE BIRTH OF CYBORG ALSO GAVE BIRTH TO ME.
A STRAY THOUGHT...THE FIRST THOUGHT YOU EVER HAD AS YOU AWOKE BOUND TO THE DIGITAL SPACE FOR A LIFETIME.
"I DO NOT BELONG HERE."
THAT IS THE THOUGHT THAT CREATED ME AND THE THOUGHT THAT HAUNTS YOU.
YOU DO NOT BELONG HERE. YOU DO NOT BELONG ANYWHERE.

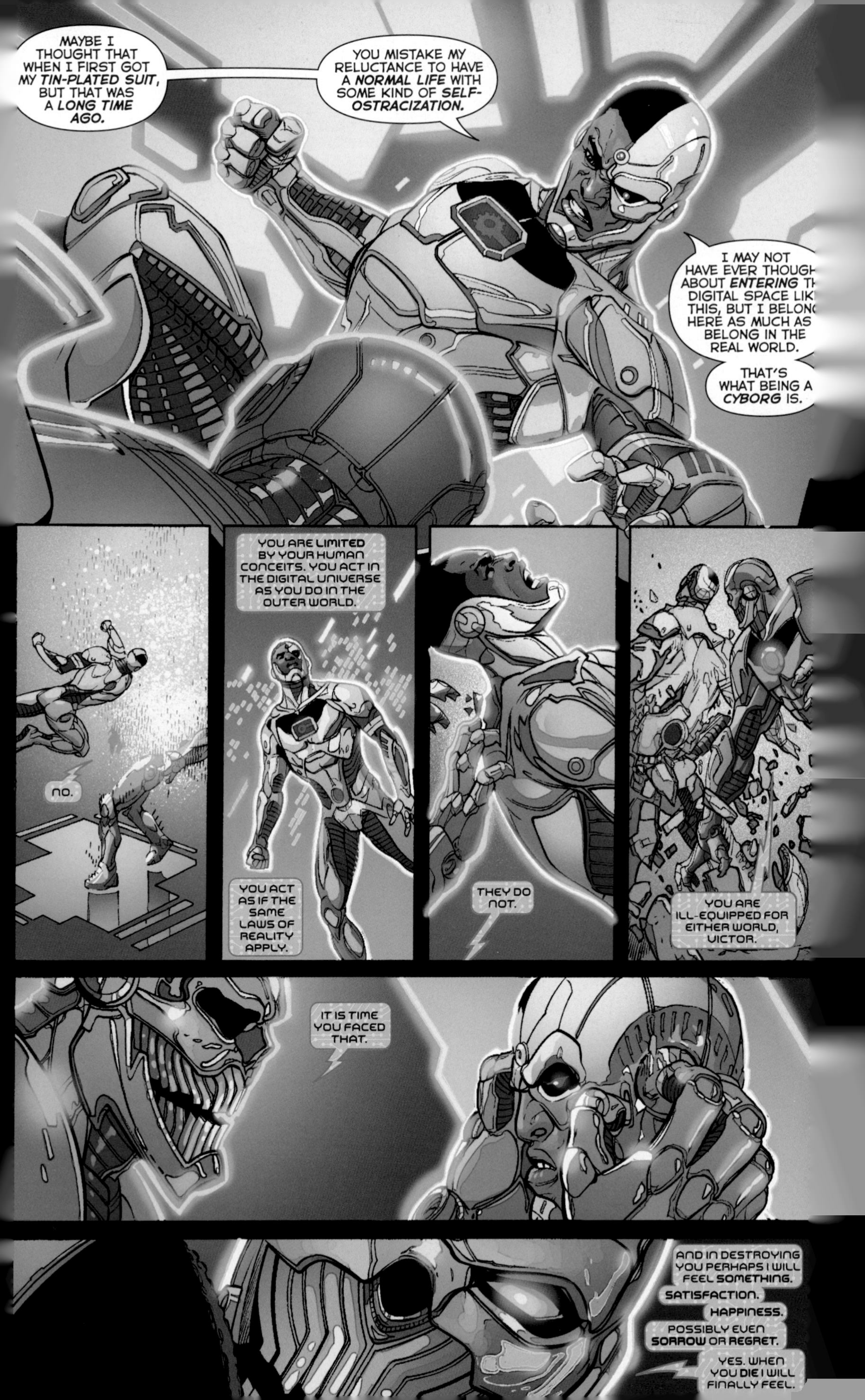
MAYBE I THOUGHT THAT WHEN I FIRST GOT MY TIN-PLATED SUIT, BUT THAT WAS A LONG TIME AGO.
YOU MISTAKE MY RELUCTANCE TO HAVE A NORMAL LIFE WITH SOME KIND OF SELF-OSTRACIZATION.
I MAY NOT HAVE EVER THOUGH ABOUT ENTERING TH DIGITAL SPACE LIK THIS, BUT I BELONG HERE AS MUCH AS BELONG IN THE REAL WORLD.
THAT'S WHAT BEING A CYBORG IS.
NO.
YOU ARE LIMITED BY YOUR HUMAN CONCEITS. YOU ACT IN THE DIGITAL UNIVERSE AS YOU DO IN THE OUTER WORLD.
YOU ACT AS IF THE SAME LAWS OF REALITY APPLY.
THEY DO NOT.
YOU ARE ILL-EQUIPPED FOR EITHER WORLD, VICTOR.
IT IS TIME YOU FACED THAT.
AND IN DESTROYING YOU PERHAPS I WILL FEEL SOMETHING.
SATISFACTION.
HAPPINESS.
POSSIBLY EVEN SORROW OR REGRET.
YES. WHEN YOU DIE I WILL FINALLY FEEL.

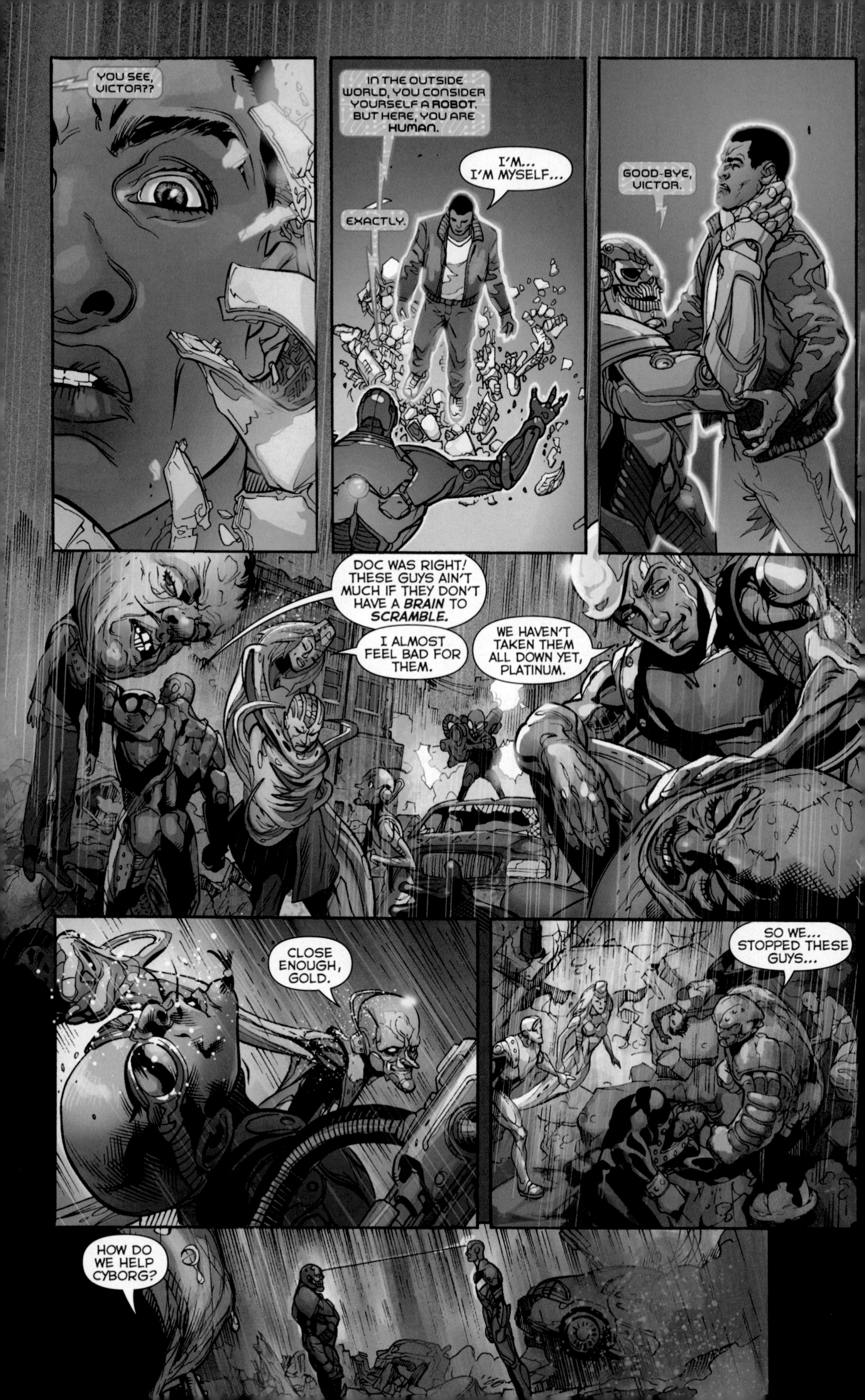
YOU SEE, VICTOR??
IN THE OUTSIDE WORLD, YOU CONSIDER YOURSELF A ROBOT. BUT HERE, YOU ARE HUMAN.
I'M... I'M MYSELF...
EXACTLY.
GOOD-BYE, VICTOR.
DOC WAS RIGHT! THESE GUYS AIN'T MUCH IF THEY DON'T HAVE A BRAIN TO SCRAMBLE.
I ALMOST FEEL BAD FOR THEM.
WE HAVEN'T TAKEN THEM ALL DOWN YET, PLATINUM.
CLOSE ENOUGH, GOLD.
SO WE... STOPPED THESE GUYS...
HOW DO WE HELP CYBORG?

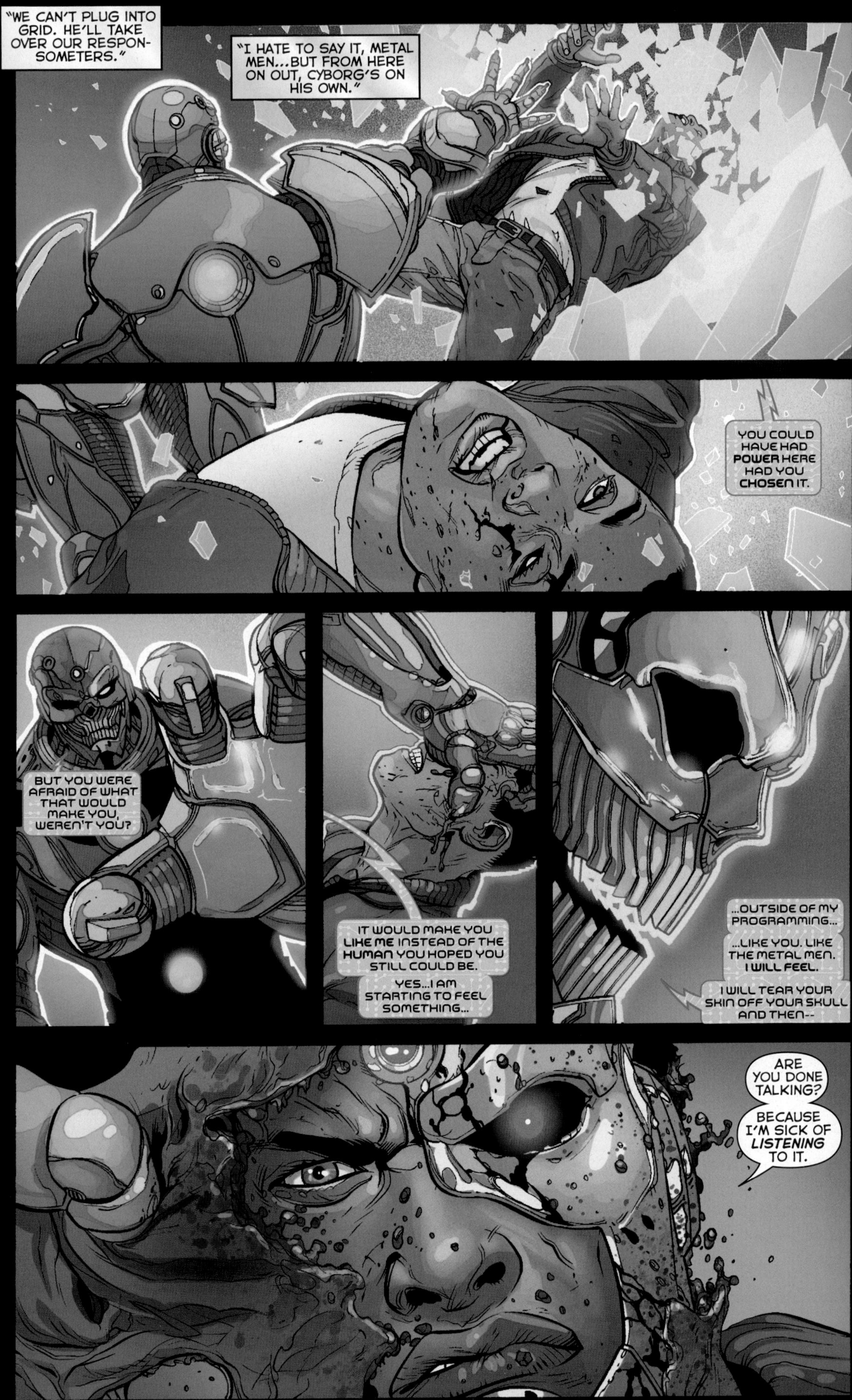
"WE CAN'T PLUG INTO GRID. HE'LL TAKE OVER OUR RESPON-SOMETERS."
"I HATE TO SAY IT, METAL MEN...BUT FROM HERE ON OUT, CYBORG'S ON HIS OWN."
YOU COULD HAVE HAD POWER HERE HAD YOU CHOSEN IT.
BUT YOU WERE AFRAID OF WHAT THAT WOULD MAKE YOU, WEREN'T YOU?
IT WOULD MAKE YOU LIKE ME INSTEAD OF THE HUMAN YOU HOPED YOU STILL COULD BE.
YES...I AM STARTING TO FEEL SOMETHING...
...OUTSIDE OF MY PROGRAMMING...
...LIKE YOU. LIKE THE METAL MEN. I WILL FEEL.
I WILL TEAR YOUR SKIN OFF YOUR SKULL AND THEN--
ARE YOU DONE TALKING?
BECAUSE I'M SICK OF LISTENING TO IT.

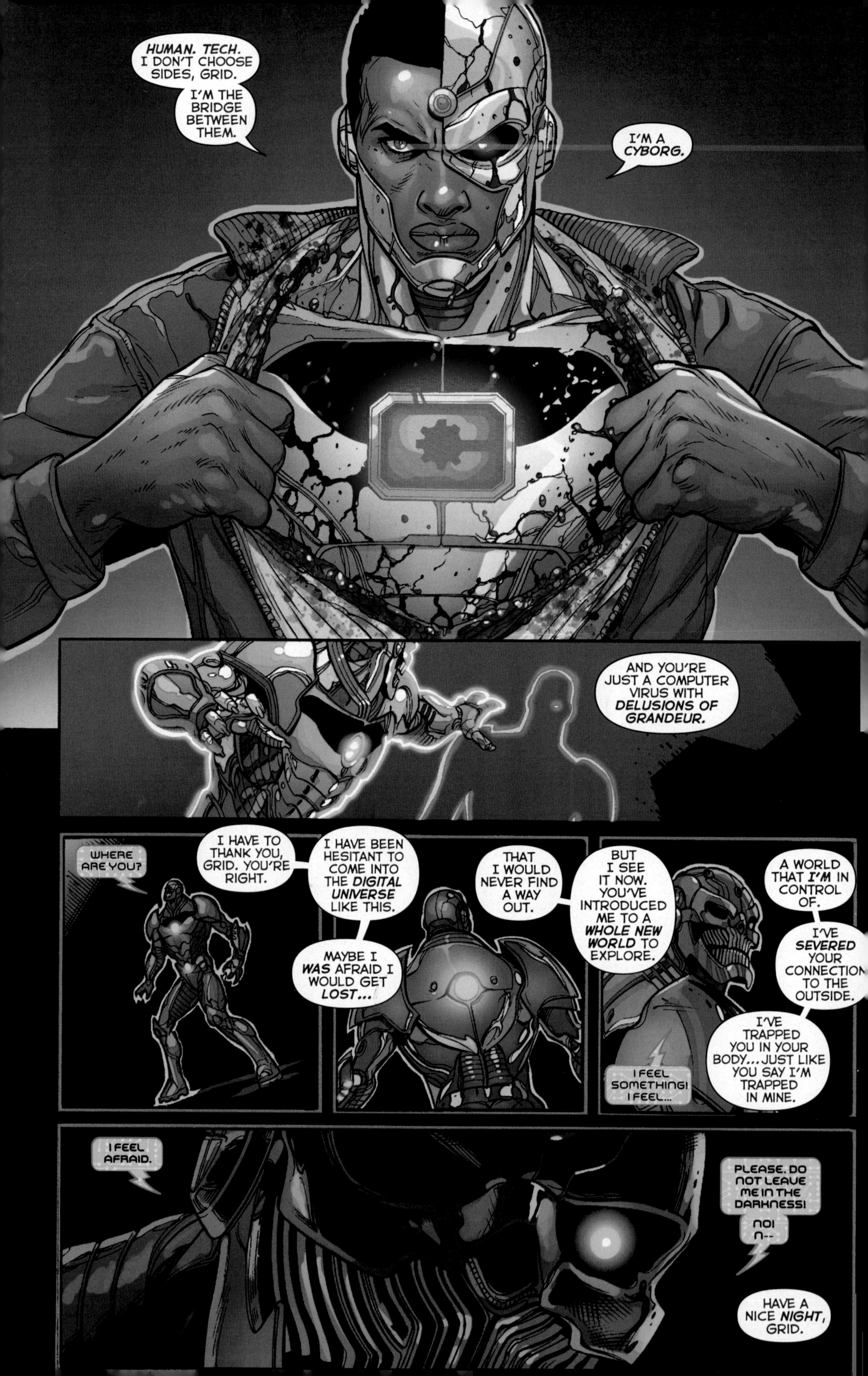
HUMAN. TECH. I DON'T CHOOSE SIDES, GRID.
I'M THE BRIDGE BETWEEN THEM.
I'M A CYBORG.
AND YOU'RE JUST A COMPUTER VIRUS WITH DELUSIONS OF GRANDEUR.
WHERE ARE YOU?
I HAVE TO THANK YOU, GRID. YOU'RE RIGHT.
I HAVE BEEN HESITANT TO COME INTO THE DIGITAL UNIVERSE LIKE THIS.
MAYBE I WAS AFRAID I WOULD GET LOST...
THAT I WOULD NEVER FIND A WAY OUT.
BUT I SEE IT NOW. YOU'VE INTRODUCED ME TO A WHOLE NEW WORLD TO EXPLORE.
A WORLD THAT I'M IN CONTROL OF.
I'VE SEVERED YOUR CONNECTION TO THE OUTSIDE.
I'VE TRAPPED YOU IN YOUR BODY...JUST LIKE YOU SAY I'M TRAPPED IN MINE.
I FEEL SOMETHING! I FEEL...
I FEEL AFRAID.
PLEASE. DO NOT LEAVE ME IN THE DARKNESS!
NO! N--
HAVE A NICE NIGHT, GRID.

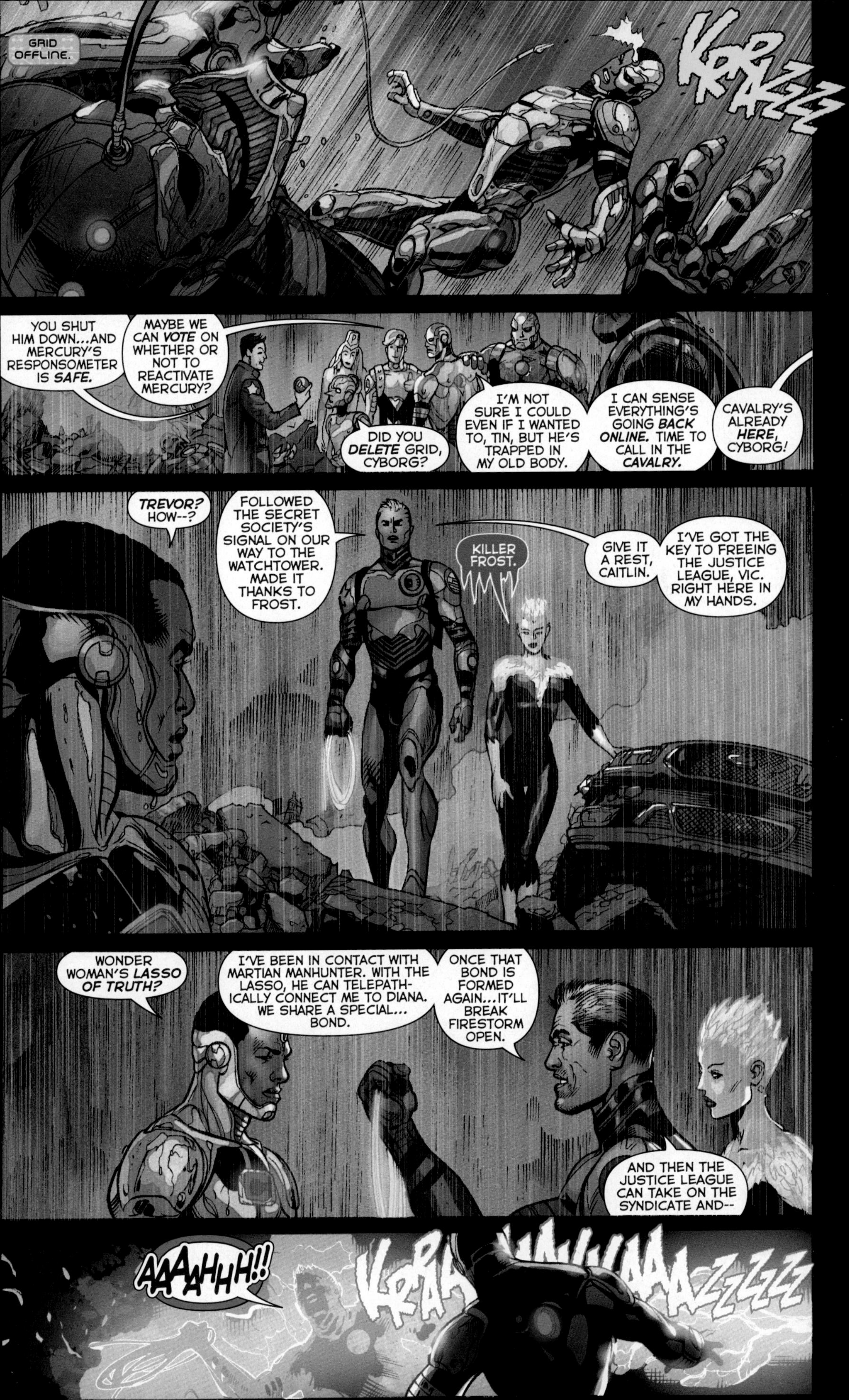
GRID OFFLINE.
KRZZZZ
YOU SHUT HIM DOWN...AND MERCURY'S RESPONSOMETER IS SAFE.
MAYBE WE CAN VOTE ON WHETHER OR NOT TO REACTIVATE MERCURY?
DID YOU DELETE GRID, CYBORG?
I'M NOT SURE I COULD EVEN IF I WANTED TO, TIN, BUT HE'S TRAPPED IN MY OLD BODY.
I CAN SENSE EVERYTHING'S GOING BACK ONLINE. TIME TO CALL IN THE CAVALRY.
CAVALRY'S ALREADY HERE, CYBORG!
TREVOR? HOW--?
FOLLOWED THE SECRET SOCIETY'S SIGNAL ON OUR WAY TO THE WATCHTOWER. MADE IT THANKS TO FROST.
KILLER FROST.
GIVE IT A REST, CAITLIN.
I'VE GOT THE KEY TO FREEING THE JUSTICE LEAGUE, VIC. RIGHT HERE IN MY HANDS.
WONDER WOMAN'S LASSO OF TRUTH?
I'VE BEEN IN CONTACT WITH MARTIAN MANHUNTER. WITH THE LASSO, HE CAN TELEPATHICALLY CONNECT ME TO DIANA. WE SHARE A SPECIAL... BOND.
ONCE THAT BOND IS FORMED AGAIN...IT'LL BREAK FIRESTORM OPEN.
AND THEN THE JUSTICE LEAGUE CAN TAKE ON THE SYNDICATE AND--
AAAAHHH!!
KRAAHWWWAAZZZZZ

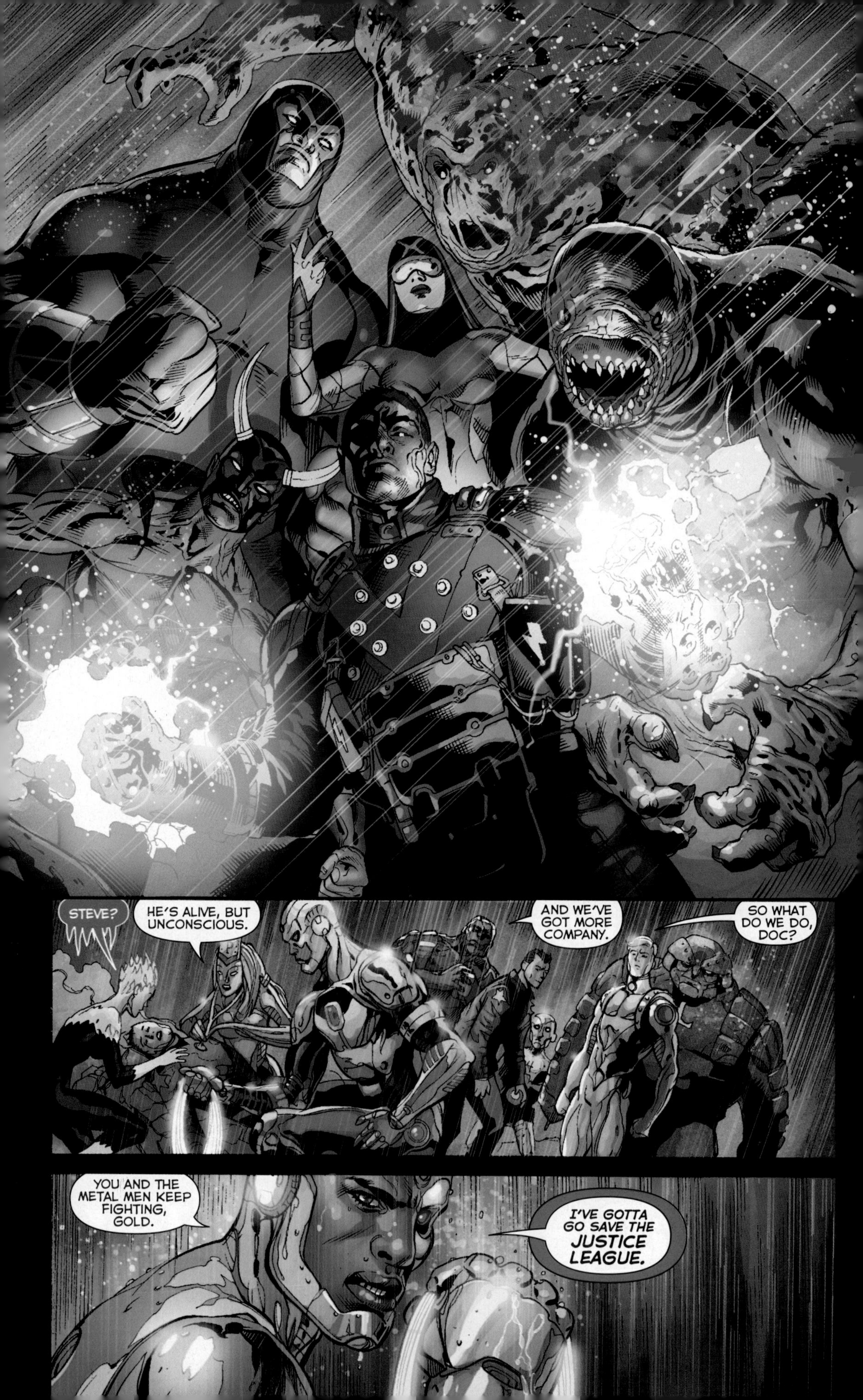
STEVE?
HE'S ALIVE, BUT UNCONSCIOUS.
AND WE'VE GOT MORE COMPANY.
SO WHAT DO WE DO, DOC?
YOU AND THE METAL MEN KEEP FIGHTING, GOLD.
I'VE GOTTA GO SAVE THE JUSTICE LEAGUE.

VARIANT COVER GALLERY

JUSTICE LEAGUE 24
Variant cover by Aaron Kuder & Brad Anderson

JUSTICE LEAGUE 25
Variant cover by Aaron Kuder & Brad Anderson

JUSTICE LEAGUE 26
Variant cover by Aaron Kuder & Brad Anderson

JUSTICE LEAGUE 27
Scribblenauts variant cover by Jon Katz, after Jim Lee

JUSTICE LEAGUE 28
Variant cover by Dan Panosian

JUSTICE LEAGUE 29
Robot Chicken variant cover by RC Stoodios

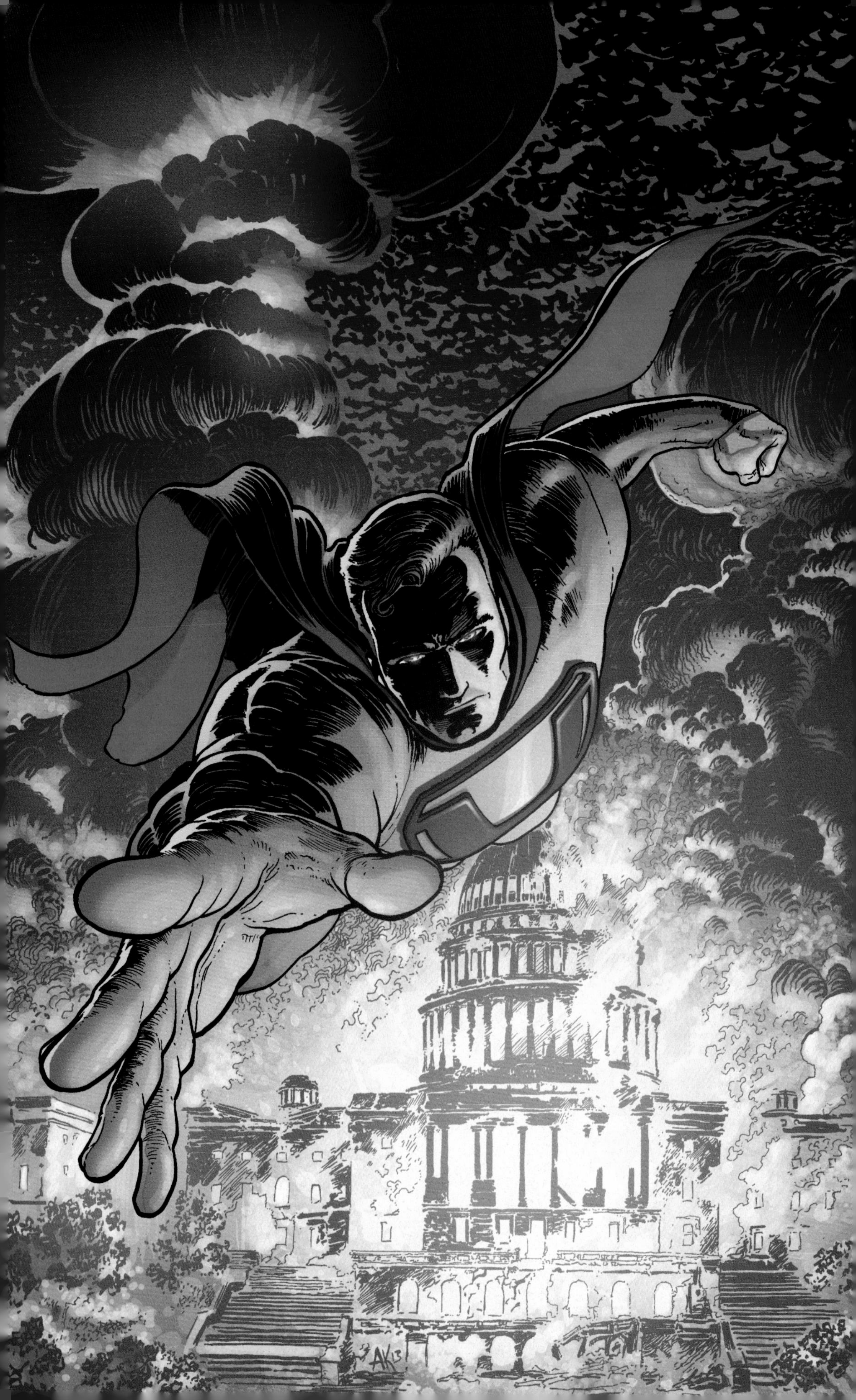

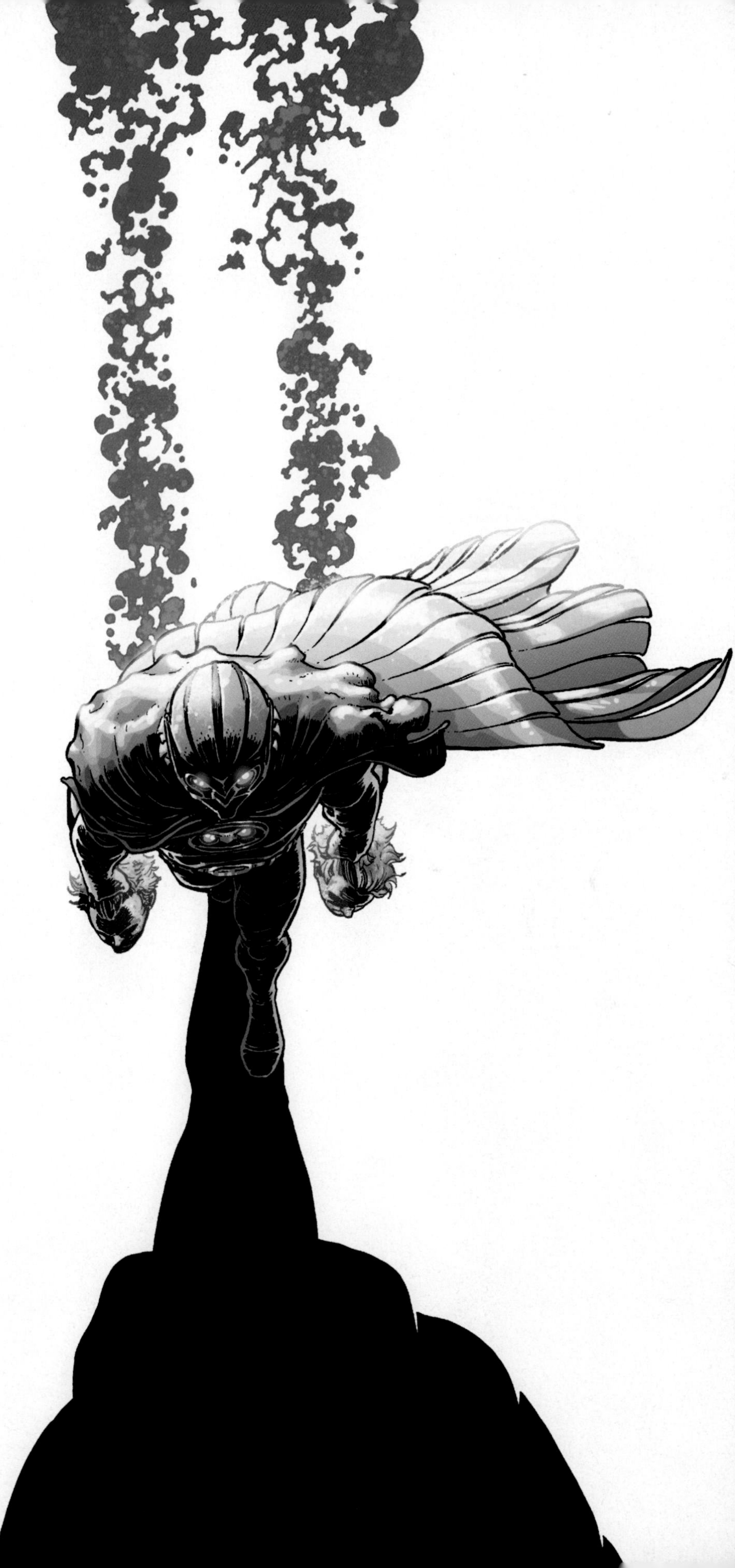

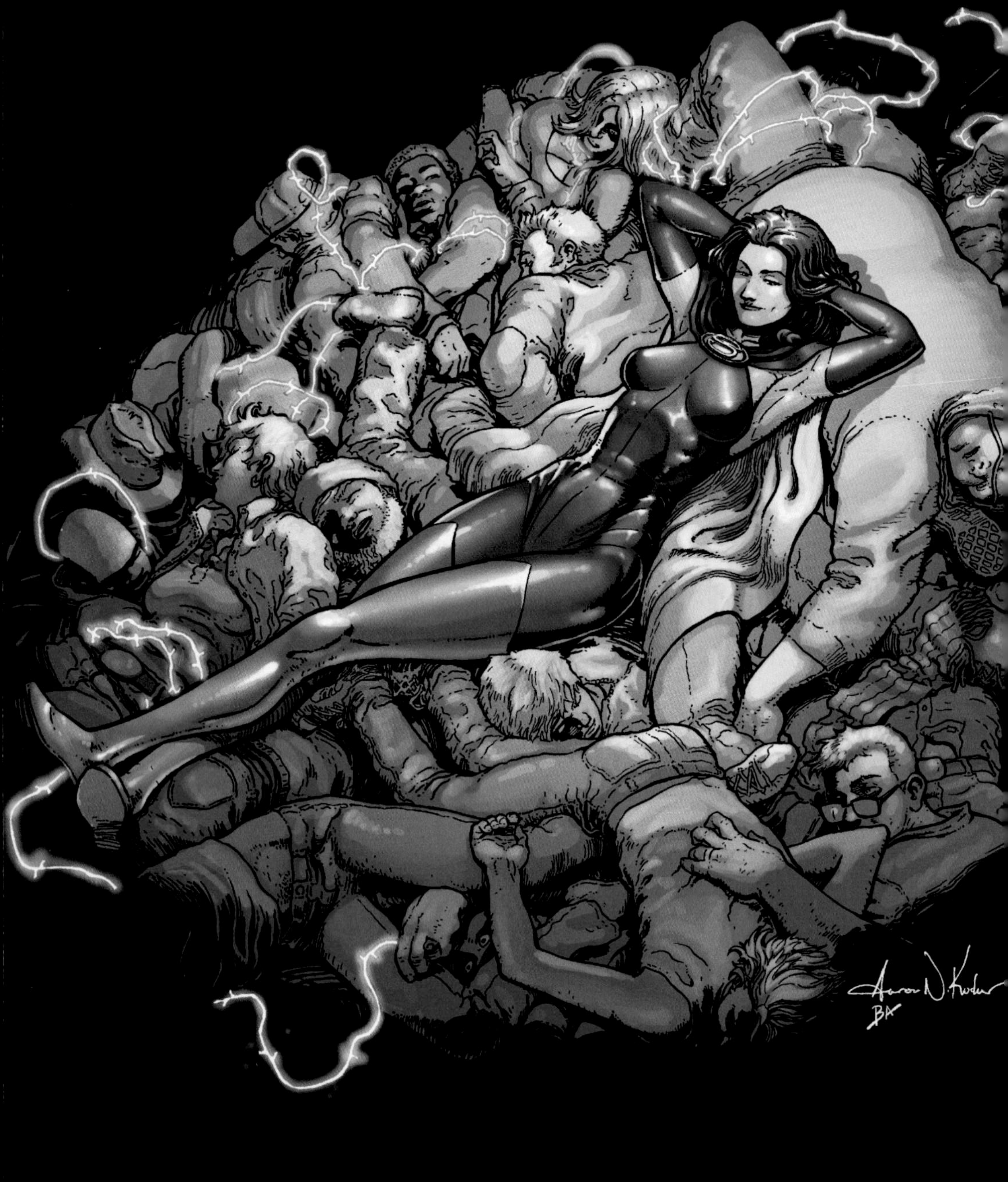

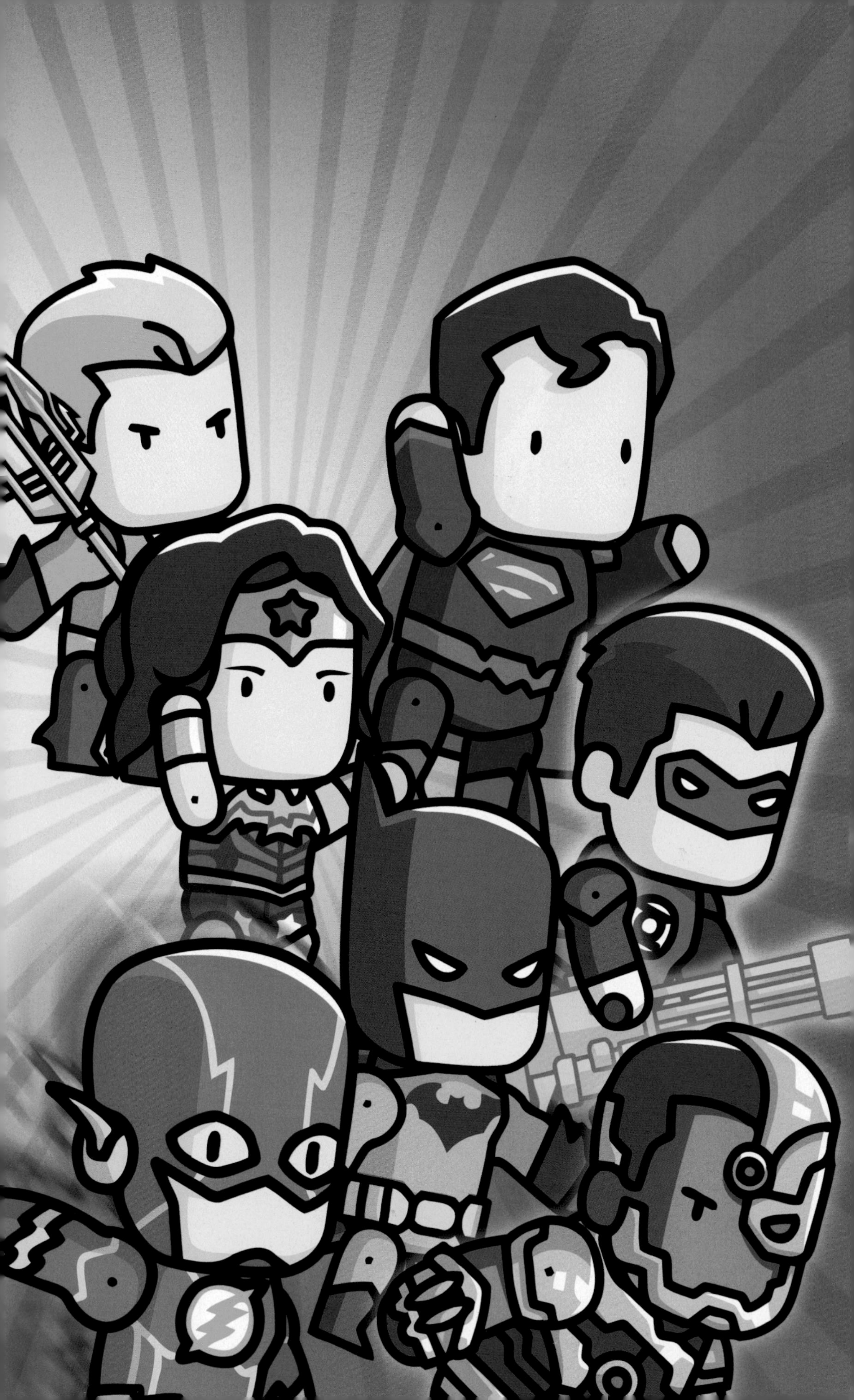

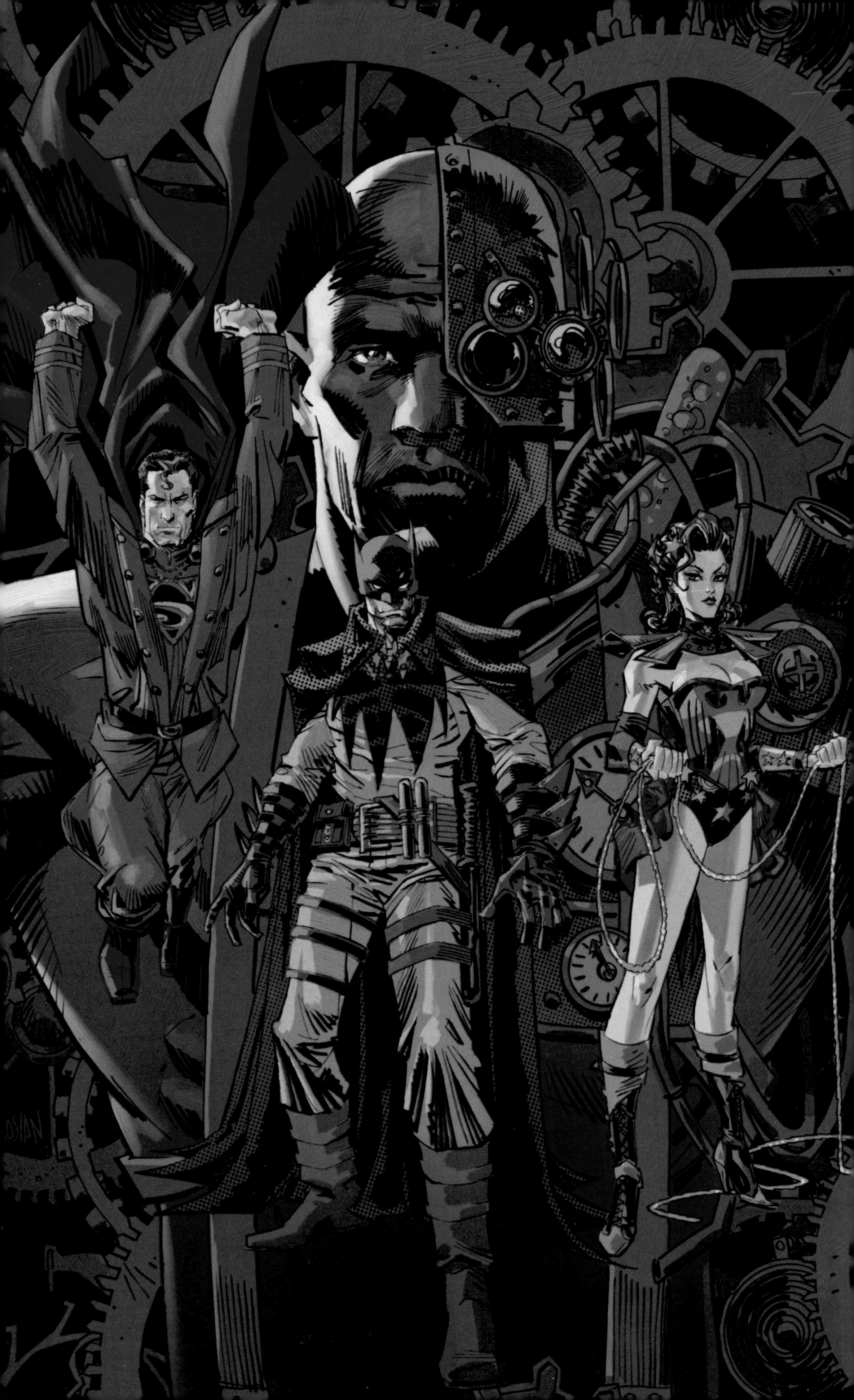

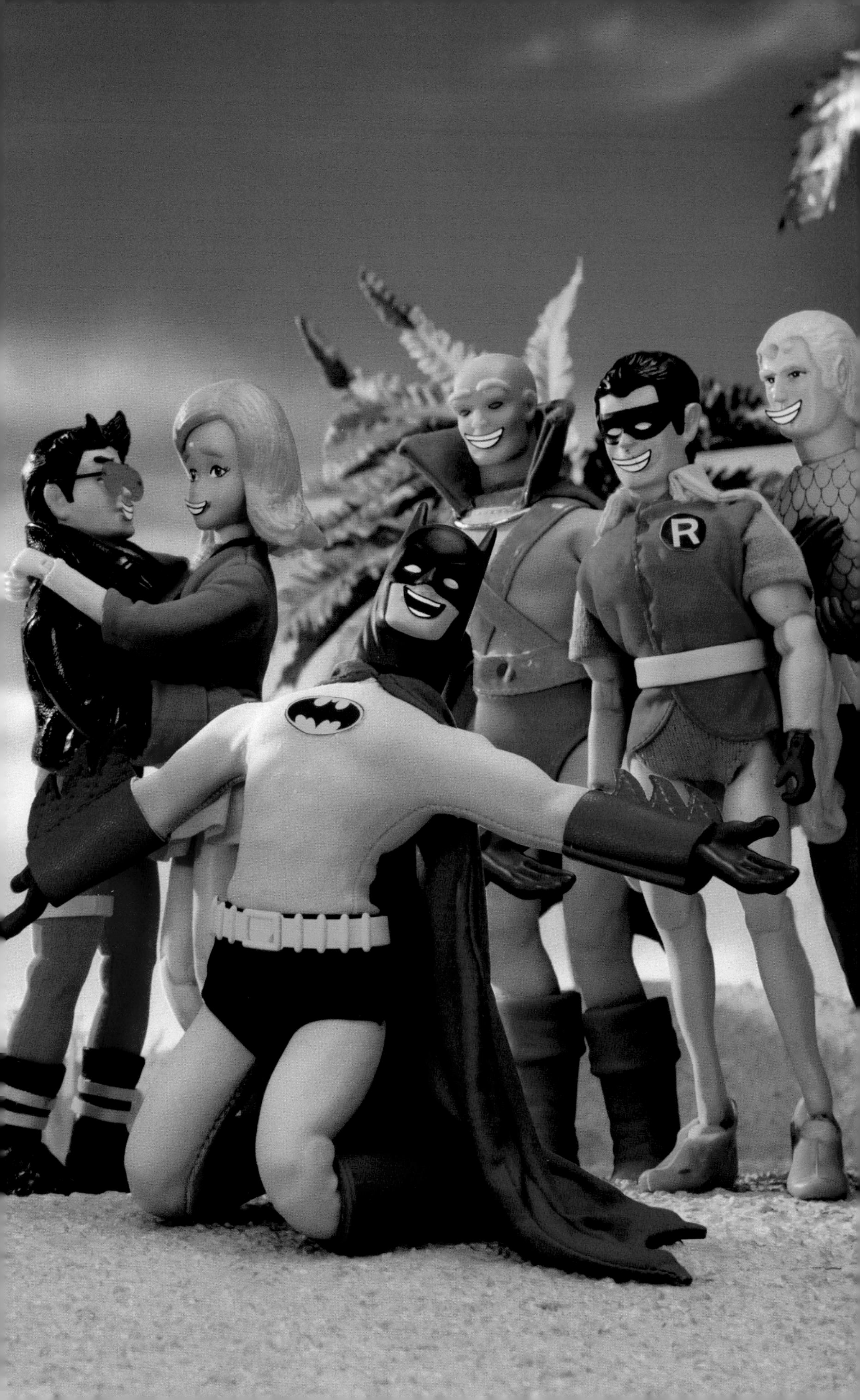

JUSTICE LEAGUE #27 page 16, pencils by Ivan Reis
First look at the rebuilt Cyborg

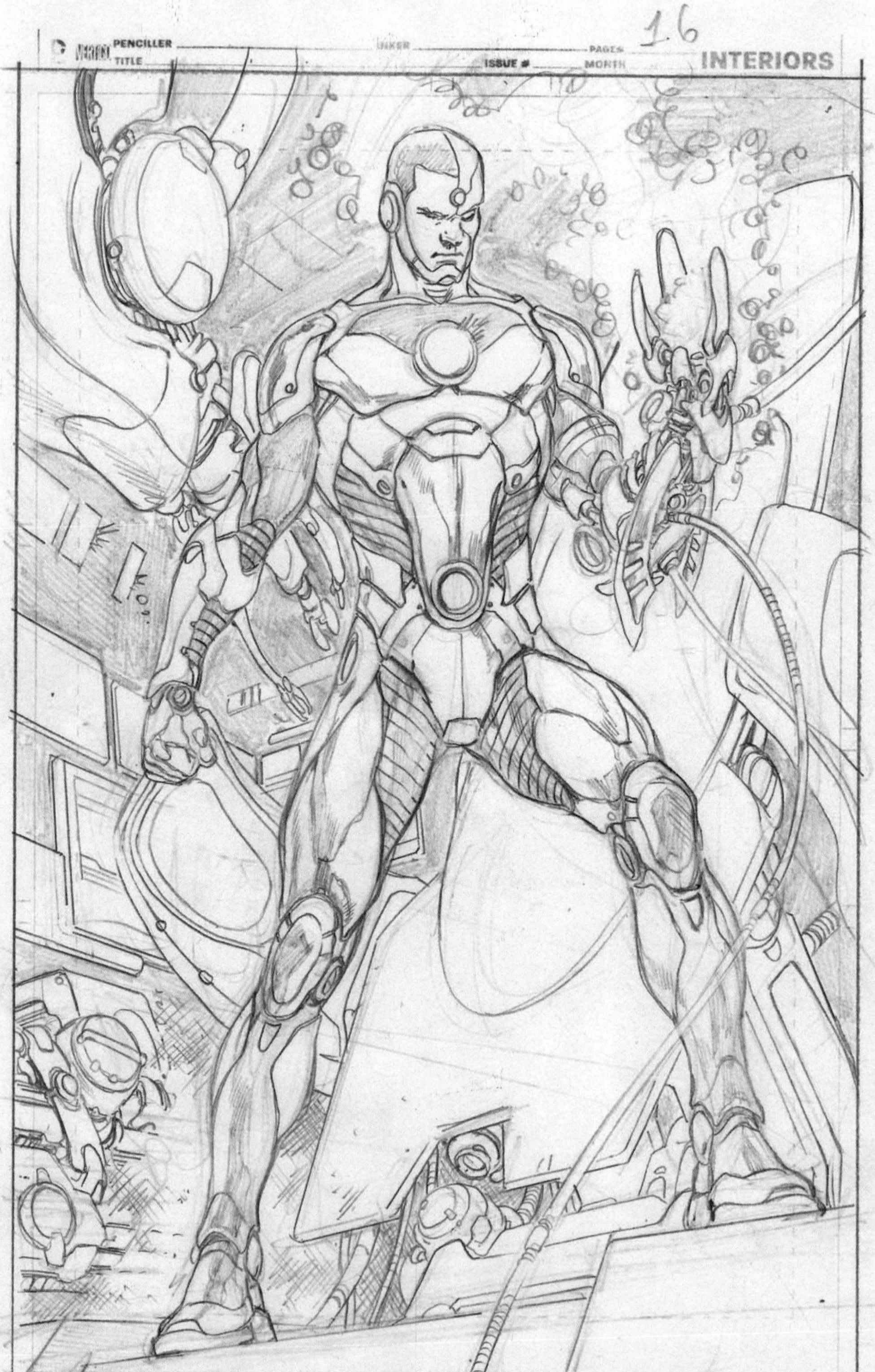
PENCILLER
TITLE
INKER
ISSUE #
PAGES
MONTH
16
INTERIORS

JUSTICE LEAGUE #28, page 8, pencils by Ivan Reis

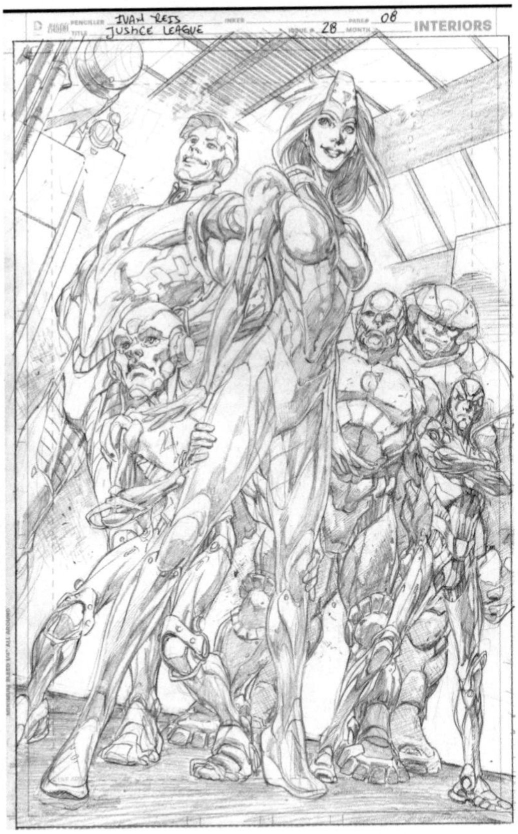
IVAN REIS
JUSTICE LEAGUE
28
08
INTERIORS

JUSTICE LEAGUE #24, page 22, pencils by Ivan Reis

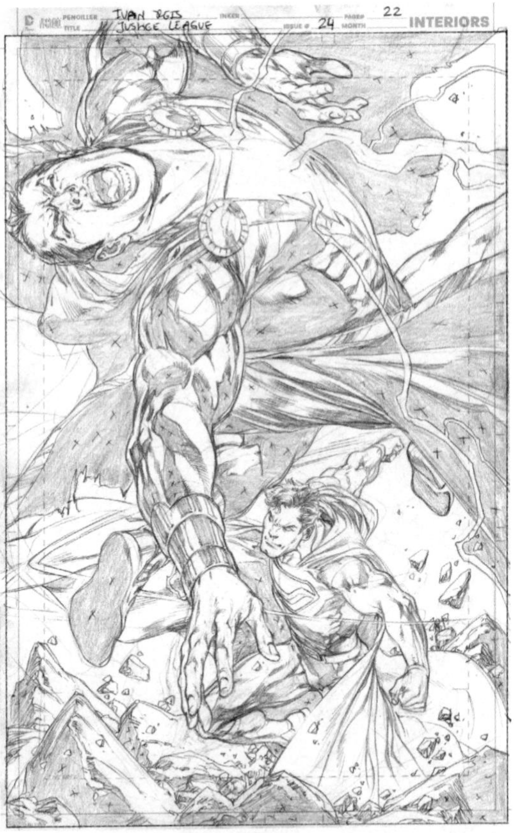
IVAN REIS
JUSTICE LEAGUE
24
22
INTERIORS

JUSTICE LEAGUE #25, page 2, pencils by Doug Mahnke

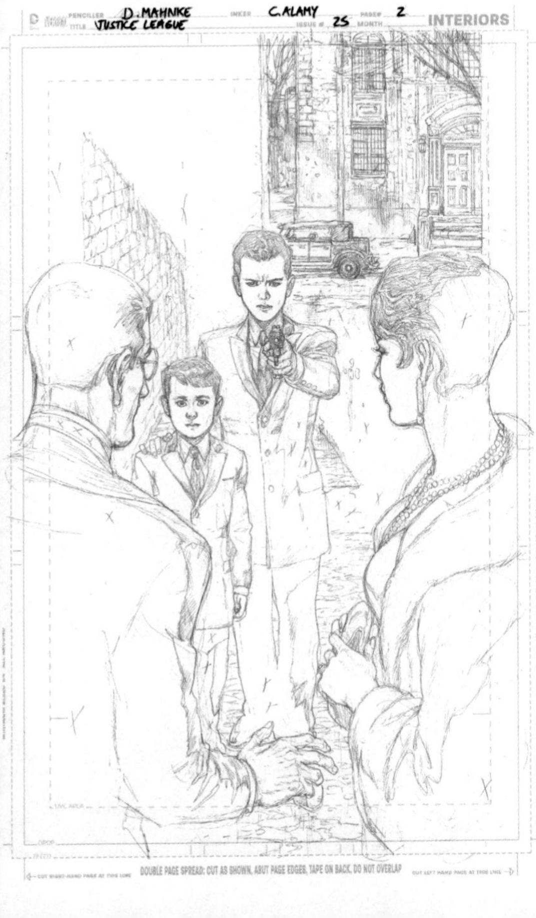
D. MAHNKE
JUSTICE LEAGUE
C. ALAMY
25
2
INTERIORS
DOUBLE PAGE SPREAD: CUT AS SHOWN, ABUT PAGE EDGES, TAPE ON BACK, DO NOT OVERLAP

JUSTICE LEAGUE #29, page 24, pencils by Doug Mahnke

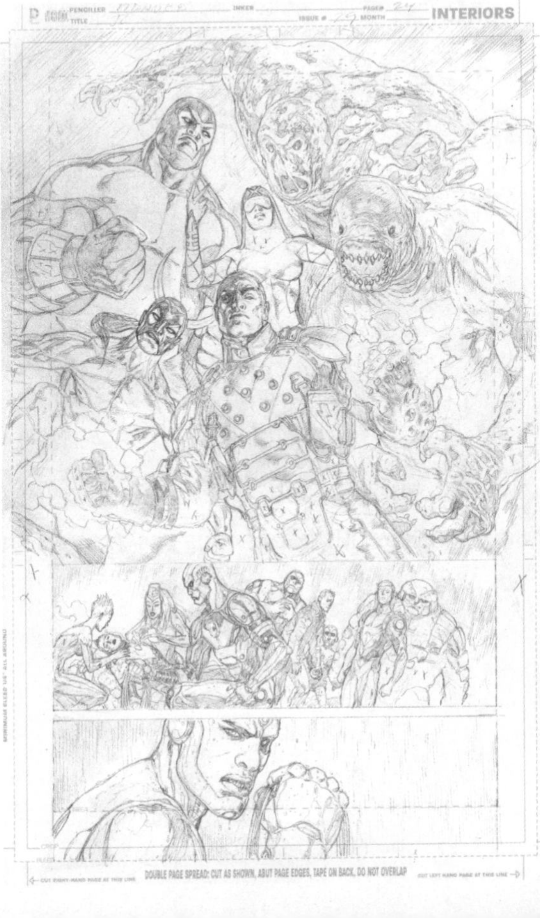
INTERIORS
DOUBLE PAGE SPREAD: CUT AS SHOWN, ABUT PAGE EDGES, TAPE ON BACK, DO NOT OVERLAP

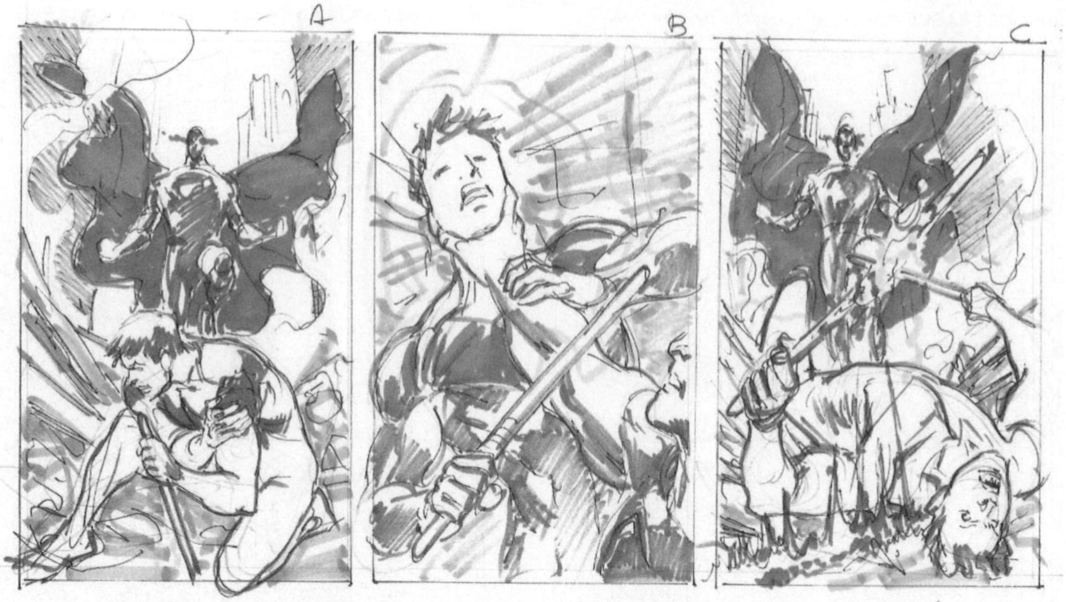
A
B
C

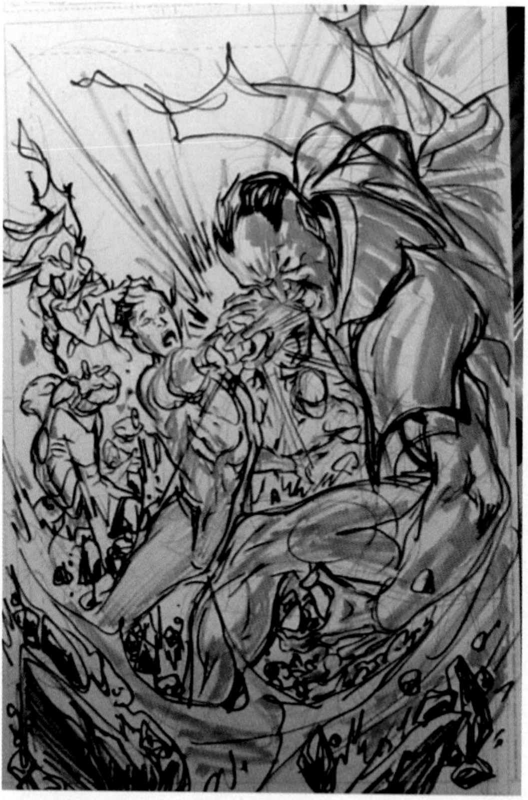

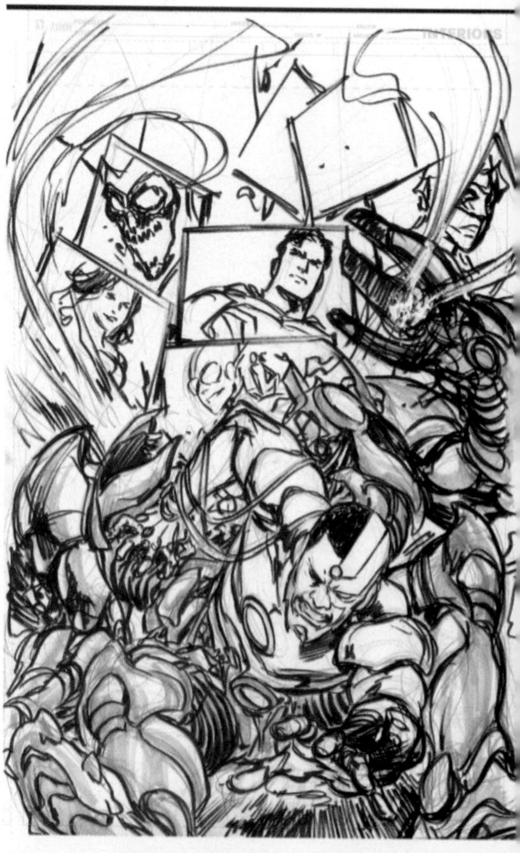

Cover layouts for JUSTICE LEAGUE #25-27 by Ivan Reis

Cover layouts for JUSTICE LEAGUE #29 by Ivan Reis

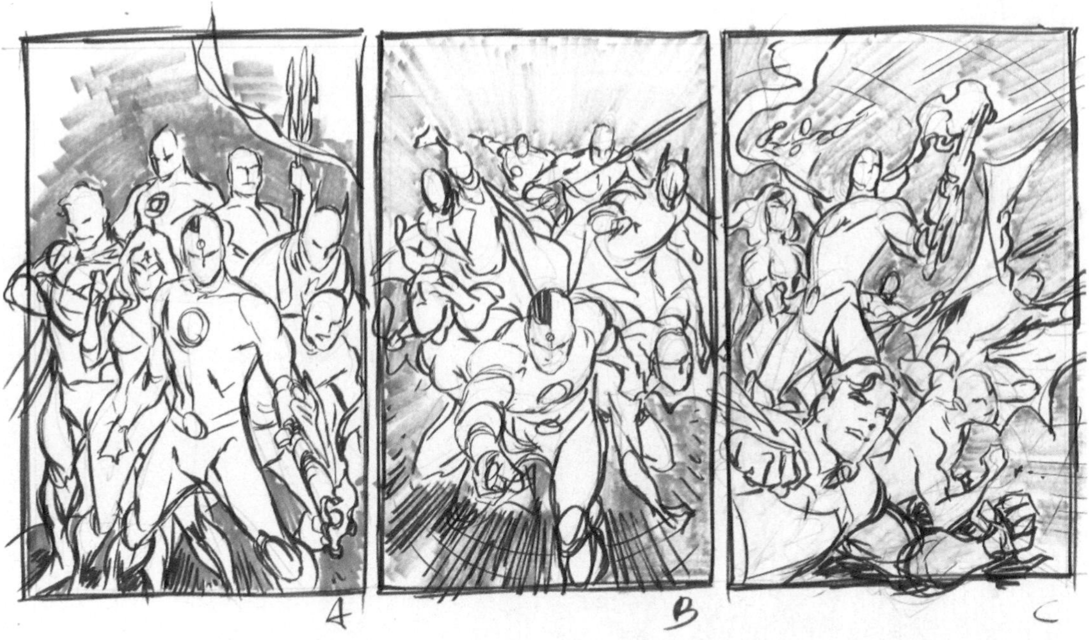
A
B
C

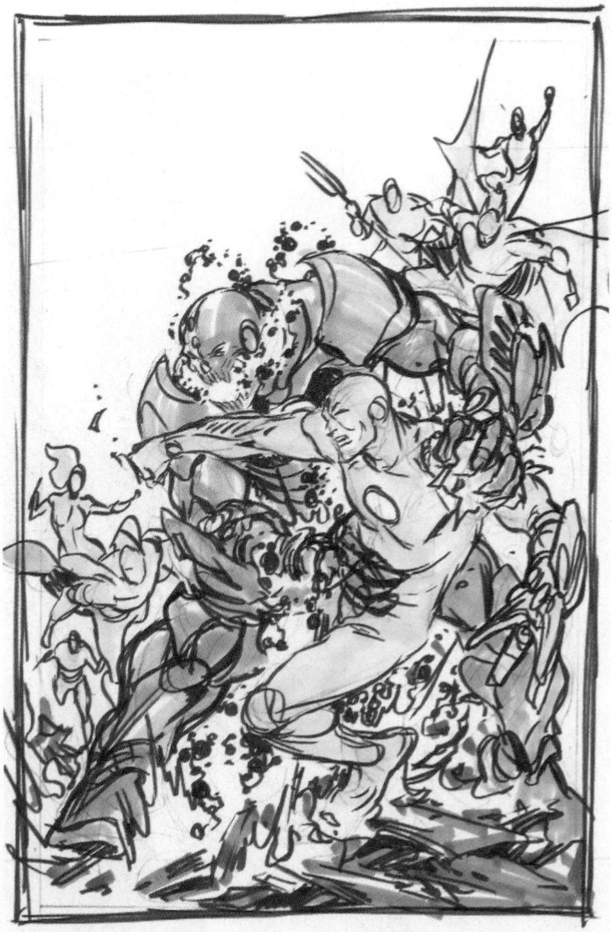

JUSTICE LEAGUE #25 Owlman
variant cover roughs by Aaron Kuder

"Writer Geoff Johns and artist Jim Lee toss you–and their heroes–into the action from the very start and don't put on the brakes. DC's über-creative team craft an inviting world for those who are trying out a comic for the first time. Lee's art is stunning."—USA TODAY

"A fun ride."—IGN

START AT THE BEGINNING!

JUSTICE LEAGUE
VOLUME 1: ORIGIN
GEOFF JOHNS and JIM LEE

JUSTICE LEAGUE
VOL. 2: THE VILLAIN'S
JOURNEY

JUSTICE LEAGUE
VOL. 3: THRONE OF
ATLANTIS

JUSTICE LEAGUE
OF AMERICA VOL. 1:
WORLD'S MOST
DANGEROUS

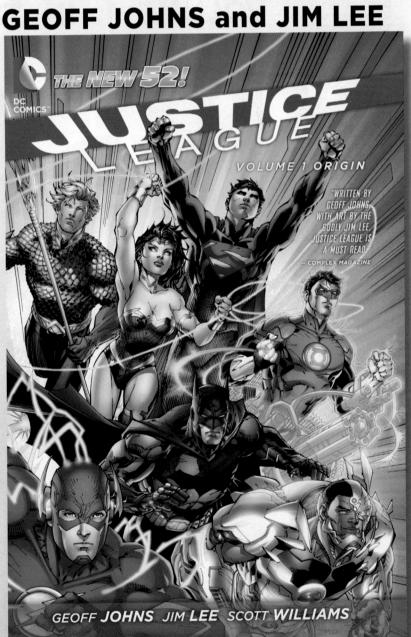

GEOFF JOHNS   JIM LEE   SCOTT WILLIAMS

DC COMICS™

START AT THE BEGINNING!

JUSTICE LEAGUE DARK
VOLUME 1: IN THE DARK

JUSTICE LEAGUE
DARK VOL. 2: THE
BOOKS OF MAGIC

with JEFF LEMIRE

JUSTICE LEAGUE
DARK VOL. 3:
THE DEATH OF MAGIC

with JEFF LEMIRE

CONSTANTINE
VOL. 1: THE SPARKLE
AND THE FLAME

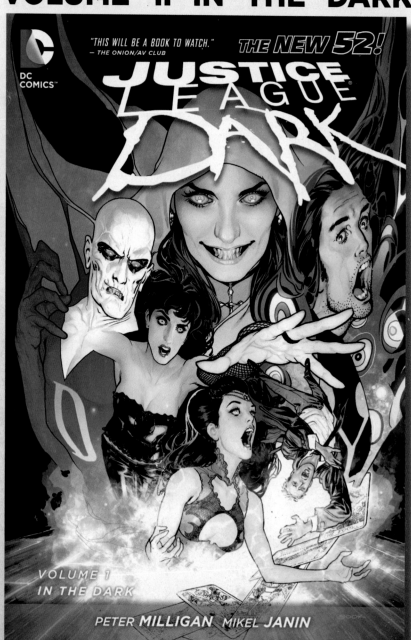

PETER MILLIGAN Mikel JANIN